Indenture Aesthetics

Indenture Aesthetics

Afro-Indian Femininities and the Queer Limits of South African Blackness

JORDACHE A. ELLAPEN

Duke University Press *Durham and London* 2025

Printed in the United States of America on acid-free paper ∞
Project Editor: Bird Williams
Designed by Courtney Leigh Richardson
Typeset in Garamond Premier Pro and Changa by
Westchester Publishing Services

Library of Congress Cataloging-in-Publication Data
Names: Ellapen, Jordache A., author.
Title: Indenture aesthetics : Afro-Indian femininities and the queer limits of South African blackness / Jordache A. Ellapen.
Description: Durham : Duke University Press, 2025. | Includes bibliographical references and index.
Identifiers: LCCN 2024017428 (print)
LCCN 2024017429 (ebook)
ISBN 9781478031345 (paperback)
ISBN 9781478028109 (hardcover)
ISBN 9781478060321 (ebook)
Subjects: LCSH: Indentured servants—South Africa—History. | Black people—Race identity—South Africa. | East Indians—Race identity—South Africa. | Post-apartheid era—South Africa. | Art, South African—Social aspects. | Feminist theory. | Queer theory. | South Africa—Race relations. | BISAC: SOCIAL SCIENCE / Ethnic Studies / African Studies | ART / General
Classification: LCC HD4875.S55 E45 2025 (print)
LCC HD4875.S55 (ebook)
DCC 306.3/620968—dc23/eng/20240828
LC record available at https://lccn.loc.gov/2024017428
LC ebook record available at https://lccn.loc.gov/2024017429

Cover art: *Family Portrait I, Chennai/Tongaat* (2017). 1999.3mm × 1000mm. Digital pigment print on fine art Baryta, 1/5. Source: Jordache A. Ellapen.

for my mother,

VELLIAMMAH ELLAPEN

(née Moodley)

and

my father,

REUBEN ELLAPEN

Contents

Preface: Mother, Memory, Movement

Indenture Aesthetics: Afro-Indian Femininities and the Queer Limits of South African Blackness is a book about the feminine, the vulnerable, and the feminized, those who unsettle the authentic and normative parameters of the postapartheid nation and sanctioned formations of postapartheid blackness. This is a book about my mother, an Afro-Indian woman, who lived her life in rural KwaZulu-Natal, one generation removed from the sugarcane plantations and coal mines on which her parents were indentured as a cheap and expendable labor force. Traversing the sugarcane plantations and coal mines, rural and urban geographies, overlapping regimes of coercive labor practices and migration routes across Southern Africa and the Indian Ocean, while troubling the common sense of race and racial categories in South Africa, *Indenture Aesthetics* is my attempt to articulate a positionality—an Afro-Indian positionality—that may possibly reframe how we understand Afro-Indian relations and South African blackness in a context where identitarian categories have coalesced and sedimented in dangerous ways. This limits the possibilities for us to imagine our collective possible futures, in a context like South Africa, where the future has largely been foreclosed, particularly for those I categorize as the *new black/ened Others.*

Much of the redrafting of *Indenture Aesthetics* has been informed by three major events: first, the death of my mother in 2019; second, the civil unrest that erupted in the country in 2021, which affected rural and semirural communities in KwaZulu-Natal, along the Indian Ocean; and third, two major storms in the first half of 2022 (April 11 and May 21 and 22) that resulted in major flooding, destruction, and the displacement and deaths of hundreds of people—black African and Afro-Indian—in oThongathi (Tongaat) and neighboring towns along the Indian Ocean. In oThongathi, the floods destroyed the water supply infrastructure, leaving hundreds of people without clean, drinkable water for almost a year. Together with regular electricity cuts—load shedding—and the collapse of various municipalities, rural and small-town South Africa reveals a different understanding of black and blackened life that rubs against the linear and progressive narrative of freedom we have come to associate with postapartheid South Africa. At first, the three events above may seem disconnected. I begin with my mother because of her positionality as an Afro-Indian woman whose life trajectory was shaped by indentureship and colonial apartheid. Indentured women were the most vulnerable within this coercive labor system, and for many descendants of indentured laborers, vulnerability and violation continue to be their collective inheritance. This is a story that has not been fully told in South Africa.

Throughout this book, I use indentureship as a hinge to understand overlapping forms of racialized labor and gendered forms of violence, connecting the past, present, and future while troubling South African racial categories to understand the deep entanglements between those who continue to live in the afterlife of colonial apartheid. The communities that were most affected by the civil unrest in 2021 and the flooding in 2022 were both black African and Afro-Indian communities living in rural and semirural small towns along the Indian Ocean. For those living in rural and small-town South Africa, the hegemonic narrative of South African freedom constantly rubs against underdevelopment, state abandonment, decay, and deterioration. People live in precarious conditions, but they continue to create livable lives alongside conditions of absolute vulnerability and violation. From rural Indianness to rural and small-town South Africa, *Indenture Aesthetics* demonstrates the ways in which vulnerability and violation not only thread together the past, present, and future but also provide a lens to understand why a new politics of solidarity is urgently needed in South Africa; one organized around the feminine, the femininized, and the vulnerable; one that prioritizes coalitional building across difference.

In 2019, my mother transitioned after a debilitating illness. I was able to take an emergency leave from the university to spend my mother's last days with her. This was the first time I spent a substantial amount of time in oThongathi, a rural area in KwaZulu-Natal nestled within expansive sugarcane plantations and often referred to as the last bastion of indentureship in Southern Africa. This time I spent with my mother taught me a lot about love, care, compassion, and the complex ways in which life and death rub against each other. We knew that we were now waiting for my mother to transition. She knew she was dying. She was not unfamiliar with death. Being the youngest girl of ten siblings, she was called upon constantly to take care of sick and dying relatives on both her side and my father's side of the family. Having spent a lot of time trying to understand her experiences as a young girl growing up under colonial apartheid, I also understood how she was intimately familiar with death and violence. This was part of life growing up in the immediate afterlife of indentureship.

I remember visits to the hospital, the numerous doctor visits, and the many invasive procedures she had to undergo before her diagnosis. I remember how she slowly became smaller and smaller as the illness progressed and ravaged her body. I cooked for her, and we spent afternoons chatting. I remember the urgency with which she recalled moments in her life and experiences that she may have still been reckoning with as her life cycle was coming to an end. She spoke with fondness about growing up in rural KwaZulu-Natal (Van Reenen's Pass and Ladysmith) with her nine siblings and their families on a farm that included horses, sheep, goats, and chickens. She talked about her father, a Natal-born Indian, and her mother, who was three years old when she arrived with her parents from British India on a coolie ship. My grandmother's parents were indentured in a coal mine in the interior of Natal. Her mother refused to speak English, preferring her mother tongue, Tamil. She did not romanticize life in rural KwaZulu-Natal. She spoke openly about gendered and racialized forms of violence within her own family and community. She revealed family secrets, and as she reckoned with her life, recognizing that her own life cycle was coming to an end, she spoke about the limited choices she had as an Indian woman one generation removed from indentureship and firmly located within the violence of apartheid. My mother understood the precariousness of life and understood futurity as solely located in the present. Living in rural KwaZulu-Natal, my parents' experiences of Indianness (Afro-Indianness) iterated differently than urban Indianness. Indenture history and its afterlives were visible all around us. We did not have the luxury of escaping this history or pretending that we had overcome this experience.

From a young age, my mother and I bonded over her storytelling abilities. When I returned home during the university holidays, we stayed up late at night as she narrated stories of her life and experiences. She had the ability to remember intricate details and scenes from the time she was a child. What I remember most fondly is our shared interest in photography and the many hours we spent talking about her photoarchive and trying to make sense of its meanings. As her illness worsened, our afternoon conversations became shorter. I watched as my mother slowly deteriorated and shrunk before my eyes. One of the most difficult things in life is watching one's parent die and waiting for death to release them from a body that had become no longer viable to host human life. When my mother passed on, my experience of time changed. In the immediate days after her passing, time slowed down and sometimes sped up. Her death disoriented me. I felt like I was orbiting in space and had no control. I felt unhinged.

I returned numerous times to the following quote from Saidiya Hartman's book *Lose Your Mother: A Journey Along the Atlantic Slave Route* (2008b, 85): "To lose your mother was to be denied your kin, country, identity." When my mother transitioned, I felt a deep sense of disconnection from South Africa. I recognized how my Africanness was intimately tethered to my mother (to the "maternal feminine"), everything she embodied, and the histories she evoked as she navigated the everyday. Every time I returned to Tongaat, which was yearly before the COVID-19 pandemic, I returned to my mother, to the home-space of the Afro-Indian family in the afterlife of indentureship. To return to my mother was to return home, to Africa. When I began this project, I did not understand what impact the feminine would have on this book. My very notion of an Afro-Indian positionality is only possible through the feminine.

Two years after my mother's death, on July 9, 2021, civil unrest swept swiftly across South Africa. The unrest was sparked by the imprisonment of Jacob Zuma, ex-president of South Africa, who defied the Constitutional Court's order to testify at the Zondo Commission. The Zondo Commission was set up in 2018 to investigate "allegations of state capture, corruption, fraud, and other allegations in the public sector" during Zuma's presidency from 2009 to 2018. Charged with contempt of court, Zuma was sentenced to fifteen months in prison. Zuma's defiance was viewed as a "politically motivated smear campaign" against the Constitutional Court, the commission, and the judiciary. Judge Khampepe accused Zuma of attempting to "corrode the legitimacy of the Constitutional Court." She is quoted as saying: "No person is above the law. . . . An act of defiance in respect of a direct judicial order has the potential to precipitate a constitutional crisis" (McKenzie, Cassidy, and Picheta 2021).

The unrest was mostly concentrated in two provinces—KwaZulu-Natal, Zuma's home province, and Gauteng, the economic center of the country. People in these communities, both Indian and black African, along the North Coast of KwaZulu-Natal from Durban to Stanger, felt abandoned by the state and an ineffective police force which quickly abdicated its responsibilities. For the first time since the end of apartheid in 1994, the South African National Defence Force deployed 25,000 soldiers to restore law and order. It was estimated that the looting and destruction of property and businesses in KwaZulu-Natal over a period of approximately eight days would impact the local economy by about ZAR twenty billion. The death toll stood at 337 in KwaZulu-Natal and

Gauteng. This event in modern South African history will go down as a failed insurrection.

What was initially viewed as an insurrection began to reveal the tears in South African society and the failures of our postapartheid "freedom dreams" (Kelly 2003). As I watched social media footage of the looting, it was apparent that those participating in these protests were from the black underclass, a class of South Africans whose experience of freedom differs significantly from that of the black political elite, those who have *arrived* through material and economic success. In one social media video circulating out of Tongaat, I watched as a man carried an entire butchered sheep on his shoulders, running through the crowd. These scenes revealed the desperate conditions of black life. The state has since tried to criminalize these protestors and has also embarked on a campaign to recover stolen goods. However, criminalization of the poor and destitute is an act of violence and violation against those most vulnerable, and it does not tackle the problem of economic injustice. These protestors were described as having *nothing to lose*, and their targeting of grocery, furniture, appliance, and clothing stores became symbolic of the African National Congress (ANC)'s failure to deliver on its promise of a better life for all.

The civil unrest erupted in a context where the unemployment rate rose to 32.6 percent in the first quarter of 2021, which is an average for the nation. In terms of racial demographics, by the fourth quarter of 2021, the unemployment rate was as follows: black African 39.1 percent, Indian/Asian 27.5 percent, and white 8.8 percent. The youth unemployment rate between fifteen- and twenty-four-year-olds was at a record high of 63.3 percent. According to an article published in *The Conversation* on September 7, 2021, by Cecil Mlatsheni and Lauren Graham (2021), the black African youth unemployment rate is the worst at 57 percent.[1] The protests revealed in very explicit ways the effects of the ANC's neoliberal economic policies exacerbated by the COVID-19 pandemic shutdowns, which have seen the closures of businesses and large-scale unemployment. What has been referred to as an insurrection begins to look very different once we focus on the economic inequalities that continue to shape the experiences of the majority black South African population.

As I watched these scenes of protests, I feared that the narrative would develop into a familiar one of Afro-Indian antagonisms. As I discuss in the introduction, from the colonial-apartheid era to the present, the Indian community has been represented as an economic success story by the media and popular representations. Indeed, among the Indian community, like the black African community, an elite and middle class has always existed in South Africa, obscuring intracommunal fissures of class within the Afro-Indian community.

KZN is the Zulu Kingdom, and because of British colonialism, the province has the highest density of Indians (people of Indian origin) in South Africa and outside of India. Many Indians from these communities along the Indian Ocean are descendants of indentured laborers. The civil unrest unfolded in a context where Indian and black African communities have long lived and worked alongside each other. However, because of the specificities of apartheid social engineering, the class distinction between these communities is significantly stark. This became an opportune context for some political parties to reignite long-existing and strategically crafted antagonisms between these two communities, which have been racialized in opposition to each other since the colonial era.

Political parties like the Economic Freedom Fighters (EFF), who have, since their inception, stoked anti-Indian sentiment in the province, saw this as an opportunity to organize a march against "racist Indians." On Twitter, the hashtag #IndiansMustFall painted a picture of a homogenous and racist Indian community alien to South Africa and intent on exploiting the livelihood of black Africans. On Twitter, members from other racialized communities in South Africa, like the coloured community, used this as an opportunity to distance themselves from Indians, anxiously asserting that they are not *like* the Indians.

The most vitriolic comments were made by Jackie Shandu, labeled by the media as a "Phoenix massacre activist." A recorded video of Shandu at a protest rally chanting "one Indian, one bullet" has been well-circulated on social media. In an interview with *Good News Community Radio*, Shandu made comments that provide insight into the complexities of how the Indian is seen and perceived in contemporary South Africa. According to him, Indians are a foreign element who have outstayed their welcome. He accuses Indians of taking advantage of black Africans who "have been good hosts." He conflates all Indians as business owners who are taking away jobs and resources from black Africans. He attributes "crime and drug abuse and those kinds of things" to Indian businesses in black African areas. According to Shandu's logic, Indian business interests, rather than the effects of the ANC's neoliberal economic policies and white monopoly capital, have strategically impoverished the black community. However, it is also important to note that all these factors work together and that business owners outside of white monopoly capital also exploit the poor in South Africa. In the video, Shandu argues that it is better to die than "be *terrorized and harassed by a foreign minority*."[2] The interview ends with Shandu asserting that "this country belongs to its *African native majority* alone." He evokes Idi Amin's expulsion of Indians from Uganda as an example of how the state should deal with the Indian problem. Shandu asserts that black Africans are the rightful "owners of the land," whereas Indians are *foreigners*, *parasites*, and *bloodsuckers*. The most recent emergence of Afro-Indian antagonism echoes early twentieth-century "race riots" between Indian and black African communities in KwaZulu-Natal. Both repeat the "unresolved questions of land and dwelling" (Hansen 2012, 102) that can be traced to the colonial era. Anxieties over the Indians emerge during times of crisis when issues of belonging and citizenship are framed around the question of who is truly entitled to enjoy the nation in the postapartheid period. Such sentiments have also circulated through popular culture. In his 2022 song AmaNdiya ("Indians"), the internationally renowned songwriter and artist Mbongeni Ngema chastises "Indians for their alleged unwillingness to accept Africans as equals, for resisting change, being interested only in making money, and being exploitative" (Vahed and Desai 2010a, 3). The song expresses fear over the increasing visibility of Indian and Pakistani immigrants post-1994, urging the Zulu nation ("strong men") to stand up against Indians (3). Interestingly, for Ngema, the *Indian* is a homogenous category. He does not differentiate between the Afro-Indian and more recent immigrants from the subcontinent. According to him, all Indians are foreign and alien Other.[3]

In the postapartheid period, the state's neoliberal economic policies created a new black middle class (across the categories Indian, coloured, and black African), replicating the problem of settler capital. The economic success of this middle class relies on the distinct demarcation between *those whose lives matter* and *those who are disposable and irrelevant* to the state's linear narrative of progress. The civil unrest once again revealed how economic and material hardships are felt most by the majority black African population, whose experience of what it means to be black is not the same as the Zumas, the Mbekis, the Ramaphosas, and the Mandelas—the black political elite and those aligned with them. The current civil unrest is one example where there is evidence that Zuma's children (part of the black elite) and those aligned with him used social media strategically to rile up the masses against the country's highest court. The protests explicitly indicate the ways in which blackness has shifted in South Africa. Today, blackness is no longer a site of collective political organization through which freedom was envisioned during the antiapartheid struggle. Blackness today is increasingly a signifier of the authentic national subject determined through autochthonous parameters that coalesce around various normativities related to class, gender, sexuality, and region. This marks a significant shift from radical oppositional political frameworks, like Black

Consciousness and nonracialism, that emerged during the antiapartheid struggle as a site where apartheid-era categories of race were challenged by the disenfranchised.

The recurring scenes of Afro-Indian antagonism reinscribe the relationship between black Africans and Indians as a "strange story of mutual nonrecognition," characterized by a "willed incomprehension derived from a lack of desire, intimacy, and respect" (Hansen 2012, 97). The civil unrest revealed the painful ways in which Indianness and blackness rub against each other in a context where apartheid social engineering strategically obscured the deep entanglements between black African and Indian communities. This "willed incomprehension" rests on the recurring trope of the Indian as the colonial middleman and the specificities of race-making in South Africa that position the Indian as alien and foreign Other. Indeed, *Indenture Aesthetics* troubles this homogenization of the Indian within the South African imaginary.

Then, on April 11, 2022, a storm raged through the KwaZulu-Natal Province, affecting the very same towns and villages that were most impacted by the civil unrest in 2021. These areas experienced the "heaviest rains in 60 years," destroying bridges, roads, houses, and other infrastructures. In June 2022, it was estimated that these communities would not have access to tap water for the next six to twelve months. The everydayness of those who live in this area, and in other areas across South Africa with similar, and sometimes even more desperate conditions, is characterized by hardship and struggle for the most basic amenities like drinkable water, electricity, and infrastructure. Largely abandoned by the state and the local municipalities, my sister describes it as a "forgotten ghost community." Such forgotten ghost communities and towns are common across the country, particularly in rural and semirural areas. For them, freedom is elusive and yet to arrive. The storms, together with the civil unrest, are powerful reminders that the majority of South Africans exist outside the linear narrative of progress and development associated with the newness of the new South African nation. These people live in desperate conditions. Their everydayness is structured around a different temporality, which could be harnessed as an alternative site of coalitional building in contemporary South Africa.

This book is an attempt to rethink and reimagine the racial categories Indian and black in South Africa by reorientating the reader to the various contours of Southern African blackness. Through the Afro-Indian positionality and that of the new black/ened Others, *Indenture Aesthetics* disrupts the narrative of postapartheid freedom by returning to indentureship and its afterlives as an intervention into black class respectability politics, which manifests through authentic blackness and the conflation of the Indian experience with that of the trader/merchant middleman class. Both these positionalities, as this book demonstrates, are unable to account for the specificities of Afro-Indianness as a particular iteration of South African blackness.

What can we learn about our entangled pasts, presents, and futures outside racial-identitarian categories, if we attune ourselves to the lives of those forgotten, rendered disposable and abject, and constructed as vulnerable by the state? What do these black and blackened people and these spaces (rural, semirural, and township spaces) reveal about embodied practices of freedom that rub against the liberation associated with, and foreclosed by, postapartheid? What can we learn differently about freedom, solidarity, and coalition-building when we prioritize the feminine and feminized, the vulnerable and violated?

This is the context out of which *Indenture Aesthetics* emerges. *Indenture Aesthetics* is committed to reimagining Afro-Indian relations and Southern African blackness by curating an archive of aesthetic practices that juxtaposes texts created by Afro-Indian and South African black artists. As a curatorial project, this method of juxtapositioning slowly erodes the hegemonic narrative of "mutual non-recognition" that has, for too long, structured Afro-Indian relations. Through the aesthetic realm, I trace lines of embodied desire between Afro-Indian and South African black communities to illuminate our deeply entangled pasts, presents, and futures as a practice of "imagining otherwise" (Chuh 2003; Crawley 2016). I am convinced that as a political project, the labor of imagining otherwise can only emerge from the positionality of those subjects who find themselves outside of the nation's linear narrative of progress and development. The urgency of this moment requires us to willingly abdicate the desire for the nation and agitate for forms of relationalities that are structured around a politics of (un)belonging as an urgent praxis of collective survival.

Acknowledgments

This book would not have been possible without the generosity, kindness, and care of a number of people who helped me cultivate my ideas and develop my voice as a writer and critical thinker. Writing this book has been a meandering journey across various countries (South Africa, the United States, and Canada) and it represents the many people—professors, colleagues, mentors, friends, family, and lovers—who have touched my life in various ways. First and foremost, I would like to express my deepest gratitude to Xavier Livermon and Vanita Reddy, whose mentorship and guidance have certainly shaped this book in ways I could not have imagined when I first embarked on this journey. Xavier, you are probably the only other person who has read every single draft of this book, and I continue to be amazed by your generosity and dedication to this project and to me as a person and scholar. I thank you for the many hours (and unseen labor) you have dedicated to this project, your encouragement when I felt that I was incapable of doing one more round of revisions, and the space you created for me to be emotionally vulnerable. You grasped the importance of this project early on and I thank you for guiding me and modeling a form of mentorship based on a practice of care and generosity. Since Vanita and I met in Bloomington, Indiana, she has mentored me through the job market and become an important interlocutor who has shaped this book in important ways. I want to thank you, Vanita, for holding me accountable, for the many hours you spent reading and rereading the introduction of this book, and gently encouraging me to slow down. Through this process you have taught me such important writing skills, and the clarity of this text is directly attributed to your (unseen) labor and your mentorship throughout this process. Xavier and Vanita, thank you. You both have provided models of mentorship and practices of care that are mostly absent within the broader academy, particularly for scholars of color.

This book would not have been possible without the artists whom I discuss in the pages that follow. Special thanks to all the artists—Sharlene Khan, Reshma Chhiba, Lebohang Kganye, Sabelo Mlangeni, Desire Marea, Fela Gucci, Mohau Modisakeng, and Githan Coopoo—who so generously made time to respond to my emails, provided interviews, and waived any fees related to the reproduction of their images in this book. Sharlene Khan recognized the importance of my own creative work as an intervention into South African art and she continues to encourage my artistic and curatorial practice. Indeed, Sharlene's creative work has been pivotal to how I have come to understand and theorize indenture aesthetics.

The ideas that developed into this book began to germinate around 2008 in the basement of Solomon Mahlangu House, a building at the University of the Witwatersrand (Wits University), Johannesburg, formerly called Senate House. My journey as an academic began in South Africa at Wits University and I would like to thank the many people who supported me during the early stages of this project—Tawana Kupe, Nobunye Levin, Trish Malone, Betty Govinden, and Pamila Gupta. Special thanks to Haseenah Ebrahim, my mentor, colleague, and friend. Much thanks and appreciation also go to Jyoti Mistry. You were my first mentor within the academy and I would not be where I am today without your guidance during those early days when I was still trying to figure out how to navigate this space. The ideas in this book began to develop in conversation with Jyoti Mistry. Thank you, Jyoti, for the important role you have played in my becoming. I will always appreciate you.

At Indiana University, Bloomington, I was intellectually nurtured and mentored by scholars who have now become important interlocutors on this academic journey. My deepest gratitude to Marlon M. Bailey for encouraging and creating the space for me to pursue a project on South Africa in an American Studies department. As an international student, Michael M. Martin provided intellectual and material resources that supported me during my time in Bloomington. I want to thank LaMonda Horton-Stallings and Cara Caddoo for encouraging my intellectual and creative endeavors. I would also like to thank Denise Cruz, Vivian Halloran, Scott Herring, Audrey McCluskey, John McCluskey, Micol Seagal, Marvin D. Sterling, and Phoebe Wolfskill. Jigna Desai became an important close reader of my work and her encouragement and commitment to this project are felt throughout the pages of this book.

A postdoctoral research fellowship in the Department of African American and African Diaspora Studies at Washington University in Saint Louis provided the time to develop this book manuscript. At Washington University, Jeffrey Q. McCune Jr. and Shanti Parikh served as my mentors and provided support, encouragement, and friendship. The research and writing of this book were also supported by an Underrepresented Minority Recruitment Program Fellowship from the University of Oregon, where I spent one year as an assistant professor. At the University of Oregon, I met some amazing folk including Sangita Gopal, Quinn Miller, and Courtney Thorsson.

The completion of this book would not have been possible without the support I have received at the University of Toronto since joining the Department of Historical Studies and the Women and Gender Studies Institute in 2018. I would like to thank Beverly Bain, Kass Banning, Andreas Bendlin, Victoria Tahmasebi-Birgani, Boris Chrubasik, Warren Crichlow, Zeinab Farokhi, Marieme Lo, Ajay Rao, Dana Seitler, Joan Simalchik, Christopher Smith, Alissa Trotz, Rinaldo Walcott, and Rebecca Whitman for your support over the years. I would like to especially thank Alissa Trotz for supporting this book in numerous ways, including providing funds for a manuscript revision workshop. Numerous fellowships from the University of Toronto, including a Jackman Humanities Institute Mellon Junior Faculty Fellowship, have supported the research for this book. Since its formation in 2021, the Queer and Trans Research Lab (housed in the Bonham Center for Sexual Diversity Studies) has become an important intellectual home. The Martha LA McCain Faculty Fellowship provided the time I needed to rethink, revise, and rewrite this manuscript. I also want to thank Chido Muchemwa, who served as my research assistant during my time as a faculty fellow. My deepest gratitude goes to Dana Seitler, who continues to provide intellectual support and friendship and who models a form of academic citizenship that is inspiring. The Department of Historical Studies' Research Committee has supported this book by providing funds to cover subvention costs that have made it possible to include full color images in the book.

Since being a graduate student, I have been sustained through the years by many friendships. I want to thank my graduate student community at Indiana University, especially Julie Le Hégarat, Heather Montes-Ireland, M. Nicole Horsley, Monica Fleetwood Black, Nandi Comer, Walter Tucker IV, Joe Stahlman, Fileve Palmer, Giselle Cunanan, Maria Hamilton Abegunde, L. Andre Bispo de Jesus, Nana A. Amoah-Ramey, and Lisa Kwong. Special thanks to Nzingha Kendall for your friendship that continues to nourish me in countless ways. Your unique approach to the world, and to the academy, continues to challenge my intellectual and creative work. I value our conversations, the times we imagine together, and the gentle ways you push me to be a better scholar, teacher, and person. I also want to thank Kaneesha Parsard and Madhuri Karak for their friendship and support over the years. Although our journeys have taken us on different paths across the world, I treasure the time we spent as Social Science Research Council Dissertation Proposal Development Fellows, and I think of you both often.

Most of the revisions of this book occurred during a period of intense mourning. While writing and revising this manuscript both my parents passed away. My mother, Velliammah Ellapen, appears throughout the book and the reader will have the opportunity to encounter her (and my father) in my artwork and curatorial practice as well as her enduring influence on how I have come to understand and enact beauty, sensuality, aesthetics, and care. Without my mother's touch, her love, her silent and enduring strength, this book would not have been possible. Whereas my mother taught me about the politics of the home-space in the afterlife of indentureship, my father's active participation in the antiapartheid struggle as a political activist orientated me toward a different, but not unrelated, kind of politics that is also evident throughout the pages of this book. My father, Reuben Ellapen, dedicated his life to teaching, and in 1988 he was elected chairman of the South African Democratic Teachers Union (SADTU) in Tongaat and launched the first branch of SADTU in the Tongaat area in 1989. Together, my parents taught me about love and care even in situations of violence and destitution. This book is for my parents, whose life experiences are theorized in the pages that follow. My notion of the Afro-Indian emerges from our positionality as rural Indians, intimately connected to indentureship and its afterlife.

My two sisters and their families have supported this project and my creative and intellectual endeavors, in ways that I cannot recount. Paula and Jo Ann, Deven and Niren, thank you for all your love and support. I hope one day that my nieces and nephews—Aeryn, Luken, Adison, and Ezra—will read this book and be able to recognize that this book is my gift of love to each one of you. I also want to thank my aunts—Galilee, Dulce, and Patricia—for your support, conversations, and encouragement over the years. As I write these acknowledgments, I also want to recognize my dad's brother, uncle David, who died from COVID-related complications in 2021. I fondly remember the many car rides through the Natal Midlands and the many ways he supported me. I want to thank my cousins Tashira and Uriev Ellapen and Mike (Mikasen) Naidoo for your support and care. I want to thank my family in Johannesburg, especially my cousin Priscilla, her partner Denzil, and her two daughters, Natania and Simone. Thank you for the love, support, and warm meals whenever I am in Joburg. Thanks also to Ashwen Singh for your support during the early stages of the research. Special thanks to my two best friends in Joburg, Charlotte Gouws and Shirda Vandeyar. Our life journeys have taken us in different directions, but we remain connected across time and space, and I love you both immensely.

Elizabeth Ault, my editor at Duke University Press, understood the importance of this project even before I fully grasped it. I appreciate Elizabeth's dedication, responsiveness, and gentle, sometimes firm, encouragement. Elizabeth's guidance through the book-writing process, her feedback on early chapters, and her overall commitment make her the kind of editor any writer would want to work with. Ben Kossak stepped in during the final stages and I'd like to thank him for his guidance through the publication process. This book has benefited from the four anonymous readers at Duke University Press whose kindness and commitment to the project were demonstrated through their thoughtful and engaged feedback. This book has greatly benefited from the review process, which has taught me so much about writing, thinking, and imagining together. Special thanks go to T. J. Tallie for offering guidance on archives and history in colonial Natal. Thanks also goes to Bongeka Buhle Selepe, who carefully language-checked and copyedited the manuscript with such care. Hershini Bhana-Young has supported this project from its earliest incarnations, and I want to thank her for her kindness and generosity throughout this process.

I want to express special thanks to my chosen (queer) family in Toronto where my research and thinking has benefited immensely from my friendship with Naveen Minai and Sarah Schroff. Sometime in 2021 I met two South African Afro-Indians, Jody and Thomas (Tom), in Toronto. We connected instantly and since then we have forged a deep intimacy sustained by our untranslatable positionalities as queer Afro-Indians navigating Canada and the United States. I want to thank you both for your love, care, and generosity. We have formed our own queer family and the completion of this book would not have been possible without your support and encouragement. As fellow South Africans, carving out a new life in Toronto, it was apparent to me that my notion of the Afro-Indian that I cultivate in this book encapsulates you both, and our deep friendship. You are the Afro-Indian I write about and theorize in the following chapters. As you read this book, I hope that you will recognize yourselves in the pages. Our friendship and commitment to one another inform the textures of this book.

My deepest gratitude and love go to Jed. You are the other person who has read multiple drafts of this manuscript with such dedication and commitment. You have taught me all about the Oxford comma and I am a better writer because of that. Every day you model for me a version of love and being together that is so expansive and generative. You challenge me to be a better person, a kinder person. You are my special person, and the work I do would not be possible without your love. You are my safe space. Our queer family also includes two nonhuman children that have moved with us across the United States and to Canada and that have been an immense source of love and comfort over the years. Tigger, my writing buddy, is big and gentle, communicates with his eyes, and keeps me grounded by reminding me constantly to take breaks. Bagheera, my partly feral cat, is fierce and independent, yet nurturing and compassionate at the same time. My love for these cats is immense; they provide forms of intimacy, care, and love that demonstrate the importance of human and nonhuman forms of relationality as essential to how we navigate and survive the world.

Blackness is still to be thought.

—KEGURO MACHARIA,

Frottage: Frictions of Intimacy Across the Black Diaspora

Introduction

AFRO-NORMATIVITY, INDENTURE AESTHETICS, AND SOUTH AFRICAN BLACKNESS

In a self-portrait titled *I Am Kali, I Am Black*, the artist Reshma Chhiba uses photography to complicate the relationship between (South African) Indianness and (South African) blackness by evoking the deviant and transgressive feminine energies of the Indian goddess Kali. *I Am Kali, I Am Black* is a medium close-up shot that frames the artist from just above the head to below the shoulders while drawing attention to her facial expressions. Chhiba stands in front of a white background gazing directly into the camera. The right half of her face is strategically blackened out by her use of lighting, while the left half is visible. Her hair is disheveled and extends from her head outward and outside of the photographic frame. In a disrespectful manner, her tongue points downward from her mouth as she gazes defiantly into the camera.

I Am Kali, I Am Black was part of a multimedia and multisited exhibition titled *The Two Talking Yonis*, imagined as a conversation between Chhiba and curator Nontobeko Ntombela. The exhibition opened on August 8, 2013, one

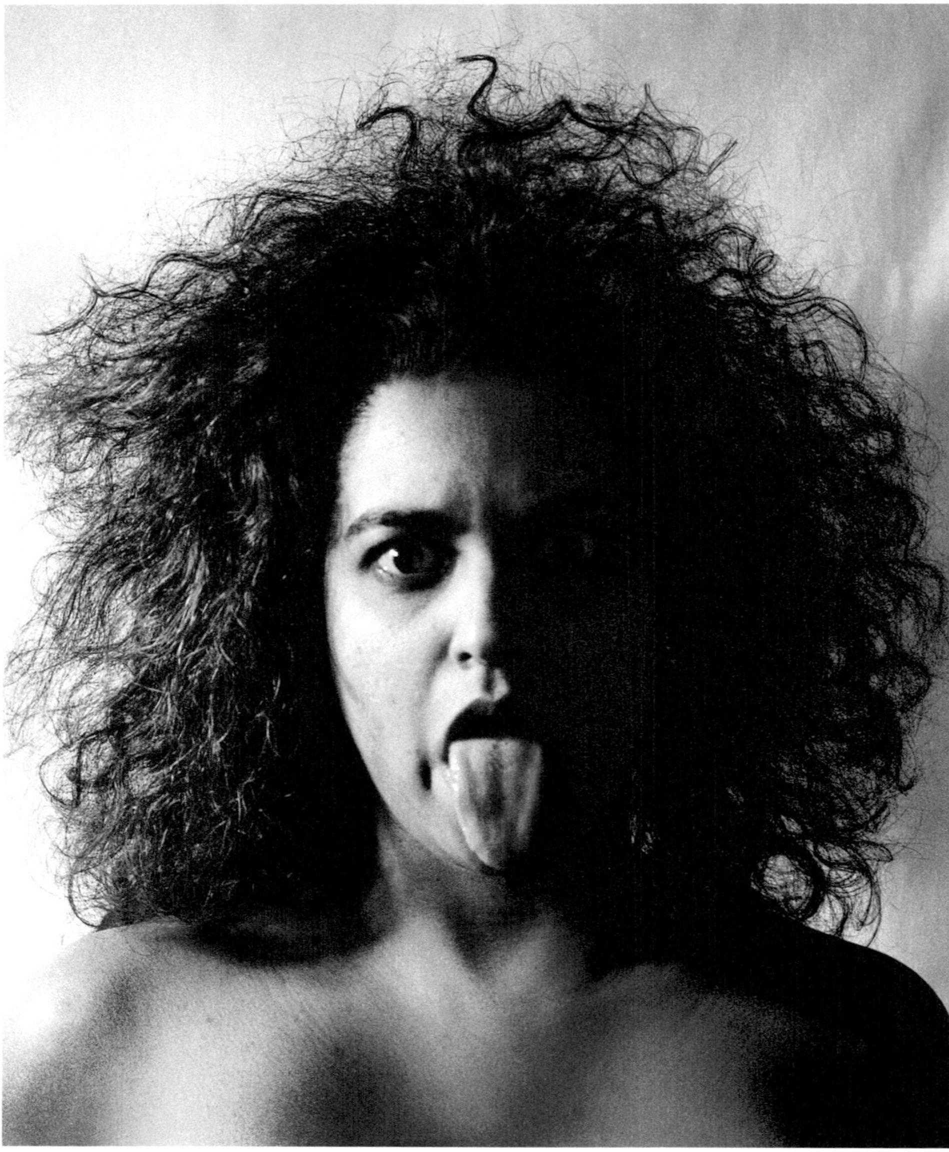

FIGURE I.1. Reshma Chhiba, *I Am Kali, I Am Black*. Courtesy of the artist.

day before Women's Day, an official South African public holiday that honors approximately twenty thousand women across the racial spectrum who marched to the Union Buildings in Pretoria in 1956 to protest the "pass laws." These laws required all *black* people to apply for a government-issued document to travel within the country. The artist located the portrait *I Am Kali, I Am Black* inside a spectacular twelve-foot walk-in *yoni*, titled "Come Inside." Yoni is a Sanskrit word that can be loosely translated to mean vulva, vagina, womb, and "sacred portal." The installation dominated the entrance to Constitution Hill, which houses the country's Constitutional Court, formed soon after the first democratic elections in 1994. As the highest court in the country, it governs all matters related to "the interpretation, protection, and enforcement of the constitution."[1] The 1996 Constitution of South Africa, recognized as one of the most liberal in the world, enshrines the protection of gender and sexual rights, disability rights, and minority group rights under the larger purview of human rights protection. Importantly, Constitution Hill was the site of a women's prison built in 1910. Prominent antiapartheid political activists, including Fatima Meer, Albertina Luthuli, and Winnie Madikizela-Mandela, as well as hundreds of other women, were incarcerated on this site.

Designed to be haunting and disruptive, Chhiba described the installation as a "screaming vagina . . . revolting against this space . . . mocking this space, by laughing at it." Chhiba's screaming yoni mocks the 1996 Constitution for its inability to protect women and children from gender-based violence, which includes rape, murder, femicide, uxoricide, and filicide. Through an aesthetic of female/feminine excess, Chhiba renders hypervisible the vulnerability and violation of South African women as a provocative critique of the limits of freedom in postapartheid South Africa. *I Am Kali, I Am Black* also critiques the shifting nature of South African blackness, mocking the repetition of colonial-apartheid logics of race in the postapartheid period. Chhiba unsettles the "visual regimes of colonial [-apartheid] modernity" (Gopinath 2018, 7) as it continues to organize South African sensibilities of race. Her portrait evokes the identification-style photograph—an instrument of state bureaucracy central to the governmentality of race in South Africa—used to "[document] and [catalogue]" physical differences (Masondo 2019, 79). Linked to the administrative and social control of native and colonized populations, the identification photo consolidated and overdetermined racial categorizations, rendering the racial hierarchy "common sense" to South Africans (Posel 2001). Indeed, South Africans live in the afterlife of the visual regimes of colonial-apartheid modernity, which continue to "determine what we see, how we see, and how we are seen" (Gopinath 2018, 7).

By titling the portrait *I Am Kali, I Am Black*, Chhiba troubles the boundaries between the racial categories black and Indian, evoking Black Consciousness (BC). Black Consciousness emerged as a politicized blackness during the antiapartheid struggle to include black Africans, Indians, and coloureds, those *blackened* by the colonial-apartheid state. Chhiba writes: Kali is "*Indian in her blackness and black in her Indianness*," referencing the deep historical entanglements between Indianness, blackness, and Africanness, obscured across time and space through the colonial governmentality of race in South Africa (2017, 48). Through her Afro-Indian aesthetic, Chhiba mocks the consolidation of postapartheid blackness through the abjection of Indians (and coloureds). This abjection secures the boundaries of the proper/authentic national black subject of the new nation.

Indeed, Chhiba draws on Kali's association with female/feminine excess and deviance to disrupt the boundaries between the racial-identitarian categories Indian and black and to trouble the binary and hierarchical relationship between Indianness and blackness. Chhiba offers a provocative representation of Afro-Indianness forged firmly within South African blackness. The artist gestures toward the importance of reimagining Afro-Indian intimacies in a context where particular performances of blackness consolidate as normative and nativist, repeating a longer history that constructs the Indian as alien to South Africa. I begin with *I Am Kali, I Am Black* because Chhiba engages the visual field to critique the shifting nature of South African blackness, while drawing on Kali's transgressive feminine energies to reimagine Afro-Indian relationalities through the aesthetic realm. *Indenture Aesthetics* is my attempt at theorizing and imagining an Afro-Indian positionality as an iteration of South African blackness, which functions as a site of reorientation to understand Afro-Indian intimacies and blackness otherwise.[2]

Indenture Aesthetics uses the term *Afro-Indian* in various ways. First, Afro-Indian refers to the indentured class and their descendants (those who continue to live in the afterlife of indentureship), troubling the homogenous racial-identitarian category Indian. This category has for a long time been conflated with that of the merchant/trader class. Afro-Indian works against this misrecognition and reminds us that the longer histories of slavery in the Cape and indentureship in Natal have emplaced the Afro-Indian differently within South African society. This emplacement necessitates an engagement with South African blackness. Even though all South African Indians (across the merchant class and indentured class) were blackened through colonial-apartheid state policies, it is important to recognize that the blackening of the trader class was significantly different from the blackening of the indentured class; and the emplacement of the trader class was also significantly different from the emplacement of the indentured class.[3] Second, Afro-Indian refers to the relationalities between Afro-Indian and black African communities, invisibilized through colonial-apartheid social engineering and racialization. Last, I use Afro-Indian not as an identitarian category but as a positionality, a site of reorientation through which we can reimagine our interconnected pasts, presents, and futures otherwise.

In this book, I work with, through, and against colonial-apartheid-era racial categories—Indian, African, coloured—because of the enduring impact it has on social life in South Africa. It is important to recognize that we, South Africans, continue to understand ourselves, our relationships with one another, and our relationship to the state through these racial categories. Within the colonial-apartheid racial hierarchy, coloureds and Indians occupied a similar positionality. However, *Indenture Aesthetics* does not engage coloured artists and perspectives for various reasons. First, coloureds occupy a different positionality within South African society, and their relationship to blackness (and whiteness) also manifests differently from Afro-Indian relations to blackness (and whiteness.) Second, unlike the Indian, the coloured is not framed as a foreign-Other through political and popular discourse, even though coloureds are abjected from postapartheid nativist articulations of blackness. Last, ongoing political calls to shift the category coloured from a racial identity to an ethnic identity (Khoi or Griqua) would refigure coloured relations to land, indigeneity, and nativism as a mode of postapartheid belonging. This would require a different contextualization than this book is able to provide. My hope is that my concept of indenture aesthetics, structured around the importance of organizing and imagining across difference, would be capacious enough for other researchers to engage the intimacies between coloured blackness and Afro-Indian blackness.[4]

Indenture Aesthetics curates an archive of aesthetic practices in order to understand the relationship between cultural politics and political culture in South Africa. It examines how Afro-Indian and black African women and queer artists turn to the aesthetic realm to examine the (queer) limits of freedom after 1994. By illuminating the aesthetic practices of Afro-Indian and black women and queer artists, *Indenture Aesthetics* seeks to displace the normative subject across the sedimented racial categories Indian and black to articulate, through a radical politics of difference, forms of intimacies that disrupt the desire for belonging to the nation. Indeed, within the South African context, Indianness is racially queer to the black-white colonial-apartheid racial hierarchy. *Indenture Aesthetics* carefully teases open the racial-identitarian category Indian, as it manifests within the South African imaginary, to reveal indentureship as the queer limit of South African Indianness. Thus, this book locates indentureship, and its afterlives, as a form of feminization that situates Afro-Indianness as always already queer. Harnessing the queer potential of indentureship as a world-making practice, I develop a queer (femme) analytic that is central to this book's queer curatorial mandate and queer-reading practice. In order to imagine otherwise, *Indenture Aesthetics* confounds what we think we know about race in South Africa by foregrounding various forms of feminization, femininities, and femme-ness, which unsettle and render pliable/queer the categories black, Indian, and African. This book examines how the aesthetic has become a site of critique and one of endless possibilities to understand the emergence of "new political vernaculars" (Macharia 2016). These "new political vernaculars" emerge out of various positionalities of vulnerability and feminization/femininity to destabilize the narrative of newness, queering the linear and progressive narrative of freedom associated with the postapartheid era.

I Am Kali, I Am Black informs two main points this book makes in relation to the aesthetic. First, I am interested in how the feminine, and its different manifestations, is central to the emergence of new aesthetic practices that become the vehicle of possibility to imagine otherwise. Second, I am interested in how the queer-aesthetic practices of Afro-Indian and black African artists, when curated together, illuminate our deeply entangled pasts, presents, and futures. Indeed, to begin with a portrait that evokes the *Indianness of blackness* and the *blackness of Indianness* is to locate this project firmly within the imperfect philosophies of Black Consciousness (BC). BC guides the ways in which I seek to rethink an ethical politics of relationality through the aesthetic and what that could possibly look like in contemporary South Africa.

In this book, I argue that it is within the realm of the aesthetic that we can trace, imagine, and rearticulate forms of intimacies between Afro-Indianness, Africanness, and blackness. In a context where the fixity of racial-identitarian categories repeats the colonial-apartheid hierarchy of race/being, the aesthetic functions as a hinge through which we can comprehend the deep intimacies between the categories black, Afro-Indian, and African otherwise. *Indenture Aesthetics* curates an archive that rubs against hegemonic and normative ways of seeing, knowing, and sensing race and belonging, agitating for an alternative politic organized around those deviant, transgressive, wild, and unruly subjects who disrupt and exceed the boundaries of the black nation and the authentic black subject. In a context where the hegemonic narrative of "mutual non-recognition" has for too long structured Afro-Indian relations, I turn to the aesthetic realm to trace lines of embodied desire between Afro-Indian and South African black communities to reorientate our understanding of race and to illuminate our deeply entangled pasts, presents, and futures. I coin the concept of *indenture aesthetics* to understand how race, sexuality, desire, pleasure, and violence become entangled with one another to open up possibilities to read and imagine South African blackness and Afro-Indiannness *otherwise* (Chuh 2003; Crawley 2016).

History and Context

Slavery, Indentureship, and the Making of Race in South Africa

In order to understand the role of the aesthetic and its relationship to the political, it is necessary to delineate some specifics of South African history as it relates to race and racialization, focusing specifically on the relationship between the racial categories Indian and black. It is also necessary to sketch some of the specifics of Afro-Indian intimacies as they relate to the making of South African blackness. Indians/Asians were relocated to Southern Africa through distinct but overlapping imperial processes: a combined Dutch and British colonial system of slavery that lasted from 1653 to 1852 in the Cape and a system of British indenture labor that began in 1860 and ended in 1911 in Natal. As colonial expansion and settlement progressed in the Cape, the need for cheap and exploitable labor arose in a context where it was illegal to enslave Indigenous peoples—the Khoi and the San. Initially, Cape slavery was tightly controlled by the Vereenigde Oost-Indische Compagnie (Dutch East India Company) that, "excluded from regions such as Dahomey and Guinea by the Dutch West India Company," sought out alternative markets in the Indian Ocean World. Scholar Gabeba Baderoon (2014, 8) writes: "The Dutch exploited nodes of an existing slave trade established by the Portuguese, and people were captured as slaves from Mozambique, Madagascar, India, and territories in South-East Asia." From the seventeenth to the eighteenth centuries, the composition of the enslaved population in the Cape shifted significantly. While in the "seventeenth century, most slaves were from Madagascar . . . early in the [eighteenth] century, almost half of the slaves were from India and Sri Lanka. Twenty percent were brought to the Cape via Batavia (modern-day Jakarta). Toward the end of the VOC's reign, the number of slaves from Asia had declined considerably as they were replaced by men and women from Mozambique" (Young 2017, 14). Lasting approximately two centuries, the enslaved population in the Cape numbered "more than 60 000 people"

(Baderoon 2014, 8) and "encompassed a large variety of languages, cultures, religions, and even phenotype" (Young 2017, 154).[5]

After the abolition of slavery in 1834, the British devised an alternative coercive labor system called "indentureship," designed to replace the transatlantic slave trade. In colonial Natal, Indian indentured workers did not replace enslaved Africans on plantations like in the Americas or in Mauritius.[6] The British introduced the indentured labor force into a context where the Zulus were "relatively secure in [their] tribal economy" and resisted marketing their labor to white colonists (Meer et al. 1980, 1). Over a period of fifty-one years, 152, 641 Indians were relocated to Natal and indentured mostly to sugarcane plantations as well as to coal mines, tea plantations, and European-owned estates in the Natal Midlands.[7] Initially, indenture contracts were for a three-year period, but by 1864 indenture contracts were extended to a five-year period. After ten years, indentured workers shifted to "free" Indian status. In this context, free signals a shift in status from being bound to the indenture contract to being able to sell one's labor independently within the colony. Some "free" Indians continued to work on plantations, while others sought work in coal mines and on railways. Many attempted to live and work independently as fishermen, market gardeners, and agriculturalists. However, determined to restrict the importation and settlement of indentured workers, Natal colonists introduced Act 17 of 1895. This act imposed a three-pound tax on Indians designed to limit new Indian immigration and restrict the movement of "free" Indians within Southern Africa. The three-pound tax forced many ex-indentured workers to reindenture, ensuring the subordinate and temporary position of the indentured class in South Africa.

In the early 1870s, "passenger" Indians began to immigrate to Natal. Passenger Indians paid their own way to the colony and were a merchant/trader class (a colonial middleman class) mainly from Gujarat and Mauritius. Even though the colonists (colonial-apartheid state) made no distinction between the passenger Indian class and the indentured class, it is undeniable that the "Indianness of the trader . . . was [and continues to be] distinct from the Indianness of the worker" (Dhupelia-Mesthrie 2000, 14). Indeed, the racialization of the indentured Indian through coercive labor practices disrupts the homogenization of these two groups into a singular racial type based on phenotype and geography. As indentured Indians moved from the official system of indentureship to other forms of labor like market gardening, for instance (overdetermined as free labor), the colonial-apartheid state invisibilized the differences between the indentured class and the passenger Indian class. Within the South African imaginary, all Indians occupy the positionality of the merchant/trader class and have become a homogenous racial-ethnic category. Through this class positionality, the colonial-apartheid state positioned the Indian as a buffer population between the European settler community and local African communities, which continues to fuel Afro-Indian antagonisms. Within this context, the abstract figure of the Indian functions as a scapegoat where anxieties over economic exploitation, of which the "unresolved question over land and dwelling" is but one element, are displaced.

In nineteenth-century colonial Natal, Europeans referred to Indians as the "Asiatic Menace." The Indian, a category conflated with that of the colonial middleman class, threatened the positionality of Europeans because they were perceived as "competing for space, trade, and political influence" within "colonial society" (Swanson 1983, 404). Indians were denied full access to political rights, which the merchant class viewed as essential to protecting and developing their capitalist interests. The trader class, unlike the indentured laborer, was able to "claim civil and economic rights as British subjects" and was "exempt from class legislation affecting Natives, Coloured persons or members of uncivilized races" (404). As passenger and "free" Indians settled across small towns and cities, anti-Indian sentiment was also driven by competition over space. Since class could not be used to restrict Indian settlement, Europeans framed Indian "habits and customs" as being "totally at variance with and repugnant to those of Europeans" (406–7), thus racializing Indians as a foreign element in the country with nothing in "common with the established South African community."

It is important to note that African voices are largely absent from early colonial archives (mid- to late nineteenth century); thus we cannot know for certain black African impressions of early Indian indentured workers. By the early twentieth century, the rift between the Indian community and the African middle class was well noted by John Dube, founder of the newspaper *Ilanga Lase Natali* and the first president of the ANC. In an article titled "The Indian Invasion," he wrote, "We know by sad experience how beneath our very eyes our children's bread is taken by these Asiatics: how whatever earnings we derive from Europeans go to swell the purses of these strangers, with whom we seem obliged to trade" (quoted in Hughes 2007, 163). In colonial Natal, Europeans and Africans blamed Indians for all sorts of social ills.[8] For many Africans, the Indian was seen as an "extension of foreign domination." Within Indian communities, it is not uncommon for black Africans to be referred to as *ravans*, a reference to the South Indian god Ravana. This derogatory term "captures the sense of the African world as alien, distant, threatening, violent and peopled by strong and violent sexual predators who are consumed by uncontrolled bodily drive" (Hansen 2012, 98). By this stage, Africans had adopted colonial attitudes toward the Indians and vice versa. The structures of colonial rule and racialization did not allow any form of recognition and desire between these two communities. However, within this context of deep racial fractures, Afro-Indian political solidarities began to emerge.[9]

With the establishment of the Union of South Africa in 1910, Indians, homogenized as an undifferentiated group, posed a problem to the national question and the creation of a "white man's land" (Peberdy 2009, 32–33). In 1925, D. F. Malan, Minister of the Interior, declared, "The Indians, as a race in this country, is an alien element in the population" (quoted in Dhupelia-Mesthrie 2000, 15). Mobilizing their rights as subjects of the British Empire, "many merchants, in an attempt to negotiate colonial hierarchies, reinforced their supposed superiority to native Africans" (Young 2017, 149). Scholars like Soske (2017) and Young have noted that within this context, "Indianness came to have meaning through ritual enactments of an imaginary culture in need of protection from the corrosive forces of modernity. These imaginary investments in Indianness did not reproduce India in various locations across time and space. Instead, they resulted in coerced performances of racialization based on difference from blackness and loss of cultural authenticity" (Young 2017, 170).

When the Afrikaner Nationalist Party came into power in 1948, one of their main objectives was "to produce fixed, stable, uniform, criteria for racial classification which would then be binding across all spheres of a person's life" (Posel 2001, 98). The colonial-apartheid state solidified categories of race mostly through the Population Registration Act of 1950.[10] With the Act of 1950, the state invested in producing a new national population register and identity documents that recorded a person's race as either white, coloured, or Native. Initially, Indian was a subcategory of coloured, a category reserved for mixed-race people that still functions as a racial category in contemporary South Africa. Indians were never imagined as a permanent population and therefore the Population Registration Act of 1950 did not initially include Indian/Asian as a distinct racial category. The racial category "Asian" emerged after South Africa became a republic in 1961 (Dlamini 2020, 21).[11] Descendants of Cape slaves were incorporated into the category coloured, flattening "South Africa's complex entanglement with Indian and South Atlantic Ocean histories" (Erasmus 2017, 6). In 1951, the Afrikaner Nationalist Party began to use the category "Bantu" instead of "Native." In 1978, this category changed to "black" (Erasmus 2012, 1). The colonial and apartheid state's use of Native, Bantu, and black referred to those who were "members of the aboriginal races or tribes of Africa south of the Equator" (Posel 2001, 90).[12] *Indenture Aesthetics* follows many South African scholars' preference not to capitalize "black," "white," and "coloured." Scholars like Asanda Ngoasheng (2021, 147) write, "This is a political statement to remind us that race is a 'social construct.'" While recognizing that there are a heterogeneity of positions regarding the use of *Black* or *black* in the United States, in this book, when referring to US Blackness, I use *Black* for two reasons. First, to make a distinction between South African blackness and US Blackness, and second, to respect US Black scholars who argue that this is a form of empowerment and respect that "honors Black experiences and speak with moral clarity about racism."[13]

Blackening and Racialization

The complex histories of coercive labor practices, indicative of overlapping regimes of racialized labor, denaturalize today's racial-identitarian categories. In the 1860s, when indentured workers arrived in Natal, the racial-identitarian categories Indian, African, and black were not firmly established categories. However, practices of racialization were already embedded in colonial society since the era of slavery in the Cape. During this period, a racial hierarchy began to congeal around a "color prejudice," subscribed to by "'respectable' whites," which "articulated a link between the inherent deviancy of the 'non-white'/less human and systems of coercive labor" (Young 2017, 6). Within this context, "whiteness became essential to the category of the human, [while] slavery and other forms of coerced labor began to be inextricable from notions of blackness" (6). Coercive labor practices like slavery and the different manifestations of indentureship that stretch from the seventeenth to the nineteenth centuries are forms of blackening that are unaccountable for within our contemporary understandings of racial formations in South Africa. My notion of blackening evokes the "deathscapes" (Mohabir 2019) associated with racialized labor and their afterlives. In the context of indentureship, the *kala pani* (black waters) has become an important metaphor to evoke the "deathscapes" of indentureship.

The journey across the *kala pani* reveals a process of blackening—a form of abjectification that is a defining feature of a labor system that not only was designed to replace transatlantic slavery, but which also saw the Indian as replaceable, disposable, and in large supply. Within the Indian Ocean World as well as the Caribbean and the Pacific, on ships and plantations, slavery and indentureship imbricated and rubbed against each other. My concept of indentureship and its afterlives draws on Saidiya Hartman's notion of the afterlife of slavery. *Indenture Aesthetics* does not argue that indentureship and its afterlives are a substitute for or new version of slavery and its afterlives. The question of whether indentureship is another form of slavery continues to be debated and is not something taken up in this book.[14] *Given the context in which the indenture system developed, indentureship is part of the afterlife of slavery*. Not only were the indentured described by colonial authorities as "of a black color" (Anderson 2009, 99) thus entering a colonial racial schema; to enter the indenture system was to enter a blackened world characterized by high mortality rates, various forms of sexual and physical violence on board coolie ships, and deadly work conditions on plantations, coal mines, and tea estates. Meer (1969, 11) notes that by "contracting to Natal, Indian workers had unwittingly chosen one of the worst conditions of labour under the indenture system."

However, these deathscapes cannot be neatly assigned to the past; they repeat into present forms of coercive labor systems like the extensive African migrant labor system that continues to blacken those who work on sugarcane plantations and coal, gold, and platinum mines, as well as the extensive labor system associated with the wine industry in the Cape. This is the afterlife of colonial apartheid, which recognizes that those black/ened by the state continue to live within the logics of the plantation, troubling the racial-identitarian categories and the hierarchy of race designed to keep us in place.

Blackening also evokes the colonial-apartheid racial hierarchy and the way labor (extraction and exploitation) has historically positioned some communities at the bottom of this racial schema while recognizing that practices of racialization shift across time and space. I am drawn to the notion of blackening because it shifts the ways in which Indianness and blackness manifest within the South African imaginary as incommensurable racial-identitarian categories. Furthermore, the homogenization of all Indians into one category, that of the merchant/trader class, was a deliberate strategy employed by the colonial-apartheid state to fracture Afro-Indian relations by positioning the Indians in the middle of the colonial hierarchy. This occurred through state-practices/ modes of governmentality as well as within the community, informed by a deep desire for respectability and belonging, submerging the history and afterlife of indentureship. Blackening evokes the death-worlds of the sugarcane and tea plantations, the coal mines, and other spaces where Indians and black Africans from Southern Africa were indentured across colonial Natal, reduced to units of labor, and rendered exploitable and replaceable. Drawing on Black studies scholars, to be blackened is to be written out of history by "being rendered abject," to evoke Darieck Scott (2010, 38). Blackening provides a framework to understand the slippery forms of intimacies formed between displaced and disenfranchised groups as they coagulate/d within the death-worlds of labor. These forms of intimacies exceed and explode the project of colonial-apartheid racialization. Blackening shifts how we understand South African blackness by troubling its nativist underpinnings. Thus, my notion of blackening also encompasses the lives and experiences of those I categorize as the new black/ened Others. Blackening reveals where the boundaries between the new black/ened Others bleed and collapse into one another, illuminating the material and psychic conditions that position the new black/ened Others—those rendered intimate strangers through the project of racialization—within a similar structural frame. Within this context, my notion of blackening functions as a site of reorientation, queering the nativist and (hetero)normative iterations of postapartheid blackness redirecting us to those who exist outside of the time-space of the nation.

The specificities of Cape slavery, indicative of the deep entanglements between different forms of coercive labor practices criss-crossing the Indian Ocean and the African continent, have a particular valence in this region that is significantly different from the Atlantic World. In the Indian Ocean World, systems of coercive labor practices like slavery, indentureship, Indigenous labor, and other forms of migrant labor overlap across time and space.[15] Young (2017, 158) argues that in the context of coercive labor systems, the distinction between "free" (indentureship as it applies to both the Khoikhoi during the era of slavery and Indian indenture labor in the nineteenth century) and "unfree"/slave labor is difficult to maintain. She argues that "all labor relations at various moments combine aspects of freedom and unfreedom. Slavery and indenture repeat the same performances on the same plantations across time and space; both systems, in their deployment of similar narratives of race, consent and force, function as surrogates for imperial labor."

Throughout this book, I foreground the iterative nature of indentureship that connects various coercive labor practices across time and space as they unfold on plantations in the Indian and Atlantic Ocean Worlds. The iterative nature of indentureship also evokes contemporary forms of coercive labor practices, like African migrant labor, which continue to construct blackened lives within the death-worlds of capital.[16] Thus, indentureship functions as a hinge through which we can understand how older forms of racialization are entangled with more contemporary forms of postapartheid racialization.[17]

Indenture Aesthetics evokes the notion of blackening to complicate and shift how we have been conditioned through the colonial-apartheid state to see and imagine the Indian in South Africa. I argue that indentureship was a form of blackening that is unaccountable for within contemporary formations of race in South Africa. Indentureship both stretches and reveals the queer limit of South African blackness (Richardson 2013). My notion of blackening reveals the making of Afro-Indianness within the longue durée of Southern African history that can be traced back to the era of slavery. Cape slavery exceeds the association between modern understandings of Blackness (via the Black Atlantic) and the notion of a "universal transparent . . . black body" (Young 2017, 7). The entanglements that occurred between Indianness/Asianness, blackness, and indigeneity during the era of slavery in the Cape unsettles contemporary categories of race in South Africa as routed through the Atlantic World and sedimented by the colonial-apartheid state.

Given this context, *Indenture Aesthetics* traces various aesthetic forms of blackening that queer the hetero-nativist parameters of South African blackness and Indianness to rethink the positionality of the Afro-Indian in relationship to South African blackness. For example, in Sharlene Khan's *when the moon waxes red*, the journey through the death-worlds of indentureship and its afterlives is a form of blackening that aesthetically engages the sugarcane plantations as well as scenes of gendered violence and death. In FAKA's performance art practice, blackening manifests as an aesthetic of bodily *excess* and *waste* through which the artists explore the violent expulsion of black queerness from the boundaries of authentic blackness. As a critique of temporality, memory, and collective national amnesia, Mohau Modisakeng mobilizes an aesthetic of blackening that references the death-world of the coal mining industry. In his photographic and video art, Modisakeng focuses on the mine worker who exists outside of nation-time. Through an aesthetic of blackening, Modisakeng emphasizes the vulnerability and fungibility of the black body in the afterlife of colonial apartheid. As a critique of Afro-normativity, blackening directs us to the afterlives of colonial-indenture-apartheid, disrupting the linear and progress narrative of development associated with the post apartheid.

From Black Consciousness to the Afro-Normative

By evoking the notion of blackening within this larger context of colonial-apartheid space-making, *Indenture Aesthetics* reactivates Bantu Stephen Biko's notion of Black Consciousness. Black Consciousness emerged as a radical oppositional political framework during the antiapartheid struggle, which attempted to redefine blackness, drawing attention to the constructed nature of race. BC emerged within the context of the South African Students' Organisation (SASO), formed in 1969. SASO initially used the word *non-white* but shifted to a new framing of blackness, recognizing that the term *non-white* reiterated the positionality of black people as nonsubjects, while centering "whiteness as the aspired-to-norm" (Desai 2015, 39). In December 1971, Biko defined black people as "those who are by law or tradition politically, economically and socially discriminated against as a group in . . . South African society and identifying themselves as a unit in the struggle towards the realization of their aspirations. This definition illustrates to us a number of things: 1. Being black is not a matter of pigmentation—being *black is a reflection of a mental attitude*. 2. Merely by describing yourself as black, you have started on a road toward emancipation, you have committed yourself to fight against all forces that seek to use your blackness as a stamp that marks you out as a subservient being" (my emphasis, Biko 2017, 52).

By redefining blackness, the movement shifted understandings of blackness from an ontological given (pigmentation) to an understanding of blackness situated within the everyday lived experiences (phenomenology) of the three oppressed racial groups, black Africans, Indians, and coloureds. BC shifted the meaning of blackness from a "racial designation" into "an antiracist political subjectivity" (Rassool 2019, 364). BC organized the oppressed "around the cause of their oppression—the blackness of their skin" in order to "rid themselves of the shackles that bind them to perpetual servitude" (Biko 1971). BC recognized that white supremacy blackened the lives of those under the weight of colonial power. Biko referred to Africans, coloureds, and Indians as the "various segments of the black community" (Biko 2017, 56). It is important to note that Biko's definition of blackness is a politicized blackness that rubbed against the colonial-apartheid state's racial categories and cultural blackness. BC "was readily accepted by the politically initiated whilst the masses in all three black communities tended to regard themselves as just Indians, coloureds, or Africans" (Mpumlwana and Mpumlwana 2014, 105). As a form of political blackness, BC was a particular strategy for coalition-building across difference.

BC emerged during a period of immense social upheaval and political repression in South Africa. The 1960s were marked by the Sharpeville Massacre, the destruction and displacement of well-established communities through the Group Areas Act. In 1961, Indians were for the first time recognized as part of the permanent South African population after the apartheid state abandoned its desire to repatriate Indians back to India. During this period, BC was attractive to a particular set of Indians who recognized the dangers of the colonial-apartheid state's positioning of Indians as a colonial middleman class. Within the context of the 1960s, some Indians "began to call themselves 'black' and embraced the Black Consciousness Movement" (Desai 2015, 37). Saths Cooper, a student and founder member of SASO, writes, "BC [Black Consciousness] was a way of identifying subjectively with the conditions we found ourselves in objectively. We rose above the narrow ethnic and tribal definitions . . . [that] remove[d] people from collective action and collective identification" (Saths Cooper quoted in Desai 2015, 42). BC introduced the term *black* into "South African political language" (Mpumlwana and Mpumlwana 2014).[18]

The BC movement failed to understand that complete liberation must tackle the deeply entrenched patriarchal roots of black liberation organizations. South African black feminists have critiqued this era for its conservative gender and class politics. Mamphela Ramphele (1991, 215) writes, "Women were . . . involved in the movement because they were black. Gender as a political issue was not raised at all." The recuperation of the black community depended on the remasculinization of the black man, rendering the specificities of black women's oppression irrelevant to the larger project of liberation.[19] The class dynamics of BC further complicated the movement. The BC movement voiced the "*specific* oppression of relatively educated Black students (predominantly men), which forms only *part* of the overall oppression suffered by all other sectors of the black community" (Gqola 2001, 136).

In 1994, Mandela's government adopted Biko's definition of blackness to include Indians, coloureds, and Africans. The category black and, indeed, apartheid-era racial categories were reincorporated into political language and institutional structures by the state as a form of racial redress against the economic and social injustices of the past. Even though the ANC incorporated Biko's notion of blackness within its policy frameworks after 1994, it is important to note that there is a heterogeneity of positions within the ANC itself regarding the place of the Indians within the postapartheid national polity. With the end of apartheid, South Africa secured itself as a fully African nation, and all who lived in it became African. This new understanding of Africanness shifted the category black to "designate those previously classified as 'native,' 'Bantu,' or . . . 'African'" (Rassool 2019, 365). This resignification of Africanness to mean blackness is played out in the public arena as it relates to capital, the economy, and who is rightfully entitled to "enjoy" the nation (Mishra 2005). This shift has also complicated the ANC's identity as a nonracial organization.[20] In 2009, Julius Malema—former ANC Youth League president and current president of the Economic Freedom Fighters—voiced his frustration that Jacob Zuma had appointed "'minorities' to strategic economic positions" in his cabinet (Malefane 2009). According to Malema, the economic cluster should be populated with "Africans," meaning black Africans. He argued that:

"We need to build confidence in the markets that Africans are also capable of handling strategic positions in the economic sector" (quoted in Malefane 2009). In this statement, Malema clearly defines the authentic national subject as black African. The ANC reacted strongly; their secretary general Gwede Mantashe expressed rage over Indian and coloured ministers being referred to as "minorities." According to former Minister of Police Nathi Mthethwa, the word *minority* is not familiar to the ANC because it is a nonracial organization, and he stated that "*There is no such thing as coloureds and Indians as they were part of the struggle*" (my emphasis, Malefane 2009). Here, Mthethwa references struggle-liberation politics as a site where old identities gave way to new, nonracial, forms of identification. This reaction failed to engage with the everyday lived experiences of race and its hold on life in South Africa.

These debates are indicative of the shifting nature of South African blackness and signal two important shifts in postapartheid South Africa. First, the postapartheid nation is imagined as a black nation in a context where blackness has shifted from an "anti-racist political subjectivity" (Rassool 2019, 363) to a signifier of the "authentic national subject" (Chipkin 2002, 571), *he* who is entitled to enjoy the new country. Second, blackness itself is a contested site, where the boundaries of the authentic national subject and authentic Africanness are played out. As the debates above demonstrate, the authentic national subject is increasingly performed through a narrow *nativism* that intersects with both *class* and *heteronormativity*.

Within this context, *Indenture Aesthetics* turns to the aesthetic realm to regenerate a feeling of BC through a radical queer African imaginary. Influenced by Chhiba's transgressive representation of the Indian goddess Kali in her portrait *I Am Kali, I Am Black* and BC's desire to redefine the political through a radical politics of relationality, *Indenture Aesthetics* articulates an alternative politics of relationality designed to unsettle the colonial-apartheid logics of race and their sedimentation in postapartheid society. My reactivation of BC is influenced by an intersectional understanding of race, class, and queerness. By queering BC through a radical and decolonial African imaginary, *Indenture Aesthetics* is committed to reimagining Afro-Indian intimacies, Afro-Indianness, and South African blackness.

Afro-Normativity and the Myth of a Better Life

Given the specific historical, social, and political context of South Africa, I coin the term *Afro-normativity* to understand how new formations of race, particularly blackness, intersect with normative notions of gender, sexuality, and class to construct the new black authentic subject of the postapartheid state. I have chosen the lens of Afro-normativity because the phrase "South African black nationalism" does not adequately reflect the ANC's positionality as an explicitly nonracial organization and postapartheid South Africa as a Rainbow Nation, welcoming everyone irrespective of race, ethnicity, gender, class, and sexuality. Indeed, it can be argued that the phrase "South African black nationalism" is the antithesis of the ANC's political identity. Thus, Afro-normativity allows me to engage with the presence of exclusive forms of black nationalism being performed, engaged, and discussed by folk who often claim nonracialism and inclusive forms of postapartheid belonging. Afro-normativity illuminates both the governmentality and nongovernmentality aspects of race and nation and how it circulates within the political and social domains to create a class of racialized outsiders. Furthermore, the making of the authentic versus inauthentic national subject must be contextualized within the context of colonial apartheid and the ANC's inheritance of a colonial-apartheid state apparatus in 1994. Thus, the logics of Afro-normativity are vestiges of colonialism and apartheid. Afro-normativity understands xenophobia and nativism as white supremacy, and settler-colonial violences that have a particular valence in the postapartheid era given our inheritances of the colonial-apartheid state. I am interested in how ideas of black authenticity and nativism attach to particular kinds of bodies to forge an authentic national subject that must abject those who are constructed through these attachments as inauthentic (the new black/ened Others). Thus, *Indenture Aesthetics* seeks to also understand Afro-normativity as a nationalist political positioning that treats black women, black LGBTIQ+ peoples, Indians, and coloureds (and those at the intersections) as outsider positionalities, hindering the ability to organize across difference.

How have we arrived at an understanding of postapartheid blackness as a racial-identitarian category representative of "the 'authentic national subject,' who manifests as elite capitalist" invested in maintaining a nationalist vision of black autochthony tethered to a (hetero)normative imaginary of the African body?

The roots of postapartheid economic inequality can be traced to the colonial era and the policies designed to displace, disenfranchise, and exclude Africans, and to a lesser extent, Indians and coloureds, from the economic mainstream. However, the transition to democracy did little to change the racialized nature of economic inequality in South Africa. Scholars have termed the transition in the late 1980s and early 1990s as an "elite transition" (Bond 2000). One of the compromises made by the ANC during the Convention for a Democratic South Africa (CODESA) meetings "allowed whites to keep the best land, the mines, manufacturing plants, and financial institutions" (Bond 2004, 45), securing the privileged position of whites through the maintenance of settler capital. After being voted into power, the ANC shifted from being a "popular-nationalist anti-apartheid project to official neoliberalism" (Bond 2000, 1). The ANC's "adherence to free market economic principles has produced a context where there has been no profound challenge to the market, but rather an affirmation of its hegemonic role in the ordering of society" (1). Invariably, this ordering maps onto racialized lines to create a context where the black majority, those who do not belong to the black elite class, find themselves at the bottom of the racial-economic hierarchy. The ANC prioritized economic development through neoliberalism, ensuring the construction of a black elite class at the expense of the black/ened majority.

Furthermore, the ANC's affirmative action policies and Broad-Based Black Economic Empowerment (BBBEE) policies, designed to redress the material imbalances of the past, have done little to change the racialized nature of capital in South Africa. BBBEE was not simply a "moral initiative." It was designed as a "pragmatic strategy to realize the country's full economic potential while helping to bring the black majority into the economic mainstream."[21] However, BBBEE policies have failed to even the playing field and have even exacerbated economic inequality, which, given the history of South Africa, maps along racialized lines. BBBEE and neoliberal economic policies have created a new black elite/middle class. According to sociologist Roger Southall (2016, xiv), the rise of a black middle class after 1994 "is one of the most visible aspects of post-apartheid society." Increasingly, the new black elite—popularly referred to as the "Black Diamonds"—have been associated with the post-apartheid phenomenon of "tenderpreneurs" and its relationship to state corruption.[22] The elite and neoliberal underpinnings of South Africa have created a context characterized by deep structural entanglements between the black elite and white capital, which necessitates the unfreedom of the black masses.[23] The making of the black elite through neoliberal economic policies, the preservation of settler capital through the negotiated settlement, and the ANC's inheritance of a colonial state structure all work together to create a class of outsiders.

The battle against the colonial-apartheid state was waged as one against racial discrimination. It was imagined that the dismantling of apartheid would restore the dignity and humanity of the black population while projecting a global image of the new South Africa as modern and civilized. Key to this new dispensation was a reframing of gender and sexual politics, even as the new nation was tasked with dismantling older regimes of race. However, in postapartheid South Africa, race became the primary marker of freedom. The restoration of full humanity to the black masses was predicated on economic freedom with little conceptualization that gender and sexuality already variegate blackness. Indeed, black masculinities scholar Kopano Ratele (2006) argues that the ANC's promise of a better life, which narrowly focuses on economic development, is limited if it does not simultaneously tackle gender and sexual politics, particularly the dangers of "ruling masculinity."

In 1996, the South African state adopted one of the most liberal constitutions in the world. The Equality Clause of the 1996 Constitution secured minority rights protection, including ethnic/racial minority groups as well as the minority status of LGBTIQ+ South Africans.[24] Disrupting the apartheid regime's race-gender-sexual politics, the new South Africa positioned itself as exceptional both within the continent and globally through a politics of inclusion that informed the Equality Clause. In 1996, when the new constitution was adopted, South Africa was "the only country in the world" to constitutionally protect LGBTIQ+ rights. The inclusion of LGBTIQ+ rights was also informed by global forces, intersecting with local aspirations (Oswin 2007). The adoption of the 1996 Constitution also marked a significant shift concerning sexual politics in Southern Africa. This was one year after the Zimbabwean president, Robert Mugabe, declared his repugnance toward gays and lesbians, shaping a broader postcolonial African discourse that positions homosexuality as "un-African," a Western contamination, and a threat to African nationalism and the authentic African body.

Herein lie the major contradictions of postapartheid society. Constitutional protections, which guarantee the protection of gender rights—particularly the protection of "women's dignity and rights to full humanity" (Gqola 2007, 62), as well as LGBTIQ+ rights, do not translate on the ground. Not only has South Africa been labeled the rape capital of the world; gender-based violence affects straight, trans, and lesbian-identified black women in disproportionate numbers, while black LGBTIQ+ folks continue to experience significantly high levels of violence and death. African lesbian activist Bev Ditsie (2019) argues that the black queer/nonnormative body remains a threat to African culture and tradition because gay people's existence is perceived as a direct intention to "destroy Africa and Africanism." However, this rubs against the positioning of South Africa as a haven for gay, lesbian, queer, and sexually nonnormative people. Indeed, it can be argued that South Africa is a haven for white queer people. African queer studies scholar Xavier Livermon (2012a, 302) argues that this paradox (one of many in South Africa) is based on the "racialization of the queer body as white and the sexualization of the black body as straight."

In other words, the white queer body is a marker of freedom and attaches to the state's exceptional positioning in terms of LGBTIQ+ politics, whereas the black queer body is an aberration of the ways in which blackness is imagined and imagines itself as normative. It is well recognized in scholarly work and activist movements that "constitutional protections regarding race, class, gender, sexuality are far from sufficient in creating . . . [an] empowered citizenry" (Hoad et al. 2005, 19).

The high levels of gender-sexual-based violence in postapartheid South Africa can be attributed to the patriarchal foundations of South African society, informed and shaped by the violent conquest, settlement, and overlapping projects of racialization that can be traced from the era of slavery to the present. These imbricated histories of "violence and violation" are informed by an "ideology of militarism" (Gqola 2009) that can be traced to the ordering of Cape slave society through sexual subjection (rape, violation, sexual labor) and other forms of coercion. Indeed, Gqola and Baderoon (2014) call upon South African scholars to "take seriously the 'trauma of slavery and sexual subjection' on which South Africa is founded" (Gqola 2010, 42). Furthermore, in the postapartheid period, black feminist scholars have examined the relationship between the state and the violence of patriarchy (Ratele 2006; Gqola 2009; Hassim 2009).

South African scholars argue that we need to understand the different phases of South African history—colonialism, apartheid, and postapartheid—in terms of continuities rather than ruptures. This approach allows us to understand "how various power systems continue to shape contemporary South Africa" (Gqola 2009, 63). Thus, "heteropatriarchal recolonization" (Alexander 2005, 25) is a defining feature of Afro-normativity. In the context of the Caribbean, transnational feminist scholar M. Jacqui Alexander (25) coins this term to map out the continuities between "white imperial heteropatriarchy and Black heteropatriarchy" where "political and economic strategies are made to usurp the self-determination of the . . . people." Performances of Afro-normativity reveal how the state operates as a "citizenship machinery in order to produce a class of loyal heterosexual citizens and a subordinate class of sexualized, non-reproductive noncitizens, disloyal to the nation and therefore suspect" (Alexander and Mohanty 1997, xxiii). My concept of Afro-normativity attempts to make sense of the realignment of race, gender, sexuality, and class in the era of neoliberal capital. Indeed, the boundaries of normative blackness are secured through the constant *violation* of those rendered most *vulnerable*. Violence and violation stitch together the colonial, apartheid, and postapartheid eras. Within this context, *Indenture Aesthetics* disrupts the logics of the Afro-normative by organizing around those who exceed the boundaries of black authenticity. If the black normative subject is defined through nativist parameters, this reframing directs us to the new black/ened *Others* of the postapartheid period. Indeed, these new black/ened Others, a term I borrow from Michelle M. Wright (2004), agitate the class-gender-sexual-erotic respectability politics that define the authentic black national subject.

It is important to note that performances of Afro-normativity are entangled with performances of Indian normativity and respectability politics that construct the passenger Indian as the good Indian. A class analysis illuminates how the alienation of the passenger Indian is significantly different from the alienation of the indentured Indian. Through class, the passenger Indian has been able to claim partial belonging, and historically, this has played out in the economic arena where passenger Indians became politicized because of the colonial and apartheid state's infringement of their economic interests. Within the South African imaginary, the category of the Indian is both conflated with the merchant class and is always imagined as heteronormative. If Indian normativity (race, class, and gender-sexual politics) is secured through the merchant class, "indenture aesthetics" reveals the queerness of the indentured class (the Afro-Indian), its nonnormative positionality, which has historically challenged the project of Indian respectability politics. It is important to note that indenture aesthetics is not reducible to indenture history.

Black and queer studies scholars have argued that respectability politics (Higginbotham 1993) and homonormativity (Duggan 2002; Livermon 2012a) uphold rather than subvert systems of power and domination, rendering LGBTIQ+ as well as black and other racialized peoples more vulnerable to forms of violence and in the process hindering progressive organizing across difference. Indeed, respectability politics and homonormativity "[police] and [preserve] the boundaries between those who are able to conform to categories of normativity, respectability, and value, and those who are forcibly excluded from such categories" (Hong and Ferguson 2011, 2). Thus, *Indenture Aesthetics* is invested in decentering the fixed unitary subject across the racial-identitarian categories Indian and black to reveal both the differences within these categories and the *strange affinities* between the new black/ened Others.

Since the Afro-Indian is always already marked as Other (alienated), the Afro-Indian reveals the (queer) limit of the nation and thus enables us to recognize how black queer subjects, refugees, immigrants, the working-class and working poor, the destitute, and township and rural dweller fall outside of the norm. Thus, this concept of the Afro-Indian is needed in order to make this larger critique of Afro-normativity. If the Afro-Indian represents the queer limits of Afro-normative blackness, "indenture aesthetics" disrupts these racial normativities by displacing the normative subject across these racial structures. If Afro-normativity structures belonging to the nation through neoliberal subjecthood that creates strict boundaries between the new black/ened Others and the authentic black subject (the new black elite), then "indenture aesthetics" is an *articulation of a radical politics of (dis)belonging that provides a blueprint to think and feel outside of sedimented racial categories.* Thus, in this book, Afro-normativity names racial normativities, and my concept of "indenture aesthetics" is committed to a queering of these regimes of race.

Indenture Aesthetics is informed by the intersectional frameworks of US and South African black feminisms, Black queer studies, queer-of-color critique, and African queer studies. Drawing on a range of feminist scholars—Pumla Gqola, Shireen Hassim, Desiree Lewis, Barbara Boswell, Filomina Chioma Steady, Betty Govinden, Audre Lorde, Cathy Cohen, Roderick Ferguson, Grace Hong, Gayatri Gopinath—I consider the construction of the new black Others as racialized subjects, constituted through the intersections of race, class, gender, sexuality, region, and a number of other vectors of difference that shape postapartheid society. An intersectional framework reveals how gender and sexuality function as key determinants of authentic blackness. The construction of authentic blackness through the normative parameters of gender and sexuality depends on and exacerbates class differences.

In South Africa, black feminism emerges out of the long history of anticolonial and antiapartheid struggles. Black women have taught us that the struggle for freedom must simultaneously tackle race, culture, gender, sexuality, and class. South African black feminism resonates with the US category "women of color" feminism. The influence of Biko's notion of blackness as a site of collective political organizing among South African women of color is significant in contemporary South Africa (see Lewis and Baderoon 2021). South African black feminists have understood the importance of BC, even as they consistently eroded its heteronormative foundations. I am particularly interested in the ethical relational framework that is foundational to South African black feminism. This framework disrupts sedimented racial-identitarian categories as the basis of our political organizing, which inevitably subtend, rather than challenge, systems of power.

Indenture Aesthetics brings into conversation the radical work of South African black feminists with a queer intersectional framework that can be traced to Simon Nkoli. Nkoli was a black gay political activist who died from AIDS-related causes in 1998. Nkoli was a founding member of GLOW, the Gay and Lesbian Organisation of the Witwatersrand. He worked closely with the black lesbian activist and filmmaker Bev Ditsie until his death.[25] In 1984, Nkoli was arrested with twenty-one other political leaders by the apartheid state and sentenced to death for treason. In prison, he came out as gay. Nkoli was initially part of the predominantly white Gay Association of South Africa (GASA). After his arrest, GASA refused to intervene on his behalf, claiming that they were an apolitical organization. As a prisoner, Nkoli was also reprimanded by his comrades for wasting his time "fighting for moffies." This revealed to Nkoli the importance of an intersectional understanding of the relationship between oppression and power and the pitfalls of identity politics. As a political and gay rights activist, Nkoli recognized the inseparability of his blackness, his gayness, and his class positionality. He stated: "I'm gay, I'm black and I'm a working class person and I'm a person living with HIV, and I'm fighting apartheid" (quoted in Davids and Matebeni 2017, 163).[26] South African studies scholars Nadia Davids and Zethu Matebeni (2017) identify this as the moment where a split occurs between white gay identity politics and a queer politic informed by an intersectional understanding of the everyday lived experiences of black gay men, disproportionately affected by HIV, living in townships, and in poverty.

If the authentic black subject of the postapartheid state is rendered legible only in relation to the new black/ened Others, a queer comparative racialization framework reveals the *strange intimacies* between the new black/ened Others. Through a queer racialization framework, it becomes possible to "craft alternative understandings of subjectivity, collectivity, and power" (Hong and Ferguson 2011, 2). For these queer and queered subjects belonging is always out of reach. Here, women of color feminisms and queer-of-color critique provide a more sophisticated framework to understand the relationship between those who constitute the new black Others. As an alternative comparative framework, women of color feminisms disrupt nationalist and identitarian modes of political organization. Solidarity emerged out of queer women of color who had to negotiate various forms of unbelonging within nationalist and cultural nationalist logics. Hong and Ferguson (3) argue that women of color feminisms and queer-of-color critique provide "an alternative method [of comparison] that, in its deep critique of the racialized, gendered, and sexualized devaluation of human life, gives us a blueprint for coalition around contemporary politics." This book brings South African black feminisms and queer African studies in conversation with US women of color feminisms and queer-of-color critique to provide a more supple framework to understand how performances of Afro-normativity mobilize gender, sexuality, and class to separate the valued from those who are disposable. Whereas Afro-normativity secures its power through performances of a particular kind of black nationalist positioning that requires the abjection of differences, I am interested in centering difference as an urgent call to rethink the political and what constitutes the political.

Indenture Aesthetics is a call to reject, to refuse, to undermine, state-ist and cultural nationalist forms of belonging, in order to activate the politics of imagining otherwise. Indeed, *Indenture Aesthetics* is an experiment in unthinking the (Afro-normative) nation and nationalism that reinscribes the categories native, immigrant, and settler, maintaining what Nandita Sharma refers to as the "postcolonial new world order of nation-states" (Sharma 2020).[27]

Notes on Archive and Methodology

Vulnerability, Femininity, and the Otherwise

This book is a call, a practice, a curatorial project, a desire (my desire) for the otherwise. This desire for the otherwise emerges out of various recognitions: (a) the end of apartheid and the onset of a negotiated democracy in 1994 has resulted in a context where black unfreedom remains a central characteristic of postapartheid society; (b) categories of race formed within the crucible of colonial apartheid continue to shape postapartheid citizenship and notions of belonging, exacerbating xenophobic violence, of which anti-Indian sentiment is but one iteration; and (c) the trope of the Indian as the exploitative merchant class relies on a strategic misrecognition of Southern African history that renders the experience of Indian indentureship and a longer history of slavery in the Cape irrelevant to the past, the present, and the future. *Indenture Aesthetics* curates an archive of aesthetic and performance art practices committed to Ashon Crawley's (2016) call that "the otherwise is the disbelief in what is current and a movement towards, and an affirmation of, imagining other modes of social organization, other ways for us to be with each other. Otherwise is the enunciation and concept of irreducible possibility, irreducible capacity, to create change, to be something else, to explore, to imagine, to live fully, freely, vibrantly."

Methodologically *Indenture Aesthetics* is a queer curatorial project that develops a queer-reading practice informed by Black Consciousness. Methodologically, my reactivation of BC is organized around the blackened worlds of those who fall outside of the nation-state's normative strivings (Ferguson 2005) in my quest to articulate, through the aesthetic, a *radical decolonial politics of relationality*. My curatorial mandate is to bring into conversation Afro-Indian and black African artists whose works have not been positioned in relationship to one another before. By juxtapositioning these artists, I reactivate BC's philosophy of disrupting and confounding colonial-apartheid racial categories as an ongoing practice of reimagining the political nature of blackness. I turn to the aesthetic realm because of the enduring legacy of the visual regimes of colonial-apartheid modernity, which continue to determine not just sensibilities of race but also how South Africans relate to one another through the visuality of racialized bodies.

In South Africa, the aesthetic has historically been connected to the political. During apartheid, legislation banned "media from explicit depictions of sex. . . . Pornography was wholly banned; the public display of eroticized nude bodies (particularly male) was unthinkable" (Posel 2005, 54). During the transitional period "an aesthetic shift [was] visible" in South African cultural production, described by Thembinkosi Goniwe (2017, 12–13) "as a radical move away from the restrictive culture of resistance to a culture of liberated expressions."[28] However, like other sectors of South African society, the arts sector—arts administration, curators, artists, critics, writers—continues to struggle to adequately transform in terms of its race and gender politics. Artist-scholars like Goniwe (2017, 2018) and Sharlene Khan (2006, 2018) have critiqued the continuing hegemony of whiteness within the arts industry that privileges white artists, curators, critics, and writers, while fetishizing a particular kind of black aesthetic.[29]

These dynamics of power construct a blind spot related to the aesthetic practices of Afro-Indian artists. Within the South African imaginary, Indians are not artists, but merchants, medical doctors, accountants, and lawyers, even though there is a longer tradition of aesthetic practices by South African Indians that can be traced back to indentureship. In South Africa, one of the problems with Afro-Indian aesthetic production is its sparsity, the absence of art education and art classes in schools in previously "Indian" areas, and the lack of official, financed spaces and institutions dedicated to the production, exhibition, curation, collection, and critical writing about Afro-Indian art. Afro-Indian artists struggle for recognition, space, and visibility within the art world. This problem is compounded within the Indian community, where art practice as a viable career is unacceptable and taboo.

Given this context, this archive gestures toward the possibilities of creating new forms of knowledge and ways of seeing from cultural objects that may at first appear disparate and incommensurable. *Indenture Aesthetics* does this through an analysis of Lebohang Kganye's digital photography projects *Ke Lefa Laka: Her-Story* (2013) and *Ke Lefa Laka: Heir-Story* (2013) in relation to my own photography projects *Queering the Archive: Brown Bodies in Ecstasy* and the *Brown Photo Album*: *An Archive of Feminist Futurities*. I read Sharlene

Khan's multimedia project *when the moon waxes red*, in relationship to various artworks by Mohau Modisakeng. I also examine Sabelo Mlangeni's photography projects *Country Girls* (2003–9) and *Men Only* in relation to my short film *cane/cain* (2011). Finally, I read Reshma Chhiba's project *The Two Talking Yonis* in relationship to various live performances, photographs, and literary explorations of black queer life by the duo FAKA. In the coda, I examine the radical work of the newly emerging Kutti Collective, a new generation of women, queer, femme, and gender-nonconforming artists organizing under the name *Kutti*. Through this method of juxtapositioning, I am interested in what emerges when these aesthetic works rub against one another.

Thus, in my quest to imagine otherwise, I curate an archive of aesthetic practices that rub against one another aesthetically, methodologically, and theoretically. What happens when these artworks rub against one another, and where do they stick to and slide apart, refusing to touch/connect? What kinds of intimacies are produced through this act of rubbing? How do individual and collective forms of pain and pleasure manifest through rubbing? How does rubbing articulate a politic where the enunciation of difference can provide alternative routes to understanding our interconnected pasts, presents, and futures? What does rubbing reveal about Afro-Indian desires for blackness and for Africanness? How does rubbing slowly erode the heteronormative ways in which the categories Indian, black, and African figure within the South African imagination?

Indeed, rubbing reactivates the queer potential of BC. My notion of rubbing is influenced by and departs from Keguro Macharia's queer concept of frottage. Macharia (2019, 4) positions frottage as "a relation of proximity" that "unsettles the heteronormative tropes through which the black diaspora have been imagined and idealized." For Macharia, frottage is an "intense longing for intimacy" (5) that is not anchored to a "genealogical tree" based on a notion of belonging through blood kinship models. Whereas Macharia is invested in the blackness of the black diaspora (intraracial experience), I am interested in interracial intimacies, produced out of what Lisa Lowe refers to as the "intimacies of four continents" (Lowe 2006, 2015).[30] For many African and Asian diaspora scholars (Macharia 2009; Reddy 2015), the relationship between intimacy and the aesthetic functions on numerous levels. According to Reddy (234), "Intimacy gives expression to tacit, minor, or ephemeral affective relations that remain difficult to locate in state or official archives and that may surface only within the domains of the aesthetic and representational." Macharia (2009, 162) argues that both queer studies and African studies historically "privileged aesthetics as a mode to access and forge ethical relations." The aesthetic has also been mobilized as a method to read for "possibilities foreclosed or absent in official political discourse."

I am interested in a concept of rubbing that recenters the body, the libidinal, the erotic, and the sensual, queering the project of race-craft in South Africa and Afro-normativity's performance of a black African kinship model predicated on nativism and heteronormativity.

Rubbing displaces the normative racial subject across the categories Indian and black and the heteronormative imaginaries that secure the sedimentation of these racial-identitarian categories. Across the chapters that follow, rubbing reroutes my notion of the otherwise through the various positionalities of vulnerability, of which the feminine is one iteration. If rubbing articulates an "intense longing for intimacy," *Indenture Aesthetics* demonstrates that this intimacy can only emerge through the feminine and the feminized, the vulnerable and the violated.

Indentured Vulnerability

Across this book, I am attuned to the various ways in which vulnerability, femininity, and femme-ness attach to racialized male and female bodies. Two photographs—first, a composite image created by the colonial-apartheid state from official indenture identification photos of male laborers, and second, a family portrait consisting of an indentured female laborer (ca. 1942/1943) shot somewhere in rural Natal (now KwaZulu-Natal)—have been pivotal to my thinking and theorization of vulnerability, femininity, and feminization. Indeed, within a colonial-capitalist society, indentureship was a form of feminization that rendered men, women, and children vulnerable and disposable. This history of indentureship, a history of sexual violence, violation, and vulnerability, is one that has not been fully told in South Africa. Within the South African imaginary and against the overrepresentation of the Indian as the merchant/trader class, the indentured laborer appears and disappears within historical and contemporary scholarly and artistic engagements with the figure of the Indian. In South Africa, indentured vulnerability and its afterlives have been strategically invisibilized, rendering it almost impossible to imagine and grapple with Afro-Indian poverty and disenfranchisement. This invisibilization both occurs at the level of the state and has been exacerbated by South African Indian historians, artists, and curators in their quest to construct a linear narrative of Indian progress and development predicated on a politics of respectability. This indexes a particular memory and forgetting about indentureship that this book seeks to unsettle.

As the colonial-apartheid state consolidated its power in the late 1940s and 1950s, it constructed an official narrative of the Indian that inevitably conflated all Indians with that of the trader/merchant class (*the state's good Indian*). Importantly, the state chose photography as its medium to consolidate this narrative of the good Indian. In order to chart how my engagement with indentureship and its afterlives departs from the existing academic and artistic work, this section offers a brief overview of the interplay between the state's construction of the good Indian and South African Indian responses during different time periods.

In 1949, the colonial-apartheid state published *Meet the Indian in South Africa: A Pictoral History*, which was the state's official response to local and international critiques concerning the introduction of the Asiatic Land Tenure and Indian Representation Act of 1946, also popularly referred to as the Ghetto Act.[31] Drawing on photographs, text, and statistics, the aim of the brochure was to "graphically show the progress, the wealth, the fundamental human rights that South African Indians enjoy" (1949, 1). It states: "The claim by Indian propagandists that, in consequence of this law, the Indian population of South Africa is oppressed and persecuted is ridiculous in the extreme, for it applies equally to both races [Black African and Indian]" (State Information Office, 1949, 1).

I want to focus on the first image that appears in this brochure. This is a composite image created from twelve mug-shot-style identification photos of male indentured laborers who have just disembarked from a coolie ship. For their mug shots—a form of identification photograph through which the indentured, similarly to those criminalized by the state, enters an elaborate system of surveillance—the laborer holds a number that corresponds with colonial ship logs.[32] The men are photographed in a state of vulnerability; they are bare-chested, and their emaciated bodies and protruding ribs, indicative of the arduous travel across the *kala pani*, are visible. In this composite image, each row consists of four photographs strategically placed next to each other, from page end to page end, with the fourth photograph in each row bleeding outside the frame of the page. The bare-chested men sit on a chair, gazing directly into the camera while holding a number. The first number is 7358, and the last number begins with 737, but the last digit has been cut out of the frame. The men vary in age from their late teens to somewhere in their forties. The numbers do not appear consecutively; there are strategic elisions in this arrangement of images. The most obvious elision is the indentured woman.

Relying on the photographic images in *Meet the Indian*, the figures of the indentured laborer are displaced for images of Indian success and social mobility

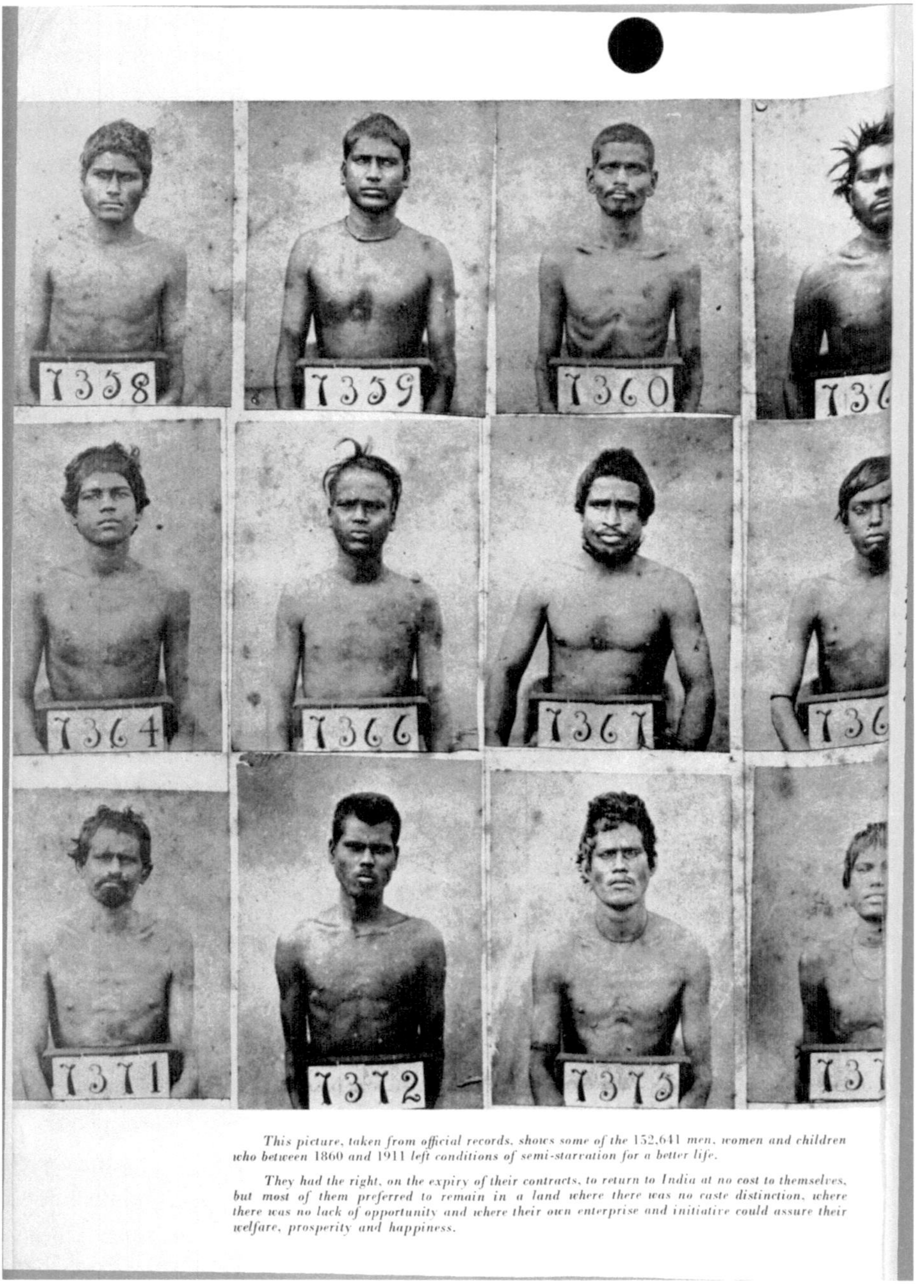

FIGURE I.2. Composite image of Indian indentured workers, reproduced as is from the book, *Meet the Indian in South Africa: A Pictorial Survey* (1949, State Information Office, Pretoria). Reproduced with permission from Historical Papers Research Archive, University of the Witwatersrand, Johannesburg, South Africa.

enabled by the colonial-apartheid state's goodwill. Through a strong work ethic, the indentured Indian can become a productive member of society—the state's good Indian—if they do not question the colonial-apartheid hierarchy that positioned the Indian between Europeans and black Africans (State Information Office, 1949). The brochure constructs the problem of racial disharmony between Indians and Europeans as a result of the Indians not understanding their subordinate positionality (their emplacement within the structure of the colonial-apartheid society) and wanting more than they are entitled to within the racial-economic hierarchy. Indeed, during this timeframe, the state was embarking on a larger project of social engineering by fixing the relationship between race and place.

One of the earliest responses to the state's good Indian is Fatima Meer's 1969 book *Portrait of Indian South Africans*, a thick sociological study of the effects of the Group Areas Act on the Indian community in Durban. Meer also uses the photographic image to complicate the narrative of the state's good Indian. Shireen Hassim (2019, 3) writes that Meer "was driven by an activist sociology *for* a common society, by a rage against injustice and by a profound belief in the value and capacity of research to convince the powerful of the consequences of their actions." Meer's book was designed to disrupt the colonial-apartheid state's policies that rendered communities with much commonality "strange to each other" (5), exacerbating artificial barriers based on perceived differences in relationship to race/ethnicity, class, culture, and tradition. *Portrait* is a fascinating documentation of the social life of Indians from the perspective of a South African Indian woman and is one of the earliest texts to delve into the gender and class dynamics of the Indian community in Durban. Throughout the book, Meer carefully distinguishes between the *indentured class* and the *trader/merchant class*, recognizing that within the South African imaginary, all Indians have been conflated with that of the trader class, invisibilizing the afterlife of indentureship.

Meer shifts her focus from the "Durban Indian business area"—an area associated with affluence and indicative of Indian economic success exploited through photos in the state's publication *Meet the Indian*—to the Indian suburbs and townships located outside of the city, where "Indian poverty predominates" (Meer 1969, 85). She argues that the signs of "visible achievement," which have been exploited by the colonial-apartheid state for their own propaganda purposes, invisibilize the *vulnerability* of the Indian worker class, those displaced by the Group Areas Act, Indian women (especially descendants of indentured laborers), and the effects of "poor schooling" on the Indian community (Hassim 2019, 9). Attuned to the dynamics of gender and class within the Indian community, Meer uses photographs to reveal conditions of Indian poverty, destitution, and vulnerability, which the colonial-apartheid state strategically worked to conceal through their publication *Meet the Indian*. Meer's attention to class stratification is significant. She stresses that wealthy Indians make up a fraction of a percent of the entire Indian population, but this "façade of influence" has been strategically mobilized against vulnerable Indian communities. Meer understood that organizing collectively around the concerns of the indentured class was important to create solidarity across racial differences. Hassim (2019, 52) writes: "She used her research skills and her network of students to document and make visible the lives of poor people, and she used her access to elites to secure support for the demands of people who were disadvantaged and in distress." She believed that the influence of the trader class was on the decline and that the indentured class was on the rise.

Meer recognized that the trader class had a different relationship to the South African nation than the indentured class. She believed that an alliance between Indians and the black African majority "was their best hope for full citizenship" (Hassim 2019, 53). For Meer, "Home was South Africa, and her people were both Indian and black." Meer's commitment to the underclass, the vulnerable, and the dispossessed across black Africans and the indentured class is an early manifestation of an Afro-Indian positionality. Meer deliberately defamiliarizes the state's good Indian, reaching outward across the racial divide to create a connection through the positionality of vulnerability. Meer reorients how we see and thus know the Afro-Indian.[33]

After 1994, the question of Indian belonging and the desire for inclusion into the postapartheid nation has been a top priority by South African Indian scholars, replicating an anxious and dangerous "longing for belonging" (Rastogi 2008, 1) to the nation.[34] This is evident in two curatorial projects: Riason Naidoo's *The Indian in Drum in the 1950s* and Uma Dhupelia-Mesthrie's *From Canefields to Freedom*. *The Indian in Drum* and *From Canefields to Freedom* reproduce the composite image of male indentured workers created by the colonial-apartheid state. Naidoo and Dhupelia-Mesthrie, like Meer, are invested in deliberately deconstructing and defamiliarizing the image of the colonial-apartheid state's good Indian. Although Naidoo and Dhupelia-Mesthrie offer complex pictoral histories of Indian social life in South Africa, mostly focusing on Durban, their curatorial projects inevitably displace indentured vulnerability. In opposition to the colonial-apartheid state's construction of the good Indian as weak and feminized, Naidoo's project inevitably recuperates Indian heteromasculinity.

Dhupelia-Mesthrie's curatorial project displaces the figure of the indentured female worker for that of the merchant-class Indian, demonstrating an investment in a politics of respectability that must disavow indentured vulnerability and its afterlives. In a striking arrangement of photos, Dhupelia-Mesthrie juxtaposes portraits of an indentured-class man and woman with portraits of a trader-class man and woman (2000, images 115–18). The arrangement of these portraits creates a linear and progressive development of the Indian from the backward and traditional indentured class to the fully modern Indian, as exemplified by the figure of the trader class. This linear placement erases the indentured laborer in favor of the trader class, the colonial-apartheid state's good Indian. The good Indian can achieve (partial) assimilation. Importantly, the series of photos begins with an indentured woman, the most vulnerable figure, who is strategically erased and replaced by a trader-class man who exemplifies proper Indian manhood and the state's good Indian. Whereas Meer was invested in deprivileging the trader class, Dhupelia-Mesthrie's curation of photos deprivileges the indentured class.

Naidoo evokes the blackness of BC, situating this archive of Indian social life in Durban as part of a broader black experience. Dhupelia-Mesthrie's book, on the other hand, focuses "on what is *Indian* about the *Indian South African*, but it also illustrates the commitment to South Africa" (2000, 28). The place of blackness within the construction of the Indian is unexplored, and her project pays little attention to South African blackness and Afro-Indian relations, other than through the realm of antiapartheid politics. The reproduction of the composite image of indentured male laborers suggests that both Naidoo and Dhupelia-Mesthrie are also grappling with the colonial archive of visuality, recognizing the unacknowledged place of indentureship in the racialized visual production of the Indian. However, Dhupelia-Mesthrie's project, as the title indicates—*From Canefields to Freedom*—maps Indian development onto the linear and progress narrative of the postapartheid nation, invisibilizing the afterlives of indentureship.

The history of Indian indentureship is a history of gender vulnerability, violation, and sexual exploitation. From the ship to the plantations, coal mines, and other spaces where indentured workers found themselves across urban and rural Natal, labor and vulnerability imbricate to produce the Afro-Indian. This is evident in the colonial photos of the indentured. In colonial Natal, indentured women were vulnerable and subject to exploitative labor conditions, the sexual needs of the master, as well as indentured men who often shared women because of uneven recruitment ratios.[35] Mariam Pirbhai (2009, 8) writes that indentured women's "vulnerable position . . . left them open to sexual assault

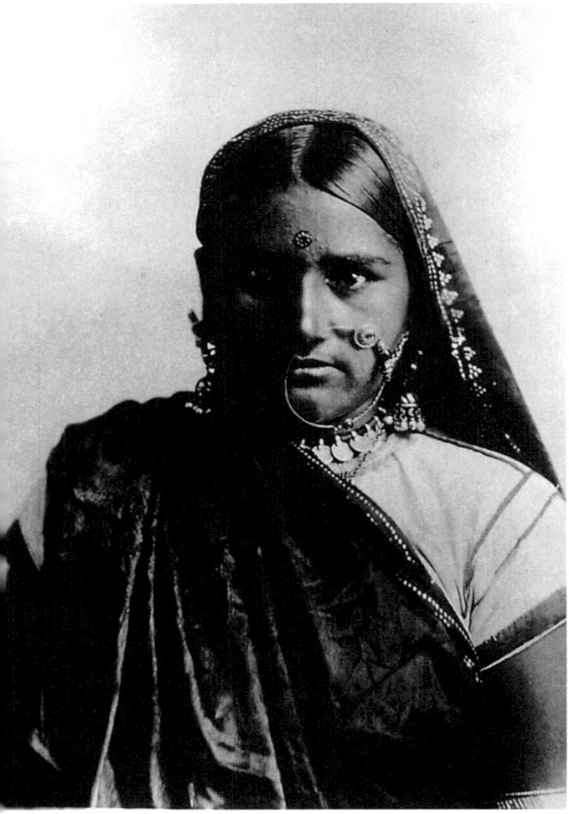

115

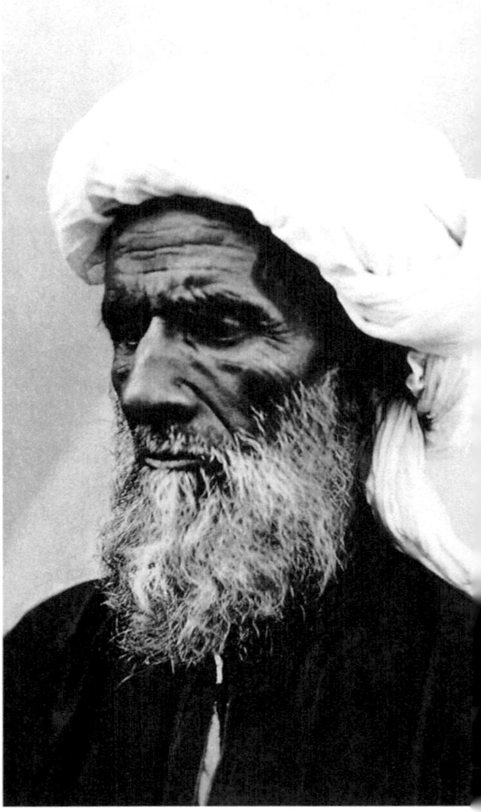

116

115. 116. 117. and 118. Four photographs reflecting the diverse regional origins and socio-economic classes of Indians and changes in dress over time. From left to right: traditional Hindu dress, possibly 1900s; a rural Indian, possibly 1900s; the wife of one of the wealthiest Indian merchants in the Transvaal, 1935; a modern Muslim businessman, 1960 – gone are the flowing robes and turban in favour of a pinstripe suit and pipe. Photos: MA

FIGURES I.3 AND I.4. Series of images reproduced from Uma Dhupelia-Mesthrie's book, *From Canefields to Freedom: A Chronicle of Indian South African Life* (2000, Cape Town: Kwela Books). Reproduced under fair use.

concubinage, prostitution, and even uxoricide." The indentured photos reveal explicitly the feminization of Indian indentured masculinity in relationship to colonial European/white masculinity. When indentured workers arrived in Natal, they entered a society with an already well-established black-white or settler-Indigenous binary. According to historian Goolam Vahed (2005, 241–42), "indenture masculinity" manifested as an in-between masculinity, positioned at the bottom of the colonial racial hierarchy. The emasculation of the indentured man

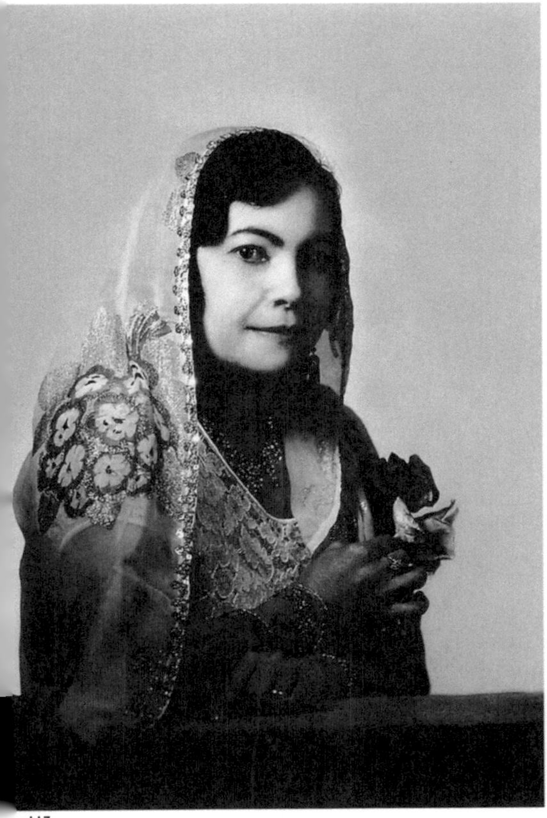
117

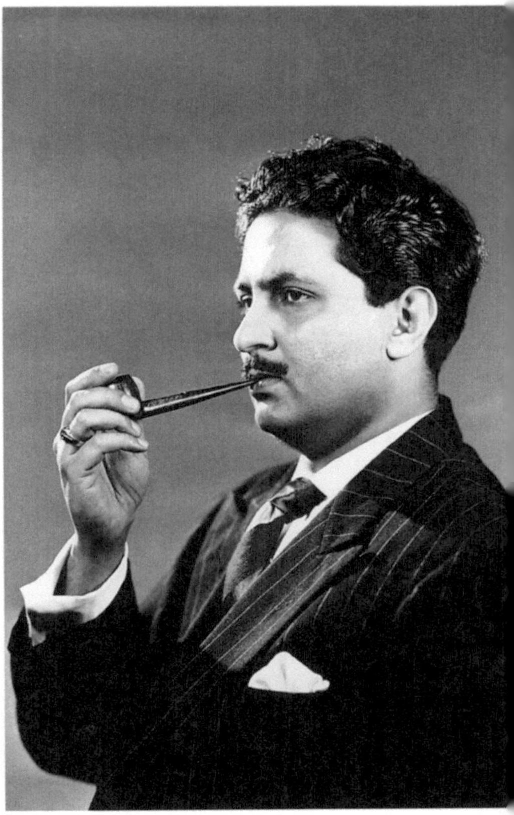
118

would have resulted in performances of hypermasculinity in the domestic arena, exacerbating violence against women, children, and one another.

But what of the femininity of indentured women and its construction within the death-worlds of labor? Since the official archive is unable to account for the indentured woman, I turn to the family album. Indeed, when I asked the librarian/archivist at the Gandhi-Luthuli Documentation Centre at the University of KwaZulu-Natal to help me locate these indenture identification photos, particularly those of women, I was told to look at family albums and that the original indenture photos have been lost.

One photo, sourced by my mother from an extended family member, most powerfully evokes the notion of blackening for me and the relationship between blackening and the Afro-Indian positionality this book imagines as a site of reorientating how we understand race in South Africa. Shot somewhere in the Natal Province, this photograph is organized around an indentured woman, her daughters, and their children. This photo is visually organized around the figure of the grandmother and tells a story about world-making on the edges of colonial society. It captures a sense of maternal intimacy and feminine energy directed toward kin- and community-making within the context of indentureship. The blackened face of the older woman radiates outward to tell a different story about Indianness in South Africa. Her blackened face is, for me, a haunting reminder of the horrors of indentureship and the blackened worlds of colonial labor extraction that rendered women and children most vulnerable. Her face tells a story deeply etched in the frown lines on her forehead, her dark eyes that are indistinguishable from her blackened face, and her tight lips.

The older woman in this photograph is my great-grandmother, Chinna Kolanthai Pillay, who was twenty-two years old when she arrived in Natal in December 1905 on the ship *Pongola LIV* from Madras. She arrived with her twenty-seven-year-old husband, Mutha Pillay, and their children, Yellamma Pillay (three years old) and Ammakanna Pillay (one year old). Like many others on this ship list, they were indentured to the Elandslaagte Collieries in Ladysmith. In the portrait photo, Yellamma, in her early forties, stands to the right of the older woman holding a girl-child approximately two years old. The young girl-child she holds is my mother, Velliammah Moodley. This photograph captures three generations of an Afro-Indian family, positioning the feminine at the center of the frame. Over time, Chinna Pillay and hundreds of indentured women like her recede from familial memory, similarly to how indentureship and its afterlives recede from South African history and the making of the nation. However, just as she haunts the family album, Indian indentureship and other forms of coercive labor practices like slavery in the Cape and African migrant labor systems, which overlap, resonate, and repeat across time and space in Southern Africa, remain an unacknowledged presence, continuously absented from the making of the postapartheid nation. My notion of Afro-Indianness is routed through the abject and vulnerable figure of this woman and the nonnormative (gritty, dark, ugly) femininity she represents, constructed within the context of indentureship. Her blackened face is haunting and a powerful reminder that indentureship was a form of blackening that is unaccountable for within our contemporary understandings of racial formations in South Africa. Her blackened face represents the coal dust that sticks to the surface of her skin, slowly permeating her body, becoming part of, and changing, the molecular structure of her cells. The coal dust filters into her lungs, staining her in unimaginable ways. This is the stain of slow death that is passed on generationally. Her body is an archive of a historical experience

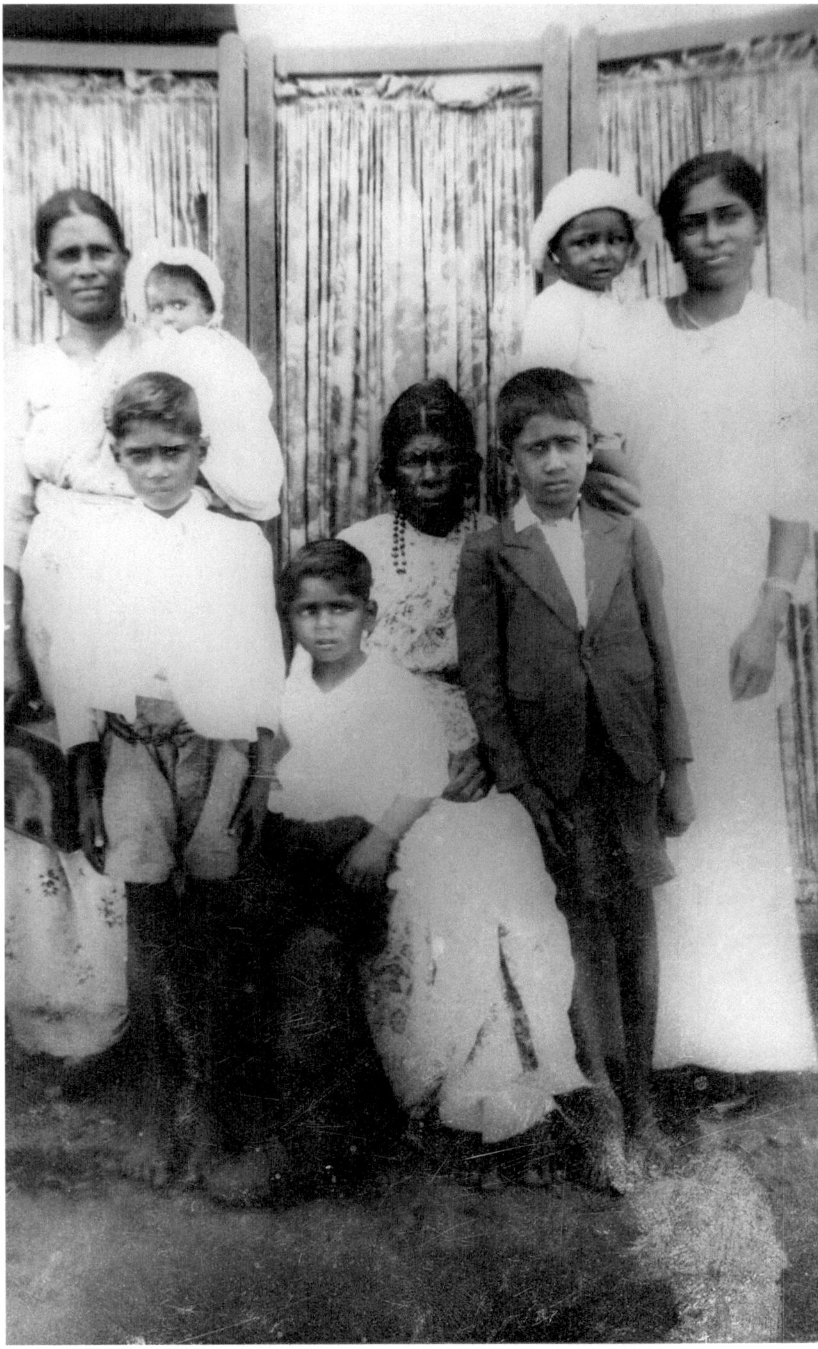

FIGURE I.5. Old family portrait photo from author's family photo album (ca. 1943).

strategically occluded from the South African imaginary, asking us to seriously think about what it means to continuously make and unmake race.

The feminization of the indentured male body rubs against the gritty, dark, ugly (nonnormative), disabled femininity of the indentured female body. Throughout this book, I follow various manifestations of vulnerability, femininity, and feminization that attach to male and female bodies, disrupting the gender binary and confounding the categories that secure proper subjecthood. The artists examined in this book, from FAKA to Modisakeng, use the positionality of male vulnerability as a form of disidentification, to evoke José Esteban Muñoz (1999), against hetero- and homonormative masculinities. Thus, this book situates male vulnerability as a feminine and feminized orientation toward the world. Femininity is a category associated with excess, fleshiness, vulnerability, and instability (Bersani 1987; Musser 2018a and b, 2023). Feminine and/or feminized bodies are sensual and eroticized (fleshiness), porous and penetrable, threatening the Cartesian divide between mind and body, self and other, male and female, masculine and feminine, returning us to various overlapping primal sites of woundedness, abjection, and fleshiness. Male femininity is particularly disruptive within what FAKA has referred to as a "cis-normative striving society." Indeed, male femininity and feminization embody the threat of penetration, challenging the notion of the ideal (masculine) body as "enclosed and autonomous" (Musser 2023). *Indenture Aesthetics* uses various manifestations of vulnerability to disrupt the ways in which hegemonic forms of masculinity organize social life and social value. Thus, throughout this book, vulnerability becomes the site to rethink an ethical politics of solidarity within and across the new black/ened Others. Drawing on the recent shift in feminist and queer scholarship, I am invested in understanding shared vulnerability as a radical openness toward otherness.

Vulnerability renders the categories black African and Afro-Indian leaky and interpenetrable. Thus, I am interested at the point where these categories bleed into each other, troubling the commonsensical nature of race in South Africa. Throughout this book, overlapping coercive labor practices allow me to further grapple with the relationship between blackness and Afro-Indianness. These labor practices reveal the ways in which black, African, and other bodies of color (Indian/Asian, coloured, Indigenous) were reduced to flesh and rendered vulnerable, a process that "depersonalizes and removes subjectivity" (Musser 2018b, 6). Hortense Spillers (2003) refers to this reduction of the body to flesh as "pornotroping." Spiller's notion of pornotroping is important because it allows us to understand, according to Musser, "the process of objectification that violently reduces people into commodities while simultaneously rendering them sexually available" (Musser 2018b, 6). Musser demonstrates how pornotroping occurs in relationship to "hierarchized systems of racialization" (6). Thus, fleshiness reveals "the ways in which power and projection produce certain bodies as other, thereby granting them a mysterious quality of desirability, which is always already undergirded by violence and the assumption of possession" (6). Black feminists have long articulated pornotroping as one of "white supremacy's tactics of domination."

Musser's turn to expand the notion of pornotroping beyond Blackness to "think about the way that the category that we understand as people of color [in the United States] is produced through late capitalism, colonialism, and globalization" is instructive to think through the politics of labor, heteronormative whiteness, and racialization in South Africa. In South Africa, labor necessitated the racialization of people of color outside of the domain of proper white citizenship; the colonial-apartheid state violently regulated the domain of gender and sexuality to protect the boundaries of white heteronormativity. The colonial-apartheid state's project of racialization constructed the racial-identitarian categories white, coloured, Indian, and black through intersecting "encounters with white supremacy" (Musser 2018b, 8). *Indenture Aesthetics* thus grapples with the violence and violation that stitches together the past, the present, and the future, while grappling with the "continuities in the forms of violence exerted by white supremacy" (Musser 2018b, 8) across racial categories. The various vulnerable, feminine, and feminized bodies encountered in this book are "highly charged affective objects" that disturb the boundaries between self and other, subject and object, male and female, masculine and feminine, and black and Afro-Indian, invested in harnessing the deep entanglements between the new black/ened Others as the foundation to reimagine coalitional-building across difference. Indeed, *Indenture Aesthetics* draws on male and female excess, abjection, and feminization to craft an "oppositional politics" (Nguyen 2014, 2) guided by an ethics of love and care for those the neoliberal state has rendered as waste and disposable.[36] Thus, I am interested in articulating a politics of difference that centers racialized femininity.

Throughout this book, I question the binary relationship between vulnerability and resistance. This binary logic is based on gendering vulnerable populations like racialized women, queer, trans, and gender-nonconforming folk as feminine, whereas resistance is gendered as masculine. Thus, the vulnerable must be brought under the paternalistic care of cisgender normative men. This binary and hierarchical logic inhibits any attempt at building solidarity across difference. In the 1960s, Fatima Meer recognized that the only way to organize across the racial categories Indian, black and coloured—to engage in a project of coalition-building and solidarity across difference—was through the indentured class. Whereas Meer was invested in collective belonging (national belonging) to a nonracial South Africa, *Indenture Aesthetics* marks a radical departure. This book is not about a desire for Indians to be included within the South African nation or within Afro-normative blackness. This book, informed by a politics of (un)belonging, offers a blueprint to reimage what organizing across difference could look like in South Africa. The politics of difference routed through unbelonging mobilizes vulnerability, femininity, and femme-ness as "other possibilities for living, for being together in common, for *feeling* injustice and refusing it without the need to engage it through forms of conquest" (Singh 2018, 21). Thus, I am interested in vulnerability and femininity as productive sites to reimagine nonstateist forms of belonging. Thus, the feminine, in various manifestations, is central to *Indenture Aesthetics* and is the condition of possibility for the reimagination of Afro-Indian relations and South African blackness.

Methodologically, *Indenture Aesthetics* is also informed by my interest in curation and art-making. I examine my own approach to art-making as a response to Afro-normativity, which structures the invisibility of Afro-Indian bodies, desires, pleasures, and erotics within South African publics. My own creative practice is influenced by the South African artist Zanele Muholi, who has dedicated her career to documenting and celebrating, through photography, the lives of black lesbian, trans, gay, and gender-nonconforming South Africans. Muholi's commitment to creating an aesthetic archive of black queer life has influenced my own commitment to an art practice that examines queer Afro-Indian sensualities and femininities, routed through the afterlife of indentureship. I am interested in using art-making and curation to wrestle with the afterlife of colonial visuality. In a swiftly changing society like South Africa where black/ened people were historically reduced to mere objects of white knowledge production, and strategically miseducated, the question of what constitutes proper knowledge production and who constructs this knowledge is important. Thus, in my research creation, I situate the body (my body) as an alternative archive of history to activate a "theory in the flesh" (Moraga and Anzaldúa 1983). Black queer studies scholar E. Patrick Johnson (2001, 3) expands on Moraga's theory to encapsulate the diversity of LGBTIQ+ people of color "while simultaneously accounting for how racism and classism affect how we experience and theorize the world." Johnson reformulates theories in the flesh as an "embodied politic of resistance" through praxis (where theory and practice come together) (4). This is a politic of survival informed by various overlapping regimes of corporeal dislocation. My theory in the flesh emerges from a space of hunger for the otherwise and situates the body (my body) as the site through which the otherwise can be glimpsed.

Methodologically, I offer close readings of various kinds of aesthetic and performance art practices including photography, video art, needlepoint-lace art, film, and jewelry-making. My close readings are also informed by artists' biographies and interviews in order to understand how these aesthetic practices emerge out of, and engage with, complex social formations. Through close readings, I trace different articulations of Afro-Indian intimacies within particular texts, while my curatorial mandate of juxtaposing an Afro-Indian artist with a black African artist creates the exact intimacies this book argues for. While focusing on the aesthetic, I also examine the ways in which artists weave their own bodies into their aesthetic practices through performance art. Indeed, from Sharlene Khan to FAKA, the artists' bodies are crafted into generative sites to examine the tensions of the postapartheid in a context where the black/ened body is under attack "by continued economic and psychic oppression" (Pather and Boullee 2019, 1). If *indenture* functions as a hinge to understand overlapping regimes of racialized labor, and the *aesthetic* functions similarly to grapple with the entanglements between Afro-Indian, black, and African, then the *body* becomes a site that "complicate[s] old [and sedimented] claims of blackness" (Madison 2014, vii). The artists I examine seek a new vocabulary, one informed by their corporeal dislocation, directing us to the multiple contours of blackness and its boundless capacities once it is untethered from the normative. Performance unveils the *now* of blackness, working with and against "economies of dislocation and disciplinary power," reaching outward and inward, stretching across time and space, to reveal not just the past and the present but also the futures of South African blacknesses as they iterate across difference, troubling the deadly imperatives of the Afro-normative (Madison 2014, viii; Taylor 2003).

Indeed, my desire (for the otherwise) and my body repeat and resonate throughout the pages of *Indenture Aesthetics*. Growing up in rural KwaZulu-Natal and coming of age—a form of critical racial-gender-sexual-class-consciousness—within the home-space of the Afro-Indian family in the afterlife of indentureship and colonial apartheid, from a young age I affectively understood that my body was an archive of history. I now realize that my queerness—my queer embodiment (of male femininity) and the queer ways in which I saw, felt, moved, and related—allowed me to comprehend and navigate the world differently. Through the violent (and often unseen and/or unseeable) regulation of my body within various spaces—the school, the church, the family, the streets—I understood (but did not have the language or the need to grapple with) vulnerability as a world-making practice. *Indenture Aesthetics* is about the importance of embodied knowledge as a decolonial praxis of (un)becoming normatively human through which we can begin to glimpse the otherwise. I am invested, throughout these pages, in forms of embodied knowledge that emerge from the positionality of vulnerability. To insert my body throughout this text, and to theorize from the positionality of my body, is to enact a particular kind of vulnerability, a form of self-shattering (to evoke Leo Bersani)—which requires us to rethink the politics of knowledge production. As the reader navigates this book, they will encounter my body in various forms—my performing body, naked and open to the world, in my artworks, my orgasmic body in relationship to the church, my body in relationship to my mother's body and to the bodies of my ancestors, my body constantly negotiating my Afro-Indianness, my blackness, and my Africanness, my body rubbing against other bodies—as an embodied praxis of navigating the past, the present, and the future.

In this book, my own artworks (and art practice) rub against that of other South African artists. These are also artists who often use their own bodies to emphasize the importance of embodied knowledge to the political project of productively unsettling the violence of the Afro-normative. To position my body and my art practice so centrally in this book, and in relationship to other artists and artworks, speaks to not just my desire but also my commitment to an ethical politics of relationality. *Indenture Aesthetics* is thus a translation in the written form—an academic text, a queer curatorial practice—of offering my desiring body (shattered, fragmented, vulnerable), my body in pleasure and ecstasy, as a relational body, one that reaches outward, one that collectively invites us to imagine otherwise. Thus, throughout *Indenture Aesthetics* I offer my body as a kind of queer Afro-Indian critical methodology, and together with the reader, I want to think about the body—the Afro-Indian body, the black and black/ened body, the queer/ed body—as methodology. This is a body constantly in the process of becoming/unbecoming and one that is willingly porous and permeable, penetrable and fuckable. This is Fanon's questioning body (1986). Indeed, the questioning body as methodology, aesthetic, theory, and as a site where pain and pleasure, memory and archive, belonging and (un)belonging, rub against one another sets the stage and makes possible racialized queer, anti-capitalist, and cross-racial coalition in South Africa, and the diaspora.

> *O my body, make of me always, a man who questions!*
> —Frantz Fanon, BLACK SKIN, WHITE MASKS

If Afro-normativity maps onto a linear and progressive narrative of the nation, throughout this book, the new black/ened Others are situated within a temporal and spatial fracture/lag. In the chapters that follow, we encounter scenes of slow death; elastic notions of time; temporal lags; haptic encounters that disrupt the past, present, and future; and alternative articulations of time and space that emerge out of positionalities of fragility, porousness, and femme-ness. Indeed, to engage vulnerability and femininity is to engage alternative visions of time and space, those that rub against and slide off Afro-normative time and its unitary fixed subject. If Afro-normativity offers a temporal and spatial framework to understand how the necropolitical structures of colonial apartheid—from slavery in the Cape, colonialism, indentureship, apartheid, and the antiblackness of the postapartheid state—live on in the present, *Indenture Aesthetics*' attention to performance and temporality hones in on quotidian, minor, and embodied acts through which black/ened people constantly create and re-create livable lives in the face of constant state-sanctioned violence.[37] Performance illuminates the "phenomenology of [South African] Blackness—that is, *when* and *where* is it imagined, defined and performed and in what locations, both figurative and literal" (Wright 2015, 3). Black studies scholars in the United States like Wright (2015), Sharpe (2016), and Quashie (2021) have relied on "temporal grammars . . . to articulate the complex and dynamic geographies of Black being, which are bound to, but not wholly bound by, the death machine of anti-Blackness" (Fleming 2022, 135). *Indenture Aesthetics* understands temporal and spatial fractures/lags as fecund nodes to grapple with our deep entanglements across time and space.

This book's curatorial mandate draws on a long tradition in queer studies dedicated to "valuing that which has been deemed without value" (Gopinath 2018, 4). Influenced by the artists curated in this book, *Indenture Aesthetics* enacts a particular kind of care-taking—a form of *wake work* to evoke Christina Sharpe (2016)—that prioritizes the vulnerable, the displaced, and the forgotten. Drawing on Erica Lehrer and Cynthia E. Milton's project *Curating Difficult Knowledge: Violent Pasts in Public Places* (2011), Gopinath argues that "the relationship between curation and caring for . . . demands that we think of curation 'not only as selection, design, and interpretation, but as care-taking—as a kind of intimate, intersubjective, interrelational obligation,' an obligation to 'deal with the past' in particular" (Gopinath 2018, 4) Thus, *Indenture Aesthetics*' curatorial mandate to focus on the afterlives of colonial apartheid offers a feminist-queer reimagining of vulnerability that prioritizes love and care-taking.

Indenture Aesthetics is the first book to develop a queer-reading practice to reimagine Afro-Indian intimacies and South African blackness. My method of juxtaposing differently racialized artists is dedicated to creating "new ways of seeing" (Gopinath 2018, 5) across difference. As a queer curatorial project, this archive is invested in "messing things up, creating disorder and disruptive commotion within the normative arrangements of bodies, things, spaces, and institutions" (Manalansan 2015, 567). Throughout this book, my use of the term *queer* moves beyond the domain of nonnormative sexuality, desires, and expressions (although I also engage queer sexuality in its multiple dimensions). By categorizing those excluded from the domain of authentic blackness as the new black/ened Others, my investment is not in creating new categories but in providing a framework to disrupt "larger normative systems" (Tallie 2019, 7; Manalansan 2015). Indeed, performances of Afro-normativity construct the new black/ened Others as *queer*; queer signals their positionalities as abject and outside of the linear narrative of progress and development associated with the postapartheid era. The disruptive quality of queer reorients our relationships with one another via the field of difference rather than the narrow confines of identitarian politics. This relational understanding of queerness necessitates a deep reckoning with "one's relationship to power" (Cohen 2005, 22). It directs us to lives lived on the margins, to those who continue to survive, organize, and thrive in the face of constant vulnerability and violation. Nkoli's vision of an African queer politic resonates with Cathy Cohen's powerful call that "one's relationship to power, and not some homogenized identity, [should be] privileged in determining one's political comrades" (22). Thus, *Indenture Aesthetics* situates queer as a site of resistance and a praxis of refusal through which we can collectively reimagine what "progressive, transformative coalition work" (22) looks likes. Prioritizing the feminine and the feminized, the vulnerability and the violated, *Indenture Aesthetics* follows the lines of flight away from the Afro-normative in order to reimagine our entangled pasts, presents, and futures. *Indenture Aesthetics* direct us to the importance of crafting nonstateist forms of belonging as an urgent political project of coalitional-building across differences as a praxis of collective survival.

Contributions and Structure of the Book

Indenture Aesthetics is informed by three important contributions. First, *Indenture Aesthetics* reanimates Black Consciousness in postapartheid South Africa through an intersectional queer-feminist framework in order to understand the entanglements between the categories Indian, black, and African. Thus, reactivating BC by bringing into deep conversation Afro-Indian and black African artists, *Indenture Aesthetics* challenges the racialized ways in which knowledge production has historically developed within the South African academy. Historically, South African scholarship maintained the racial divide, constructing knowledge about racialized communities within the silos inherited from colonial-apartheid logics. This is evident in studies that deal with Indian and black African communities. Historian Heather Hughes (2007, 156) argues that in South Africa "the political context weighted heavily on scholarship"; except for "moments of extreme racial tension . . . there has been little published on everyday relations between Africans and Indians."

Second, *Indenture Aesthetics* responds, writes, and imagines against the overrepresentation of the Indian as the merchant/trader class as it manifests within the South African imaginary. This work is indebted to South African scholars who have studied Indian indentureship through disciplines like history, anthropology, sociology, and literature. Black feminist scholar Betty Govinden positions much of this as part of the "memory work" that has emerged since the late 1980s, as the apartheid project begins to unravel. Govinden suggests that the history of Indian indentureship is inseparable from the indenture narrative and, more broadly, "any South African narrative" (Govinden 2009, 286). This body of work "recounts suppressed histories" and offers a fuller account of the South African experience (288).

However, *Indenture Aesthetics* works against the romance of the archive to give voice to subjugated people and communities (Arondekar 2009), recognizing the limits of history's methodological approaches to the archive and its focus on what counts as legitimate primary sources and objects of study. In South Africa, black subjects were historically written out of history, or where they do appear, they emerge as fragments and statistics, often rendered through the imperial/colonial gaze. In the postapartheid period, history often maps onto the recuperation of heroic figures or spectacular events, often focusing on cisgender males. This constructs a hegemonic narrative of the nation that must strategically erase vulnerable populations like women of color, the poor, the working class, the destitute, and gender and sexual nonconforming subjects. In South Africa, Indian histories have overwhelmingly focused on figures like Mahatma Gandhi and Indian participation in antiapartheid politics. Indeed, this focus privileges an elite understanding of the Indian experience that emphasizes an anxious "longing for belonging" (Rastogi 2008) to the nation. Within this context, *Indenture Aesthetics* is the first book to examine the Afro-Indian positionality and Afro-Indian relations outside of the structure of longing for belonging to the nation.

Studies of the indentureship narrative through literary forms have significantly shifted a largely social science approach to the study of Indians in South Africa. Literary scholars have been interested in how "indentureship, paradoxically, allows us to see South African literature beginning to move beyond its somewhat parochial and exclusive concern with events in this country toward current transnational investigations of an Indian Ocean map of South/South interactions, as well as to other Indian diasporic sites" (Govinden 2009, 288). Most of this work overemphasizes the transnational turn (South/South interactions as well as connections to the African and Caribbean diasporas), producing a blind spot into which this book intervenes. This emphasis on the transnational risks obscuring local Afro-Indian relations. The routing of Indianness through transnational and diasporic routes (which privileges the Atlantic World) renders illegible the ways in which the Afro-Indian positionality can only be understood through a complex understanding of South African blackness. Thus, *Indenture Aesthetics* situates the aesthetic and performance art as interventions into dominant histories and literary narratives about Indianness and blackness in South Africa.

Historically, the Indian in South Africa has been imagined as straight/heteronormative, and this is evident in the different genres of scholarship and archival and aesthetic practices concering Indianness in South Africa. *Indenture Aesthetics* marks a significant shift from this line of inquiry by mapping the queer positionality of the Afro-Indian and prioritizing the queer Afro-Indian subject. *Indenture Aesthetics* also challenges the whiteness of queer South African studies, while deepening the emerging field of queer African studies. Within both contexts—queer South African studies and queer African studies—the queer Afro-Indian positionality has been largely erased, reflecting the contested positionality of the (Afro-) Indian both in South Africa and the continent. This book deepens our understanding of racialized Africanness, even as it attempts to deconstruct the racial hierarchy and the making and unmaking of race in South Africa.

Third, *Indenture Aesthetics* shifts the study of race in South Africa from an Atlantic to an Indian Ocean framework. Throughout this book, I am cautious about using the term *diaspora* as a mode of identification and form of belonging. Given South Africa's history of struggle/liberation politics informed by the imbricated regimes of exclusion that Indian, black African, and coloured South Africans have experienced in relationship to the nation, and the purchase that blackness held during the antiapartheid struggle in rescripting the terrain of belonging outside of the logics of colonial-apartheid era race categories, the term *diaspora,* as a descriptor of the Indian experience, has been at best tenuous and contested as a form of identification. For Indian-identified political activists, artists, and scholars, diasporic modes of belonging are incompatible with belonging to the *new* nation. Furthermore, the Afro-Indian positionality, formed out of the long history of imbricated coercive labor practices in Southern Africa, reveals the limits of both the North American category "South Asian" and the category "Black" as they are informed by the Atlantic World. The Afro-Indian is not South Asian, and Afro-Indian blackness, like coloured blackness, formed within the specific histories of slavery, colonialism, indentureship, and apartheid and is rendered illegible within Atlantic Blackness, North American South Asianness, and subcontinental South Asianness.

Indenture Aesthetics seeks to understand Afro-Indian relations and Southern African blackness through an Indian Ocean studies framework, rather than an Atlantic framework, which is the hegemonic framework to understand race, and particularly Blackness, in the Global North and South Africa. An Indian Ocean studies framework directs us to a world of entangled coercive labor diasporas, confounding the racial categories Indian and black. The Black Atlantic has significantly impacted the study of black culture in South Africa.[38] Paul Gilroy's Black Atlantic framework has also been critiqued for erasing Africa in the production of a transatlantic Black modernity (Masilela 1996; Hofmeyr 2007). South African literary scholars have also been interested in how the Black Atlantic framework emerges in South African Indian fiction. Scholars like Young (2017, 150) critique the ways in which South African Indian fiction writers evoke transatlantic slavery to "locate Indian claims of belonging in the performance of coerced labor." Through this strategy of conflating transatlantic slavery and indentureship in Natal, the Canefields unfold in an "Atlantic register" (Samuelson 2010, 272; Young 2017, 150). Literary scholar Meg Samuelson (272) argues that the evocation of the Atlantic register translates "oceanic routes" into "territorial roots" where the mobilization of tropes similar to the Middle Passage and plantation existence rescripts the indenture experience as another form of slavery. This can also be read as a disidentificatory strategy to "distinguish South African Indians with various histories from the stereotype of... 'oppressive traders' and thus work through African Indian historical antagonism" (Young 2017, 150). However, territorial roots translate into a "deep longing for belonging" to a nation that abjects the Indian. Furthermore, by working through the specificities and complexities of Indianness in South Africa through the Atlantic framework—where diasporic Blackness and South African Indianness relate to each other because of intimacies shared between transatlantic slavery and Asian/Indian indentureship—such works erase the positionality of black Africanness within these structures of identification and affiliation. An Indian Ocean studies framework offers a more supple understanding of the specificities of colonialism and coercive labor practices, migration, and nationalism, as well as processes of race and racialization that are significantly different from the Atlantic World. Importantly, an Atlantic framework forgets that the system of Asian/Indian indentureship was designed to replace the trade in African bodies and has been largely silent on the deep entanglements between these two forms of coercive labor practices.

In Southern Africa, the Black Atlantic framework has been the dominant mode to engage with the transnational turn in the humanities and social sciences (Hofmeyr 2007). This has privileged North-South modes of transnationalism, obscuring histories of contact, migration, and movement, and overlapping labor diasporas within the Indian Ocean World that both intersect with and depart from the Atlantic World. In the Indian Ocean World, the relationship between slavery and blackness and Indianness/Asianness and indentureship does not hold in the same way as in the Atlantic World. As I have discussed earlier, in the Cape it was almost impossible to distinguish between the enslaved, the indentured, and those, like Indigenous peoples, under other forms of coercive labor practices. These Indian Ocean labor diasporas require a different understanding of diaspora and race. Loren Kruger (2001) employs the term *black Indian* as a counterpoint to Paul Gilroy's Black Atlantic. The black Indian Ocean directs us to forms of entangled coercive labor practices complicating how we understand the African diaspora; this is an African diaspora that includes the African continent, the Indian Ocean, and the Red Sea (Young 2017, 13). The notion of the black Indian directs us to how imperial labor *blackened* the lives of those enslaved and indentured—Indian, Asian, East African, Madagascan, Indigenous—across time and space. Indeed, throughout this book, I gently untangle South African blackness from an Atlantic framework to offer a conceptualization of blackness that considers multiple entangled routes across the *kala pani* of the Indian Ocean as they intersect with Southern African labor migration routes.

The specificities of South African slavery and other forms of coercive labor practices only gained academic traction since the 1980s as the apartheid state began to dismantle (Gqola 2010; Baderoon 2014; Young 2017). By this stage, the racial categories Indian, African, and black were well-sedimented in the apartheid state's official policy. The "dualistic constructions of Indianness and blackness" naturalize slavery and African migrant labor "as black and 'forgetting' those Asians whose presence in South Africa predated 'coolie' indenture" (Young 2017, 156). However, Cape slavery and the regimes of overlapping coercive labor practices that repeat across time and space require a different framework. Loren Kruger writes: "Narratives of migration, diaspora, settlement and naming on and around the 'Cape of Storms' bursts the bounds of apartheid racial classifications, or, indeed, of anti-apartheid categories" (2001, 35). Thus,

Indenture Aesthetics is committed to both a global black studies and a black queer studies that reorients the field toward the multiple contours of African blackness, while being in conversation with blackness elsewhere.

Chapter 1, "Afro-Femininities: Maternal Archives as Sites of Queer-Feminist Futurities," examines the aesthetic practices of two artists, myself and Lebohang Kganye, whose works are influenced by maternal archives. This chapter focuses on the maternal feminine and the home-space of the black/ened family in the afterlife of colonial-indenture apartheid. I focus on my interrelated projects *The Brown Photo Album: An Archive of Feminist Futurity* (2019) and *Queering the Archive: Brown Bodies in Ecstasy* (2013–present), which I read alongside Kganye's project *Ke Lefa Laka: Her-Story* (2013) and *Ke Lefa Laka: Heir-Story* (2013). Influenced by our mothers' photoarchives, I am interested in maternal archives as sites of feminist and queer possibilities that illuminate the making of Afro-femininities otherwise.

Chapter 2, "Afro-Vulnerabilities and the Aesthetics of Slow Death: Memory, Trauma, and Labor," examines overlapping regimes of racialized labor by reading Sharlene Khan's project *when the moon waxes red* in relationship to various performance art and aesthetic practices by Mohau Modisakeng. Whereas Khan's project takes us on a visual and affective journey through the sugarcane fields, emphasizing the experience of the Afro-Indian female subject in the afterlife of indentureship, Modisakeng focuses on the figure of the African migrant laborer in relationship to the coal mining industry. This chapter situates vulnerability as a feminine and feminized orientation toward the world. This chapter examines the making and unmaking of black/ened life within the death-worlds of the sugarcane plantation and the coal mine, two geographical spaces indicative of slow death. The queer aesthetic of slow death in these practices brings time to a halt as an urgent call to deal with the colonial-apartheid past and the ongoing violence that shapes black/ened life in postapartheid South Africa.

Chapter 3, "Afro-Intimacies: Queer-Kinship Formations and African Rurality," examines the emergence of black/ened queer life-forms in and alongside the death-worlds of capital, the sugarcane plantations, and the coal mines. This chapter analyzes Sabelo Mlangeni's photoseries, *At Home* (2004–9), *Country Girls* (2003–9), and *Men Only* in relationship to my short film *cane/cain* (2011). Mlangeni and I return to small towns and rural South Africa to offer complex articulations of queer world-making practices within these spaces. This chapter theorizes rural and small-town South Africa as feminized spaces where those who live in these spaces are still waiting for freedom. This chapter reads Mlangeni's femme aesthetic of temporality alongside my aesthetic of sensuality. We both explore the entanglements between pain and pleasure as constitutive of queer world-making. This chapter considers how alternative queer life-forms and queer social worlds emerge when time slows down.

Chapter 4, "Afro-Transgressions: Queer Femininities and South African Sex Publics," focuses on two bodily spaces—the black queer anus and the Afro-Indian yoni—associated with female/feminized sexual excess and deviance. I examine the performance and aesthetic art practices of FAKA, a black queer femme duo consisting of Desire Marea and Fela Gucci, in relation to Reshma Chhiba's multimedia and multisited project, *The Two Talking Yonis*. This chapter examines FAKA and Chhiba's use of both abjection and erotics through performances of sex as art. FAKA's radical femme-ness rubs against Chhiba's Afro-Indianness in a context where the black queer and the Afro-Indian are both abjected from the nation through performances of Afro-normativity. Through these positionalities, Chhiba and FAKA reimagine the authentic parameters of postapartheid blackness to reveal the multiple contours of blackness as it is continuously made and unmade.

The coda, "Afro-Queer Diasporic Femininities and Emergent Imaginaries of Freedom," focuses specifically on the multimedia artist Githan Coopoo, a founding member of the Kutti Collective. The Kutti Collective, an emerging art collective consisting of femme, queer, womxn, trans, and gender-nonconforming artists, represents a new generation of performance and aesthetic art practices by Afro-Indians. Unlike earlier generations of Afro-Indian artists, the collective deliberately uses terms like *desi* and *South Asian*. In their art practice, Coopoo uses clay as their chosen material/medium. Clay, Coopoo reminds us, is symbolic of fragility, vulnerability, and porousness. Symbolic of the queer black/ened body, the nature of clay reveals the potential to reimagine the body outside of regimes of normativity and mastery.

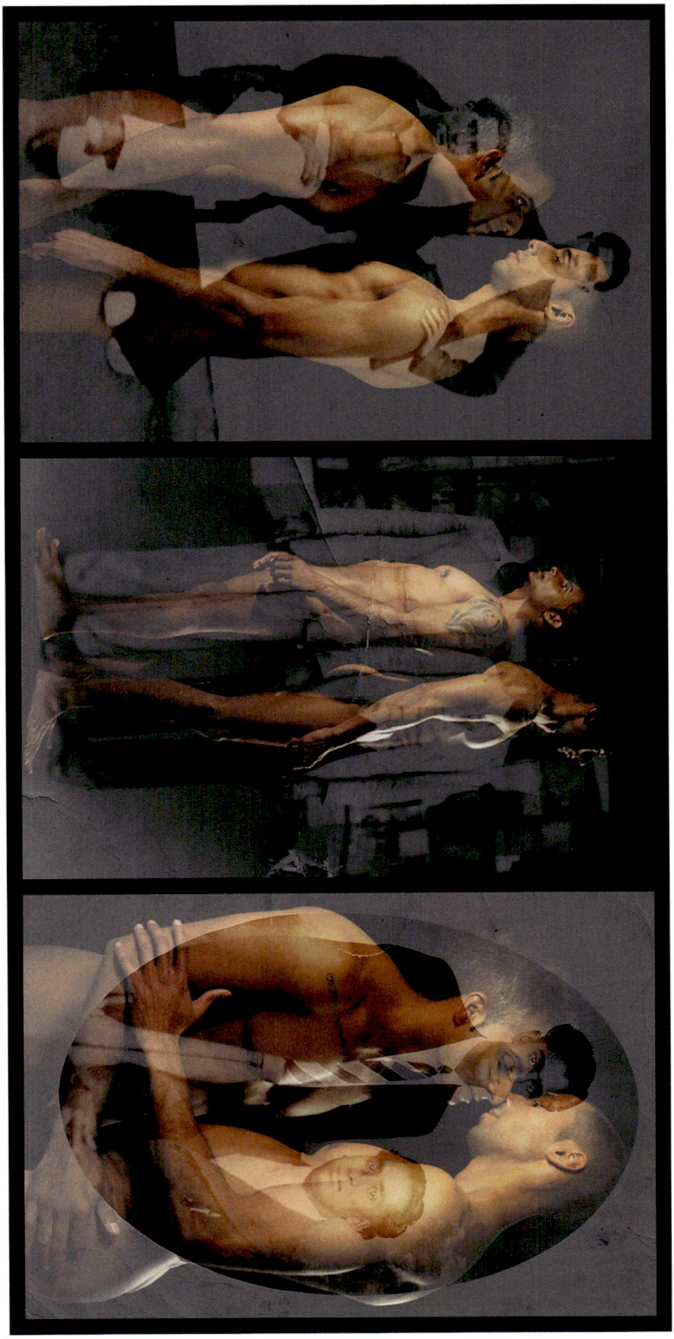

PLATE 1. Jordache A. Ellapen. *Brownflesh II* (2017). 1000 mm × 666.7 mm. Digital pigment print on FineArt Baryta, 1/5. Source: The author.

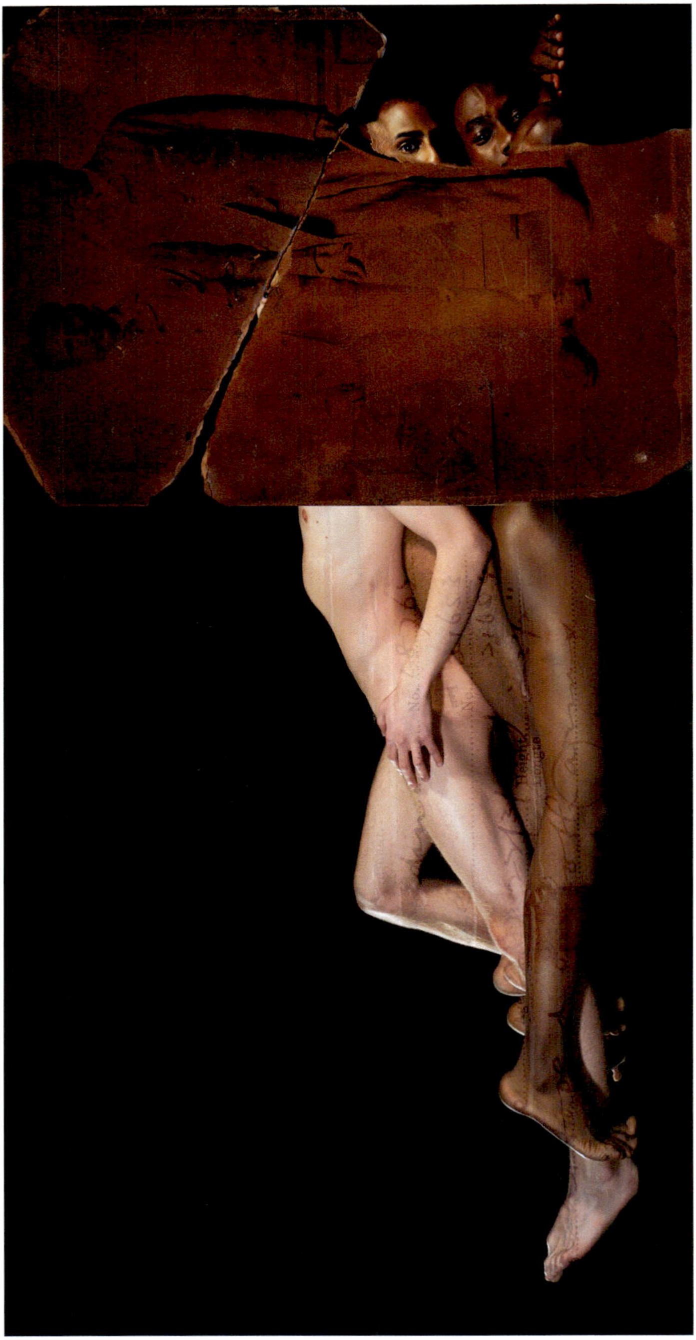

PLATE 2. Jordache A. Ellapen. *No. 21653* (2016). 549 mm × 1052 mm. Digital pigment print on FineArt Baryta, 1/5. Source: The author.

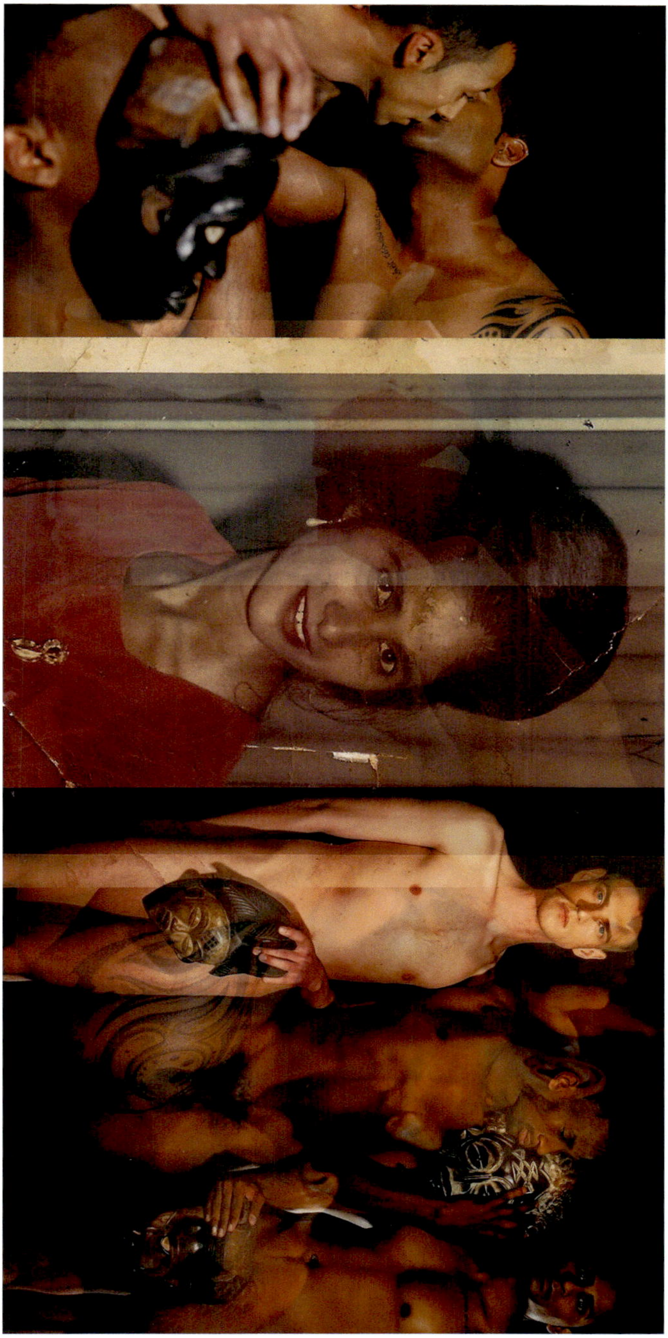

PLATE 3. Jordache A. Ellapen. *Brownflesh I* (2016). 549 mm × various sizes. Digital pigment print on FineArt Baryta, 1/5. Source: The author.

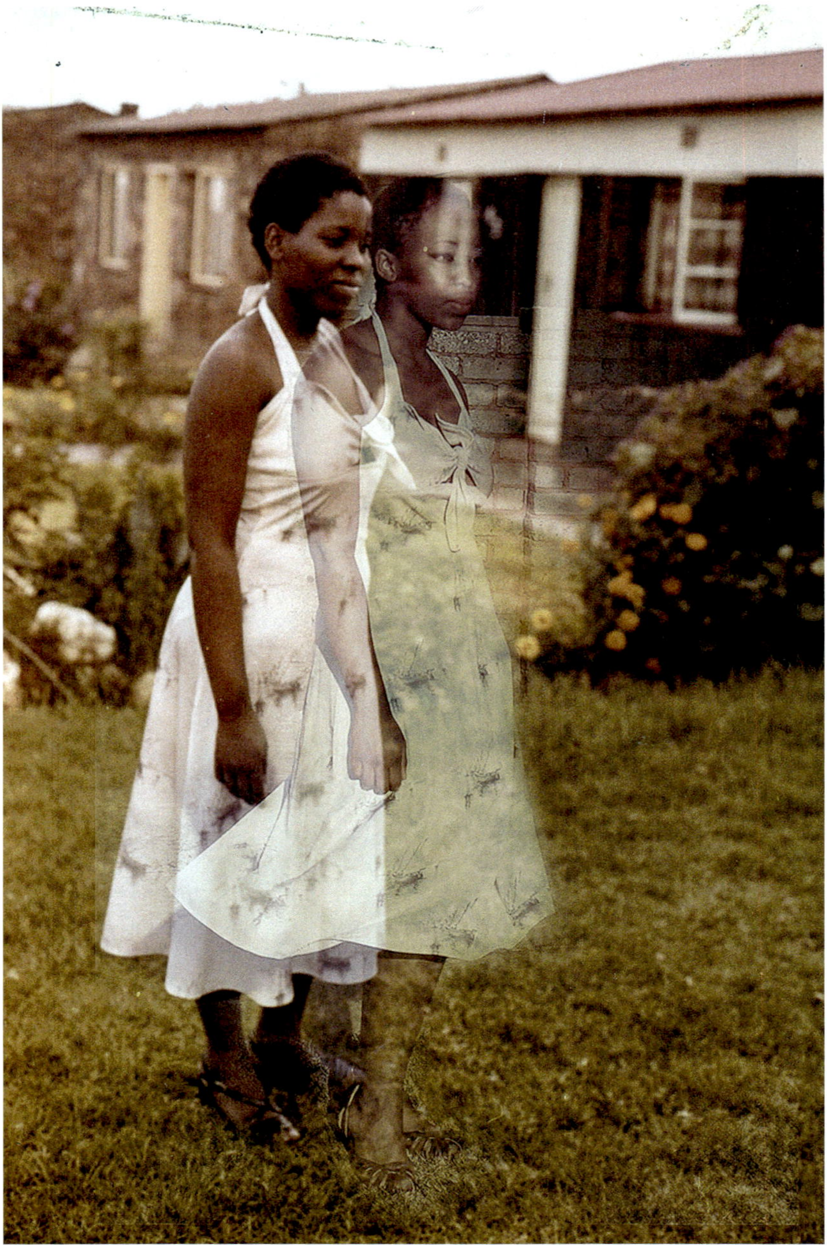

PLATE 4. *Ka mose wa malomo kwana 44 II* (2013, *In a Floral Dress*). Source: Lebohang Kganye.

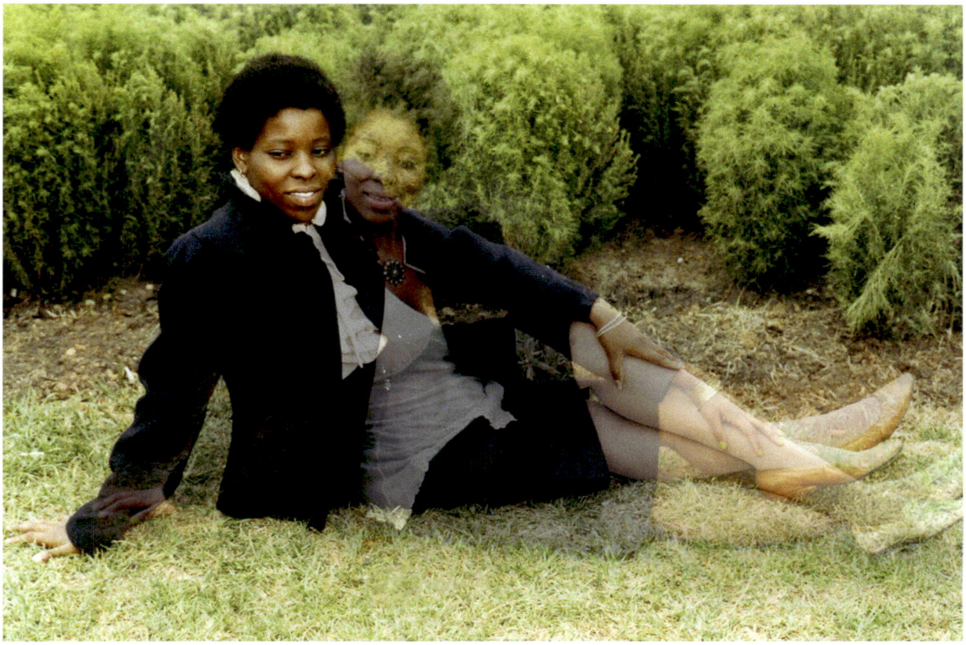

PLATE 5. *Tsimong ka hara toropo II* (2013, *In the Garden in the Middle of Town*). Source: Lebohang Kganye.

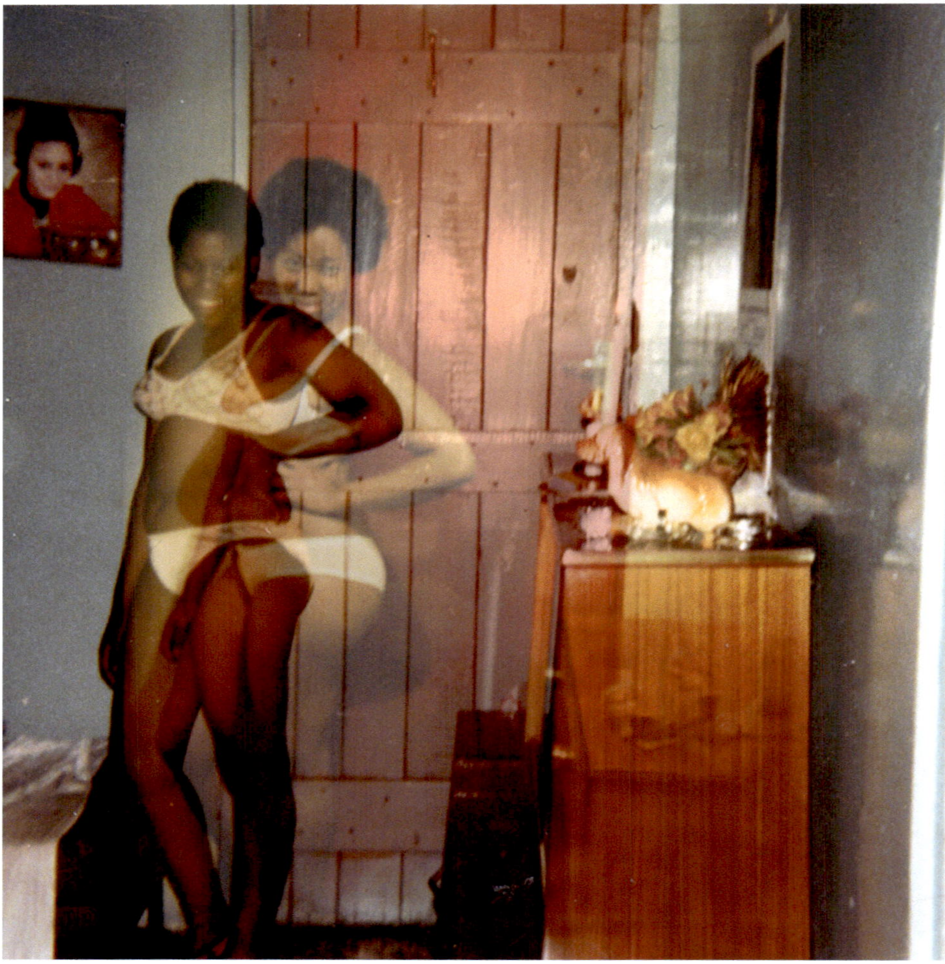

PLATE 6. *Ke le motle ka bulumase le bodisi II* (2013, *I Was Beautiful Wearing a Panty and Bra*). Source: Lebohang Kganye.

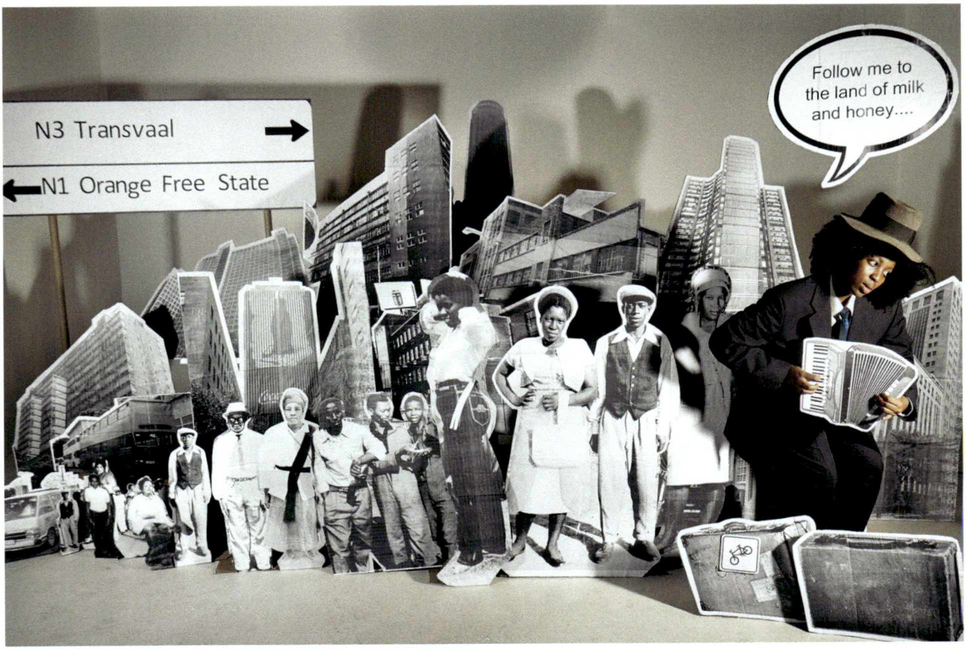

PLATE 7. *Pied Piper* (2013). Source: Lebohang Kganye.

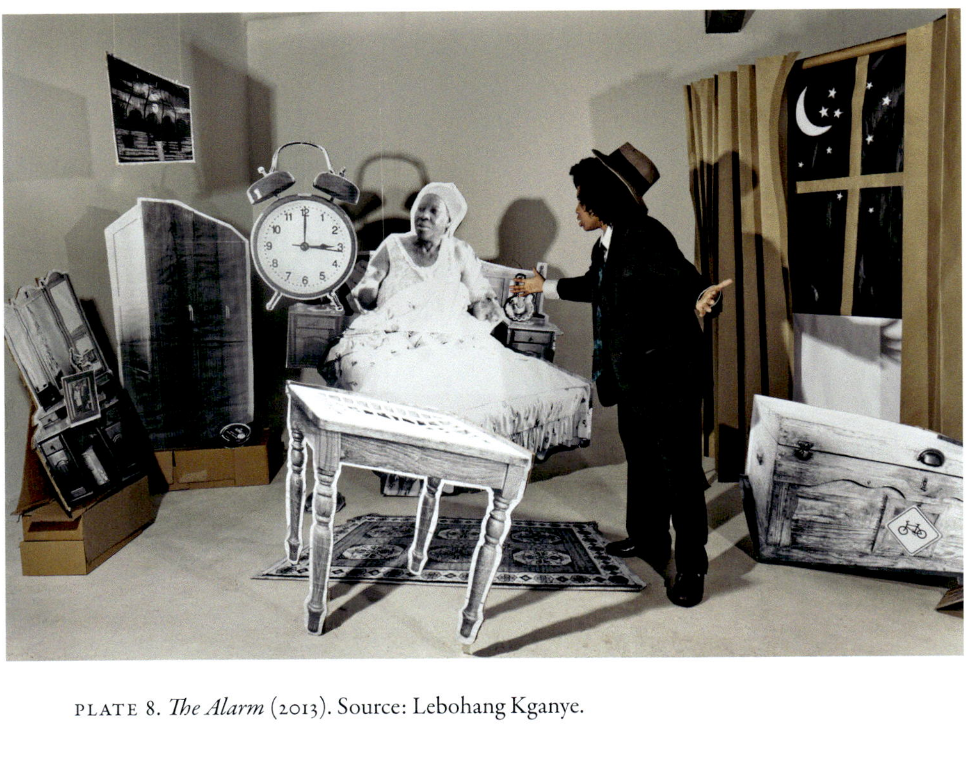

PLATE 8. *The Alarm* (2013). Source: Lebohang Kganye.

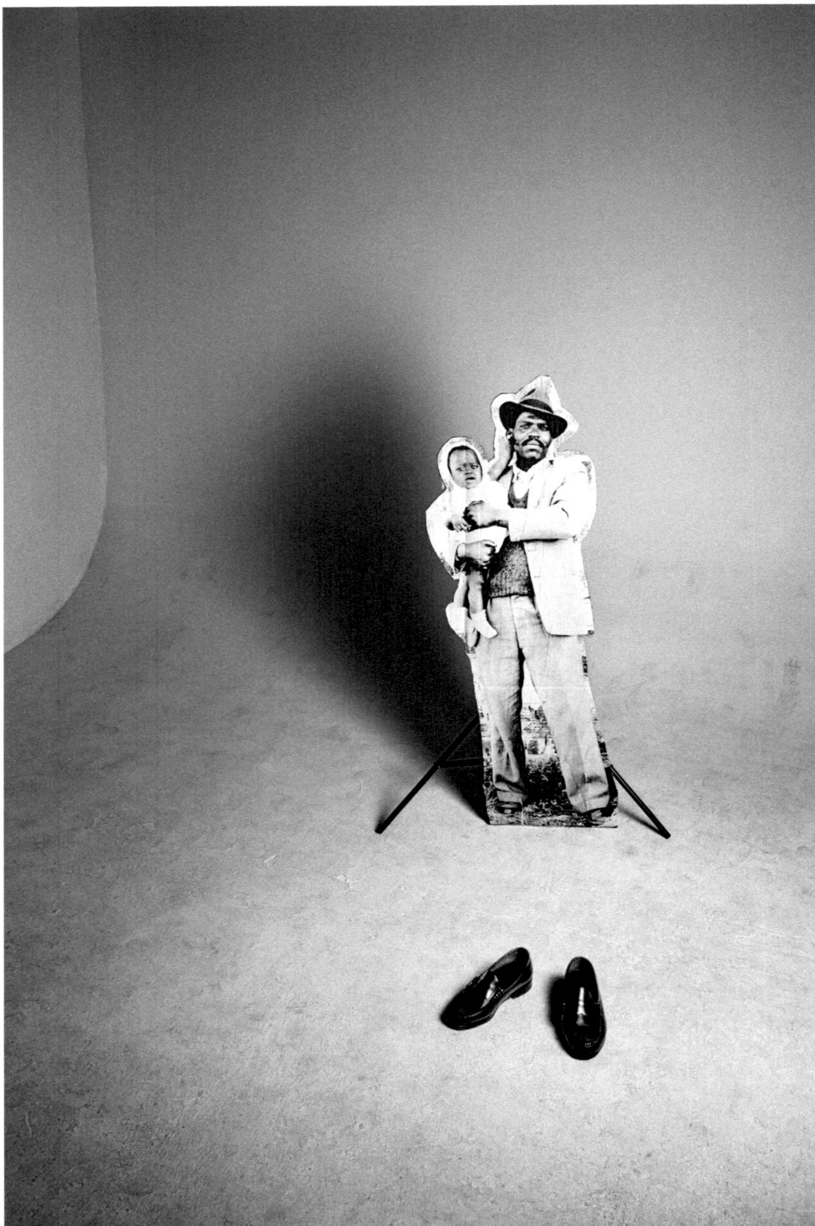

PLATE 9. *The Suit* (2013). Source: Lebohang Kganye.

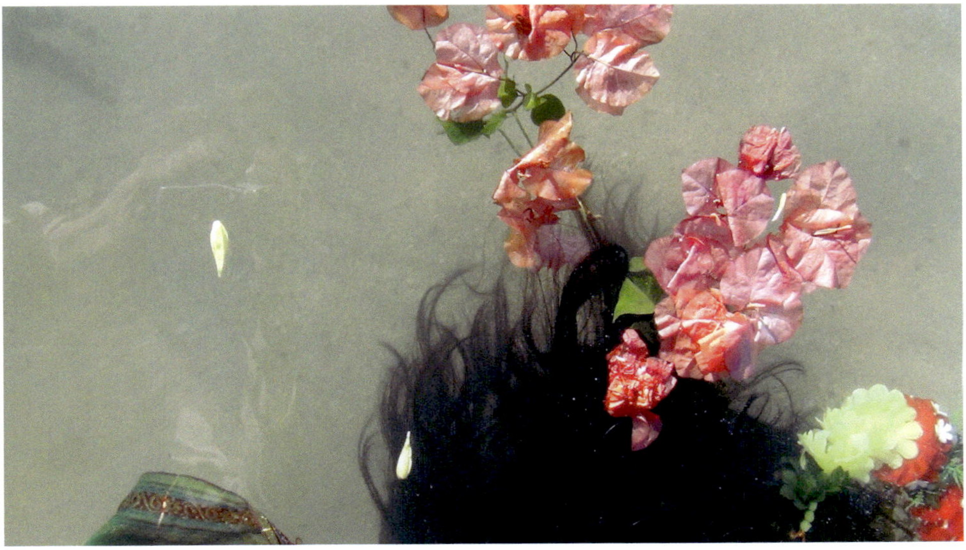

PLATE 10. Sharlene Khan. *Drowning Durga VII* (2015). 61 cm × 91 cm. Individual hand-painted digital color photograph on Sihl Persomural. Photo credit: Nicola Gear.

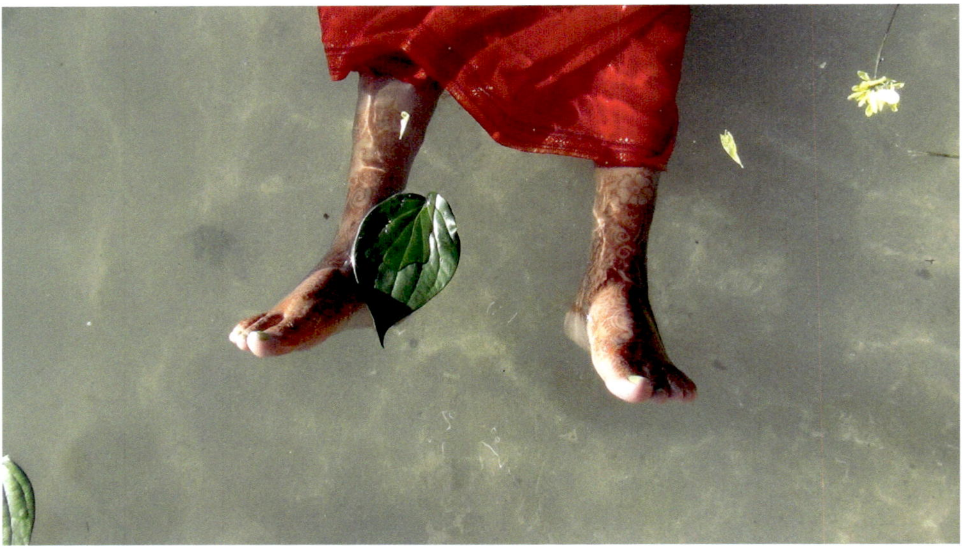

PLATE 11. Sharlene Khan. *Drowning Durga IV* (2015). 61 cm × 91 cm. Individual hand-painted digital color photograph on Sihl Persomural. Photo credit: Nicola Gear.

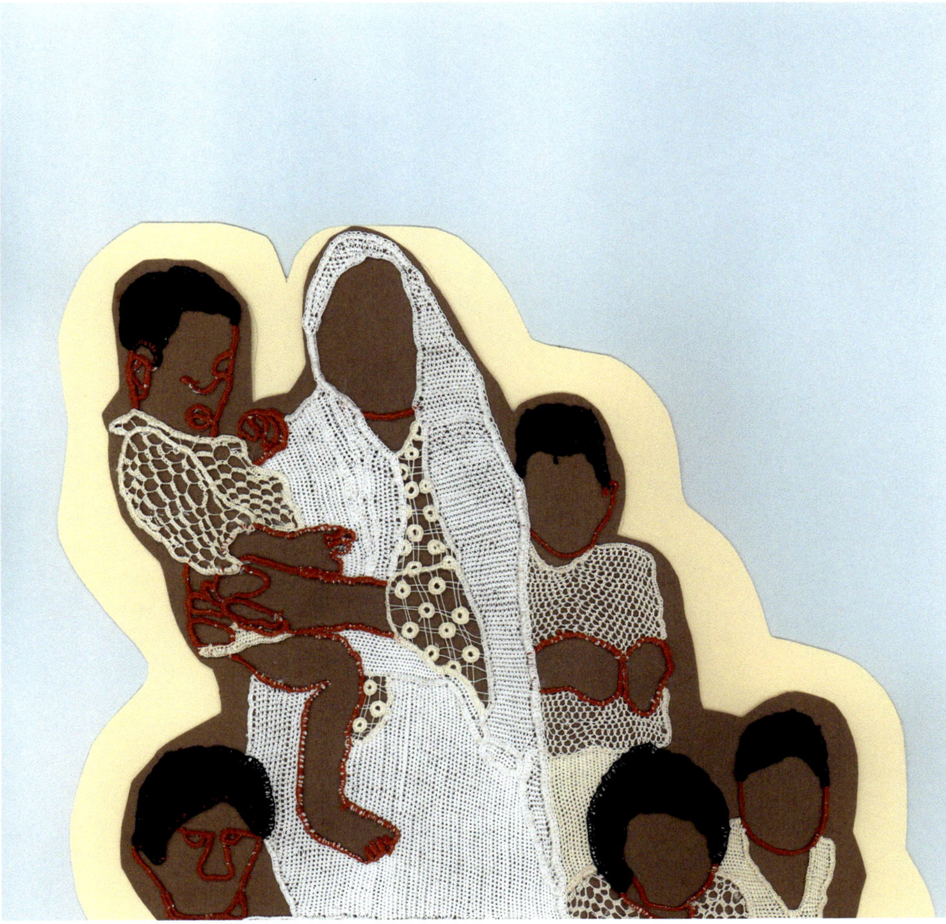

PLATE 12. Sharlene Khan. *Family Portrait* (2016). 29 cm × 37 cm. Mixed media (cotton, cardboard). Collection: Iziko South African National Gallery.

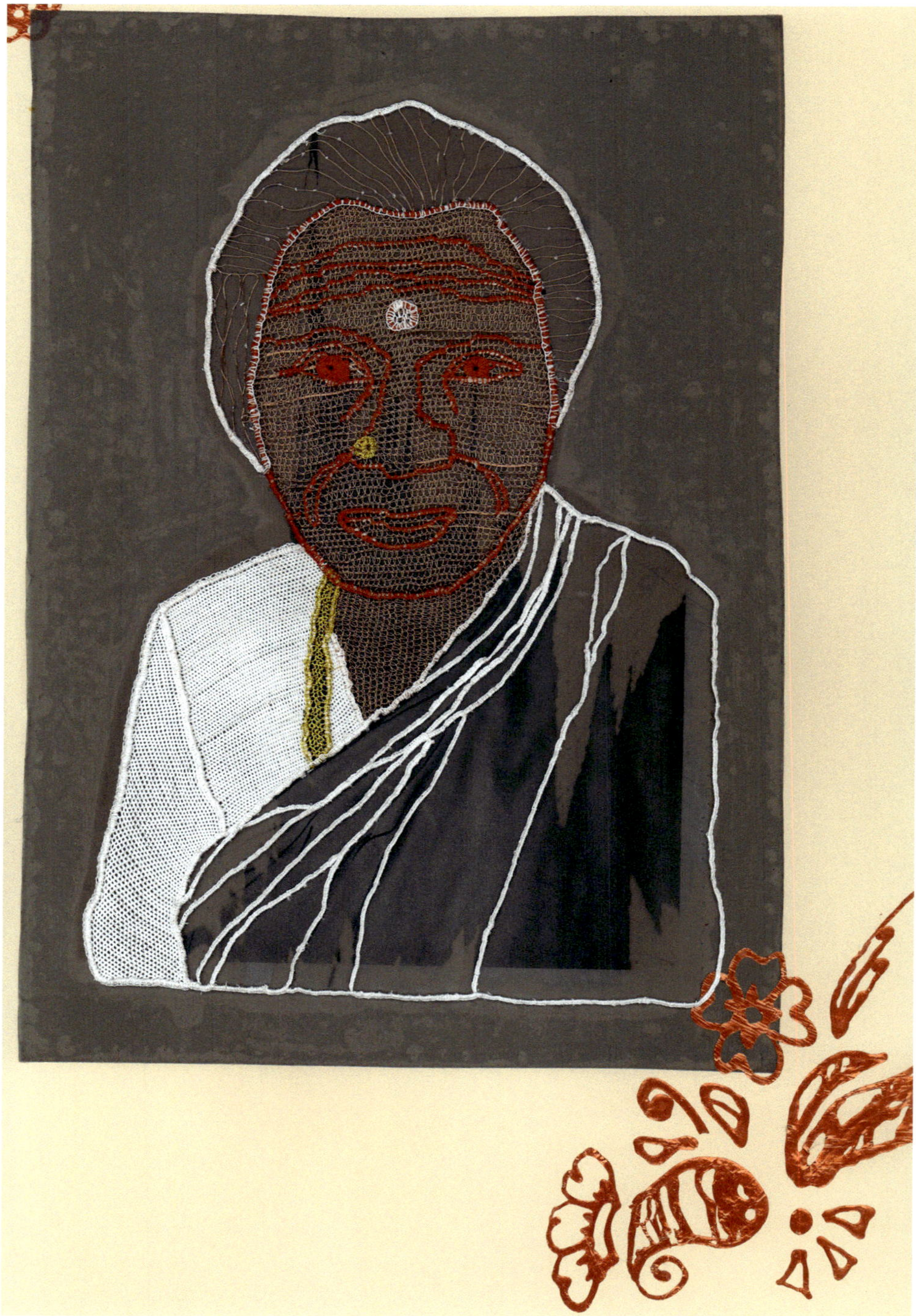

PLATE 13. Sharlene Khan. *Aya I* (2015). 50 cm × 37.5 cm. Mixed media (cotton, wire, acrylic paint, cardboard, photocopy). Collection: Iziko South African National Gallery.

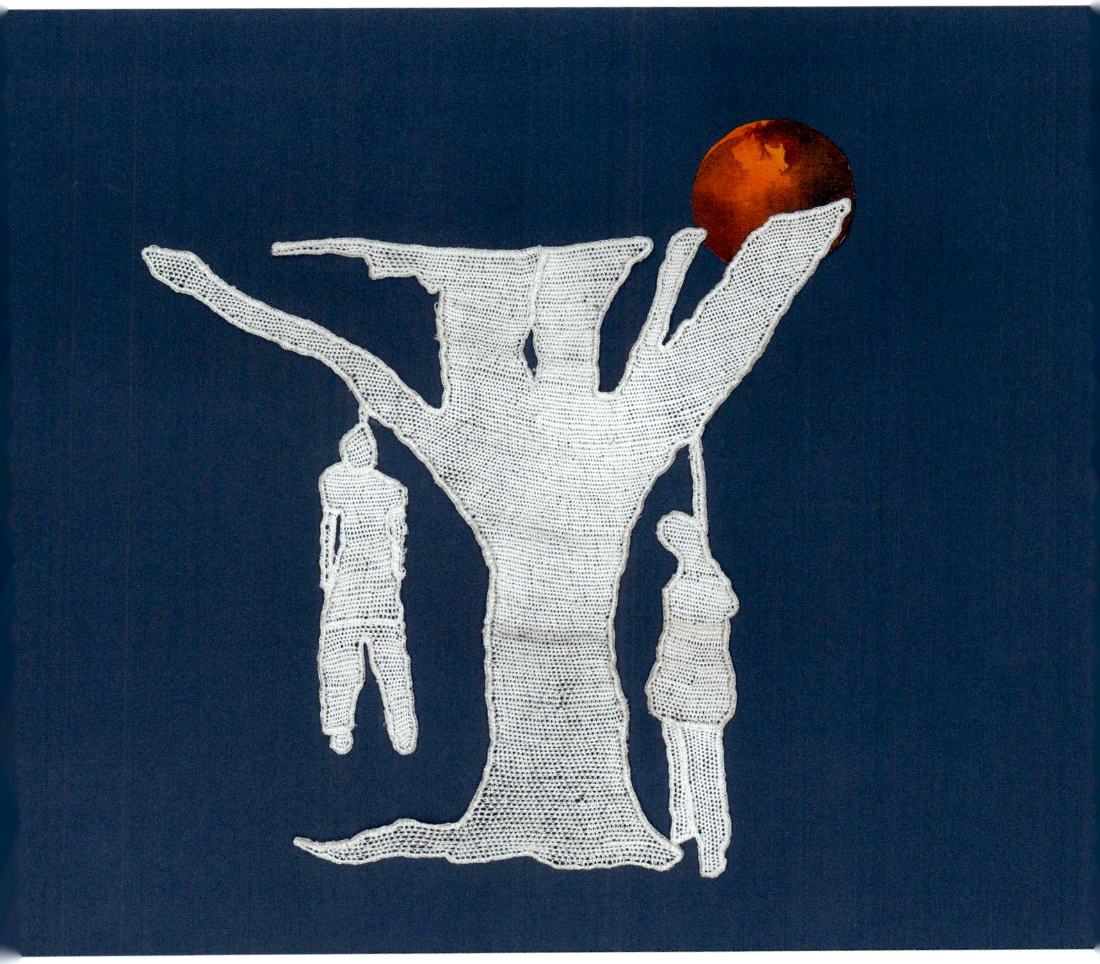

PLATE 14. Sharlene Khan. *Strangefruit II* (2016). 36.5 cm × 36 cm. Mixed media (cotton, cardboard, ink, handmade paper). Collection: Iziko South African National Gallery.

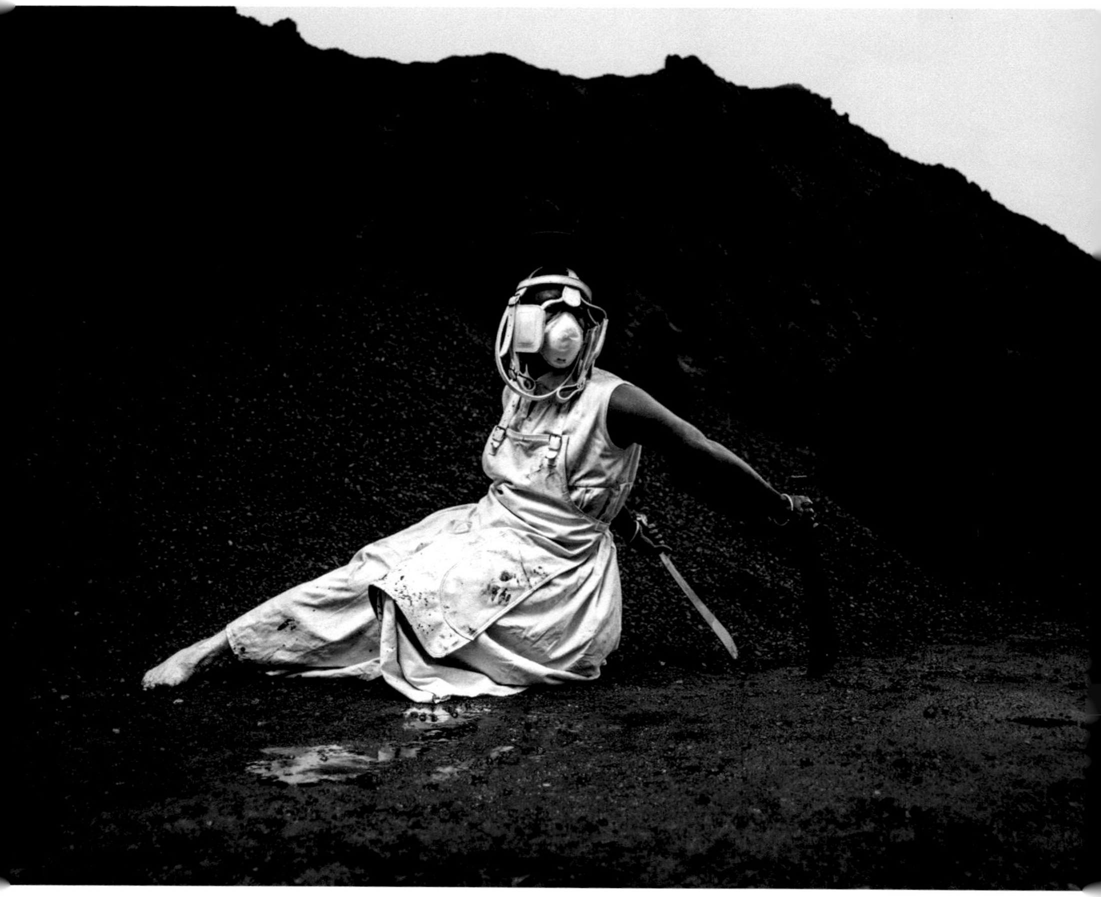

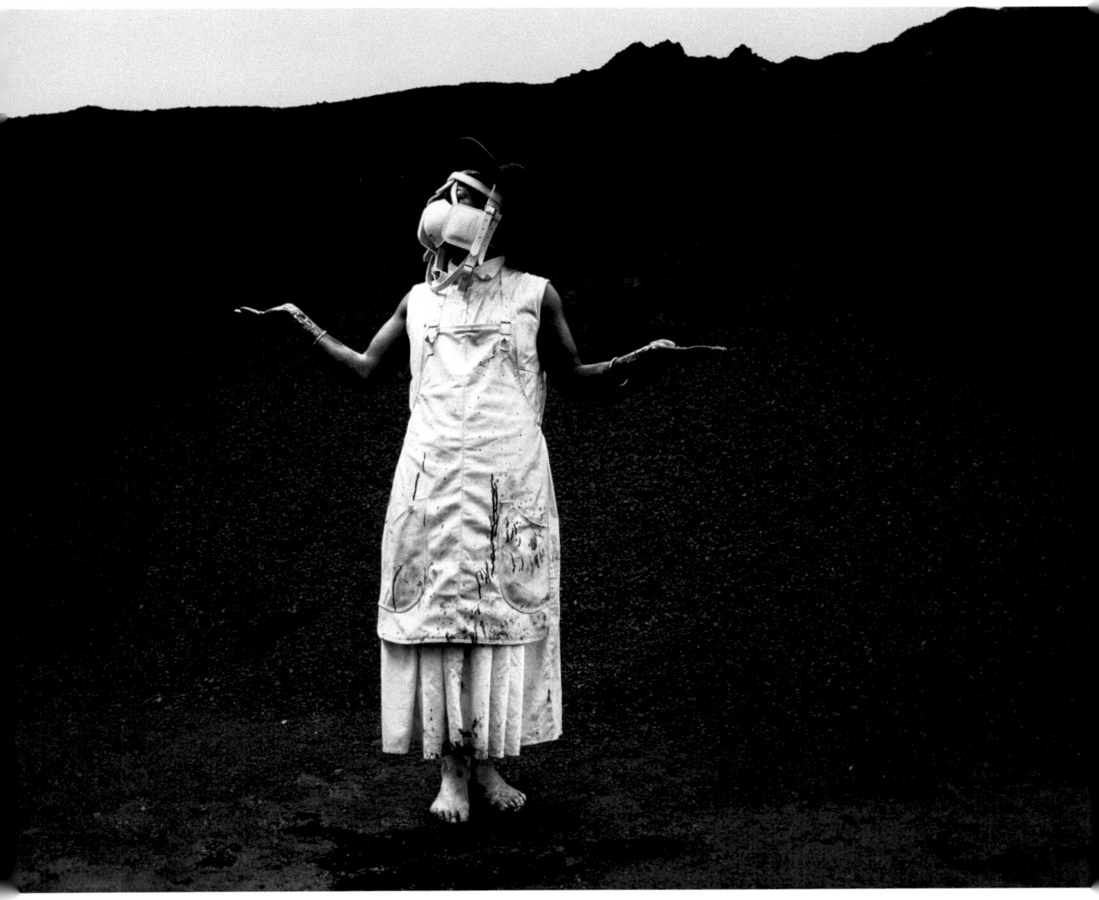

PLATES 15 and 16. *Kwa Ndabeni* (2016). Source: Mohau Modisakeng.

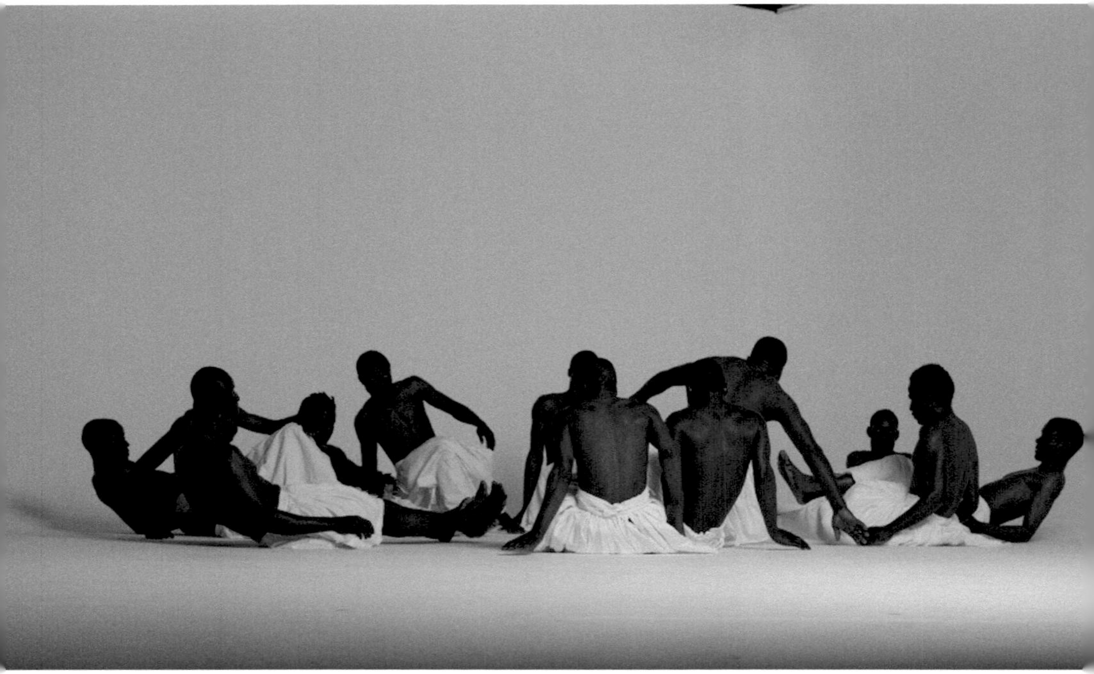

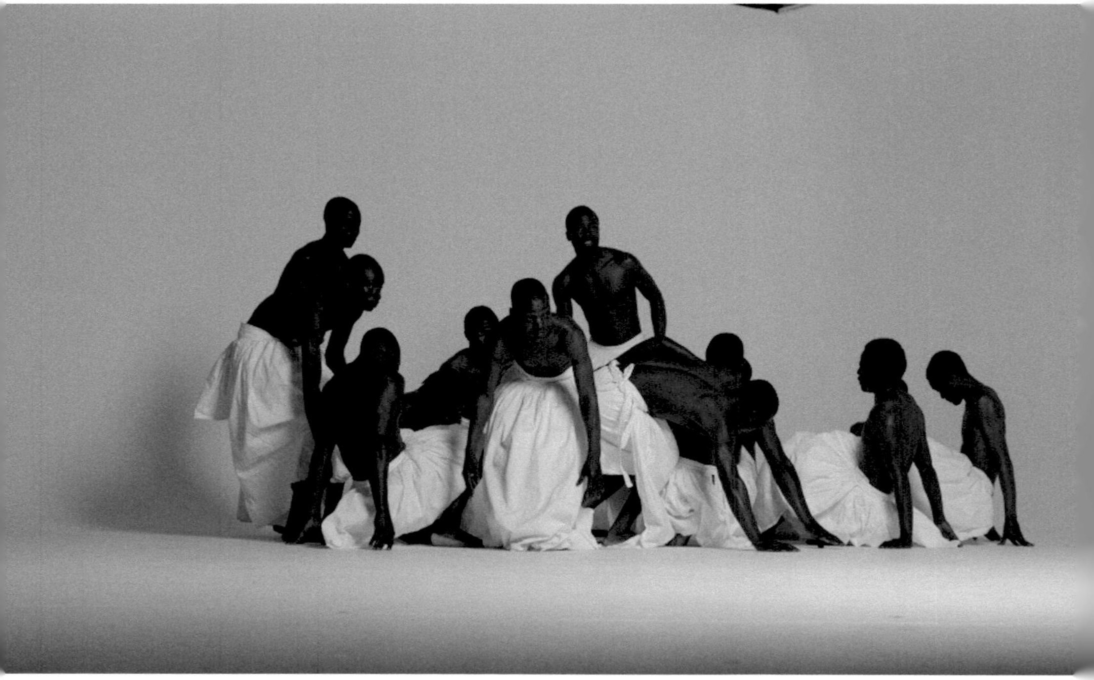

PLATES 17 and 18. *Ga bose gangwe* (2014). Image stills. Source: Mohau Modisakeng.

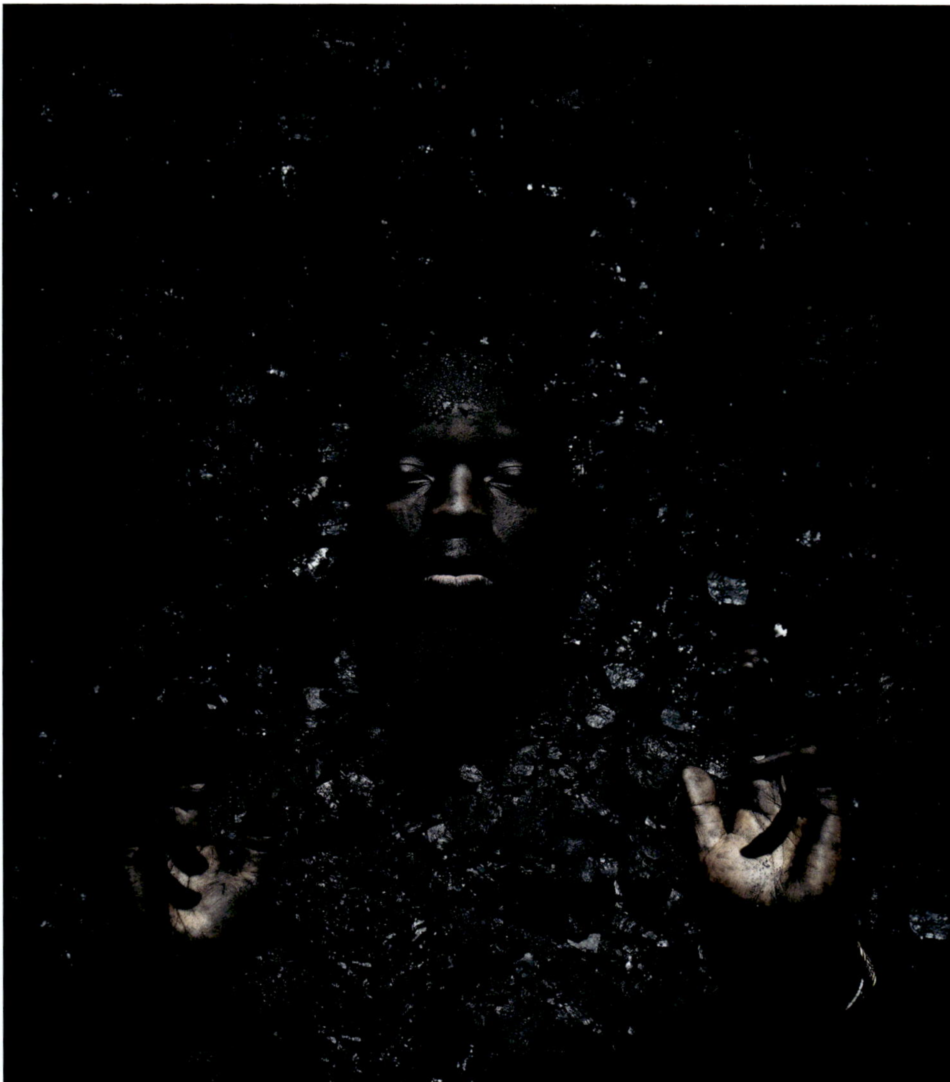

PLATE 19. *Lefa La Ntate* (2016). Source: Mohau Modisakeng.

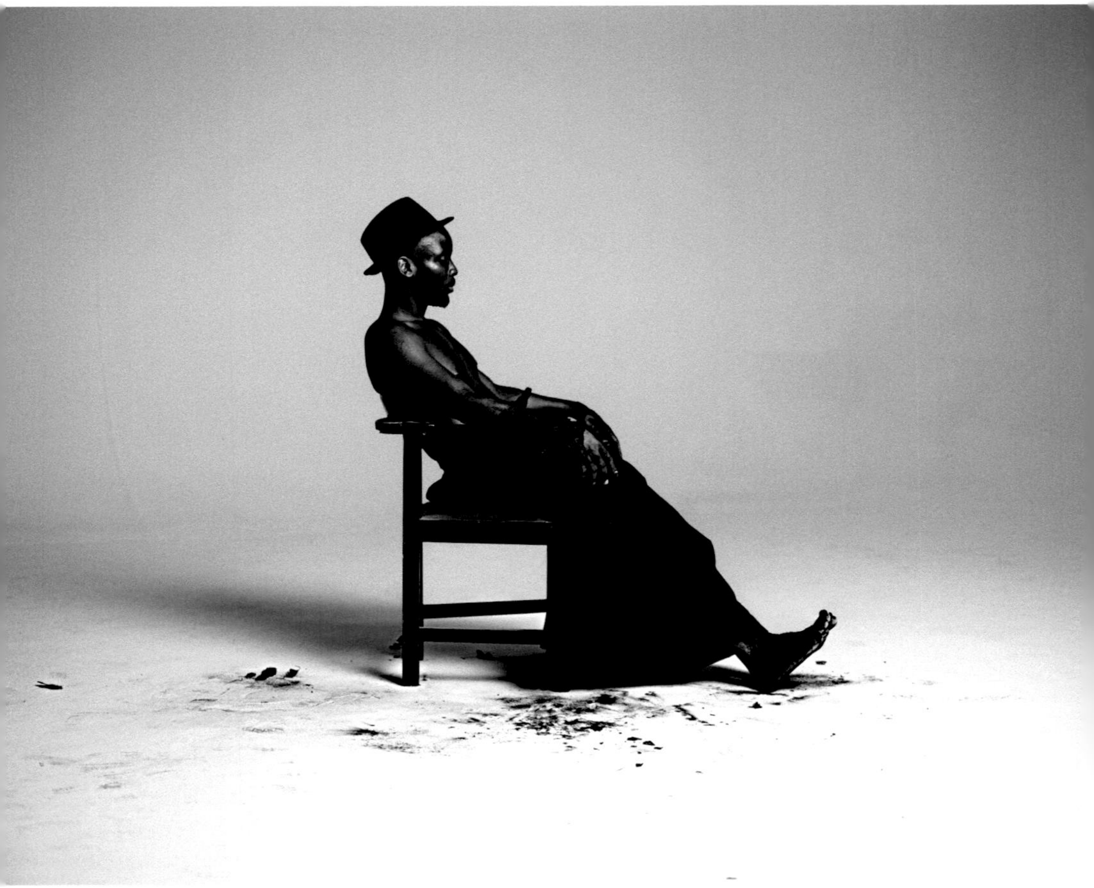

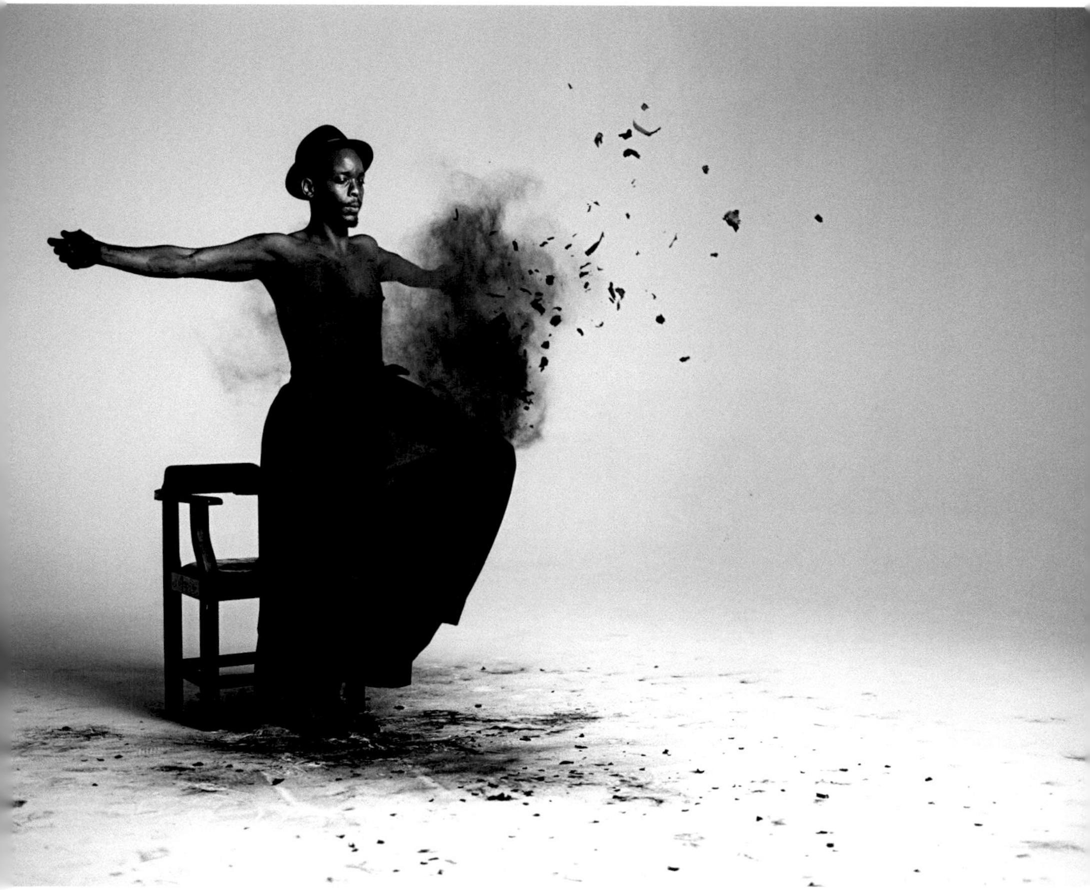

PLATES 20 and 21. *Inzilo* (2013). Image stills. Source: Mohau Modisakeng.

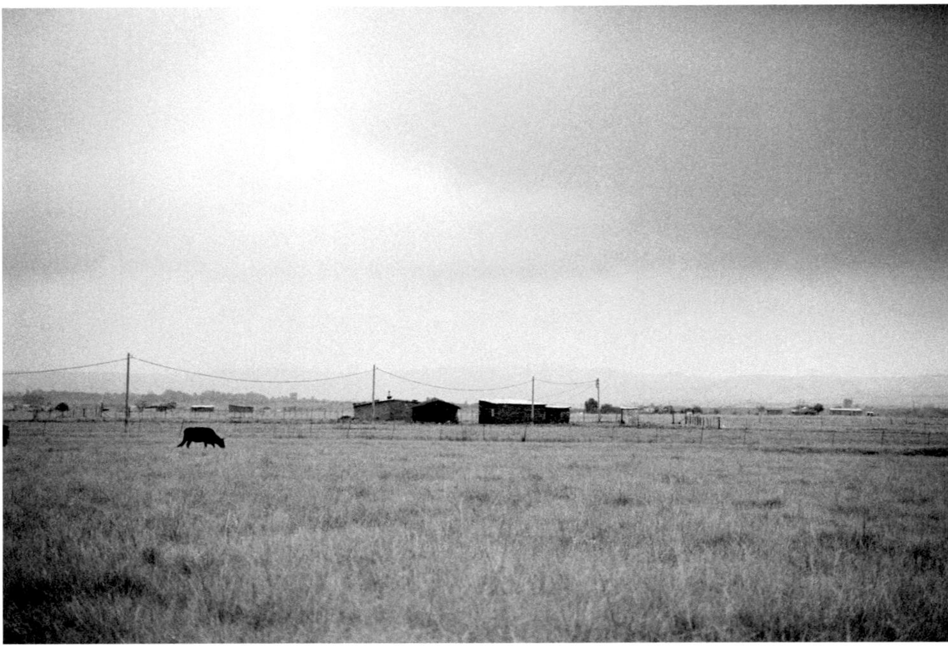

PLATE 22. *Msobotsheni* (2006). Image courtesy of the artist and blank projects, Cape Town. © Sabelo Mlangeni.

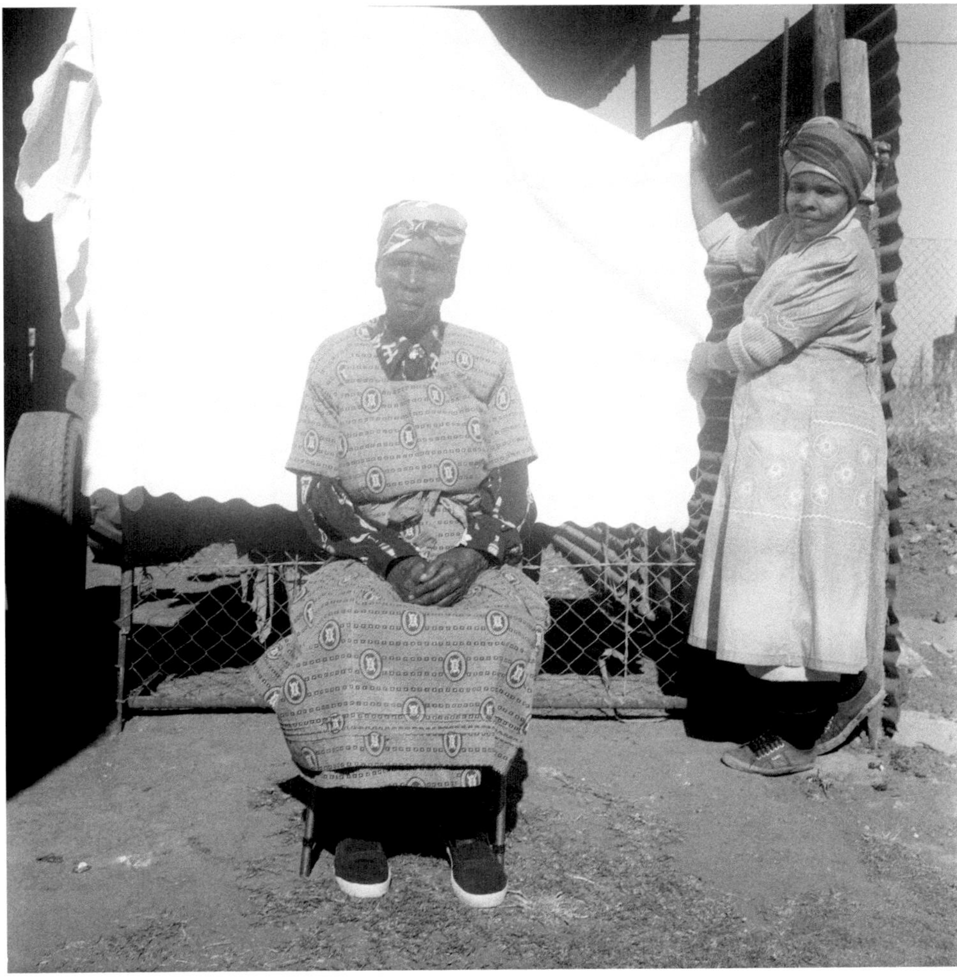

PLATE 23. *Portrait of a Family, Msibi* (2008). Image courtesy of the artist and blank projects, Cape Town. © Sabelo Mlangeni.

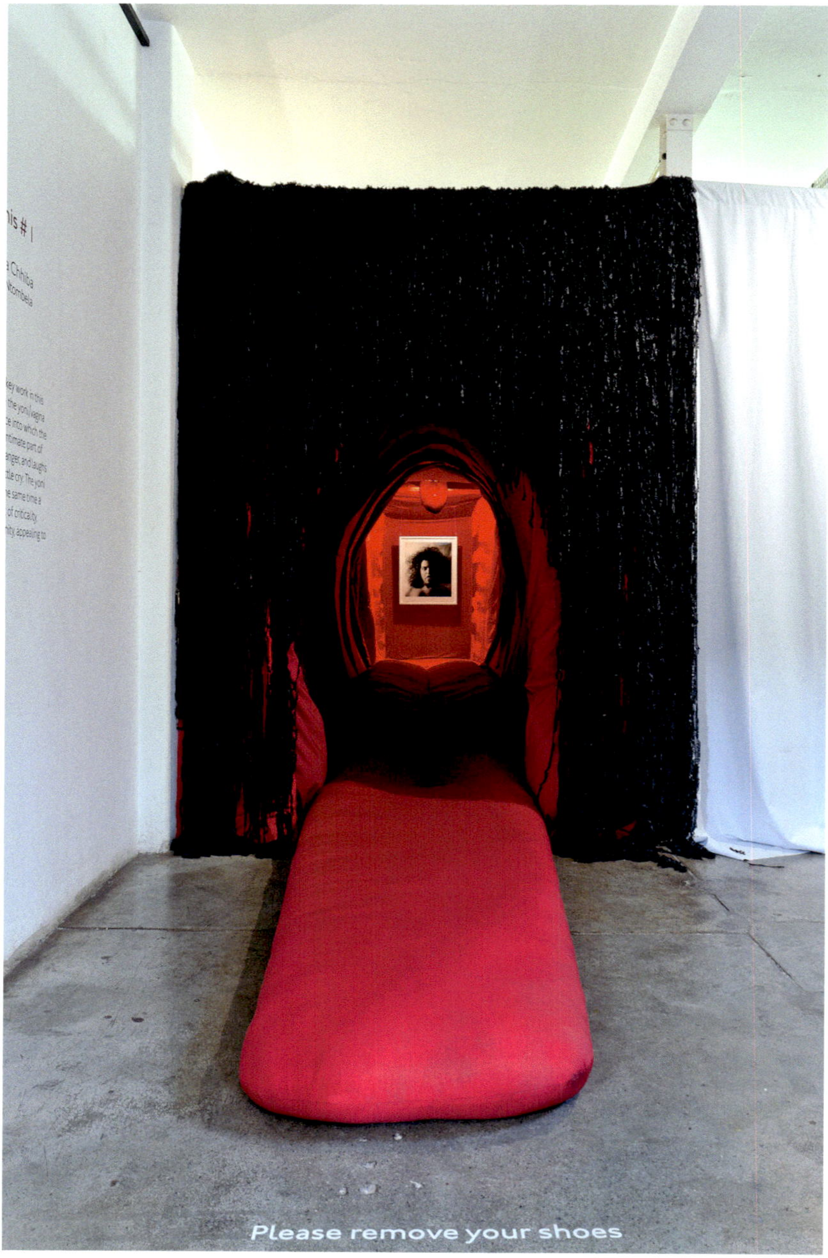

PLATE 24. Reshma Chhiba. *Come Inside*. Installation view. Photographed by Anthea Pokroy. Image courtesy of the artist.

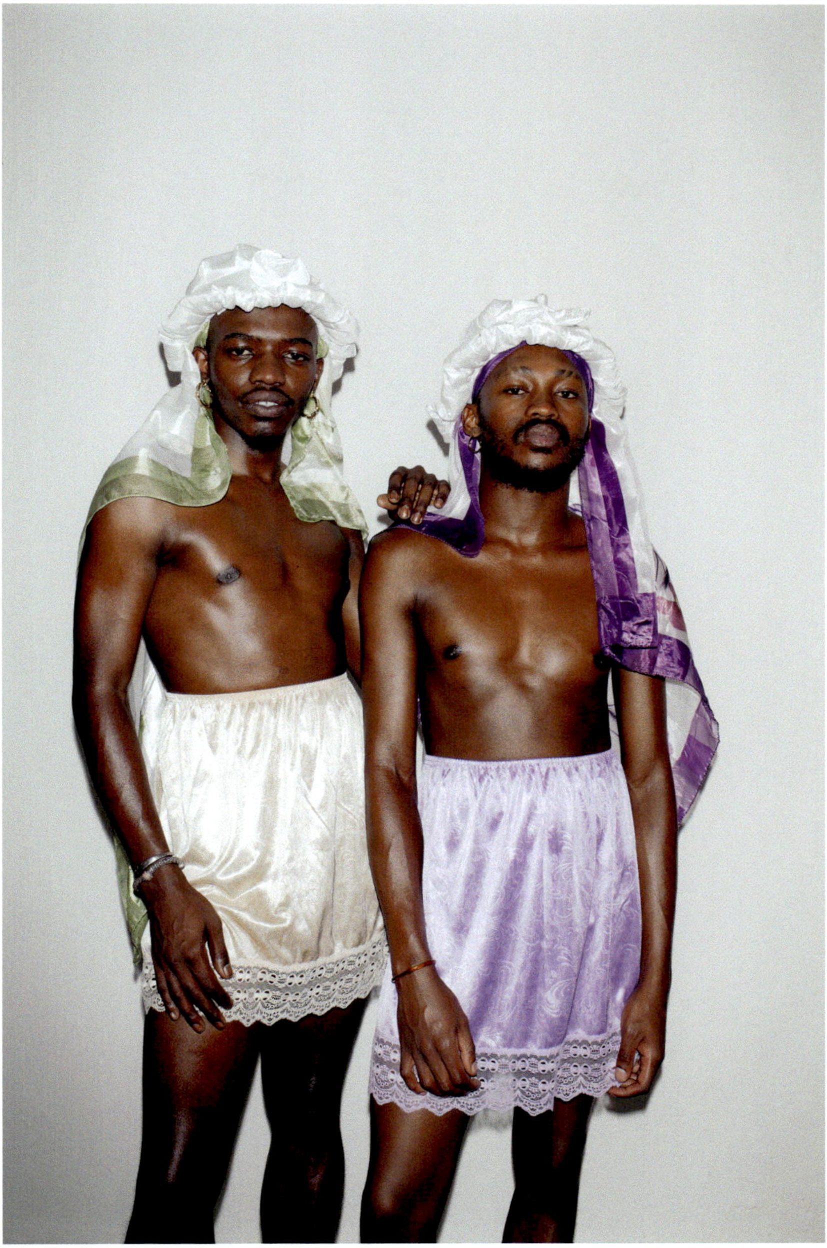

PLATE 25. Portrait of Fela Gucci and Desire Marea for *Cakeboy Magazine* (2006). Image courtesy of Nick Widmer.

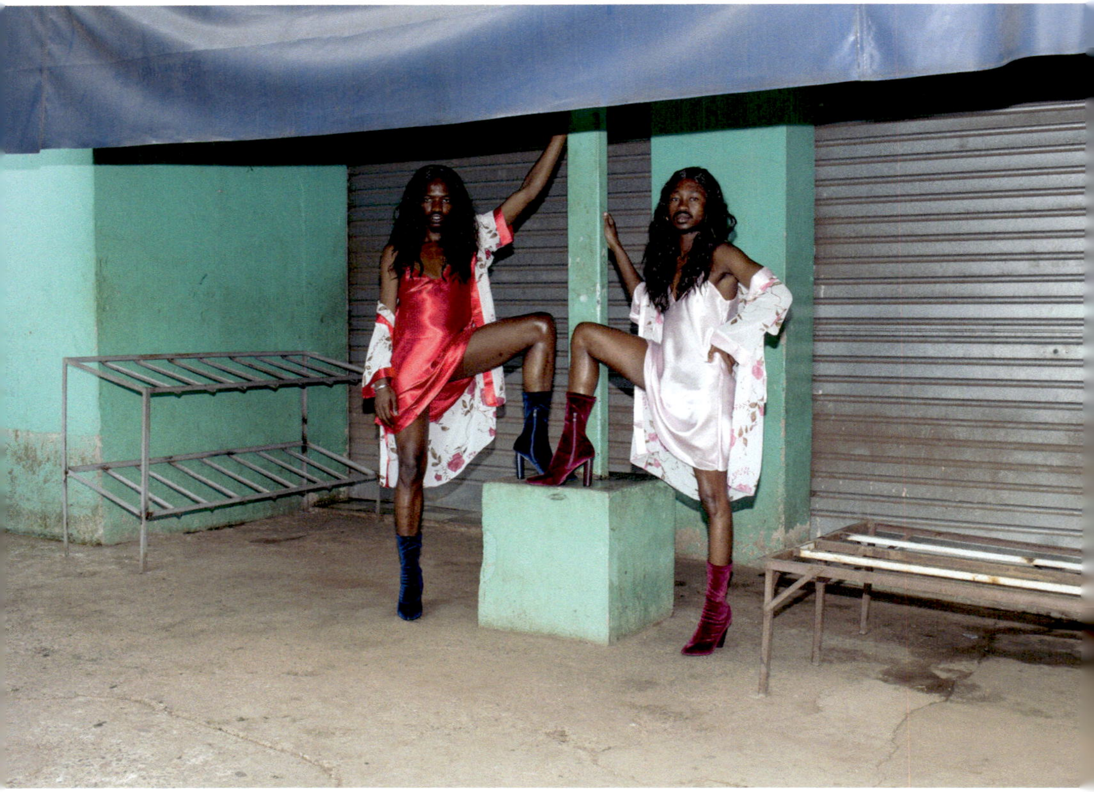

PLATE 26. *Ngizokuzingela* single cover (2018). Image courtesy of Nick Widmer.

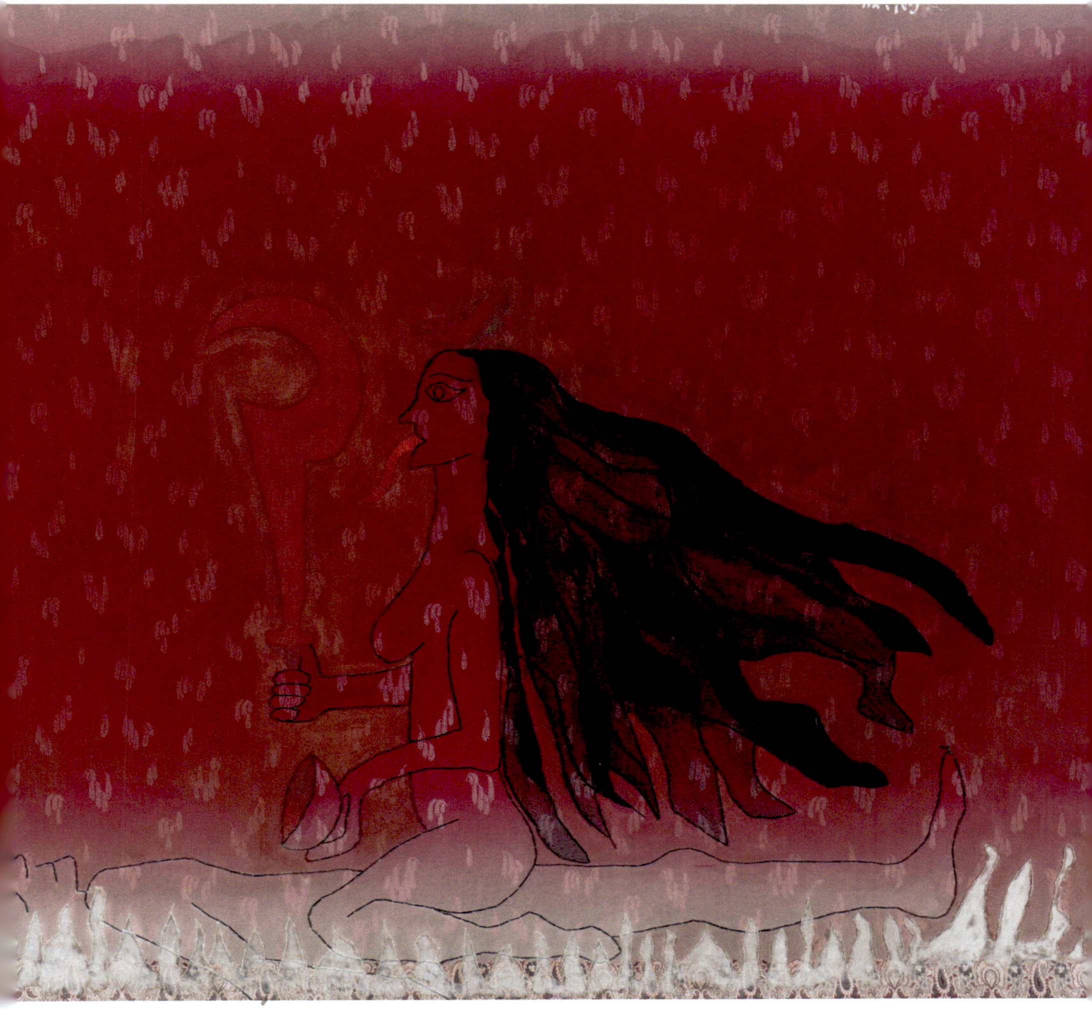

PLATE 27. Reshma Chhiba. *Divine Copulation* (2013), 1 m × 1.2 m. Kumkum powder and thread on sari. Image courtesy of the artist.

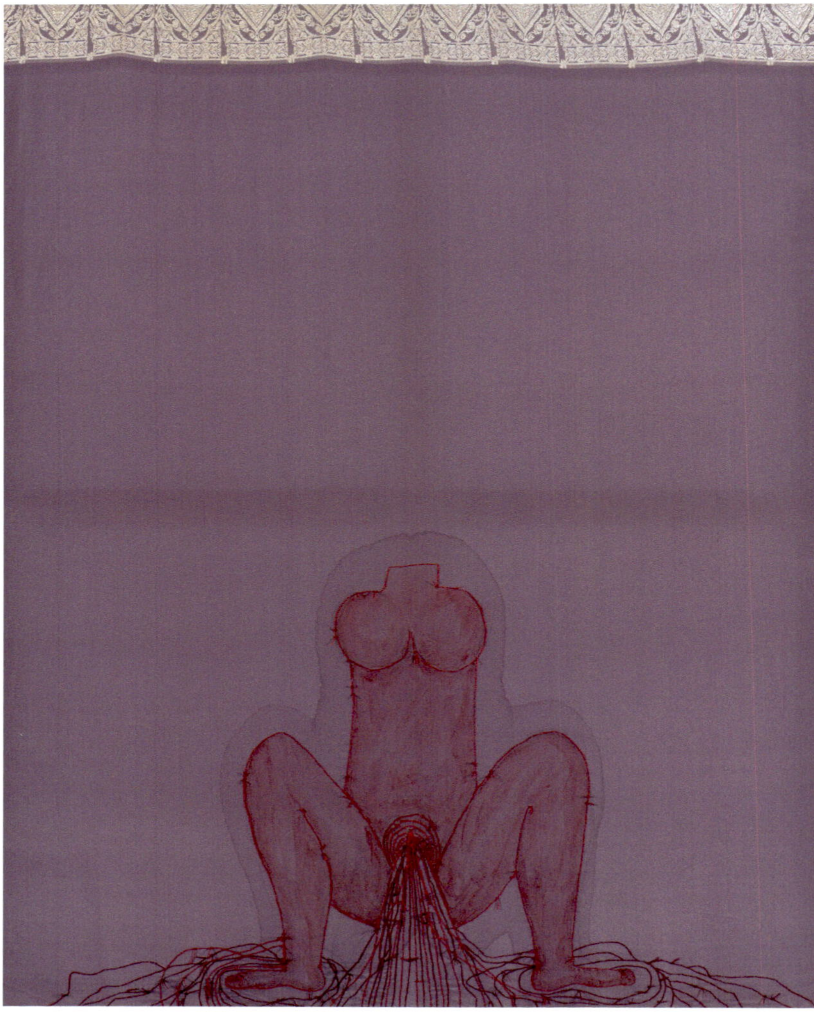

PLATE 28. Reshma Chhiba. *Sublime Essence* (2013). 1.2 m × 1 m. Kumkum powder and thread on sari. Image courtesy of the artist.

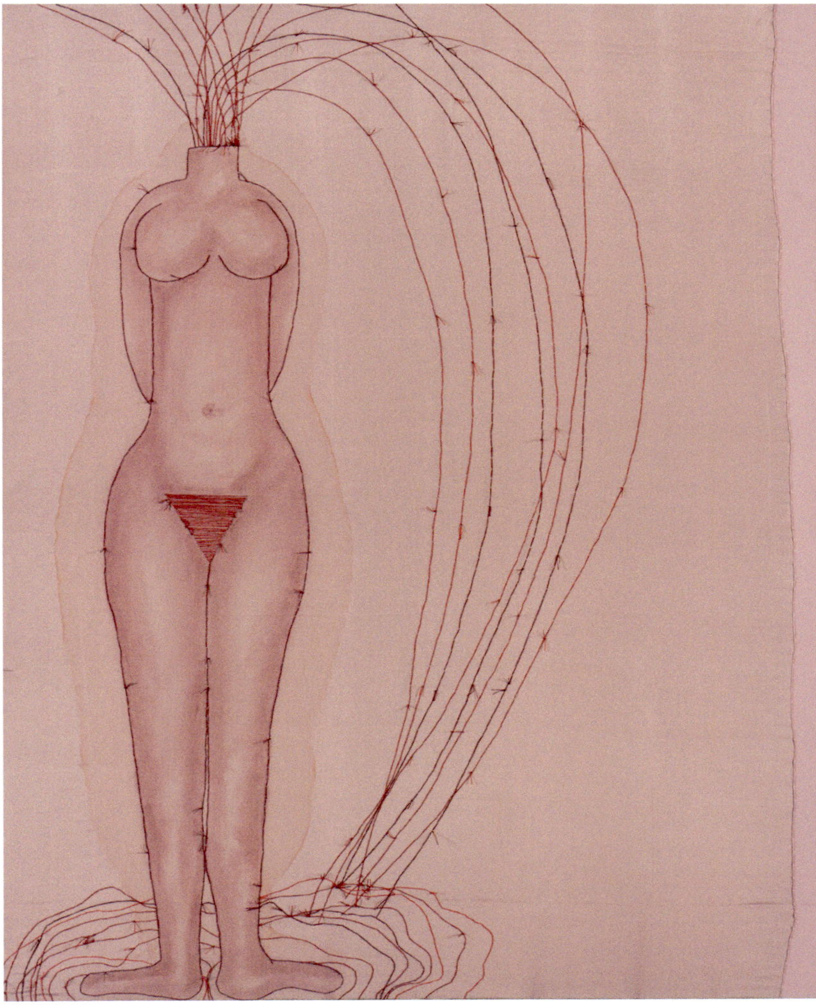

PLATE 29. Reshma Chhiba. *The One Who Is All That Has Been* (2013). 1.2 m × 1 m. Kumkum powder and thread on sari. Image courtesy of the artist.

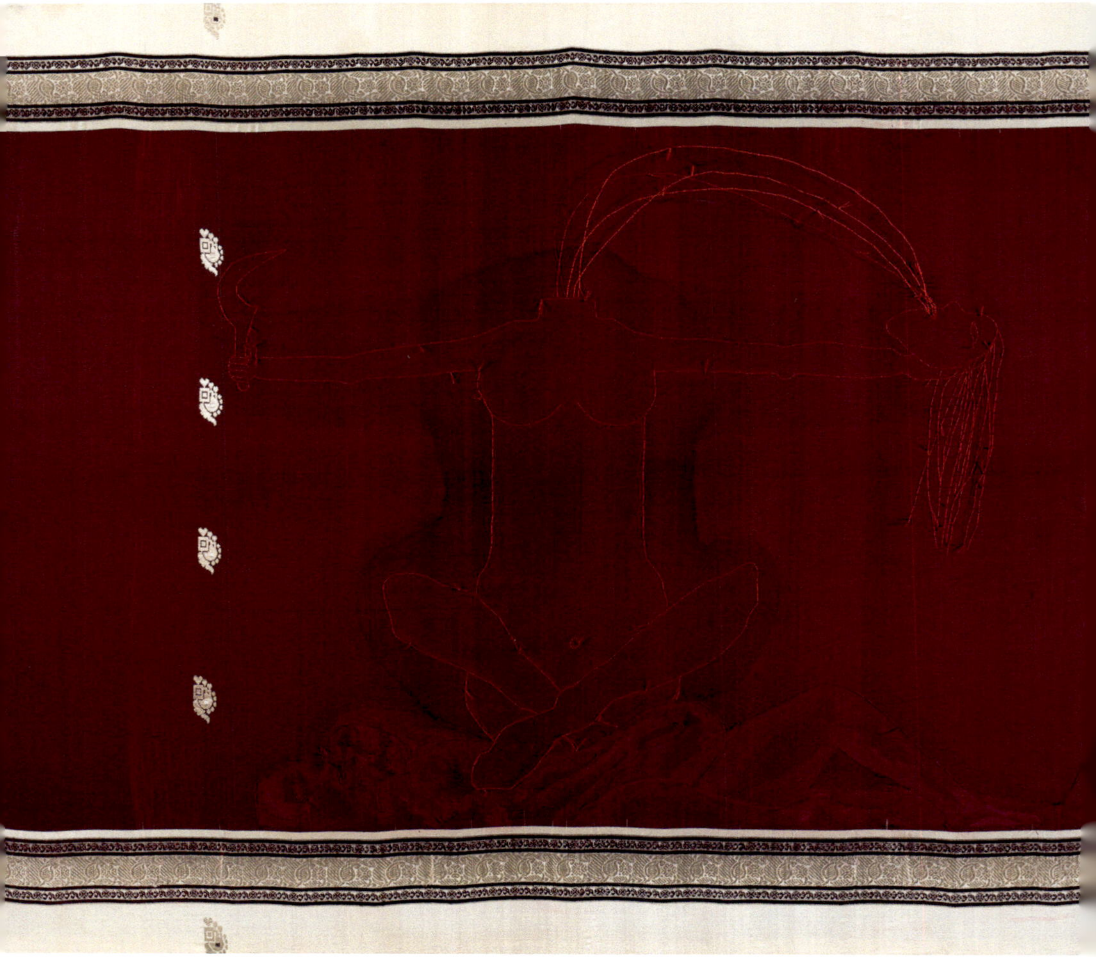

PLATE 30. Reshma Chhiba. *Ultimate Reality* (2013). 1 m × 1.2 m. Kumkum powder and thread on sari. Image courtesy of the artist.

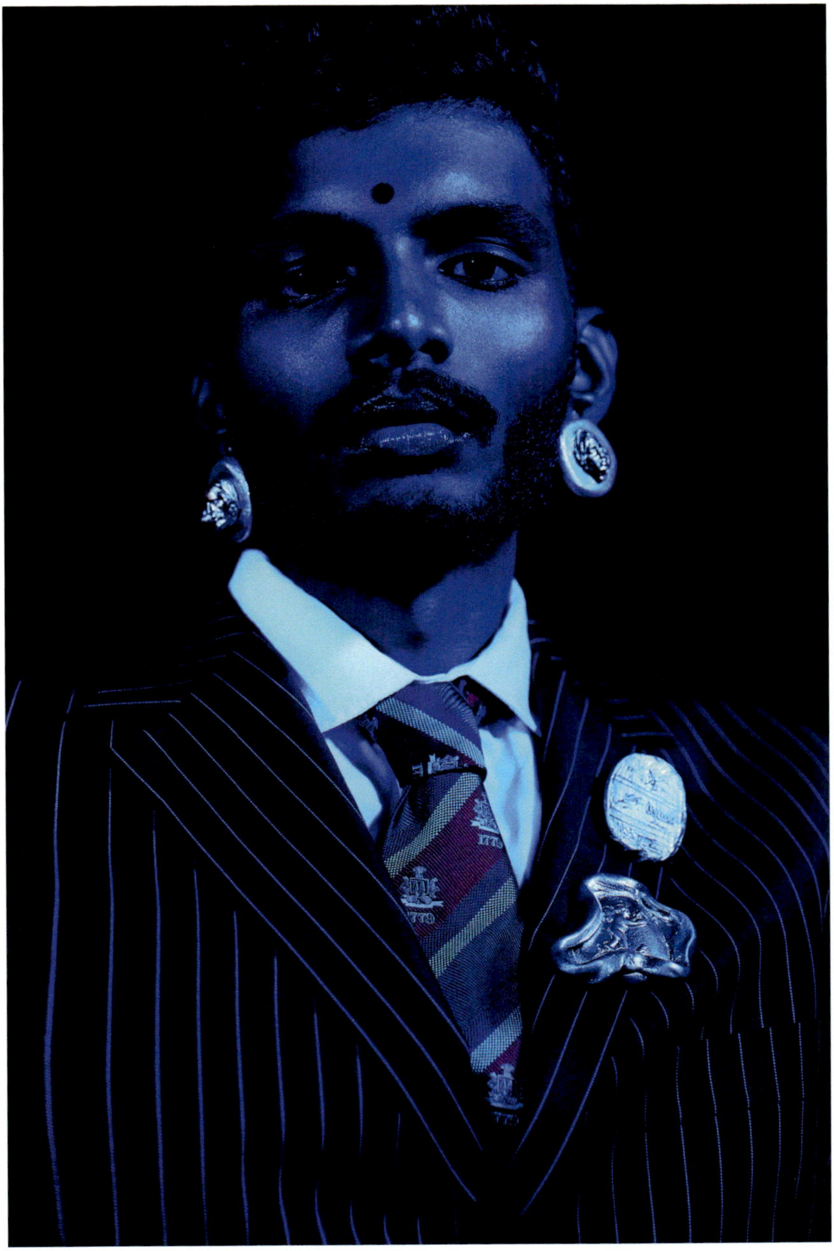

PLATE 31. Githan Coopoo. *Byzantine Collection* photoshoot (2018). Photographed by Jarred Figgins. Image courtesy of the artist.

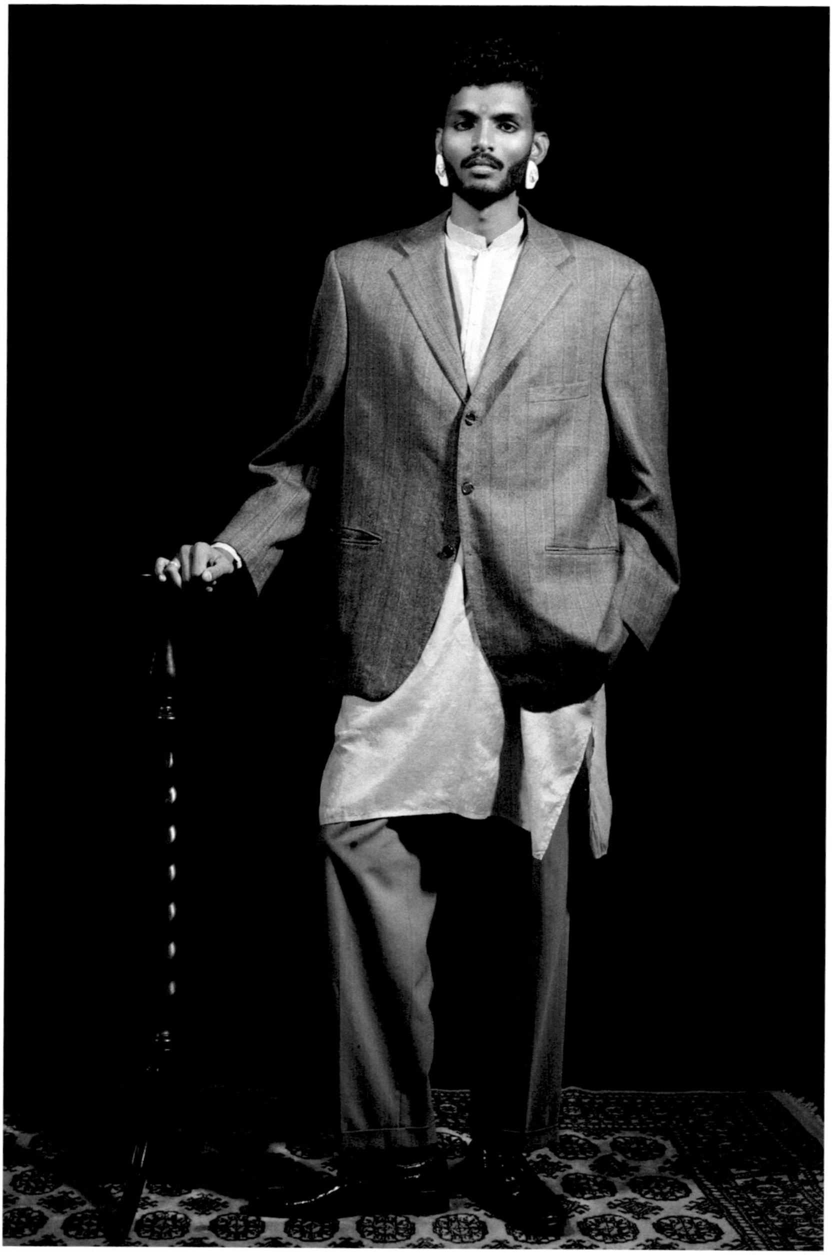

PLATE 32. Githan Coopoo. *Byzantine Collection* photoshoot (2018). Photographed by Jarred Figgins. Image courtesy of the artist.

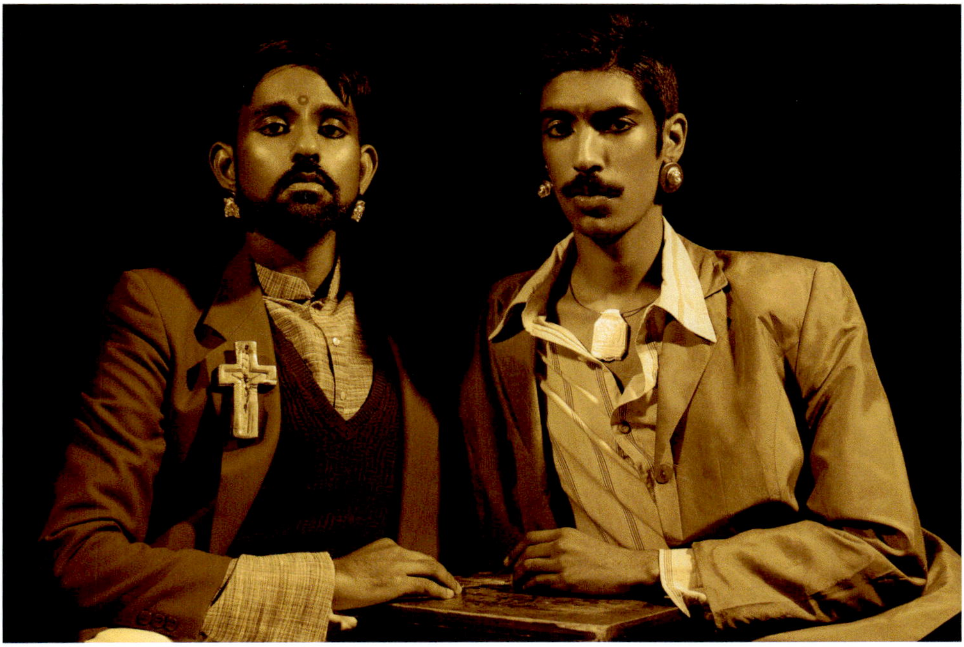

PLATE 33. Githan Coopoo. *Byzantine Collection* photoshoot (2018). Photographed by Jarred Figgins. Image courtesy of the artist.

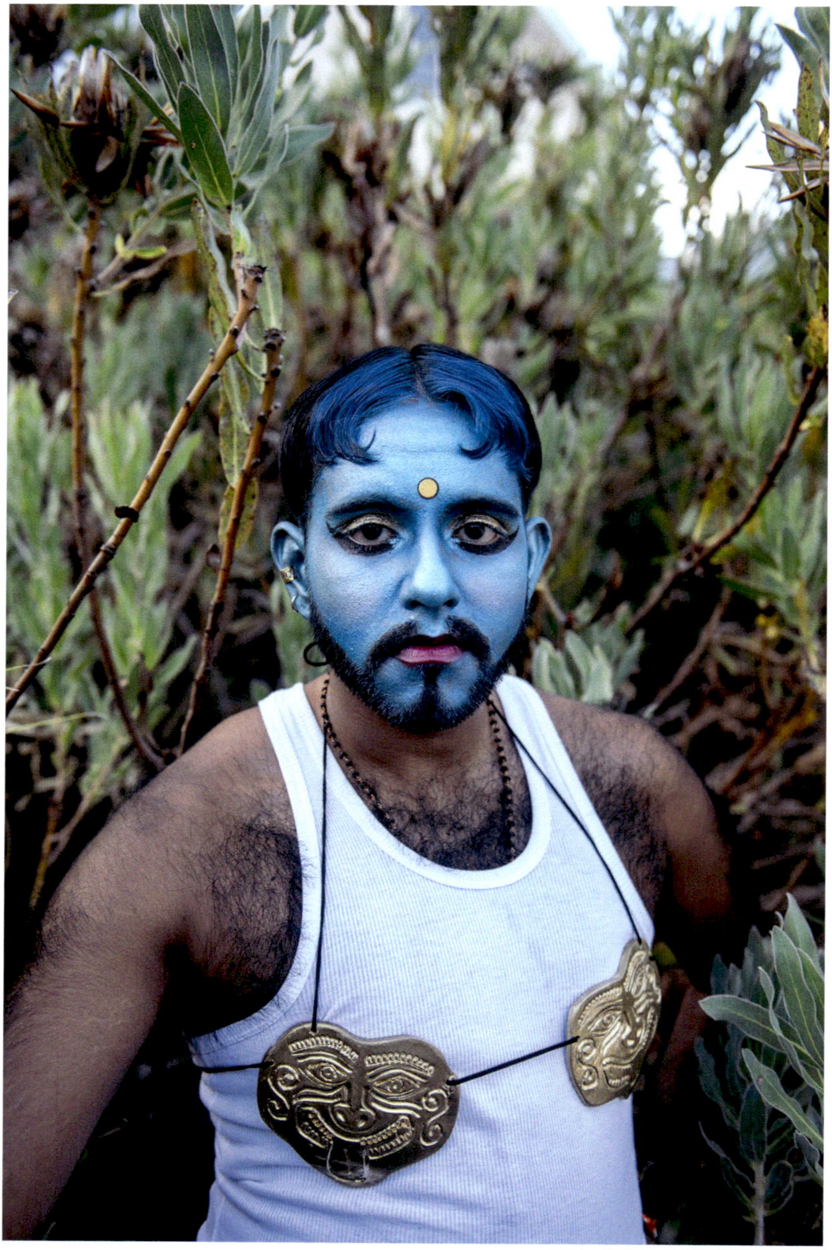

PLATE 34. Githan Coopoo. *Mail and Guardian* photoshoot (2020). Photographed by David Harrison. Image courtesy of the artist.

1

Afro-Femininities

MATERNAL ARCHIVES AS SITES OF QUEER-FEMINIST FUTURITIES

Given this book's central emphasis on the feminine, the vulnerable, and embodied knowledge as routes to rethinking Afro-Indian intimacies, Afro-Indianness, and South African blackness, this chapter examines the aesthetic practices of two artists—Lebohang Kganye and myself—who engage maternal archives (the family photoarchive) as sites to examine the formation of Afro-femininities in the afterlife of colonial apartheid. Our art practices are shaped by the figure of the black/ened mother (the "maternal feminine") and their positionalities within the home-space. This chapter examines the relationship between the maternal feminine and the quest for queer-feminist futurities. The home-space is a contradictory space; it is inherently feminine and feminized, but simultaneously a site of gender-sexual regulation and surveillance. Whereas the nation submerges the feminine to secure its cohesive narrative of post-apartheid mastery, the home-space, centered around the maternal feminine, disrupts nation-space and nation-time. Indeed, this disruption occurs within the aesthetic of the artworks where the past and the present, the living and the dead, memory and history, racialized bodies touch and rub against one another in our quest to understand the afterlives of indenture-colonial-apartheid and the making of Afro-femininities across regimes of racial difference.

This chapter enacts my queer curatorial practice and queer-reading practice by bringing into conversation two differently racialized artists, one born in the early 1980s and the other in the early 1990s, to examine our interconnected interests in the figure of the mother and family photo albums as alternative sites to grapple with gender, sexuality, memory, migration, and kinship. Routed through a queer reading of the maternal feminine, this chapter creates, through juxtapositioning, the Afro-Indian intimacies that this book argues for, reading across the artworks—across regimes of difference—to examine our entangled pasts, presents, and futures.

By manipulating family photos and positioning them into an aesthetic conversation with recently shot digital photos through digital technologies, our projects create an aesthetic that engages and disrupts spatial and temporal frameworks through an aesthetic of touch. Thus, this chapter engages the importance of memory and touch across our interrelated bodies of work. Touch manifests through our (the artists') affective and haptic engagement with this archive. Touch activates the realm of memory and processes of remembering—between mother and son, mother and daughter, and grandmother and granddaughter—and emerges aesthetically within the photographic frame through an aesthetic of time that I refer to as *elastic*. Routed through the figure of the mother, the aesthetic of touch reimagines, while actively generating "relations of care and pleasure, ways of inventing and sustaining being together" (Macharia 2019, 53; Tinsley 2008).

Weaving together narratives through photographs, memories, and oral histories, our aesthetic practices can be considered "memory-work." As a genre memory-work takes on many forms, including experimental video and film, photography, exhibitions, curatorial projects, autobiographical writings, and performance art. The slippery nature of memory and processes of remembering renders the genre of memory-work fluid and fragmentary, resisting genre conventions. In both our practices, we literally cut up (physically and digitally) family photos, disrupting, reinterpreting, and recreating narratives from the fragments of familial memories as mediated through the maternal-feminine. Annette Kuhn writes, "Memory-work is a method and a practice of unearthing and making public untold stories, stories of 'lives lived out in the borderland, lives for which the central interpretive devices of culture don't quite work.' These are the lives of those whose ways of knowing and ways of seeing the world are rarely acknowledged, let alone celebrated, in the expressions of a hegemonic cultures" (1995, 80).

Born in 1990 and raised by a single mother in Katlehong, a township situated on the East Rand of Johannesburg, Lebohang Kganye uses aesthetic practices like film, animation, and digital photography to reanimate quotidian encounters of black life. Kganye's practice mobilizes the family photograph as an alternative site to examine the experiences of South African blacks as they relate to histories of migration, displacement, urban settlement, and freedom. This chapter examines two interrelated bodies of work, *Ke Lefa Laka: Her-Story* (2013) and *Ke Lefa Laka: Heir-Story* (2013), two visual culture projects in which Kganye uses family photos and performance to reactivate the realm of memory to create an intergenerational dialogue that positions her and her mother (Dimakatso) and her and her grandfather within the same photographic frame, disrupting the linear time-space of the postapartheid nation. The death of her mother further estranged her from her extended family and the particularities of her familial history. The loss of her mother propels her on a journey across the country, tracing the movement of her grandfather and other family members from the farms and homelands to Johannesburg. Her memory-work shifts from attending with care to the death of her mother, in a context where her memory and her image begin to fade as time passes, to attending to the afterlife of colonial apartheid and its impact on the black family structure.

Her-Story emerged after Kganye's mother's death and was her way of mourning and celebrating her mother's life. Her mother's life experiences were intimately connected to the histories of African labor migration, and in *Heir-Story* she examines the gendered impact of labor migration on the construction of black womanhood and femininities. Kganye's practices shift from literally embodying her mother's feminine beauty through performance and by restaging her mother's photographs (*Her-Story*) to photomontages where she performs the positionality of her grandfather, subverting gender norms, displacing the patriarchal figure through which family is organized and remembered. Indeed, Kganye's maternal figures—mother and grandmother—become the impetus to examine the slippery nature of memory and remembering. I am interested in how Kganye's reverse migration from the city to the "homelands," as well the aesthetic compression of time and space engendered through performance, disrupt the forward-looking trajectory that shapes postapartheid nationalism, reorienting the desire for nation-state forms of recognition that foreclose a more complex understanding of the black experience.

The death of my mother in 2019 also informed my curatorial project *The Brown Photo Album: An Archive of Feminist Futurity. The Brown Photo Album* is an experiment in reading and reanimating the photoarchive of a woman born one generation removed from the sugarcane plantations and coal mines where her parents (my grandparents) were indentured. *The Brown Photo Album* is an ongoing project related to my digital photography project, *Queering the Archive: Brown Bodies in Ecstasy*, also invested in family photos/archives as a method to grapple with the afterlife of indentureship and Afro-Indian queer embodiment. My interest in family photography intersected with my parents' interest in family history, and together we embarked on a journey to find as many family photo albums as we could. We drove from town to town, traversing rural and urban KwaZulu-Natal, visiting extended family members, seeking out our history within the sleeves of deteriorating albums. I understood that these family photos revealed a different history of Indianness, a history of the Afro-Indian experience as shaped by rural Natal. We reconstructed "familial maps" trying to understand the movement of my ancestors from the Indian subcontinent to Southern Africa, from the sugarcane fields along the Natal Coast and the coal mines in the interior of the province, from rural to semirural towns and Indian townships. Collectively, these photos articulate a rural Indian positionality shaped by the indentured class, which has not been fully examined within the South African context.

I did not know it at the time, but as I encountered, looked at, touched, and felt these photos, I was engaging in a queer-reading practice that would inform my art practice. Even though there was some form of delight and pleasure in finding photos of my great-grandparents and other early ancestors, the photos revealed forms of intimacies, particularly between men, either still under indentureship or in the early days after the abolition of the system in 1911, that shifted my relationship to this archive. The curation of this archive by my grandparents represented the deep desire for stability routed through marriage and heteronormativity. Examining these photos closer, I became attuned to the subject's attention to style, posture and comportment, attention to beauty, and forms of intimacies that required a different set of reading practices. There was something *queer* about these photos, which became the basis for my project *Queering the Archive: Brown Bodies in Ecstasy*.

In *Queering the Archive*, I create digital visual assemblages that queer family narratives in order to open up the archive and our reading practices from the (hetero) normative impulse through which Indian histories and memories have been historically narrated. Whereas Kganye subverts gender norms to reenact encounters with her mother and grandfather, I re-create fleeting moments of male-male intimacies from old family photos through digital photography to explore the relationship between the archive, touch, memory, and sexuality.

These assemblages use sex acts (sex as art) between men as an aesthetic to erode the racial-gender-sexual normative parameters of family to reimagine kinship across regimes of racial difference. As the reader encounters my artworks, they will notice that the term *brown* appears in many of the titles of my visual assemblages and that brownness and Afro-Indianness rub against each other. This rubbing is indicative of my own wrestling with terminology and language, and I more fully contend with these productive tensions later in the chapter. Initially brownness was a way for me to articulate an Indian positionality outside of the merchant/trader class. However, I have since come to recognize that brownness can sediment in dangerous ways through the disavowal of blackness. As I worked with and against brownness, it did not hold the same possibilities for thinking and feeling relationally that have emerged through my notion of Afro-Indianness as a site of reorientation.

Like Kganye, I insert my own body into these assemblages. Exposing oneself to the public in such a manner is to "show [our] vulnerabilities, [our] desires, [our] contradictions," which becomes the basis to imagine kinship otherwise. Through photomontages and assemblages, performance, and narrative reconstruction, Kganye and I are invested in queer-kinship formations that situate the home-space as a productive space to think through questions about routes and roots across black African and Afro-Indian communities. Our aesthetic practices are not framed around the desire, or longing, for belonging. Instead, these maternal archives point to the possibilities of feminist and queer world-making in a context where freedom, as routed through the nation, is at best fragmentary and illusive. I recognize that the experiences of Kganye's mother and my own mother are different, and the differences can be significant. Indeed, they were separated by generation, region, the rural/urban divide, and notions of womanhood as determined by racial formations and class. However, a critique of the Afro-normative nation needs both these black/ened women to understand the differences within the category "black" and the strange intimacies between the state's new black Others. These maternal archives decenter the normative racial-gender subject within the black African and Afro-Indian communities.

This chapter begins by examining the emergence of a memory industry in postapartheid South Africa and the role of memory, through the Truth and Reconciliation process, in creating a national archive through which the new South Africa was negotiated and imagined. I situate our memory-work projects as critical interventions for three reasons. First, the memory industry engendered after 1994 has had a complicated relationship to women's experiences under apartheid, particularly marginalizing black women. Second, the timeframe of the Truth and Reconciliation Commission (TRC) has occluded violent historical events like African migrant labor schemes and Indian indentureship and the ways they continue to inform processes of racialization, intersecting with gender, sexuality, and class, after 1994. Third, much of this work assumes the heteronormativity of the subject, producing archives that can be characterized as "straight." By turning to the family archive and the home-space as an alternative archive, I am interested in how our aesthetic practices, when read in relationship to one another, queer the archive through aesthetic form. I first examine my curatorial project *The Brown Photo Album* and *Queering the Archive: Brown Bodies in Ecstasy*. I then analyze Kganye's photomontage projects *Ke Lefa Laka: Her-Story* and *Heir-Story* and her short animated film *Pied Piper's Voyage*.

Memory-Work

Family Archives, Feeling, and Embodiment

The negotiated transition from apartheid to democracy resulted in the explosion of a "memory-industry" in South Africa. In the early 1990s, the postapartheid state embarked on a project of constructing a "repository of South African memory" (Nuttall and Coetzee 1998, 1) through the Truth and Reconciliation Commission. Since then, the expansive records of the TRC hearings, contested, incomplete, and limited, stand in for the country's official memory. The TRC was pivotal to the larger postapartheid project of "imagining ourselves anew" by "processing the apartheid past" (Gqola 2010, 3). Indeed, through the public act of confession, based on a Judeo-Christian model, the state engaged in a project of constructing historical memory by negotiating the memory of the past. This inevitably produced "a few master narratives that offer a sense of unity at the cost of ignoring the fracture and dissonance" (Nuttall and Coetzee 1998, 14). The 1996 Constitution and the TRC were premised as the primal site/scene for the emergence of a unified South African nationalism.

The TRC's focus on "incidents of gross human rights abuses" (Coombes 2011, S92) between 1960 and 1994 necessitated the strategic forgetting of earlier traumatic historical events like slavery in the Cape, the violence of Indian/Asian indenture labor and African labor migration, and the genocide of the Khoi and the San, the First Peoples of Southern Africa. Coombes (S93) writes: The "proscriptive demands that the testimony be confined to incidents of gross human rights abuses effectively diminished the legitimacy of accounts of more insidious daily erosions of personal liberties and dignities through, for example, the implementation of the Pass Laws and the constant forced removals" (S93). Importantly, the public nature of the TRC and its focus on the spectacular resulted in the "silencing of women's experiences because of the lack of attention to the distinctive ways in which apartheid affected women across all sectors" (S94). Analysis of women's testimony reveals that "most women recounted incidents of human rights violations experienced by others, not by themselves" (S95). Even though the TRC process was at best limited and parochial, the extensive archive is a record of events that were "otherwise unrecorded during the long apartheid years" (S93).

The state's project of negotiating historical memory and constructing a post-apartheid archive reiterates its desire for a narrative of progress and development that is forward-looking. Within the South African art world, many artists have engaged historical memory and modes of remembering. I am interested in how artists, like Kganye and myself, shift the focus from the construction of memory within the public domain to the home-space as a site to engage with memory-work. Kganye's engagement with her family's histories of migration and displacement and my own engagement with indentureship and its afterlives—routed through the family photo album—extend beyond the circumscribed parameters through which South Africans were invited to imagine themselves anew in the early days of democracy. Our projects privilege the quotidian experiences of black/ened women as an alternative way to understand memory and historical experience. We understand memory and history as narrative and performance: open to constant interpretation and reinterpretation.

According to Kuhn, storytelling, particularly "about the past, our past, is a key moment in the making of the self" (1995, 2). Personal memories, mediated through family photographs, are entangled and informed by larger sociopolitical structures, like colonial apartheid and indentureship. Kganye articulates these entanglements as such:

> My work speaks about my desire to understand history and politics in an attempt to mediate my position. I explore the trajectories of family memory and history within the collective, through my visualisation of how I imagine the memories and the stories that are shared with me, carrying them with me and transmitting them so that I become an active participant in keeping these memories alive, as well as identifying with and contributing to them. *Ke Lefa Laka* becomes a substitute for the paucity of memory, a forged identification and imagined conversation. It allows me to create a space where the past and the present converge to create alternative versions of history and memory—exposing the complexities of

memory, the personal and collective. Admittedly, our history is complex and manifests in the everyday (Bakhit 2021).

As objects that are touched and felt, family photoarchives exceed the visual. After my grandfather's death in 1996, the albums remained in the cupboard, and I slowly brought them under my care. I remember my desire to touch the photos under the plastic covers; I remember one day peeling back the plastic skin and slowly running my hands over the photos, my fingers tracing the outline of the images of the people who posed in front of the camera—in studios, kitchens, gardens, churches, on the street, in front of shops—dressed impeccably to have an image of themselves preserved as a record of a particular time, space, and environment that now existed as a memory of a memory of a memory. . . . Who were these people? What were their relations to me? What were their dreams and desires?

Why did I feel the intense need to touch the photographs, and how was I to rationalize the intense feelings and emotions that these images activated in me as I became the caretaker of this archive? These family photos pricked the surface of my skin, unravelling my sense of self to open up my body to the sensorial regimes of sensuality and pleasure. These experiences conveyed to me the immense bodily pleasures of being disorientated, allowing me to glimpse other possibilities; other ways of engaging with the past, the present, the future; and other ways of imagining kinship, community, and the body across the various regimes of race that continue to structure belonging and (un)belonging in the postapartheid period.

Family archives are collections accumulated across generations, and their status as personal collections rather than public archives complicates their "archival status" (Cvetkovich 2014, 274–75). As time passes, and as familial memory recedes, retracts, and is regenerated, the album is both a significant part of family history and a site where these histories are constantly imagined and reimagined. I understand the family archive as an "archive of feelings" (Cvetkovich 2014, 274). They are created through acts of care and "forms of love" that rub against institutional archives, which function as objective and official repositories of history. Family archives, like institutional archives, are created through processes of selection and curation. Both construct silences and elisions and shape how forgetting and remembering are constitutive of constructs like nation and family. Ann Cvetkovich writes: "The term 'archive of feelings' puts pressure on traditional notions of the archive because emotional experience and intimacies are frequently ephemeral and hence not always assumed assessable via the print records and other documents conventionally found in institutionally based archives" (274). Our individual aesthetic practices emerge from our haptic and affective engagement with family photographs/archives. Our affective relationship to the photographic archive became the impetus for us to reconstruct familial narratives and reimagine forms of kinship by focusing on those "shadow subjects" (Brown and Phu 2014) that are often marginalized within traditional frameworks of photographic analysis.

For Kganye and myself, family photo albums became "vehicles to a fantasy" to deconstruct this notion of "familyness" through performance. In our projects, family photographs are the foundational building blocks to understand the performative nature of memory and the selective processes that shape how remembering and forgetting are constitutive of family as a construct. Through performance and embodiment, we offer new ways of understanding and accessing the past. Performance studies scholar Diana Taylor writes that, "Performances act as vital acts of transfer, transmitting social knowledge, memory, and a sense of identity through reiterated... 'twice behaved behaviour'" (2003, 2–3). I have always understood the body—my body—as an archive of history and historical experience; the body remembers. Performance becomes a method to access these memories and make them available in the present. Performance allows us to "manipulate, extend, and play with embodiment" (4), disrupting time and space. Through our bodies, we reach into the past to complicate the present in our quest to develop routes to imagine the future. In these two different, but entangled bodies of work, gender subversion and queer erotics are sites of possibility to reimagine kinship in the afterlife of indentureship and colonial apartheid. Central to this is the figure of the maternal-feminine and a return to the home-space.

The Brown Photo Album

Afro-Indian Femininities and Embodied Futurities

My relationship to the feminine has always been complicated. Growing up in an Indian community and evangelical Christian household, male femininity was a site of constant shame and failure. I embodied male femininity and as a child—frail, fragile, small—I represented failed masculinity. I failed to perform and embody proper regional Indian masculinity, associated with fast cars, liquor, a local slang dialect and accent, and homosocial bonding with heterosexual males. I was drawn to color, texture, and pattern. Instead of playing cricket or soccer with the "boys," I stayed indoors, crocheting with my father's aunt, creating colorful patterns on tablecloths and pillowcases with fabric paint, and watching my mother machine knit our winter sweaters and sew dresses for my sisters and sari blouses for friends and family.

My mother invested a lot of attention to creating beauty within the home-space out of the barest of necessities. I also understood how my mother, a dark-skinned Tamil woman, and her dark-skinned children were excluded from notions of beauty within this rural community and my extended paternal family, where colorism, as it intersected with colonial-apartheid notions of race and a local reinvention of caste, determined proper female beauty. In New York City, a South Asian female friend once commented on the bodies of the women in my family album, when she casually commented that she was surprised that the women, including my mother, looked *masculine*. Years later, I understood that this comment was about notions of South Asian beauty and femininity and revealed much about my friend's own class and caste positionality. It did not register to her that these women were indentured workers and their descendants. These female bodies were constructed through regimes of labor within the household, on plantations, mines, and gardens. The musculature of their female bodies was a sign of slow death under the conditions of a coercive labor system. My feminine body (a symbol of failed male masculinity) rubbed against the masculine bodies of the women in these photos (symbols of failed female femininity). Like my mother, I wanted to be surrounded by beautiful things, I wanted to be beautiful.

My mother's creativity became the basis to reimagine the home-space. As a housewife, the home-space was her domain. She paid careful attention to small details; she created tablecloths and sewed covers for the sofa cushions; she created curtain ties with extra materials and beads; she saved money by sewing sweaters and clothes for friends and family and selling Tupperware from house to house to supplement the allowance my father provided monthly to run the household. The creation of my mother's feminine aesthetic within the home-space is located within the economy of indenture labor and its gendered afterlives. My access to the feminine is undoubtedly routed through my mother and the home-space in the afterlife of indenture and apartheid. It is an understanding of the feminine as a site of creativity amid scarcity; it is a femininity routed through labor and the laboring female body rather than leisure and disposable capital; it is an articulation of the feminine that informs my understanding of Afro-Indianness and shapes my articulation of *Indenture Aesthetics*.[1]

My mother's attention to beauty, both as a form of self-fashioning and as a creative practice within the household, was also visible within her extensive archive of studio photos. These photos were not displayed in the home. They were hidden away in cupboards. I was particularly drawn to a collection of professional studio photos shot between the mid-1950s and late 1960s. This collection was taken at the now defunct Victory Studios, in a town in rural KwaZulu-Natal called Ladysmith. My mother's family moved from a small farm in Van Reenen's Pass to Ladysmith in the early 1950s. The photos were shot by Bully Narandas, who was a friend of both my parents. How do we read the photoarchive of an Indian woman born in 1941, one generation removed from the sugarcane plantations and coal mines where her parents and grandparents were indentured as a coercive labor force? What do her photographs reveal about "the nature of the conditions under which [she] lived" (Wexler 2017, 100) and about her labor of *imagining freedom* in a context where black/ened women's lives were severely curtailed by the violence of the colonial-apartheid state? What can this archive reveal about indentured women and the gendered afterlives of indentureship? What does it mean to create a visual archive that centers the indentured woman and her descendants, in a context where indentured femininity rubbed against that of the passenger Indian class women, who embodied proper Indian femininity?

Since I was a child, I was particularly drawn to my mother's collection of studio photos shot before she married in the late 1960s. As she grew older and as we explored this archive together, I realized that this collection was anything but quiet, mundane, and minor to her sense of self and her processes of becoming. With age, her photoarchive became a portal into another world; she talked about the pleasures of growing up on a farm among animals and the hills and valleys of Van Reenen's Pass. They also activated memories of being raised in a context defined by various forms of racial and gender-based violence within the home-space. Even though her portrait photos, and her careful attention to style and beauty, concealed the violent social worlds that informed her positionality as an Afro-Indian woman, I realized that they could not be understood outside of the context of indentureship and its afterlives. I recognized that my mother's photos were precious to her. They revealed a part of her that had become distant with the passage of time. This collection includes photos of her twenty-first birthday party, a trip she took with her best friend to Cape Town on a ship in the 1960s, her participation in beauty pageants, and studio portraits. Together we spent many hours engaging this archive—touching, feeling, holding the photographs—as I prodded my mother to remember, to tell me more. The repetition of her stories and the sharpness of her memories, even as she grew older, demonstrated for me that being photographed was important to her. I began to understand that this was her practice of refusing the violence, regulation, and death that marked the quotidian experiences of women within this community. I wanted to understand what photographs meant for these colonized subjects and their descendants born into a world defined by racial hierarchies that exacerbated gender inequalities.

The Brown Photo Album is an attempt to make sense of my mother's desire to be photographed against the backdrop of indentureship and the tightening grip of apartheid-era policies. As I engaged this archive, I recognized that these photos revealed my mother's "creative practices of refusal" (Campt 2012, 9) against the gender-racial-sexual-class violence that informed the positionality of indentured women and their descendants. Family photos offer "alternative accounts" of marginalized subjects, where vernacular photographic practices can be read as an "everyday strategy of affirmation and a confrontational practice of visibility" (32). As I became more intimate with my mother's photos and focused on her embodied performances, I began to understand her desire to be photographed as a practice of refusal invested in creating lines of flight away from the various overlapping regimes of violence that informed her everyday experiences. It is evident to me that my mother's collection of photos attests to her understanding, as the sitter, of the importance of visuality and representation. Stuart Hall writes, "It is only through the way in which we represent and imagine ourselves that we come to know how we are constituted and who we are" (1993, 111).

The Brown Photo Album: An Archive of Feminist Futurity is a curatorial project that consists of approximately seventeen photos from my mother's archive. Most of the photos are shot indoors in a professional photo studio. The backdrops are unassuming: in some photos my mother stands in front of curtain drapes, in others she stands in front of a background that provides the illusion of exploding into a burst of light. Except for a wrought iron side table in the corner of one photo (shot in Nigel by Bisman), there are no props in these photos.

For this curatorial project, I chose a variety of photos. In some she appears alone. In others she poses with a childhood friend. They appear together in several photos, suggesting that they visited the studio together on numerous separate occasions. I also chose three photos that were shot outdoors by an amateur photographer. In addition, I included two photos where she poses with family members; in one, she poses with her older sister and a family friend, and in another, she carries her young niece on her lap. In this photo, she is around fifteen years old. Included in this collection are two composite images that I created using her identification-style photos that also lived as part of this maternal archive. In the studio photos, the simplicity of the background and the absence of props direct the viewer's gaze to the subject's attention to

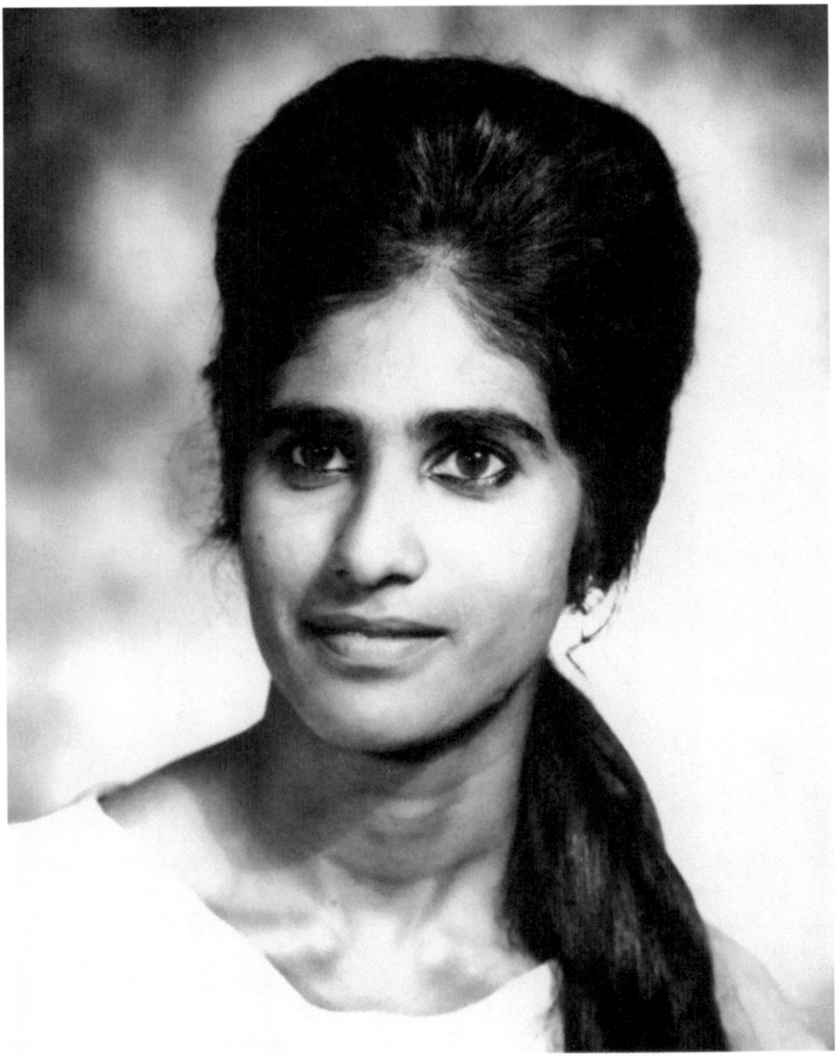

FIGURE I.1. Portrait photo from the author's mother's photo collection (ca. 1960s).

fashion and style, comportment, and posture, as well as her attention to beauty as a practice of self-fashioning. In some photos she wears Western clothing (blouses, knee-length skirts, tailored dresses) and in others, traditional Indian clothing like the sari and *salwar kameez*. She wears makeup—lipstick, eyeliner, and foundation. Her 1960s beehive hairstyle—which aesthetically threads together this archive of photos—is indicative, for me, of her desire to be beautiful, to be seen as beautiful. She understood beauty, as it relates to fashion, style,

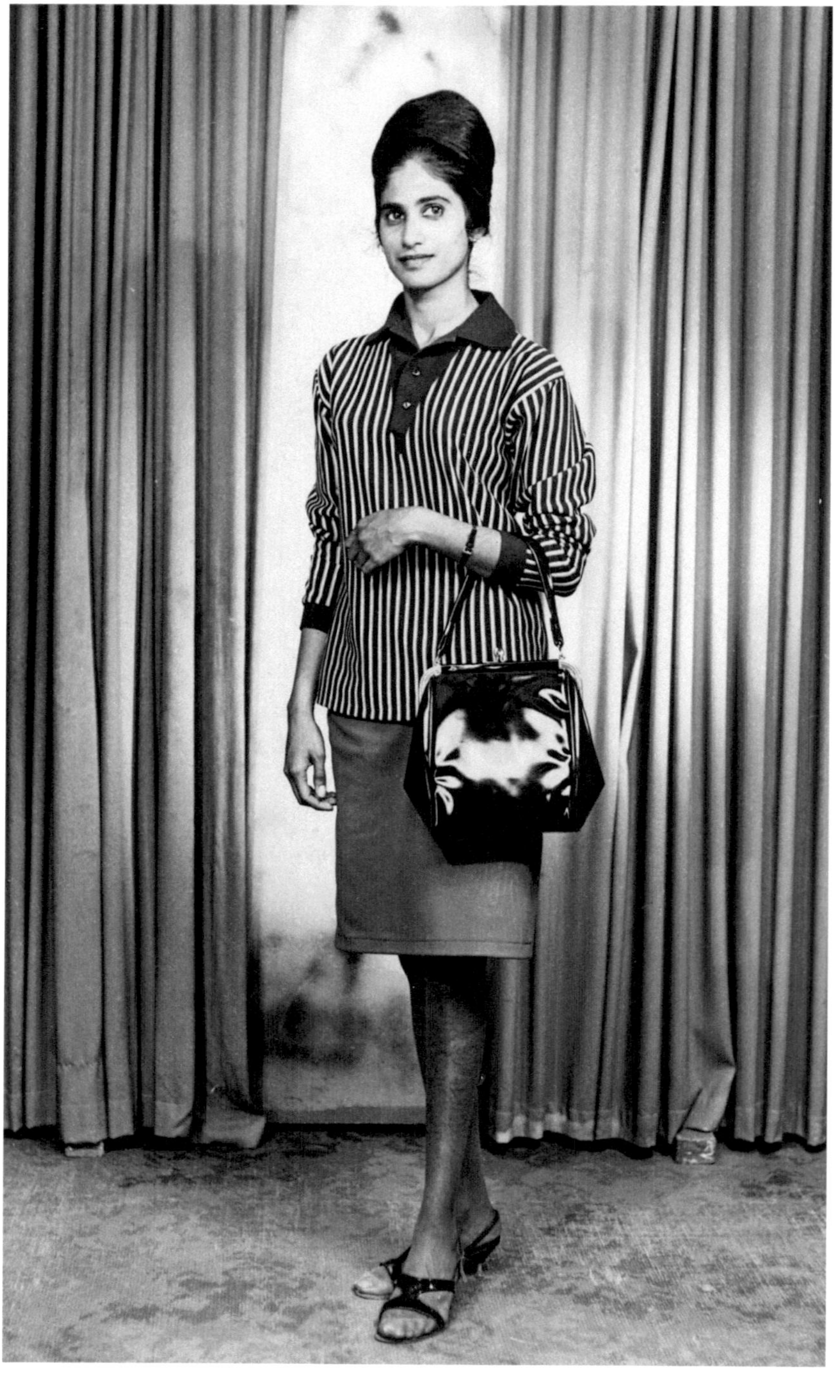

FIGURE I.2. Portrait photo from the author's mother's photo collection (ca. 1960s).

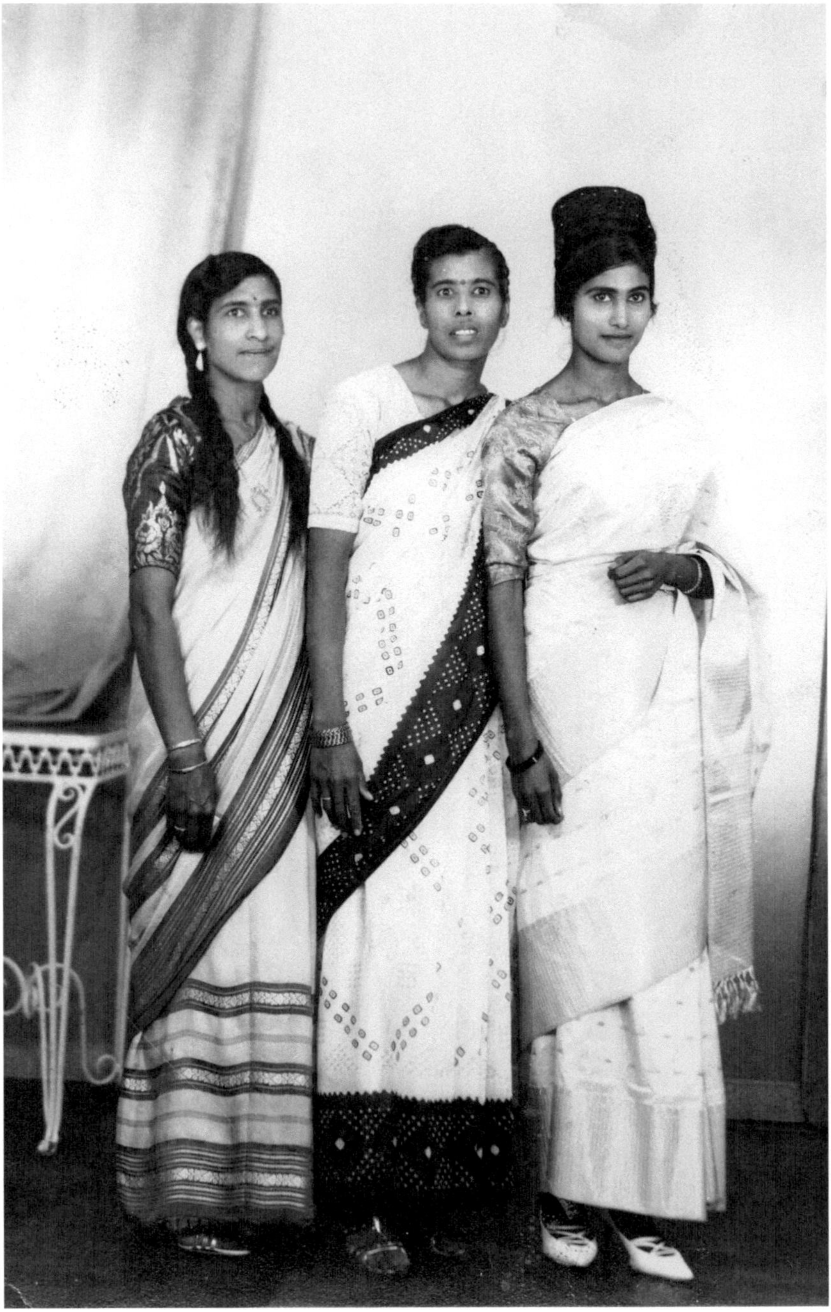

FIGURE I.3. Portrait photo from the author's mother's photo collection (ca. 1960s).

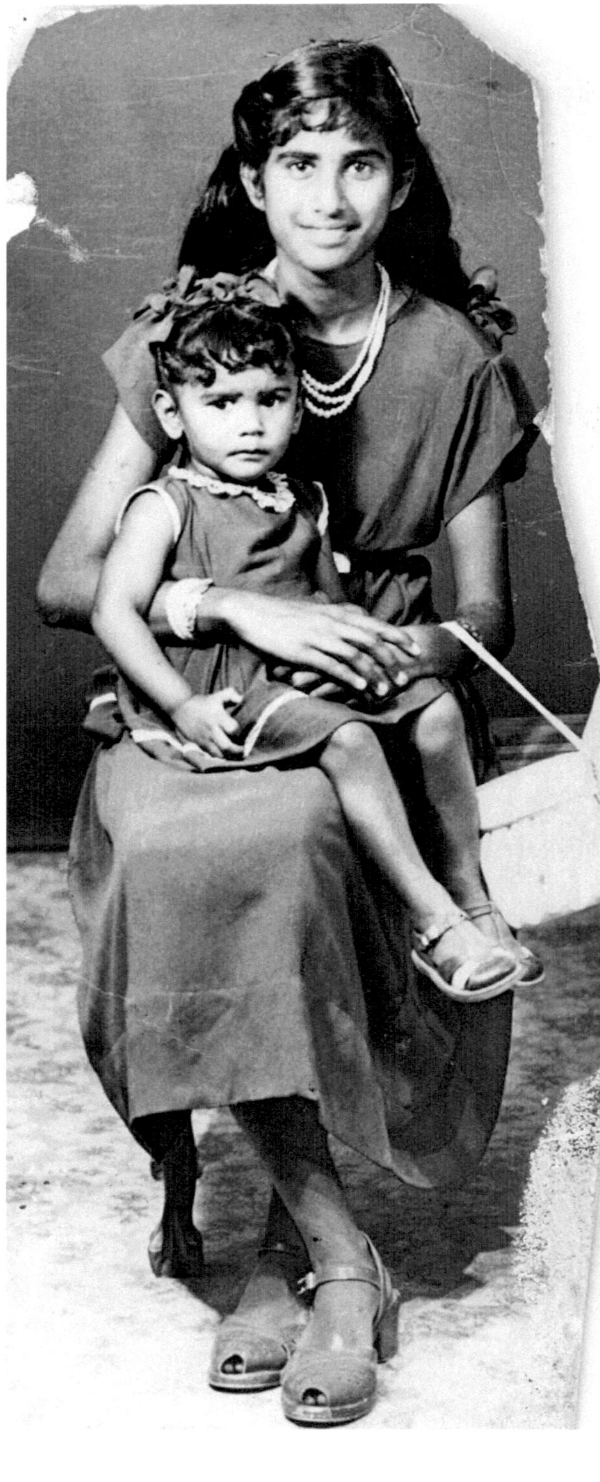

FIGURE 1.4.
Portrait photo from the author's mother's photo collection (ca. 1950s).

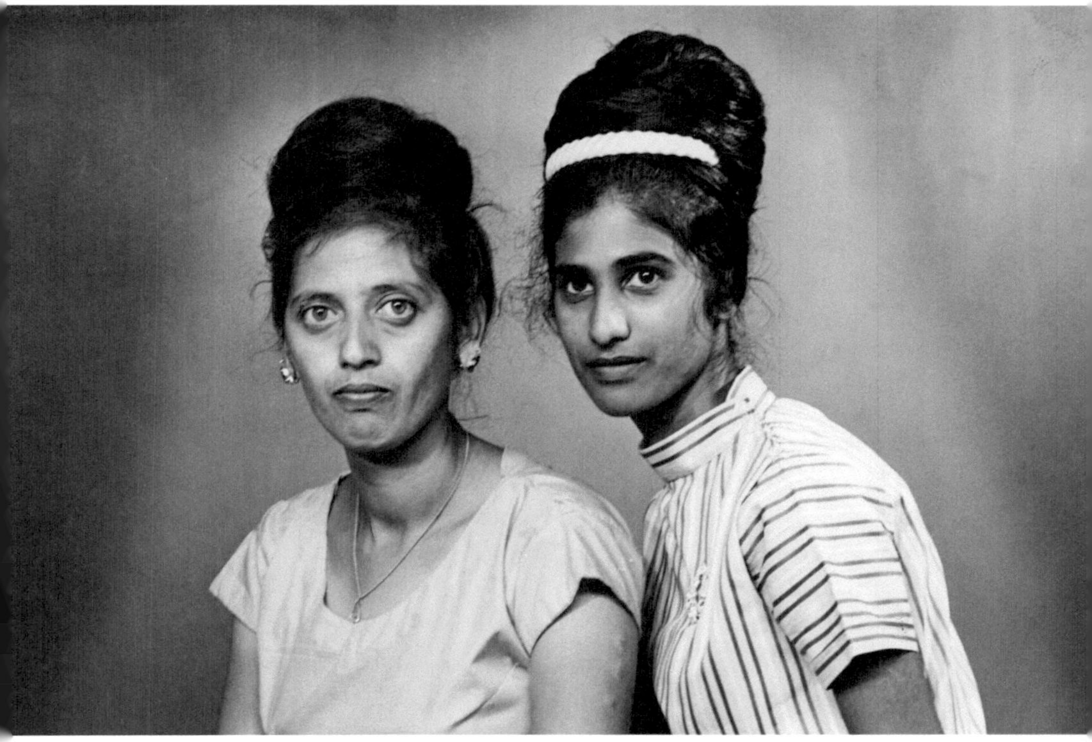

FIGURE 1.5. Portrait photo from the author's mother's photo collection (ca. 1960s).

and femininity, as an embodied practice of self-making and self-realization in a context of everyday violence and erasure. She smiles, gazing directly into the camera or slightly out of frame, appearing relaxed, playful, and flirtatious. Her attention to style is explicit in the range of hairstyles—from the photo of her long hair cascading down her back to her neatly tucked up-style to the unruly hair of her identification photo when she was in her early twenties. In the earliest studio photos, she wears a triple-strand pearl necklace and holds a handbag on her left arm. Her dress is held together with a belt, creating a high waist. Her shoes are large and clunky with a small heel.

Although there is an absence of scholarship on women and practices of beauty and fashion within the context of Indian indentureship, the research conducted by Vanita Reddy on fashion, beauty, and diaspora within urban and elite South Asian expressive cultures in the Global North is helpful to think about what beauty is and what beauty does within the diasporic context. In her book *Fashioning Diaspora*, Reddy writes:

> Beauty . . . refers to a mode of aesthetic judgment and a diasporic mode of embodiment—a physical attribute either earned by or conferred on the diasporic subject . . . sometimes with the goal of producing aesthetic pleasure; and a style or performance of racialized femininity. These modes of judgement and embodiment are at times linked to the way that beauty operates as a form of aesthetic and sexual capital—the possession of beauty as a way to gain access to privilege and prestige. At other times, beauty operates as a form of labor and care—both the labor of self-beautification and the labor and care of beautifying an(other) or others. (2016, 6)

Reading my mother's archive, it is apparent to me that my mother was unconsciously disrupting a visual archive that excluded the indentured women from the boundaries of proper and respectable Indian femininity as represented by the merchant-class women (see brief analysis of Mesthrie's curation in the introduction). In Mesthrie's curation of images, through dress and adornment the indentured class is represented as traditional and backward, whereas the merchant class is represented as modern, civilized, and upper-middle-class. Indeed, my mother's portrait photos rub against the primitivism of the indentured-class woman as represented in Mesthrie's curation. My mother's photoarchive is indicative of her desire to step out of the death-worlds of indentureship and its afterlives as she used portrait photography as a method to imagine otherwise.

What does my mother's attention to beauty and fashion reveal about the making of Afro-Indian femininity in the immediate afterlife of indentureship? My mother worked as a seamstress in a factory after high school, and I watched her create dresses for herself and my sisters. I would not be surprised if she created the dresses and blouses worn by her in some of the photos. Beauty for her, as evident within these photos, functions as a "form of care and labor." Her labor of self-beautification positions beauty as a method and as an act of black political resistance. Saidiya Hartman (2019, 33) writes: "Beauty is not a luxury; rather it is a way of creating possibility in the space of enclosure, a radical act of subsistence, an embrace of our terribleness, a transfiguration of the given. It is a will to adorn, a proclivity for the baroque, and the love of *too much*." Self-fashioning can be read as a form of resistance and refusal. Her attention to style and to the aesthetic of selfhood directs us to her "quiet but resonant claims to personhood and subjectivity in the face of dispossession" (Campt 2017, 65). I now understand her performances as small, intimate, and quotidian acts of refusal against the various overlapping regimes that rendered her, as an

Afro-Indian woman, an "impossible" subject (Gopinath 2005). It is evident that being photographed was a site of immense pleasure for her and these photos capture her desire to want to be seen, to be rendered visible and beautiful against the apartheid state's regulation and surveillance of black/ened women. She was creating a feminist archive of futurity in a context where "the history of colonial indenture labor meets Indian patriarchy meets South African racism" (Khan, 2019). This became evident when I realized that my mother's photos activate both scenes of pleasure and gender-based violence within her family and community.

As my mother grew older, she became bolder about the ways in which she narrated her experiences of growing up in an extended family and of married life. She spoke about the women in her family with an urgency that suggested she intuitively understood her limited life expectations and trajectory from a young age; but within this context, she was determined to create a livable life, recognizing that the pain and violence of the everyday existed alongside moments of pleasure and ecstasy that are evident in her photographs. As my mother and I engaged her photoarchive—as we touched and felt the photos together—she transmitted to me her embodied experiences. She repeated several stories that gave me access to her memories. I understood this as an alternative form of knowledge about the afterlife of indentureship. Even though my mother was only about seven years old at the time, she vividly remembered the tragic death of her oldest sister from untreated meningitis at the age of twenty-nine. Her sister was married to an older man who had children from a first wife who had passed away. This man treated her sister like a servant; she had borne seven children by the time she was twenty-nine. She was forced to work in a garden planting and harvesting vegetables that they sold to the local community to support their family. After the birth of her seventh child, she developed meningitis after being forced to return to the fields. Her husband refused to take her to a medical doctor. He also refused to allow her to return to her father's house so that they could seek out proper medical treatment. My mother remembers the night her sister died. Her mother and older brother were indoors taking care of her, trying to get her fever to break. Even though she was delirious, she recognized that she was going to die and blamed her parents for forcing her into marrying an older man who treated her as property. Her husband's refusal to relinquish control over her life led to her untimely death. My mother remembers her sister telling her parents in Tamil that she was going to die because of them. She died that night.

My mother also recalled memories about her oldest brother's wife who attempted suicide by setting her *sari* on fire in the bathroom of their home. This incident occurred when my mother was in her mid-teens. She remembers visiting her sister-in-law in the hospital as she lay dying, her body covered in burns. She talked about poverty and the everyday struggle for access to food and other necessities. She did not shy away from the fact that her brother was abusive. Her sister-in-law died in the hospital, leaving behind five young children, one only nine months old. My mother oversaw the care of these children even though she was only in middle school. As my mother grew older, she talked more openly about her limited options as an Indian woman and her deferred dreams and desires. She wanted to enroll in the police force and thought about becoming a flight attendant, but these options were not available to her. Instead, she resigned herself to fulfilling the normative role of wife, mother, and grandmother.

It is against stories such as these that I approach my mother's archive of studio photos. These oral narratives—subject to the complex processes of remembering and forgetting—draw out the relationship between the violence of indentureship and how it determined both "gendered and raced identities" that would otherwise remain forgotten (Gqola 2010, 10). When I prodded my mother into revealing why she was so invested in being photographed, all she said was that she did not know and that when she was paid at the end of the month, she visited the photo studio. She simply liked being photographed. Against these spectacular stories of everyday violence, I understand her studio photos as deliberate performances of futurity, a "performance of a future that hasn't yet happened but must. . . . It is the power to imagine beyond current fact and to envision that which is not, but must be. It's a politics . . . that involves living the future now . . . as striving for the future you want to see, right now, in the present" (Campt 2017, 17). I read this performance of futurity through her careful attention to beauty, fashion, and aesthetics. This is evident in the professional studio photos as well as in the photos shot outdoors.

As shown in figure 1.6 she stands on a dirt road, against a concrete wall, with a large section broken off. Two children—one barefoot and both wearing clothes that appear a little too big for their small bodies—play in front of the broken wall. The break in the wall provides depth to the photo, revealing a building structure with tin barrels on a roof. This could have been a local water supply. I read the broken wall as symbolic of the broken, fragmented, and neglected lives that circulated around her. She does not stand in front of the broken wall; instead, she stands next to it, revealing how beauty coexists with deterioration and fragmentation within the blackened social worlds of these descendants of indenture labor. Her attention to beauty can be read as her attempt to stitch together the *tear* in her world in the afterlife of indentureship and colonial

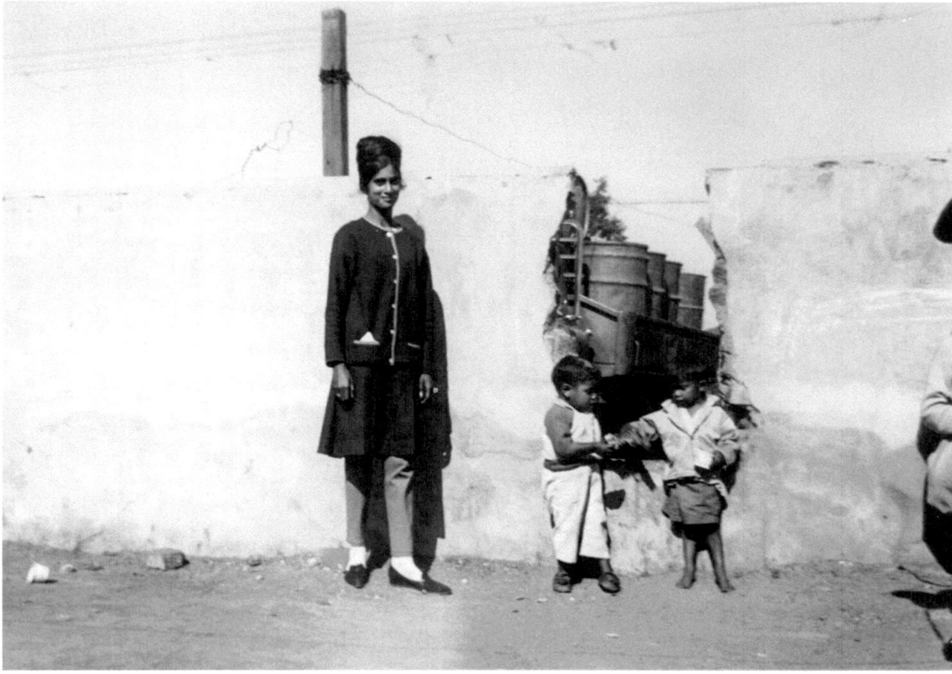

FIGURE 1.6. Vernacular photo from the author's mother's photo collection (ca. 1960s).

apartheid (Brand 2001). The repetition of her performances across these different spaces—from the studio to the outdoors—tells us something about her approach to beauty as a method, a form of unacknowledged female labor, committed to creating livable lives.

These photos point to my mother's desire for the otherwise; her performances of futurity can be read as lines of escape, quiet and creative practices of refusal, away from the overlapping regimes of the colonial-apartheid state and the heteropatriarchal family structure. These photos suggest that for my mother and other black/ened women like her, violence and precariousness stitch together the past, the present, and the future. Her performances can be understood as the desire for a "futurity realized in the present" (Campt 2017, 17). In a context where the future was rendered impossible, through photography my mother was negotiating and creating "new possibilities for living lives that refused a regulatory regime from which [she] could not be removed" (33). These photos reflect her desire to live and imagine a future in the present, a *future-present*, as an everyday practice of creating and performing freedom, thus positioning this as an embodied archive of feminist futurity.

Queering the Archive

Ecstasy, Race, and Embodiment

Through *The Brown Photo Album*, I examined how my mother negotiated her impossible positionality as an Indian woman from the indenture class by weaving beauty into her life through the spectacular (as evident in her attention to self-fashioning and style in her studio photos) and the mundane (her labor of beautifying the home-space). I understand that my mother was creating a visual archive of Indian indenture femininity. Unlike my parents, I was born in the early 1980s and came into political consciousness, and race-gender-sexual awareness, as the apartheid state was being systematically dismantled in the late 1980s and early 1990s. My consciousness of the world was informed by the violence of colonial apartheid and the promise of freedom from the strictures of race. This movement from the rural to the urban—from the sugarcane plantations of KwaZulu-Natal to the most densely populated urban area in South Africa and the economic hub of the country—was both pleasurable and disorientating. I began to understand the textures of Indianness in South Africa differently and was confronted with a deeply anti-Indian public sphere. Furthermore, there was an absence of Indian South Africans within South African film, television, and visual cultures more broadly. When my short film, *cane/cain* (2011) was first screened in Johannesburg in 2011, I spoke about my own desire to see brown bodies on screen—this film began as a pedagogical practice in learning how to desire my own brown body and to position the brown body as desirable. Thus, I began to develop an aesthetic practice as a response to the "under visibility of South African Indians and especially brown intimacies . . . on the country's screens" (Ebrahim 2017). I examine *cane/cain* more fully in chapter 3.

My understanding of beauty, fashion, sensuality, and sexuality was deeply informed by my mother's femininity and creativity within the home-space as well as the sensual and sublime beauty of the sugarcane plantations. My constant return to the home-space and to the maternal feminine enabled me to realize how racialized and marginalized queer subjects rescript the trauma associated with the home-space because of their encounters with a racist queer culture that produces shame for not being able to embody proper queer (read: white) culture. Queers of color rework dominant (white) narratives of exile from the home, where the queer white child must be exiled to come into gender-sexual-queer wholeness. José Muñoz, in his book *The Sense of Brown*, emphasizes the "deeply reductive" characterization of the family as "an oppressive totality." He writes, "On the one hand, it is true that not all families of color affirm their queer sons and daughters. On the other hand, the generalized gay community often feels like a sea of whiteness to queers of color, and thus the imagined ethnic family is often a refuge. It is a space where all those elements of the self that are fetishized, ignored, and rejected in the larger queer world are suddenly valorized" (2020, xviii).

My mother's positionality of impossibility was sutured to my own, creating an opening that reorientated me to the world. I understand my queer sexuality as part of a larger web, inseparable from how the entanglements of race, history, diaspora, memory, beauty, and desire have shaped my subjectivity and understanding of Afro-Indianness. Against a racist and femme-phobic queer public culture, my paternal grandparents' family photoarchive become an alternative site to examine Afro-Indian masculinity, where through aesthetic and archival practices, I reimagine and resituate the Afro-Indian male body as desirable. This project began to reimagine small, quotidian, and minor moments of male-male intimacies in old family photos. In this project, I use my own body to examine queer pleasure and desire as it relates to history, memory, diaspora, racial formations, and notions of beauty. By creating digital visual assemblages, I reorient my racialized queer body in a way that reaches out and touches the past (ancestral history), while creating lines of flight that desire different forms of relationalities and intimacies rendered impossible by the logics of Afro-normativity. Indeed, my pleasure in being photographed maps onto my mother's pleasure in being photographed, both indicative of our hunger for the otherwise. By rescripting the Afro-Indian body into a site of pleasure and sensuality, I am interested in how pleasure can "open up affective circuits" between the past, present, and future, while it creates "lines of relationality between queer bodies of color" (Wahab 2018, 389, 152).

Queering the Archive: Brown Bodies in Ecstasy is a digital photography project consisting of approximately fifteen images. If the composite image of indenture identification photos represents the feminization of the Indian laborer, *Queering the Archive* reimagines the feminized Afro-Indian male body into a site of desire and pleasure. In this series of assemblages, I work with and through excess. Queer bodily pleasures and desires, particularly as they relate to black/ened bodies, have the potential to exceed and disrupt "the colonial (or postcolonial) 'order of things'" (Gopinath 2018, 8–9).

In *Brownflesh II* (plate 1), I create a triptych using three old portrait-style family photos, strategically chosen because of the minor and quotidian traces of intimacy between the Indian men who appear in these photographs. These three portrait-style photos informed this series of assemblages. In the first studio photo, a man sits on a wooden stool with his left leg over his right leg and his right hand resting on his knee. A younger-looking man stands next to him. His left hand is resting on his left hip. His right foot crosses over his left foot to stabilize his pose as his left hip juts outward. Whereas the man who is seated holds his body tightly, gazing into the camera, the body of the man who stands next to him creates a fluid and playful movement in the photo, which suggests that there is something else happening in this photograph. In the second photo, two men stand, gazing directly into the camera. Their arms touch, blurring the boundaries between them as the photo is taken. In the last photo, two men of approximately the same age pose in a studio. One man stands and the other is seated on a chair. Their bodies also merge into each other as they gaze into the camera.

In *Queering the Archive*, I reimage these homosocial expressions of male intimacy as homoerotic expressions through digital photography. With *Brownflesh II*, I layer posed nude photos of Afro-Indian men onto the archival photos to construct an aesthetic conversation between the past and the present, in a context where I am also creating an archive of the Afro-Indian queer positionality and Afro-Indian queer desires and pleasures. In the center image of the triptych, the two Afro-Indian men stand naked with their backs to each other. They gaze directly out of the frame. Their glistening brown bodies create a visual contrast with the black and white archival photo and the two men standing directly in front of the camera. In the left image of the triptych, the two Afro-Indian men face each other. They gaze into each other's eyes, the one looking up, while the other looks down. Their bodies don't touch. But the act of looking at each other, while nude and in such close proximately, renders these bodies vulnerable to each other. In the third image of this triptych, the two bodies embrace intimately and erotically. Their noses touch and their lips open for an anticipated kiss. Their hands touch each other's bodies, drawing each other closer. The photos tell a story about learning to desire the Afro-Indian body, which occurs from the positionality of vulnerability. The images create a visual contrast between the naked bodies and the well-dressed men from the archival photos. The method of layering creates a conversation between the past and the present, reimagining the traces of bodily intimacies evident in the archival photos to shift how we understand the feminization and abjection of the Indian indentured male body as produced within the visual regimes of colonial-apartheid modernity.

In image *No. 21653* (plate 2), I create a digital assemblage by layering and juxtaposing an old torn portrait of two men standing next to each other, a digital photograph of three differently racialized men—black African, Afro-Indian, and white—whose bodies are piled on top of one another, and an

Indian pass document, belonging to my grandfather. In the archival photo, the two men stand facing the camera with their hands overlapping. I use this trace of intimacy to examine how colonial apartheid obscured the deep intimacies between differently racialized bodies, and instead used racial differences to solidify a racial hierarchy that positioned whites at the top, black Africans at the bottom, and Indians in the middle. In this assemblage, the fragmented archival photo is positioned on the right, obscuring the faces and the upper bodies of the three men. However, we see their eyes, gazing into the camera. The black African model is on his stomach and carries the weight of the other two models. The Afro-Indian model lies on his stomach, on the back of the black African model. The white model lies on his back on top of the Afro-Indian model, facing upward. The black African and Afro-Indian bodies fit intimately into each other; their buttocks are perfectly aligned. This positioning opens up an affective and intimate circuit between black Africanness and Afro-Indianness, positioning my own Afro-Indianness in an intimate relationship to blackness. In this assemblage, the white body faces upward and away, pressing down onto the Afro-Indian and black African bodies, revealing how the weight of whiteness—the afterlife of colonial apartheid—continues to inform how we relate to one another, obscuring the intimacies between the Afro-Indian and the black African. The white body is relaxed and open to the world, emphasizing how white comfort in the postapartheid period continues to rely on the exploitation and discomfort of black/ened bodies. The maintenance of white comfort was pivotal to the negotiated democracy South Africans inherited in the early 1990s.

In this assemblage, the indenture pass document is layered over the legs and torsos of the three racialized bodies, receding into the background, functioning as a haunting reminder of a coercive labor system that reduced the indentured to numbers and bodily marks. The indenture numbers appear across all three racialized bodies, suturing them to one another, functioning as a hinge to demonstrate how older and newer forms of racialization occur in relationship to one another. Even though logics of apartheid were based on separateness, determined through the visuality of the body, skin-to-skin contact opens an alternative sensorial circuit to understand how overlapping processes of blackening construct the Afro-Indian and black African within the carceral logics of the colonial-apartheid state. The pass document and the photo show signs of visible deterioration. The pass document is held together by tape—notice the darkened cross-like figure that sutures the document together—while the broken photo is positioned on the right, strategically placed to reveal the eyes of the white model and the partial faces of the black and Afro-Indian models.

Read from left to right—from the entangled legs to the more clearly visible racialized faces—this assemblage plays with the relationship between the gaze and skin, the preeminent sign of racial difference. Indeed, in South Africa, like the African diaspora, "skin [is] a master signifier for the specificity, the particularity, of race" (Stephens 2014, 1). According to Frantz Fanon, the white gaze reduced him to his black skin, the site of his "crushing objecthood." If the white gaze constructs black/ened skin as the primary site of racial difference, I am interested in touch—skin-to-skin contact—as a site of reorientation. I am interested in an aesthetic of skin as felt rather than seen, permeable and porous, not "a hard and impermeable container but rather a sensual form of relationality, a 'threshold, a point of contact, a site of intersubjective encounter, between the inner and outer self and between the self and the other'" (Stephens quoted in McMillan 2018, 3).

The assemblages shift to performances of sex-as-art to foreground sexual desire and pleasure as pivotal to reimaging Afro-Indian masculinity and Afro-Indian intimacies. Within the archive of the Indian South African, sexual desire, pleasure, and the erotic are largely absent. Indeed, sex, sexuality, pleasure, and the (naked) body disrupt Indian desires for respectability and social standing. Thus, the creation of my Afro-Indian archive positions (deviant/transgressive) bodies, desires, pleasures, and differences as a method to decenter both the normative Indian and normative black African subject. In *Brownflesh I* (2016) (plate 3), I create a triptych that layers archival photos of my mother (in her early twenties) and a portrait from my parent's wedding that includes my grandparents from both sides, onto *tableaux vivants* of men engaged in the act of sex. To the left, three figures are visible in the image. Two models kiss while the hand of one model is firmly placed on an African mask that covers the face of the third model. To the right, three models—white, black African, and Afro-Indian—stand directly facing the camera. Two models gaze directly into the camera, while the third holds an African mask against his left cheek. The other two models also hold African masks covering their genitals.[2] As you gaze at this part of the image, two figures appear as they reach toward each other to kiss. In this image, my mother's studio portrait sutures the different elements and layers together. The portrait provides a point of contact between the past, the present, and the future. This image routes my understanding of sensuality and beauty through the maternal archive, which continues to inform how I understand pleasure and beauty as methods of survival.

Whereas in my mother's archive, I focused on her attention to fashion and her desire to be beautiful, in *Queering the Archive*, I seek to understand beauty and sensuality through the nude body and the aesthetics of skin.[3] In a context where dark skin is perceived as a site of ugliness, evilness, and dirtiness, I used digital photographic techniques and studio lighting to create a visual surface effect that renders the Afro-Indian and black African bodies, through skin and shine, sensual and beautiful, luminous and radiant. The lighting illuminates the skin tones across the differently racialized bodies. In these assemblages, I use an aesthetic of shine (Thompson 2015) to create a form of relationality between Afro-Indian and black African bodies, recognizing their imbricated construction within the death-worlds of labor. The shine, a thin and sticky film of sweat covering these bodies—a site of abjection and eroticism—binds these bodies together and is a reminder of the histories of racialized labor in South Africa and their afterlives. It is undeniable that Afro-Indians and black Africans labored together on sugarcane plantations and coal mines, working side by side, sweating together, their bodies deteriorating under the deadly conditions of labor. However, these bodies become racialized differently within the logics of colonial apartheid and are inserted differently within the racial hierarchy. In these assemblages, the shine—the sweat—connects these bodies, bleeding across time and space, across regimes of difference, to remind us of our deep relationalities obscured through projects of racialization. The body always remembers.

Skin-to-skin contact creates a different regime of intimacy and a different kind of affective opening to understand both Afro-Indianness and Afro-Indian relations. To allow oneself to be naked with another person is to allow oneself to be vulnerable and fragile in ways that generate bonds of intimacy that reveal practices of care: caring for, caring with, caring together across difference. The sex scenes between men create lines of flight away from the heteronormative institution of marriage designed to manage the feminine and regulate the feminized. In this assemblage, I map my own queer desires and pleasures onto that of the maternal figure, suggesting that even though the home-space figures as a site of gender-sexual-erotic regulation, particularly for women and nonnormative children, it is often a site where the queer child of color learns to see, listen, and feel differently and counterintuitively. For me, this was routed through the maternal feminine within the home-space.

Through performances of sex-as-art, I am interested in creating an intergenerational dialogue to understand how both my mother and I have used performance as forms of embodied knowledge to fuck with race-gender-sexual hierarchies. Inserting photos of my mother, father, and other family members into this project was risky and provocative. I wanted visually to capture how my understanding of queer erotics was informed by my mother's attention to beauty, sensuality, and performance. I wanted to explore what it meant to understand queer erotics and pleasure through the figure of the maternal feminine in the afterlife of indentureship. Indeed, this is an erotic informed by Audre Lorde, who teaches us that the erotic is "a resource within each of us that lies in a deeply female and spiritual plane" (Lorde 2007, 54). The erotic, as a female/feminine source of power, can take us to the realm of joy and pleasure (within the quotidian and mundane), creating a connection across difference. Lorde writes that the erotic has the potential to "lesson the threat of . . . difference" (56). Accessing the feminine—the maternal feminine—through the erotic created a connection to my mother and other women in my family across generational, gender, and sexual differences, allowing me to connect with the world—to desire to connect with the world—differently. For me, this connection was routed through the maternal-feminine. I understood that this connection was fluid and constantly being made and remade, activating a circuit that shifted from desire (my desire to connect across racial-gender-sexual-erotic differences) to pleasure and ecstasy. Indeed, the aesthetics of the project—the shiny skin tones, the performances of sex, the different levels of touch—direct us to an aesthetic of pleasure routed through the feminine and the feminized.

The Brown Photo Album and *Queering the Archive* seek to engage and rethink the entanglement between the visual regimes of colonial-apartheid modernity and the racialized production of the Indian, the role of indentureship in the racialized production of the Afro-Indian, and the gendered dynamics of diasporic homemaking. Through these projects, I wish to unsettle and open up the thick silences embedded within this South African-specific entanglement.

In both projects, femininity, feminization, and vulnerability become routes to imagine Afro-Indian futurities otherwise. Initially, I used the term *brown* as a deliberate form of disidentification from Indianness and to negotiate my effect of displacement.[4] If Indianness represents a homogenous identity, conflated with that of the trader/merchant class, through brownness I began to grapple with Afro-Indianness. Brownness was my attempt to reactivate and queer Biko's notion of Black Consciousness. Although my terminology has shifted from brownness to Afro-Indianness, I wanted to activate a "Sense of Brown" that resonates with José Muñoz's work (2020). Echoing Muñoz, my understanding of brownness was shaped by a desire to disrupt the fixity of race in South Africa that continues to produce "individualized subjectivities." Brownness was a sense of movement away from the logics of Afro-normativity toward understanding our shared commonality across difference. It was a way of grappling with "not only [our] shared indignation but also a process of thinking and imagining otherwise in the face of shared wounding" (6). Muñoz writes, "Brownness is being with, being alongside" (2). This idea of being with and being alongside fundamentally holds together my notion of indenture aesthetics and Afro-Indianness as a site of reorientation. Thus, I follow the movement away from the atomized identities, our collective inheritance of colonial apartheid, to read Kganye's art alongside my own, sitting with the fragments, the overlaps, and the tensions to grapple with our entangled pasts, presents, and futures.

Lebohang Kganye

Colonial Legacies and the Making of Black Femininities

In her 2013 body of work, *Ke Lefa Laka: Her-Story*, Lebohang Kganye engages her dead mother's photoarchive, through performance and aesthetic practices, as an experiment in reanimating quotidian encounters of black life. Using family photographs, Kganye activates the realm of memory and the labor of remembering by aesthetically compressing the past and the present to create an intergenerational dialogue between herself and other family members, particularly her mother and her grandfather. *Her-Story* emerged organically three years after the death of her mother. *Ke Lefa Laka*, translated from Sesotho to English, means "it's my legacy."[5] Her mother's loss propelled her on a journey across South Africa to understand "where [her] family originated from and how [they] ended up in these different spaces that we now call home." Kganye's grandmother, Maria, was the main source of information. Having grown up in Johannesburg, Kganye's link to her family's history and relatives in rural spaces had been severed. Maria helps Kganye construct a "familial map," connecting her with relatives across the country. Kganye embarks on a reverse migration, revisiting the many farms her family lived and worked on, in search of a more complex understanding of her positionality as it continues to be shaped by the textures and contours of historical experience. Along this journey, she encounters family photo albums, many of which contained photos of her mother. This was important to Kganye because her mother "has always been the connection to the extended family and historical roots."[6]

Migration and movement, as it shapes everyday black life, informs Kganye's aesthetic practices. In an interview, Kganye recalls that her grandfather was the first person in her family to move from "'di'plaasing,' which means 'homelands,' in the Orange Free State to the city in Transvaal to find work because he didn't want to be a *farm labourer* like the rest of the family." Through conversations with her grandmother, she learned about the family's "history of migration around South Africa." Many family members worked as laborers on farms and were "forcibly removed under colonial regimes and relocated after tribal wars." These histories of labor exploitation and migration, removal, displacement, and relocation have had significant impact on the notion of the black family structure and kinship formations. For her grandfather, and other family members who left the homelands as apartheid was ending, the city promised freedom from exploitative labor conditions in rural areas. Whereas I engaged with my mother's photos in order to understand this archive as one of feminist-queer futurities, Kganye's engagement with her mother's photos became a way for her to understand her familial history by tracing her "ancestral roots." Reimagining and recreating an aesthetic connection to her mother was pivotal to her desire to connect more deeply with her history and roots. Importantly, for both Kganye and me, the maternal archive and the maternal feminine become counterintuitive sites to understand what she refers to as "'her-our' histories." The death of her mother caused her to feel disconnected from her extended family and distances her from the histories of displacement, migration, and settlement that is constitutive of her intimate experiences of blackness in South Africa. The maternal feminine provides the adhesive to connect her to histories of blackness that have been strategically obscured by the state's emphasis on a progressive and linear narrative of development.

Through her journey of mourning her mother's death, she noticed that all around her, within the home-space, lived traces of her mother, left behind after her death. Through material objects like photographs and clothes she begins to reconnect with her mother. In her mother's archive of photographs, she was drawn to her mother's smiles, her attention to style and self-fashioning, as well as her performance and pose. After realizing that her mother's clothes would fit her, they became a conduit to connect with ancestral memory to understand how the past continues to inform her positionality as a black African woman in postapartheid South Africa. In *Ke Lefa Laka: Her-Story* she wears her mother's clothes while emulating her mother's performances within the photographs. Through photomontages, Kganye creates new visual narratives that conflate the past and the present, while drawing out the complexities and fragmented nature of memory and remembering. In a post on the PhMuseum's website concerning her projects *Ke Lefa Laka*, Kganye writes, "I juxtaposed old photographs of my mother retrieved from the family archives with photographs of a 'present version of her'—me, to reconstruct a new story and a commonality—she is me, I am her and there remains in this commonality so much difference, and so much distance in space and time. . . . The photomontages became a substitute for the paucity of memory, a forged identification and imagined conversation."

Kganye reflects on the fragmented nature of memory and remembering and the relationship between memory and fantasy. She troubles the notion of time as linear and progressive. In a different post on the PhMuseum's website regarding *Ke sale teng*, Kganye states: "Such [family photo] archives do not reveal easy answers, for me they reveal that time can break apart and reconnect and not quite fit back into one another." I am interested in how the maternal feminine becomes the vehicle of possibility through which time is negotiated. Kganye's attention to time, space, and fantasy offers an alternative articulation of black temporality, one that rubs against and disrupts the time-space of the postapartheid nation and Afro-normative blackness.

Ke Lefa Laka: Her Story,

the Maternal Feminine, and the Photo Album

Ke Lefa Laka: Her-Story consists of approximately thirty-nine photomontages. Kganye created *Her-Story* in collaboration with her younger sister and her grandmother. Her grandmother helped her identify the physical spaces in Soweto where many of her mother's photos were shot. Kganye then restaged her mother's photos in these same physical spaces, both indoors and outdoors. Her younger sister would hold the original photo and direct Kganye's performances—the movement of her arm, the placement of her body within the frame, her posture and comportment, her smile, and lips. Her sister would then take the shot. This process, involving her sister and grandmother, created a space for them to celebrate her mother's life and to mourn collectively as daughters and mother of the deceased. Kganye chooses a range of photos from her mother's albums. In some, she is photographed posing outdoors standing or sitting on the grass, leaning against a tree or a concrete fence, and sitting on a brick wall. In others, her mother is photographed indoors. She wears silky nightdresses, lacy underwear, and in one photograph she is seated at a table with her books open and a school bag visible under the table. The rest of the photos are group photographs, including a wedding, a child's birthday, and other kinds of family gatherings. In some photos, the artist appears with her mother as a toddler. Men are largely absent, except for their appearance within a couple of family group photos.

In these photos, Kganye's mother's attention to fashion and beauty is visible. In *Ka mose wa malomo kwana* 44 II (2013, *In a Floral Dress*), Kganye's mother wears a flowing white halter-neck dress, with gentle imprints of a design that is not clearly visible (plate 4). She wears black strappy sandals with a slight heel.

She poses in what appears to be a front lawn. The grass is green and luscious, the shrubs creating a boundary wall between the properties are in bloom, and in the background, we see the uniform houses of the township. Her mother's gaze is directed downward as she smiles slightly. Her hands rest at her sides. She appears relaxed and firmly in place, but the photo is full of kinetic energy, almost as if she is about to leap forward. In another outdoor photo (plate 5) titled *Tsimong ka hara toropo II* (2013, *In the Garden in the Middle of Town)*, Kganye's mother sits on the grass, wearing a skirt suit and a ruffled white blouse. She gazes down at the grass as a smile crosses her face. She poses in front of green bushy shrubs, revealing the lushness and richness of her environment.

In this project, Kganye recreates both these photos by dressing like her mother and posing similarly to her. She reenacts the positionality of the maternal feminine, copying her mother's pose and wearing her clothing. She then layers her digital photograph onto the original photo of her mother to create a new photographic narrative. This digital photography technique is evident in *Ka mose wa malomo kwana* and *Tshimong ka hara toropo II*. Kganye's layering aesthetic does not conflate the image of her mother with her. Instead, she creates a ghostly effect where her image pulls away from but sticks to that of her mother's. Throughout this body of work, it is not apparent whether she (the artist) or her mother is the ghost.

The indoor photomontages reveal glimpses of the home-space and the interior intimacies of black life. In *Ke le motle ka bulumase le bodisi II* (2013, *I Was Beautiful Wearing a Panty and Bra*) Kganye creates a photomontage from a picture of her mother wearing silky underwear and posing seductively for the camera (plate 6). She poses in a bedroom; to the right is a wooden dresser stacked with ornaments and she stands in front of a door, alongside a bed. On the wall is a framed image (perhaps an advertisement?) of what appears to be a white woman. The framed image appears to the left of the photomontage, slightly askew on the wall. The white woman is fully dressed wearing a black high-neck top and a red jacket over that. Her hair appears to be in an up-style. Her lips are set in a tight smile. The shine of her white skin is indicative of normative standards of (white) beauty. The white woman gazes down on Kganye's mother as she stands in a lacy bra and panties. Her hair is in a short Afro style. Her smile reveals her teeth. Her right leg is slightly bent as she poses with her left arm on her left hip. We do not know who shot this photograph. Is she posing for a lover or a friend? Or did she take this photo herself, for herself? Kganye's mother gazes downward, shy yet confident in her body and sexuality. Her mother's pleasure in this photo is evident as well as her desire to be photographed as beautiful, desirable, and sexy. In this photomontage, Kganye superimposes an image of herself wearing similar kinds of underwear, posing with her left hand resting on her left hip, but changes the texture of the image by gazing directly into the camera, rather than downward, like her mother. Kganye's natural hair is in a fuller Afro-style. She captures her mother's playfulness and her mother's desire to be photographed, to leave a record, or imprint of beauty, in a context during the apartheid era where blackness (particularly black women) was not a site of beauty. The juxtapositioning of the white woman (in the framed image) gazing down at two generations of black women speaks to the complex ways in which white femininity and black femininity manifest in a dialectic relationship to each other. Indeed, Kganye's mother plays with racial-gender-sexual excess to challenge the ways in which whiteness has historically controlled and regulated black bodies. Through this series of images, Kganye's understanding of beauty, femininity, and sensuality is routed through the figure of the maternal feminine and shaped within the home-space.

The layering and superimposing technique creates an effect where the artist touches her mother, reaching across time and space. This regime of touch manifests through her aesthetic technique as well as through memory and embodiment, where the artist literally wears her mother's clothes. Through this series of photomontages, Kganye attends to the loss of the maternal feminine. She both mourns and celebrates her mother's life, with care and love, teaching us something about black love in a context where gender-sexual-class violence continues to structure black women's experiences of the everyday. Through this technique of layering, Kganye conflates her mother's timeline with her own (and with that of her grandmother's and her younger sister's) to create an intergenerational dialogue structured through three generations of women. The ghostly effect blurs the distinction between the dead and the living, the past and the present, memory and remembering, and mother and daughter. In some images, we are unable to discern the ghost in the photomontage. Through this technique, Kganye questions the notion of black freedom in postapartheid South Africa as it is organized along the new nation's linear and progressive narrative.

Most probably shot in the late 1970s and 1980s, Kganye's mother's photographs of quotidian life in Soweto rubs against the genre of "resistance documentary photography" or "struggle photography" that emerged during this period (Newbury 2009, 5, 220). The family photo album and vernacular photos provide an alternative account of black life and black temporality.[7] In Kganye's mother's photoarchive, I read resistance in the small, minor, and inconsequential: her attention to self-fashioning, beauty, and sensuality; her flirtatious gaze into the camera; her posture and comportment; and her playfulness as she is being photographed resonate with my own mother's photoarchive and her quiet but resonant claims to imagining freedom in a context where black/ened women's lives were one of containment, lived continuously under regimes of labor, violence, and death. Reading across the artist's mother's photoarchives, beauty functions as a method, an act of black political resistance, that sutures blackness and Afro-Indianness across regimes of difference.

Kganye's aesthetic is inherently *queer*. Here I use the term *queer* to signal the ways in which her technique disrupts time and space, past and present, subject and object, mother and daughter. These disruptions can be read as a form of resistance against the very logics of Afro-normativity that continue to render black life a commodity within the context of global capital. Kganye offers an aesthetic of touch, where through touch she forges "connections in ways that commodified flesh was never supposed to, loving your own kind when your kind was supposed to cease to exist, forging interpersonal connections that counteract imperial desires for Africans' living death" (Tinsley 2008, 192).

Ke Lefa Laka: Heir-Story, the Maternal Feminine, and the Photo Album

In her related projects *Ke Lefa Laka: Heir-Story* (2013) and *Pied Piper*'s *Voyage* (2014), a short film version of *Heir-Story*, Kganye shifts the focus from her mother to her grandfather. Once again, this memory-work project is mediated through her grandmother, who is the conduit of familial history and memory. In this series of images, Kganye reconstructs and deconstructs the home-space of the black family. By creating photomontages using old family photos, *Heir-Story* examines the impact of colonial-apartheid-era policies on black familial life. In this series, Kganye subverts gender norms by performing the positionality of her grandfather, further *queering* the family archive. Kganye's research and her travels across various farms revealed to her the importance of her grandfather—the patriarchal figure—to how familial narratives are remembered, reconstructed, and transmitted across generations. As extended family members left the farms for the city, her grandfather's home became a meeting point. She was also born in his home, but she cannot remember him. In *Heir-Story*, she conflates the past and present by embodying her grandfather through performance. She wears a black suit, tie, white shirt, top hat, and oversized shoes. She wears the suit because her grandfather often appeared in family photos wearing a suit.

Aesthetically different than *Her-Story*, in *Heir-Story* she creates *tableaux vivants* by cutting up and blowing up old family photos and creating elaborate stage sets. *Heir-Story* appears as still images from the short film *Pied Piper's Voyage*. She is the only real character, moving across the set in a manner that is representative of early film characters. Using animation and performance, the film unfolds in six short scenes. In the first scene, the cityscape moves into place as Kganye walks across the stage playing a accordion (plate 7). She looks backward, inviting others to join her. A long line of family members follows her grandfather to the city. In the background, we see the cityscape of Johannesburg, casting shadows on the stage props, revealing its expansiveness. There is also a minibus taxi and a double-decker bus. A conversation bubble above Kganye reads: "Follow me to the land of milk and honey." A street sign to the left provides directions to the Transvaal and the Orange Free State. The line of relatives following Kganye's grandfather suggests movement toward the Transvaal. As Kganye exits to the right, the mise-en-scène changes. We now enter the home-space and the privacy of her grandparent's bedroom (plate 8). Her grandmother lays in bed, positioned in the center of the room. A wardrobe and dresser appear on the left and a window appears on the right. It is nighttime. The moon and stars are visible through the window. An alarm clock appears in the frame and goes off. It is 3 a.m. She/her grandfather stands next to the bed as her grandmother wakes up. He is animated and moves around almost like he is berating her.

The next scene transitions to an outdoor scene. An open door is positioned almost center frame. In the distance we see the uniform houses of the township stretching toward the horizon. Three women appear in the frame. Two chat with each other, while one stands behind a wall. To the right is a cut-out of Brenda Fassie, a South African singer and entertainer, standing in front of a radio. Kganye, dressed like her grandfather, is wheeled into the scene by a younger black man, drinking from an alcohol flask. In the next scene, Kganye lays on the ground, having passed out from consuming too much alcohol. The scene is fragmented. Trees, concrete pipes, roads, skyscrapers, and other structures appear. A black man wearing a hoodie over his face appears on the scene, holding a knife. Two black men appear and rob Kganye in their state of drunkenness. This scene is reminiscent of old South African films like *Jim Comes to Joburg* (1949) and *Come Back, Africa* (1959) that chart the movement of the African country bumpkin (a male character) to Johannesburg, and their rude awakening to the realities of city life.

In the next scene we return to the home-space. Kganye sits at a table with extended family members all around. It is suppertime, and the only person not eating is the grandmother. She stands to the side of the frame holding a bunch of flowers in a vase. Although the other characters hold plates of food and enamel cups, they gaze directly at the audience as the grandfather eats. The last scene is an enlarged cut-out photograph of her grandfather holding a baby (plate 9). A pair of black shoes appears in front of the cut-out, and it is the only animated/moving object in the image.

The project offers complex representations of black masculinity as it is negotiated differently within the public and domestic spaces. The grandfather holds the promise for future generations; he is the first person to migrate to the city, and other family members follow his trajectory. However, in public spaces he appears inebriated and emasculated as he navigates a hostile environment where black people were constructed through colonial-apartheid policies as out of place. Within the cityspace, his masculinity has been undermined and he is a feminized character. Her grandfather negotiates his feminization within the public arena by asserting his authority within the home-space. Within this space, the grandmother is both the anchor of the family and rendered vulnerable. It is significant that, in the end, Kganye prioritizes the portrait of her grandfather holding a baby. The sex of the baby is unknown. This can be read as a commentary on intergenerational inheritance. The baby will inherit the grandfather's legacy as it has been shaped through colonial apartheid. The grandfather's feminization will be passed down from generation to generation, reiterating the queer positionality of the black family within the afterlife of colonial apartheid. Thus, Kganye's gender subversion is important because she reveals, through performance, the ways in which the long history of colonial apartheid ensured that black/ened people were always excluded from normative claims to gender and sexuality.

Heir-Story and *Pied Piper's Voyage* are two iterations of the same narrative. Both examine the gendered impact of colonial-apartheid-era policies, which forced black African men to leave their homes and families to work as a cheap labor source "on the mines, in homes and the cities" (Phillips and James 2013, 410). This "male-model" of migrancy has historically "erased women's experiences from view." Black African women also migrated to cities, many finding work as domestic servants. Often, children were left behind on farms and homelands to be cared for by their grandmothers. In a context where the apartheid state strategically and deliberately broke up the black family, the absence of black men required women to often assume the role of the man within the family. Kganye reflects on this as follows: "As a young woman enacting a patriarchal figure in a family, I address the shift in my role as a woman, having to be a provider and protector of the family since my mum's death, by assuming the role of a man that most of the women in my family have had to take on because of the absent father figure. So, we have had to learn to become these roles and by taking on the persona of my grandfather, I also perform a degree of masculinity associated with certain provisional roles."[8] Kganye reflects on how, in the context of colonial apartheid, black African women were strategically excluded from normative femininity and womanhood, as represented by white women, within the context of these coercive labor schemes. This is her heritage and her legacy, passed down from generation to generation. This is the afterlife of colonial apartheid, which directs us to other modalities of being black and embodying blackness.

Across these projects—*Her-Story*, *Heir-Story*, and *Pied Piper's Voyage*—Kganye complicates our understanding of black femininity and the clear separation of the feminine and the masculine, as binary and dichotomous. Colonial apartheid rendered black women and men queer/nonnormative to secure the boundaries of whiteness and the utopia of a "whites-only" nation. In a context where African migrant labor continues to center black men and masculinity, Kganye's gender subversion is important. By destabilizing the normative black patriarchal subject, Kganye offers a critique of labor extractive economies as it relates to black womanhood and the construction of black femininities. Kganye is forthright about her grandmother's role in these interrelated bodies of work. Her grandmother is the keeper of familial memory and history. This shapes the queer aesthetics across her interrelated projects. The grandmother is a figure who exists outside the boundaries of normative, reproductive womanhood. She is a queer figure, whose queerness sticks to the figure of the dead mother. These maternal femininities imbricate and become the site of possibility to examine the impact of migration, displacement, and urban settlement on the making and unmaking of black femininities and womanhood in postapartheid South Africa. Similarly to how I attend to the afterlife of Indian indentureship and its formative role in my understanding of sexuality, sensuality, and the (queer) Afro-Indian body, Kganye attends to the afterlife of African migrant labor systems and its impact on black womanhood and femininities.

Through her art practice, Kganye offers us an aesthetics of time that is elastic, creating a tension that exceeds and explodes the time of newness associated with the postapartheid and new formations of blackness. Kganye's reverse migration from the city to the farms and homelands—all indicative of black displacement within the larger arch of South African history—maps onto the ghostly effect she creates to disrupt the linear and progressive ordering of nation-time. Across our bodies of work, the past and the present, the dead and the living, history and memory, pain and pleasure coexist within the same frame. Through memory-work and our engagement with maternal feminine archives, we reorient our relationship to the world, mining different but interrelated regimes of difference and scenes of (un)belonging, following the lines of flight as they direct us to the otherwise. In this chapter, I position the maternal feminine as central to these emergent imaginaries and feminist-queer social worlds.

Whereas in this chapter, I focused on queer-feminist futurities and the making of Afro-femininities, in chapter 2, I examine the aesthetics of slow death in the artworks of Sharlene Khan and Mohau Modisakeng. Chapter 2 examines the relationship between overlapping coercive labor regimes (indentureship and the African migrant labor system) by exploring the relationship between labor, trauma, and gendered vulnerability. Chapter 2 takes us on a journey through the death-worlds of capital through the vulnerable bodies of the Afro-Indian female and the black African migrant male worker. I situate gendered vulnerability as a feminine and feminized orientation toward the world that brings time to a halt, disrupting the linear and progressive narrative of development associated with the postapartheid nation.

2

Afro-Vulnerabilities and the Aesthetics of Slow Death

MEMORY, TRAUMA, AND LABOR

I remember the first time I saw Sharlene Khan's multimedia project, *when the moon waxes red*, exhibited at the KwaZulu-Natal Society of the Arts Gallery in 2017. I walked into the darkened space, drawn to the video-art piece, as the following lines echoed through the room:

> Do you think it's possible to hate even before you are born?
> Do you think it's possible to want somebody to die even before you are birth?
> I think I did, even while in my mother's womb. Before my eyes could see, my ears heard. Her screaming and begging for him to stop. I felt her distress.
> And I hated.

These words literally caused me to stop moving and to stand still as time slowed down and fragmented, and space extended outward, even as I was drawn inward toward the speaking voice, as it took me from the gallery to the Indian township and the sugarcane plantations. As my eyes slowly adjusted to the dim lighting, I became aware of the numerous photographs lining the walls of the gallery space. In this series of photographs, a dead female body—wearing a red and green sari, with blue makeup/paint covering her face, bangles on her wrists, flower garlands around her neck, and *mehendi* patterns visible on her hands and feet—floats in a body of water. The woman's body is fragmented and broken up across the walls (plates 10 and 11). In some, we see a medium close-up of her painted face; eyes tightly shut and facing upward (*Drowning Durga VII*, 2015). In other photos, we see fragments of body parts, a hand with painted nails extending in the frame of the image, slightly submerged, as flower petals, ripped apart, float in the water (*Drowning Durga V*, 2015).

This project offered a visualization of the very same oral narrative histories of domestic abuse, violence, and the vulnerability and disposability of the Afro-Indian female body in the immediate afterlife of indentureship that my mother had passed down to me as she and I reckoned with her own archive of studio photos and their complex meanings. Thus, for me and many others, the gallery space became a sacred space, one where we (artists, curators, audiences) attended to these scenes of violence and death, with care. Khan's attention to beauty and care play with the duality of women's bodies as sites that are simultaneously revered and reviled.

The narrating voice in the video-art piece, as well as the woman photographed floating in the body of water, is the artist, Sharlene Khan. Her body becomes an archive of history; the black/ened body remembers across time and space, extending beyond and disrupting the boundaries of the postapartheid nation. *when the moon waxes red* is an aesthetic exploration of memory as it relates to and is informed by the trauma and afterlife of indentureship. Through embodied knowledge, she weaves together her grandmother's and mother's memories into visual narratives that confront the ongoing legacy of gendered violence, sexual assault, poverty, hunger, and displacement—the afterlife of indentureship. In this project, the vulnerable Afro-Indian female body is the site through which memory, history, violence, and death converge across time and space, across generations of women, impacted by the deathworld of the sugarcane planation. Through the positionality of vulnerability, Khan explores the cyclical nature of trauma and its ripple effects/affects across generations.

This is also evident in the aesthetic practice of Mohau Modisakeng. Whereas Khan's project emerges out of the historically Indian township, Newlands West, in KwaZulu-Natal, Modisakeng's art practice is informed by his experiences of growing up in a Zulu settlement in Soweto in the 1980s and 1990s. In an online article titled "Mohau Modisakeng: Memories of a Murder" written by Tom Seymour for the *Financial Times* in 2016, Modisakeng states, "I remember seeing people who had been killed, their bodies still in the street. Death was part of my every day. So when I reflect on violence today, it's based on those experiences, filtered through my own memories and emotions." As a photographer, sculptor, and video artist, Modisakeng's aesthetic practice is informed by his memories of township violence, trauma, and loss.

Like Khan, Modisakeng positions his body as an archive of history and a site of remembering. His work draws on his intimate experiences of violence, "loss and trauma." Modisakeng states, "I started to work with photography and to put my own body into the images, layering narratives over the top of it. I saw my body as a way of describing my own struggle with loss, but also reflecting on the collective black experience in South Africa and the trauma and loss that is such a part of our history" (Seymour 2016). Modisakeng's aesthetic examination of the afterlife of colonial apartheid emerges from the positionality of male vulnerability. Through costume, performance, gesture, and props, Modisakeng offers a complex representation of the vulnerable black male body—sometimes feminine, and other times feminized. Modisakeng examines the relationship between trauma and labor, taking the audience on a journey into the death-worlds of the coal mines. Through gender vulnerability, he examines the impact of the mining industry and migrant labor, a coercive labor system, on the construction of the black male body. Gender vulnerability allows him to make this larger aesthetic critique of the impact of the afterlife of colonial-apartheid-era labor regimes on African immigrants, the working class, and working poor, those who exceed and explode the boundaries of the authentic national black subject.

This chapter brings into conversation two artists, Sharlene Khan and Mohau Modisakeng, to think through overlapping regimes of racialized labor and the making and unmaking of black/ened life within the death-worlds of the sugarcane plantation and the coal mine. Khan's and Modisakeng's aesthetic practices allow me to deliberately stage an encounter between Indian indentured labor and African migrant labor, two overlapping forms of coercive labor practices that have become racialized in opposition to each other within the South African national imaginary. I am interested in how Khan and Modisakeng mobilize *gender vulnerability* and an *aesthetic of slow death* to attend to the afterlife of colonial apartheid. Through the aesthetic realm, Khan and Modisakeng examine the relationship between memory, trauma, and labor, bringing to an abrupt halt the narrative of linear and progressive development that organizes postapartheid nation-time and the space-time of the new black normative subject. Their aesthetics of gender vulnerability direct us to the new black/ened Others: those who live on the margins in the afterlife of colonial apartheid—the immigrant, the township dweller, the coal miner, the plantation worker—those whose everyday experiences continue to be shaped by slow death.

The newness of the postapartheid nation promised to disrupt and reverse the slow death of those rendered black/ened that began with the conquest and settlement of the Cape in 1652.[1] "Slow death," a phrase coined by Lauren Berlant (2007), describes the "unglamorous quotidian wearing down of life necessitated by capital" (Young 2017, 153). Berlant argues that slow death occurs in the ordinariness of "everyday activity," where the erosive qualities of capital are a "*fact of life*" and occur in "*ordinary time*" (Berlant 2007, 759–60). Those who live in the afterlife of coercive labor regimes understand slow death as intimate and continuous, passed down from generation to generation, rubbing against the narrative of newness promised by the ANC in 1994. For the new black/ened Others "dying and the ordinary reproduction of life" coexist, directing us to alternative modalities of humanness carved within the death-worlds of racial capital (762). Through gender vulnerability, Khan and Modisakeng reorient our senses toward feminine and feminized modes of being. In this chapter, I position vulnerability as a feminine and feminized orientation toward the world. Thus, read together, across racial-gender-sexual-regional differences, I am interested in how Khan and Modisakeng mobilize feminine vulnerability to articulate a politics of (un)belonging that enables us to grapple with the multiple, contested, and layered manifestations of South African blackness, while understanding Afro-Indian intimacies otherwise.

In feminist theories, *vulnerability* is a contested term. Vulnerability is often positioned in opposition to resistance. Vulnerable populations and bodies enter the dominant gaze through tropes of "passivity and victimization," and are associated with inaction, or the lack of agency. The assumption, feminist scholars like Judith Butler, Zeynep Gambetti, and Leticia Sabsay (2016, 1) remind us, is that "vulnerability requires and implies the need for protection." This reinforces "paternalistic forms of power at the expense of collective forms of resistance and social transformation." Such dominant modes of thinking about vulnerability and resistance (as binary oppositions) presuppose that "paternalism is the site of agency" (Butler et al. 2016, 1). Within this binary logic, women are constructed as weak and must naturally come under the paternalistic control of men. Positioning vulnerability in opposition to resistance reinscribes the gender binary and the hierarchy of male/masculine over female/feminine. Thus, vulnerable populations, often racialized women, and other disenfranchised groups are gendered as feminine, whereas resistance, associated with action, is gendered as masculine. As a feminized concept, I am interested in how vulnerability can be mobilized to deconstruct hegemonic forms of "power and agency" (2), moving away from "liberal forms of individualism" as they coalesce around "capitalist concepts of self-interests and masculinist fantasies of sovereign mastery" (2).

To allow oneself to be vulnerable is to willingly open up one's body to the world in a way that renders one "susceptible, . . . receptive, . . . and [ambiguous]" (Gilson 2016, 72). Vulnerability softens the surface of the body, rendering it subtle and mutable, mobile and flexible. Vulnerability contracts the space between self and other and can potentially suspend the desire for mastery over the other. It "enables us to recognize how shared vulnerability constitutes the basis for ethical responsiveness, which may be elicited through experiences of vulnerability as a fundamental condition and a process of accepting and reckoning with one's own vulnerability" (72). Gilson writes that vulnerability "is also the ground for our responsiveness to one another. It is because we are vulnerable that we need ethics and social justice, but it is also because we are vulnerable—because we can be affected and made to feel sorrow, concern, or empathy—that we feel any compulsion to respond ethically or seek justice" (72).

In their aesthetic practices, Khan and Modisakeng decenter the normative Indian (merchant/trader class Indian) and normative black masculine subjects, respectively. Indeed, Khan's project seeks to disrupt the trope of the merchant/trader class. In this project, she explicitly asks: "How to speak and not be a type, 'representative,' 'indicative,' 'archetypal'? How to tell a story of an Indian when you are not a Gupta, a Mahatma, a middle-class intellectual?" The story she tells of "an Indian" is the story of the Afro-Indian experience routed through the vulnerable female body. In a context where the Afro-Indian represents the queer limits of authentic and nativist blackness, I am interested in how vulnerability, routed through feminine and feminized bodies, reorients us—Afro-Indians and black Africans—toward one another. Feminine vulnerability reveals forms of intimacies between the new black/ened Others. This chapter further develops my concept of indenture aesthetics by positioning feminine vulnerability as a site of possibility to examine our entangled pasts, presents, and futures.

when the moon waxes red

Female Vulnerability and Afro-Indianness

when the moon waxes red is a multimedia project consisting of three distinct visual components.[2] The first component is an experimental thirty-minute digital video consisting of footage shot indoors and outdoors. The video component consists of a voice-over narrative that weaves together various kinds of footage including the artist's performance on a stage, shots of sugarcane, and scenes of a dead woman floating in a body of water. This is a story that takes us on a journey into the violent intimacies of the home-space in the afterlife of indentureship. This narrative is informed by the sugarcane plantations, the site of Indian indentureship, as well as by the Indian township, a site of continued displacement and impoverishment.

The second component consists of two photographic series: *Drowning Durgas* and *After Ana*. *After Ana* is a series of digital photos (discussed in the opening segment of this chapter) of a disembodied female immaculately dressed and adorned.[3] In these photos, the violence of death by suicide rubs against the beauty of the woman's costume and adornment. Adorned like a traditional Indian bride, her ultrafeminine costume reveals something about femininity, vulnerability, and the institution of marriage within the context of indentureship and its afterlives. The digital photos titled *Drowning Durgas* reference the Durga Puja Festival, dedicated to the Indian goddess Durga. On the last day of the festival, devotees submerge an effigy of Durga in a body of water. Historians and scholars of Indian religious practices have traced the ways in which the figure of Durga has transformed from her "non-Brahaminic and non-Hindu origins" where she is "described as a fearless virgin, hunting and living in mountains . . . , craggy terrains, and caves. Her companions are ghosts and wild beasts, and she is dressed in peacock feathers" (Bhattacharya 2007, 925). Consuming alcohol and meat, she is described as "primarily . . . a war-goddess who is fond of battles and destroys demons—especially Mahisasura, is endowed with a variety of weapons . . . and protects her devotees" (Chakrabarti 2001 quoted in Bhattacharya 2007, 925). By the sixth century, Durga is "seen as the manifestation of Sakti, that very Vedic notion of divine energy." By the nineteenth and early twentieth centuries, the image of Durga navigating the familial and embodying political agency is well established. Bhattacharya writes, "She is both the ideal daughter/mother and the valiant slayer of demons. Thus, she is 'good' in the small sense of the domestic, as well good in the more cosmic sense of the eternal struggle between good and evil" (924). Manifestations of Durga within the Indian subcontinent and in the diaspora shift to take on local inflections.

However, the Durga Puja Festival emphasizes Durga's embodiment of the mother/maternal figure. She is "surrounded by her children and combines the 'martial with the maternal image'" (Skoda 2019, 225). On the tenth day of the festival, clay idols of Durga are submerged into a body of water. The submersion is "symbolic of her return to the divine cosmos and her marital home with Shiva."[4]

The third component is a series of family portrait photos created from needlepoint-lace art. The needlepoint-lace art is a direct reference to Khan's grandmother and the resourcefulness of Indian woman within the impoverished home-space. Needlepoint-lace art evokes the history of colonial missionary intervention into the home-space of the colonized. Missionaries encouraged Indian women, particularly from the lower castes, to develop skills in feminine practices like lace, embroidery, and stitching, for instance, as ways to embody respectable femininity, asserting the importance of the gender binary to the civilizational process (Kent 2004).

The family photoarchive and the home-space emerge once again, emphasizing their importance to indenture aesthetics. In the previous chapter, I examined Kganye and my own engagement with family photos and maternal archives as sites of feminist-queer possibilities. Kganye and I used family photos as building blocks to examine our own relationships to history, movement, displacement, memory, and freedom. By transforming family photos into needle-lace art, Khan pays homage to her grandmother, who created needle-lace as a way of supplementing her income. Within the gallery space, Khan curates the needle-lace art into a family photo wall, alongside the series of digital photos of the dead and fragmented female body. In an interview with the artist, she revealed that unlike my family's collection of photos and other documents, her family did not accumulate such an archive. She vaguely remembers seeing photos of her grandparents as a child.

The lack of family photos took Khan on a journey to an official state archive, the Gandhi-Luthuli Documentation Centre (GLDC) at the University of KwaZulu-Natal, where she sourced family portrait photos from their collection. She uses these family portraits to create needle-lace art. I do not read Khan's relationship to the state archive as recuperative. In other words, she does not reach back into the state archive out of a sense of loss, as a way of articulating a deep longing to belong to the nation as evident in Riason Naidoo's relationship to the archive. Unlike Naidoo's approach, Khan and I are more suspicious of the archive, particularly as it relates to "minoritized knowledge formations" (Arondekar 2009, 2–3). Khan complicates our relationship to the colonial visual archive by literally weaving it into her aesthetics of slow death. She implicates the archive and its uses in the violent erasure of black/ened women. Khan's archival practice, which works with and against the official visual archive, is a commentary on the impossibility of articulating an Afro-Indian positionality.

Unlike my family archive, in Khan's context the family photo is absent. It is not the conduit to remembering, even though this project is based on her grandmother's and mother's memories and experiences of violence within the family. Whereas I mine the family photoarchive for queer-feminist possibilities/futurities, Khan complicates this relationship to reveal the limits of the archive. Whereas I am interested in how the family archive can provide a different articulation of Afro-Indian history and experience that rubs against the hegemonic narrative that erases indentureship and its afterlives, Khan disrupts the promise of the family archive to do this. How does one reconstruct a story, an experience, and a history when all that remains are fragments of memories and oral narratives?

If we understand the family archive as a site of "historical orientation" (Nair 2020), a sort of compass that provides genealogical continuity, as well as an "archive of feeling" (see chapter 1) created through acts of care and "forms of love" (Cvetkovich 2014, 214), then what does an absence of such an archive of feeling reveal about the afterlife of indentureship within the space of the Indian township? Positioned in relationship to the surplus of family photographs in my family archive—a rural Afro-Indian family—what does the lack of family photographs reveal about the making of Indianness within the South African township in the immediate aftermath of forced removals, relocations, and resettlements of differently racialized groups, within spaces racialized to contain and restrict the movement of these groups? How does township Indianness rub against rural and urban Indianness?

Through this visual project, Khan reveals the impossibility of normativity for the Afro-Indian family. This project charts how this impossibility maps most violently and insidiously onto the bodies of women and children.[5] When indentured laborers entered the hold of the ship, they entered the death-worlds of capital. Their slow death began during the recruitment process. It continued aboard the coolie ships and was repeated on the sugarcane plantations and in coal mines. The end of the system did not repair the broken and fragmented bodies and subjectivities of the indentured and others also entangled within this coercive labor system. *when the moon waxes red* allows us to track the continuation of slow death across various geographies: from the home-space of the Indian family to the plantations, shanty towns, and townships (strategically located on the peripheries of major urban centers like Durban), as well as to rural and semirural areas, a process exacerbated by the desire to create stable and normative familial life in a context where such stability and normativity were structurally and strategically denied by the colonial-apartheid state.

when the moon waxes red is informed by memories and stories the artist heard growing up and "reluctantly witnessing" (Khan, *when the moon waxes red*). Khan creates visual aesthetics held together by the delicate nature of memory and remembering. These are the tenuous threads that hold together the past and present, public and private, black and black/ened, grandmother, mother, and daughter, and artist and audience. Through the positionality of female vulnerability, Khan uses the aesthetic realm to connect with other black and black/ened women across time and space. Khan's attention to vulnerability resonates with Fatima Meer's commitment to crafting an alternative Afro-Indian politics through the positionality of the vulnerable and disposable. Khan states that this project is "for all those women who came before, trapped between racism, colonialism, patriarchal religiosity and poverty, able only to free themselves from sugarcane and hardship by death. Hanging, drowning, burning." She asks, "How did you survive?"

Geographies of Slow Death in *when the moon waxes red*

It is almost impossible to imagine Afro-Indian poverty and the vulnerable lives of the indentured and their descendants, who make up the majority of the Indian population in South Africa. This is an effect of the colonial-apartheid state's strategic use of visual culture to construct a narrative of Indian social mobility and economic success. Khan's multimedia project invites us to imagine what Afro-Indian poverty and vulnerability look like and how structural conditions in the Indian township exacerbated forms of gender-based violence within a collective theater of slow death. Fatima Meer's sociological study of Indian life in Durban in the 1960s is an important intertext here. In her study of Tin Towns, informal settlements in Springfield, Durban, along the Umgeni River, which sprang up to temporarily house "those (non-white families) displaced by the Group Areas Act and the Slum Clearance Act" (Meer 1969, 108), Meer offers thick descriptions of the material conditions under which non-white people from a lower socioeconomic class existed and attempted to carve out livable lives. Meer's term *non-white* includes Indian, coloured, and black Africans. This was before she mobilized the term *black* in the spirit of Biko's Black Consciousness.

Describing a Tin Town on the banks of the Umgeni River, Meer writes:

> Contiguous and on the same plane are factories, quarries, refuse dumps and scrapyards. The houses . . . each a patchwork of tin and wood from the nearby demolisher's yard, stand back to back on four streets, two reasonably wide, and two, too narrow for vehicular traffic. There are no street lights, no pavements and no telephone booths. Taps sprout at intervals . . . about one, for every seven or eight homes, to provide residents with their only water supply. There are no shops, no churches, no temples, no mosques, no playgrounds, no evidence of any institutions that serve and bind the community or any of its component groups.
>
> So privies cluster close to kitchen and living rooms, ventilation is poor, and the large puddles which flood the hollows in wet weather lie about for weeks breeding mosquitoes. The flies from the nearby sewerage farm hover thickly over food and dirt and children's sores. (113)

She goes on to describe the quotidian wearing-down of the bodies of those who lived in these deadly spaces. "The poverty and pain," she writes, "is often excruciating to watch." She encountered "Children, pot bellied and unhealthy, with festering sores and running noses" and a woman with a "face riddled with fungus" unable to visit the hospital because of a lack of funds (Meer 1969, 113). Meer's thick sociological descriptions resonate profoundly with the memories of poverty and violence that saturate *when the moon waxes red*. As Meer experienced first hand in the late 1990s, and as noted by other scholars like Desai (2002), these conditions have changed very little in the postapartheid period.[6] The descendants of those displaced in the 1950s continue to live in abject poverty and are still waiting for freedom to come.

At the KZNSA Gallery in 2017, *when the moon waxes red* was exhibited in an enclosed, darkened room, designed to emulate a womb-like environment. The video was projected on one wall; another wall consisted of the artist's needlelace reproductions of family photos, which were installed adjacent to the video projection; and the digital photos of the dead woman in a body of water were installed on the remaining walls of the room. The artist curated the space to deliberately subvert the meaning of the womb as a space of safety and intimacy. The artist's voice, with her distinctly Durban Indian accent, echoes through the room as she weaves together the memories of trauma and violence experienced by the women in her family. Khan's distinct voice pushes toward and against the viewer, turning the womb into a claustrophobic space of slow death and "monstrous intimacies" to evoke Christina Sharpe (2009). Khan's narrative voice-over sutures together the different visual elements. Through her voice, Khan's personal emotions vibrate outward, bouncing off the walls, attaching to the viewers across differences of race, class, gender, and sexuality, drawing us into a world we uncannily recognize as constitutive of the postapartheid present. We are compelled to respond to the artist's vulnerability and the vulnerability of the generations of Afro-Indian women who came before her and those who will come after her. Through the positionality of feminine vulnerability, we become entangled within this world and recognize that this story belongs as much to the past as it does to the present; this narrative explodes the racialized ways of seeing and knowing that continue to structure postapartheid South African society. This is a story of black/ened life that the postapartheid nation's desire for linear and progressive development is unable to contain.

Before we see any visuals emerging from Khan's video, we see blackness. The artist's voice emerges from the darkness, drawing us into this blackened world, displacing the visual. We hear the following: "Do you think it's possible to hate even before you are born? Do you think it's possible to want somebody to die even before you are birth?" We are transported into a time-space (in one's mother's womb) before the visual becomes a primary mode of knowing, before language begins to structure the world, before consciousness begins to shape our understanding of self and other, before categories of race, gender, sexuality, class, and geography are supposed to have any material weight. By displacing the visual as the primary way of knowing and being in the world, the artist foregrounds emotion and affect. She reveals that she *felt* before she *saw*; she felt her mother's distress as her father violently kicked, punched, and slapped her; she felt her mother's distress as she begged him to stop. *She felt the weight of history even before she was born.* She emerged into an unjust world fearless and learned to navigate this world without fear. Even though she felt, she tells us that this is not her story. How do we deal with the memories of trauma as passed down from generation to generation? How do we deal with the inheritance of trauma in a context where our memories and our modes of feeling and navigating the world continue to be informed by the weight of historical experience, which has been strategically elided in a postapartheid society?

Khan's video narrative introduces us to the abject worlds of the Afro-Indian working class and poor from the perspective of women across three generations. In this thirty-minute video, Khan stitches together fragments of memories that link the home-space to the sugarcane plantations and the journey across the *kala pani*. She begins by recalling her mother's abusive relationship with her first husband. At the age of thirteen, her mother was forced into a marriage after her father owed money from a gambling bet. Her mother was sold as payment for this debt. She reveals the extent of her mother's abuse by her first and second husbands, which left her with physical and mental scars she lived with for the rest of her life. She introduces us to her "dark skinned" grandmother, and philandering grandfather, who worked as a barman at a local hotel. She recounts his numerous affairs with white colonial women. He treated his dark-skinned wife as a maid. Khan remembers her maternal grandmother as a silent woman with "no voice and whose existence was exacerbated by a life of poverty," revealing that even when her grandmother appears in her dreams, she is silent.

Indeed, in this project, the home-space is a space of slow death. The shame and humiliation of poverty, hunger, and sexual and physical abuse within this extended family led to women committing suicide and attempting pedicide. Slow death is embedded within the structures of these communities. She recalls stories of her mother's aunt, who set herself on fire using paraffin; her children witnessing the flames engulfing her body, the smell of burning skin filling the home. The effects of these cycles of trauma and abuse reverberate across generations. Her aunt's son commits suicide by the time he is eighteen and her daughter has a mental breakdown. Suicide is the ultimate outcome, and within these death-worlds of labor, Khan understands it as an enactment of freedom.

The significantly high levels of suicide among indentured workers in Natal were historically attributed to the inherently "weak" nature of the Indian (physical and mental) and to a "crisis of tradition" (Young 2017, 170) emphasizing suicides as "exceptional examples of crisis premised on individual notions of 'free will"' (26). In her analysis of high suicide rates among indentured laborers in Natal, Young argues that "suicide allows us to see the plantation and its various surrogations as a space that routinizes violence, overestimates the differences between enslavement and free labor, and underestimates the violence of 'free labor'" (26). The memories of violence and death enacted within the plantation weave indentureship to the violent conquest and settlement of Southern Africa that begins with slavery in the Cape. Indeed, as South African black feminists argue, "violence and violation" is a common thread that stitches together the past, the present, and the future, stretching back to the era of slavery in the Cape. Slavery in the Cape in the sixteenth century and indentureship in Natal in the eighteenth century depended on the fungibility and fleshiness of the Indian/Asian female body. This reorientation disrupts the oppositional relationship between slavery (unfree labor) and indentureship (free labor), reminding us of the "monstrous intimacies" (Sharpe 2010) between the Indian/Asian women enslaved in the Cape and the Indian women indentured on plantations, coal mines, tea estates, and Europeans' houses. Indeed, Afro-Indianness functions as a site of reorientation that draws these historical experiences and overlapping regimes of racialized labor into the same frame, complicating how we understand the entanglements between black, African, Indian, Asian, Indigenous, and other racialized groups whose collective labor across various plantations and mines created European bourgeois respectability and domesticity.

The video cuts from footage of the artist weaving on a stage to scenes of sugarcane stalks dancing in the wind against a bright blue sky and a dead woman floating in the water. The sugarcane is symbolic of the violence of indentureship and the relationship between labor and trauma. The various scenes of sugarcane—sometimes dancing against a clear blue sky almost mockingly, and other times, the camera moving through the cane, drawing the viewer into a monstrous intimacy (Sharpe 2010) with the cane fields—directs us to the vulnerability of the laborer's body within the plantation. Sugarcane leaves are sharp and literally cut into the body, slowly wearing it down. Sugarcane was also given to indentured workers and enslaved Africans to consume as a source of energy to fuel their bodies. Thus, the body under conditions of coercive labor practices is fueled (and built up) to be slowly broken down. Thus, the muscularity of the women in my family album is a sign of a deteriorating body under the conditions of slow death. The slow wearing-down of the laborers' bodies—enslaved and indentured across the Indian Ocean and Atlantic Worlds—"founded the formative wealth of the European bourgeoisie" (Lowe 2006, 196).

As Khan recalls the stories of her grandmother's attempted suicide and pedicide, the camera moves frantically through the sugarcane. The urgency of this moment is reinforced by the sound design where the audience hears a rapid heartbeat. The scene increasingly becomes claustrophobic and anxiety producing. Aesthetically reproducing the urgency in her grandmother's intention to kill herself and her children through camera movement and voice-over, Khan captures the intimacy, violence, and slow death of plantation life. She says, "cutting through the cane, the cane cutting through you," capturing the nature of "proletarian labor." The metaphor of the sugarcane leaves literally cutting through the body speaks to the ways in which "plantation work constitutes a form of necropolitical labor that necessarily incurs physical and mental injury on a continuum with death" (Young 2017, 26). These images evoke the forgotten, injured, and disabled bodies of indentured women, men, and children who worked and died on sugarcane fields across KwaZulu-Natal. Afro-Indian history and experience in Southern Africa cannot be displaced from the sublime beauty of the sugarcane plantations along the Indian Ocean coast. This is an alternative site of Afro-Indian history and one through which an alternative understanding of Afro-Indian intimacies can emerge.

when the moon waxes red reminds us that the slow death of indentured women begins on the coolie ship, continues on the plantation, and repeats across generations.[7] Indentureship imputed onto these women's bodies the moral stain and sins of history, transforming them into abject and fleshy sites that must be violently disavowed to maintain the gender hierarchy of man over woman, masculine over feminine. The death-worlds of the sugarcane plantation resonate with the ocean as a site of violence and death. In the series of photographs, the audience is confronted with the drowned, fragmented, and decomposing body of Durga. The body of water is simultaneously scripted as a site of death and reverence. Floating alongside the woman's body are betel leaves, split coconuts, petals, clay lamps, and garlands. This is a ceremonial site and the dead woman's body occupies its center.

Khan photographed these images in Mauritius in 2014 while she was participating in the Partage residency program. Mauritius was one of the first colonies to receive Indian indentured workers in 1834. In Mauritius, Khan visited Grand Bassin (Ganga Taloa), a lake considered to be one of the most sacred Hindu pilgrimage sites outside of India. The lake is surrounded by Hindu temples and statues of Hindu gods. She recalls encountering a local custom in which clay figures of the goddess Durga, covered in cloth, are submerged in water. According to local folklore, the Durgas are drowned in order to cleanse their bodies of sin. This ritual is performed as the moon waxes. In an email communication with Khan on October 19, 2015, she indicated that the use of the female body (as represented by the goddess Durga), simultaneously as a site of reverence and violence, resonated with her. For Khan, this ritual performance of submerging Durga in a body of water was a violent enactment of drowning. She read this as symbolic of patriarchal violence that also emerges within sacred religious practices. Khan refigures the meaning of this ceremony. The image of the drowning Durgas resonated with her memories of the violent deaths of women in her family and community. These women were constantly navigating the role of mother and wife, even as they resisted the violence of "patriarchal religiosity" through small and quiet acts. Their survival within the context of slow death positioned them as fearless warriors. Khan evokes the feminine-warrior energy of Shakti as embodied by these women. Suicide is a release from the death-worlds created by capital and is considered a fearless act, rather than a cowardly one. Interestingly, Khan's link between Durga and the recurring figure of the Indian woman and her descendants in the afterlife of indentureship reconnects the goddess Durga to the abject (ghosts, wildness, fearlessness, a warrior goddess consuming meat and alcohol). Khan reminds us that even though women's bodies can be honored and worshipped within the home because they are the repositories of authenticity, tradition, culture, and religion, they are still vulnerable to paternal violence. During the Durga Puja Festival, clay statues of Durga are kept and worshipped within the home for the first nine days. On the tenth day, adorned, dressed, and painted, Durga is removed from the home and drowned.

Needlepoint-Lace Art and Afro-Asia

In the absence of a family photoarchive, Khan created her own through needlepoint-lace art. Needlepoint-lace art, a finely honed skill, disrupts the idea of the indentured household as a site of lack, loss, and emptiness. It directs us to quotidian practices of beauty and care within the everydayness of violence, poverty, and desperation. In the womb-like space of the gallery, she curates as a family photo wall, adding another layer of meaning to this complex project.

Needlepoint-lace art, like embroidery, sewing, knitting, stitching, and crocheting, can be described as one of the "feminine arts" (Outar 2016, 193) and is mostly considered a feminized creative expression related to the home-space. Such feminine art forms were introduced into the Indian home-space by colonial missionaries and were used to bring "low caste women" into the fold of civilization (Kent 2004, 15).[8] Indeed, those lower-caste women described by Kent could have found themselves aboard a coolie ship bound for Natal as indentured laborers. In his book *Christian Indians in Natal 1860 to 1911*, J. B. Brain notes that 1.4 percent (2,150 out of 152,184 indentured laborers) of the indentured laborers identified as Christian. Khan's reference to needlepoint-lace art evokes this larger colonial history of Christian conversation that reorganized Indian social life, confining Indian women within the home-space under the patriarchal authority of men. The construction of respectable Indian womanhood and femininity maps onto the "retraditionalization" of Indian social life after indentureship. In a study on the kinship structures among Indian South Africans in the 1960s, Hilda Kuper described the idealized "kinship model" among Indians as consisting of "well defined roles for parents and elders, brothers ranked in a defined seniority system, functional separation of men and women, strong notions of female purity and modesty, and the emphasis of the family home as an ever-growing compound of adjoined or adjacent units of couples and their children" (quoted in Hansen 2012, 61).

Through needlepoint-lace art, Khan evokes an often-forgotten history of colonial intervention into the home-space. The quest to construct proper female and male colonial subjects through the gender binary reinscribed the vulnerability of women. After indentureship, "the social organization of gender" as binary and hierarchical "became a crucial measure of [this] community's relations of power and status with respect to other groups" (Kent 2004, 2). Khan's needlepoint-lace art sheds light on the impossibility of the colonized woman, from a lower social class, to ever achieve respectability and genteel femininity. Enclosing women within the home-space robbed them of their autonomy and subjected them to various forms of physical, emotional, and sexual abuse as retold by Khan. In *Family Portrait* (plate 12) and *Aya I* (plate 13), Khan centers the figure of her grandmother. In *Family Portrait*, an image of a woman carrying a child and surrounded by four other children, the women and two children to her right are faceless. The outlines of eyes, ears, and nose offer facial features to the child she holds and the one positioned on the bottom left of the image. We are drawn to the intricate and delicate work of the needlepoint-lace art in the image. Khan creates her grandmother out of white thread. She is dressed in a sari that frames her faceless head. The design shifts to a more complex pattern in the center of the image. The needlepoint-lace clothes that Khan creates for the children are more basic, giving form to their formless bodies and faceless heads. In the portrait *Aya I*, the needlepoint-lace art is more focused on the face. With red and white thread, she creates the outlines of her grandmother's lips, broad nose, and eyes. She carefully draws out the wrinkles in her forehead and the chin. She adorns her grandmother with a nose ring and chain, created from gold thread. She wears a simple white blouse. Her hair appears to be neatly tied at the back of her head. Her gaze is direct, and its intensity is heightened by the color of the thread—burnt sienna—used to create her eyes.

The mundaneness and ordinariness of the images are represented by titles like *Great-Grandmother* and *Great-Grandfather*. In one image titled *when the moon waxes red II*, her grandmother is hunched over a sewing machine, her hands touching the machine as she sews. In this mixed-media piece, the moon, burnt orange and white, appears against a red background. In another image, titled *when the moon waxes red I*, the grandmother faces the red moon, with her hands in a prayer position. The red moon is a recurring symbol of feminine energy and the divine. The mundaneness of some of these images is fractured by others titled *Til Death Do Us Part*, a portrait of a man and a woman standing awkwardly next to each other—created from a wedding portrait she sourced from the GLDC—and *Mt Edgecombe Cemetery*, where the grandmother appears to be either cleaning a gravesite or using a hoe to fill a gravesite. To the right of the image, Khan included a cross elaborately created from needlepoint-lace art. The faceless grandmother in *Family Portrait* as well as the images titled *Til Death Do Us Part* and *Mt Edgecombe Cemetery* add another aesthetic layer to Khan's rendering of the home-space in the afterlife of indentureship as a space of female violation and feminine vulnerability. The portrait with the faceless grandmother captures the violent ways in which women—their bodies and desires—are rendered an impossibility within the home. If it is not even possible to represent the face of a woman within this space, what is Khan revealing about the positionality and representability of the Afro-Indian woman? Through this wall she captures the intimate forms of slow death that are weaved into the structures of kin and community in the afterlife of indenture-colonial-apartheid.

Apart from capturing the ways in which men negotiate their feminization within the broader structures of indenture-colonial-apartheid through the enactment of violence on women's bodies, Khan also uses needlepoint-lace art to create a transnational connection between the United States South, Southern Africa, and India. One of the most striking and evocative images in this family photo wall is one titled *Strangefruit II* (plate 14). In this image, we see two figures, presumably female, hanging from the branches of a tree. The needlepoint-lace art image is set against a murky blue background. The red-orange moon appears to the right, slightly covered by a tree branch. The size of the tree dwarfs the hanging bodies, one on the left and one on the right, emphasizing their vulnerability and highlighting their violation and death. This image resonates with a digital photograph also titled *Strangefruit II*. In this photo, we see the lower part of a woman's body hanging from a tree. Her feet are visible. In these images, Khan evokes Billie Holiday's song "Strange Fruit," positioning *when the moon waxes red* as an aesthetic form of protest against racism, heteropatriarchy, misogyny, sexism, and poverty, which imbricate to position women as disposable, abject, and exploitable. Angela Davis describes Holiday's song "Strange Fruit" as a "personal protest against racism," specifically referencing the lynching of African Americans in the Jim Crow South. Davis argues that "Strange Fruit" evokes "the specter of lynching inevitably conjur[ing] up other forms of racism" (Davis 1998, 194). By evoking the specter of transatlantic slavery through this image, Khan connects the afterlife of indentureship to slavery.

Khan notes that she created the *Strangefruit* series in 2014 to commemorate and honor the number of women who continue to be killed by men across the world. In an interview I conducted with the artist, she stated that *Strangefruit* evokes the sexual violation and death of black and black/ened women. She specifically connects the murder of Tanisha Anderson, an African American woman who died in 2014 while being restrained by a white police officer, to reports of gang rape, murder, and the suicide of Dalit women in India around the same period. These murders and suicides evoked memories of women who died by suicide in her own family and community. Khan also remembers her mother recounting a story of suicide that occurred in the Durban community where seven sisters hanged themselves. She could be referring to the mass suicide of the Toplin sisters in the 1950s, who hanged themselves from a tree because their father could not afford to buy them silk dresses. All he could afford was cotton. The girls wanted silk in order to fit in with other girls, to feel beautiful and to embody luxury. Cotton was a sign of poverty and a sight of shame. Suicide was their only line of escape from a life of desperation and gender-sexual vulnerability. *Strangefruit* directs us to plantation histories of coercive labor practices through which black/ened women's bodies were reduced to flesh. Drawing on Hortense Spiller, Jennifer Nash (2014a, 40) writes: "Fleshiness is a state of sexual availability and use; it is having one's body located as the preeminent site of racial-sexual difference." Through the image *Strangefruit*, Khan emphasizes how white supremacy and patriarchy (Afro-normativity and right-wing Hindu nationalism, for instance) use fleshiness as a "tactic of domination" (Musser 2018b, 60) that ensures the vulnerability of women from lower racial-class and caste backgrounds.

Against this backdrop, Khan's attention to stitching and weaving takes on a different resonance. *when the moon waxes red* is filled not only with images of dead, decaying, abused, vulnerable female bodies, but also with rage. As a form of protest against racism, sexism, misogyny, and heteropatriarchal religiosity, Khan's needle can be read as a metaphor of patriarchal violence—the needle pricks and violently punctures the surface of the cloth.[9] The cloth must be slowly destroyed in order for the beauty of the needlepoint lace to emerge. Across the various media, Khan sutures the slow death of black/ened women to an aesthetic of beauty, indicative of care and love. These women are *Strangefruit*, trapped within the logic of the plantation that necessitates their slow death. *Strangefruit* is the condition of racial-sexual vulnerabilities that holds them together across various regimes of difference. Through needlepoint-lace art, Khan activates "a diasporic feminist poetics of 'speaking nearby'" (Reddy 2016, 190).[10] Developed by Trinh T. Minh-ha, postcolonial feminist and filmmaker, "speaking nearby" counters the epistemic violence of "speaking for" or "speaking about," silencing the "racialized or colonized Other" (Reddy 2016, 190). Khan's close attention to form, aesthetics, and performance positons her embodied experiences, as informed by the afterlife of indentureship, in relation to other violent historical experiences to foreground the vulnerability and violation of black/ened women across time and space. The performance of stitching represents the ways violence is a quotidian fact of life for marginalized women across the globe. In her essay "Age, Race, Class, and Sex: Women Redefining Difference," Lorde (2007b) writes, "But Black women [and other women of color] and our children know how the fabric of our lives is stitched with violence and with hatred, that there is no rest. . . . For us, increasingly, violence weaves through the daily tissues of our living—in the supermarket, in the classroom, in the elevator, in the clinic and the schoolyard . . . the waitress who does not serve us" (119).

Through performance, Khan transforms her body into a fleshy archive of history and situates feminine vulnerability as a form of embodied knowledge. The memories of violence, death, vulnerability, and abuse stick to her body, cutting into her like the cane cutting into her ancestors, slowly extracting the life force out of her. The moral stain of indentureship, unacknowledged and invisibilized, is her inheritance. This is the intimacy of slow death, which occurs as a fact of everyday life. *when the moon waxes red* offers no redemption; she doesn't emerge from the watery grave triumphant and without sin. Instead, at the end of the video she removes the red beaded necklace from her neck and encloses herself in a white shroud onto which she has stitched her needlepoint-lace recreations of family photos. The shroud covers her body under the weight of patriarchal violence. The video ends with Durga's body slowly decaying and deteriorating in the water. Khan's *kala pani*, a womb that births death and decay, disrupts readings of the *kala pani* as a site of hybridity, transformation, reinvention, and social mobility where older identities disintegrate to give birth to new ones as an escape from inherited oppressive social hierarchies. *when the moon waxes red* reminds us that this desire for autonomy and mastery over this abject historical experience submerges and disappears the Afro-Indian female body. Such narratives of mastery, indicative of neoliberal forms of subjecthood, inevitably continue to keep the wheels of capital turning. Failure, fragmentation, and unbelonging are facts of life for those who exist within the death-worlds of capital; indeed, capital requires these fragmented and deteriorating bodies. Left to decay and deteriorate, these bodies become part of the molecular structures that are a vital lifeforce, a form of feminine energy, that can remake the cosmos. She demands that we attend to these women, and the gendered afterlives of indenture-colonial-apartheid history, with care and love. Attending to history requires the suspension of nation-time and the linear and progress narrative of development. Feminine vulnerability disrupts straight time, directing us to the queer and fungible lives of those who exist on the peripheries. Through female/feminine vulnerability, Khan's project is a powerful reminder of the queerness of Afro-Indianness. This queer positionality allows her to reach outward and to connect with other black/ened women across differences of race, ethnicity, language, class, geography, and nation.

Though Khan's routing of Afro-Indian intimacies through US Blackness is provocative, it also has limitations. Aesthetically, Khan attends to the various imbricated regimes of sexual violence against women from the US South to India through transatlantic slavery. Khan's desire to activate a transnational Afro-Asian circuit through the vulnerability of black/ened women's bodies erases the everyday forms of violence (sexual assault, murder, poverty, homelessness) experienced by black African women, lesbians, and gender nonconforming people in South Africa. Khan evokes the sugarcane plantations as the point of stickiness between the Afro-Indian and the African American, erasing the gritty relationship between the Afro-Indian and black African, formed within the death-worlds of the sugarcane plantations and the coal mines. Khan's evocation of US Blackness evokes a longer history (see the introduction) of comparison in South Africa. In an interview in 1999, Hugh Masekela, for instance, suggests that there is no difference, for him, "between African Americans" enslaved on Southern plantations and "Africans who were taken from their lands, into the plantations which is where we live in South Africa right now" (Masekela quoted in Livermon 2012b, 177). Here, Masekela evokes the history of the mines that removed thousands of black African men from their rural homes, and displacing them within Southern Africa. He connects the carceral logics of the plantation during slavery in the United States to the carceral logics of the colonial-apartheid state and its afterlives in South Africa.

Khan does not unsettle the relationship between indentureship and Indian racial formation, which necessitates the erasure of the black African subject. This erasure resonates with the ways in which coal mining attaches to African migrant labor and racial blackness, which must occlude a history of mining that included Indian indentured workers on coal mines in Natal and Chinese indentured workers in the gold mines of the Transvaal.[11] Indeed, in some of the literature, African migrant labor is referred to as indentureship (see Oakes 1992; Josephy 2018). A photograph shot at the Simmer and Jack Gold Mine in Germiston by David Goldblatt in 1965 evokes the intimacies between black miners and Chinese laborers indentured on the same mine. The caption reads: "David Goldblatt, Miner's bunks in the abandoned Chinese compound, so called because it probably housed indentured Chinese labourers between 1904 and 1910, after which it accommodated black miners. Simmer and Jack Gold Mine, Germiston, July 1965."

Mohau Modisakeng and Black Male Vulnerability

In an interview in 2014, Modisakeng stated, "South Africa's past affects the conditions under which people practice and experience culture today" (Modisakeng 2014) and that "the body is indifferent to social change, so it remembers" (Modisakeng quoted in Mqombothi 2014, n.p.). This is a powerful commentary on the postapartheid present illuminating the myth of the ANC's promise of a better life underpinned by the state's project of constructing official memory through the TRC. If the state is invested in managing national memory, and producing, through the TRC, an official "repository of South African memory" (Nuttall and Coetzee 1998, 1), then Modisakeng's attention to aesthetics and performance art, like Khan, works against the national imperative that must violently excise and submerge bodies, histories, and experiences that deviate from the nation's desire for progress and development. Modisakeng's statement that "the body is indifferent to social change" directs us to those who don't have the luxury of forgetting, those black and blackened subjects who are suspended between the past and the present and whose futures have been foreclosed. These are the new black Others, constructed as nonnormative/queer. These are those who continue to experience slow death as a fact of everyday life. Whereas Khan returns to the sugarcane plantations and the moral sin imputed onto female bodies, the inheritance of those who continue to live in the afterlife of indentureship, Modisakeng returns to the coal mines and engages the slow death of the black male body within this space. He evokes, through the figure of the mine worker, the history of African migrant labor in Southern Africa and its afterlives. Through the aesthetic realm, he examines the relationship between trauma and labor, routed through complex articulations of black male vulnerability. Through this feminized positionality, Modisakeng queers the nativist and hetero-Afro-normative black male subject. In this section, I first offer a brief overview of African migrant labor and its afterlives in postapartheid South Africa. I then examine Modisakeng's aesthetics of slow death in his interrelated projects *Lefa La Ntate* (2016), *To Move Mountains* (2015), and *Inzilo* (2013).

The modern history of Africa is one of displacement and disruptions caused by external and internal forces.[12] Forced labor practices are a defining feature of colonization in Africa, directly related to territorial expansion, remapping, and the exploitation of natural resources. Leopold's greed for rubber in the Congo, the extermination of the Herero peoples in South West Africa (Namibia) by the Germans, and the need for cheap labor on gold mines in the

Witwatersrand are indicative of the ways in which African blackness is produced out of coercion, exploitation, and the fungibility of the African body. After the Anglo-Boer War (1899–1902), mine owners in desperate need of a cheap labor force turned to Portuguese Mozambique after the reluctance of local Africans to enter the labor system (Cohen 1995, 160). By the late nineteenth century, South Africa's gold and coal mines were filled with African migrant laborers, recruited through a sophisticated scheme and networks of rural depots that reached "deep into Angola on the west coast, and Tanzania on the east" (Crush 1995, 172).

The recruitment of African migrant laborers resonates with the strategies used across India to recruit indentured laborers.[13] The Protector of Indian Immigrants was formed as a response to complaints by returning indentured workers, "in terms of overwork, punishments, unhygienic accommodation and poor food" (Kaarsholm 2016, 445). The protector's job was to ensure that indentured workers were not overexploited. However, the contradiction is that the "Protector of Indian immigrants was meant to protect the colonial state and give it legitimacy" in a context where the British imperial government "was very actively involved in campaigns to suppress the slave trade along the African Indian Ocean coast." Similarly, recruiters used coercive and violent means to "round up groups of Africans, often at gunpoint, in order to sell them on for a contracted period to the various mining companies." Many local chiefs were complicit and were paid "to exert customary and more spontaneous forms of compulsion over the reluctant recruits" (Cohen 1995, 160). African migrant mine labor, like indentureship, is a condition of slow death. Crush (1995) writes, "Between 1945 and 1984, over 50,000 miners died on the mines. Others—some 110,000 between 1972 and 1976 alone—were injured or permanently disabled. The workforce was also regularly decimated by occupational disease such as tuberculosis and pneumonia. Wages were low and did not rise at all in real terms between 1910 and 1970" (172). Not only did migrant miners return home "physically maimed and crippled with lung disease," but also "a lifetime of work in South Africa never qualified a single miner for permanent residence" (Crush and Tshitereke 2001, 50). Crush and Tshitereke (51) trace the ways in which the African migrant labor system has been left intact in the postapartheid period. South African scholars have demonstrated that mining companies "benefited from the draconian labor and movement laws central to apartheid," emphasizing the collusion of the "mining industry with the apartheid regime" (51). In 1998, the TRC criticized the "Chamber of Mines' actions in shaping the migrant labor system," arguing that this "'is the clearest example of business working closely with the (minority) white government to create the conditions for capital accumulation, based on cheap African labor . . . the mining industry harnessed the services of the state to shape labor supply conditions to their advantage. Thus, the mining industry bears a great deal of moral responsibility for the migrant labor system'" (51). The postapartheid state has left unchanged a system designed to create wealth for a small minority at the expense of black/ened life. The ANC now operates in the interests of global capital and multinational corporations rather than being a representative of the people, the majority black population.[14]

Within this context of coercive labor practices and their afterlives, the Afro-Indian and the African migrant laborer are familiar strangers. While Khan examined the afterlife of Indian indenture labor through the figure of the Afro-Indian women, Modisakeng examines the abject positionality of the black working class through the figure of the mine worker. Khan and Modisakeng explore the collective inheritance of those who exist outside of the space-time of the Afro-normative nation. I am particularly interested in Modisakeng's attention to black male vulnerability and time. In an interview in 2011, Modisakeng stated: "*I want to bring time to a halt*."[15] Through the trope of black male vulnerability, a feminized positionality, Modisakeng's aesthetics of slow death disrupt the temporality of Afro-normativity. His art practice is invested in time as a way of attending with care to black life on the margins, iterations of blackness that have been strategically forgotten in our collective quest for progress and development. He demands that we attend to the past, which "has not been dealt with properly" (Modisakeng quoted in Simbao 2017, 70). Thus, his attention to the relationship between labor and trauma and its afterlives is significant because this continues to stain what we think we know about South African blackness.

The Weight of History

Black Masculinity, Temporality, and the Afterlife of Colonial Apartheid

Modisakeng's concern with the relationship between labor, trauma, and the construction of blackness is routed through the coal mining industry. *To Move Mountains* is a commentary not only on the long history of colonial exploitation and extraction in Southern Africa that relied on the labor of black bodies, but also on the ways in which such extractive practices extend into the postapartheid period, creating a continuity that stretches from the nineteenth-century Scramble for Africa to the Marikana Massacre in 2012. Modisakeng's work thus deals with the traumatic weight of history. This is the inheritance of the present generation and future generations to come. Throughout his work, Modisakeng inserts his body into the artwork. From his portraits to his video artwork, Modisakeng uses performance, dress, adornment, and props and tools associated with violence to "draw attention to the corporeality and vulnerability of the body."[16] By rendering his body vulnerable through performance, his body becomes malleable, fluid, flaky, and sticky. His body becomes a site of excess, drawing the viewer's gaze to the various ways in which labor and trauma continue to blacken the black body. The black body that Modisakeng foregrounds in his artwork is not the black body of the proper Afro-normative subject. This is a black and blackened body associated with the abject—the black and blackened body that can be read as a metaphor for the new black Others, those who exist on the margins, outside the boundaries of normative and respectable blackness. It is therefore significant that Modisakeng's work engages the mine worker and the African migrant laborer through an aesthetic and performance practice that is queer.

Consisting of various interconnected scenes, *To Move Mountains* is a ten-minute, four-channel video that takes the viewer deep into the physical and psychic landscape of the coal mine. The video begins with a tracking shot moving forward into a coal mine. The audience is immersed into the blackened environment of the coal mine and all we see are mountains of black coal. A beam of light falls on coal, which shines eerily. The shine emphasizes the value of the coal, which is often referred to as black gold. The landscape is desolate, isolated, and devoid of life. This is further signified by the sound of wind that is eerie and ghostly. In the next scene, we see a medium close-up shot of feet stained white (plates 15 and 16). The figure wears white overalls stained black. We hear the sound of steel scraping the coal. The figure—the artist, the mine worker, the African migrant laborer—holds a chopper as he walks through a puddle of water in this desolate landscape. Stepping onto the coal, he pauses for a moment as his foot sinks into the coal and as he adjusts to the sharpness of the coal against his bare feet. *The coal cuts into him*. The sound of a bell cuts across the landscape and brings to an abrupt halt this forward-moving trajectory. In the next scene we see the artist standing in front of a mountain of coal, clenching a machete in both fists, the blades pointing downward. This is the first time the audience sees a full shot of the miner. He wears long white overalls, a black trilby hat, a white mask covering his mouth and nose, and blinkers designed to block his peripheral vision. The camera slowly zooms in, bringing the clenched fists into focus. The fists are encased in black earth. The coal and earth render his fists gritty and sticky. The miner's forearms are tense, this muscular tension extends to his arms and neck. He then moves his fists toward his body. The shot then cuts to a close-up of the miner's hands, where a black viscous liquid, like oil, is being poured into his cupped hands and falls toward the ground. In the next scene, the miner stands in front of the asphalt heaps in a Christ-like position. It is now raining. We hear the ululation of women's voices in the background. Rain falls onto his hands and onto the mountain of coal, causing the coal to fall dangerously to the ground in the background. The coal threatens to collapse onto the miner, burying him. As the water falls over the miner's hands, we see the blackened water dripping off it. The miner's body is rendered vulnerable within this death-world.

In the next scene the miner runs up a mountain of coal; as he attempts to run upward, his feet sink into the ground and moves downward in the opposite direction. He uses the chopper to support him. He eventually reaches the top and sits on the mountain of coal for a minute. He then begins to slide down the mountain, the metal from the chopper providing some resistance. In the next scene, we see the miner lying on his back on the blackened earth; the sounds of waves, birds chirping, and a moving train overlap. Is he dead or is he resting? Has he been shot down for protesting? The sounds blend to become incoherent as the camera moves backward over the landscape, taking us to the beginning, to where the film started. As the camera tracks backward, we see torn and stained pieces of white cloth littering the landscape, stained black by the coal dust. The coal mine is a graveyard, and the cloth—tattered, torn, buried deep and forgotten in the coal mines—represents the hundreds of thousands of miners across Southern Africa who died while extracting black gold to enrich the pockets of the colonizers. The mine is a death-world, one that has been invisibilized within the South African postapartheid national imaginary.

To Move Mountains was shot in Ndabeni, an industrial site located outside Cape Town. Modisakeng focused on terrain and landscape as important elements of this project in its initial stages. He writes, "I knew I wanted the idea of landscape/topography to be prominent but I kept coming back to an image of an arid, extraterrestrial, post-apocalyptic, Black landscape" (Modisakeng quoted in Jamal 2016, 117). In *To Move Mountains* the asphalt creates a Black and Blackened world that is deep, intense, and overwhelming. The black terrain itself disrupts spatial and temporal logics of postapartheid nationalism that has failed to resolve the violent history of this country. Ndabeni's history reflects the long trajectory of race-based social engineering. Modisakeng's research on this location revealed that:

> This location was established in 1902 by the civil authorities as a field hospital and isolation camp for victims after an outbreak of the bubonic plague in Cape Town which spread due to the importation of Argentine horses by the British military during the course of the South African War. It was this outbreak that justified and made way for the mass removal of black people from Cape Town's urban centers to what became the first permanent location for the black labouring class. Ndabeni is therefore at the center of the genesis or the origins of the segregated settlements of the apartheid system. (117)

Across Khan's and Modisakeng's work, landscape is significant. In *To Move Mountains*, Modisakeng, similar to Khan, creates a womb-like environment. This is a womb that swallows up black laboring bodies and births death and destruction. Across both bodies of work, the artists also use memory to connect racialized bodies to landscape. In South Africa, space and landscape still remain central to how we understand race. In an interview given to the St. Louis Public Radio website on November 17, 2016, Modisakeng states, "I would like viewers to understand that memory has a way of connecting our bodies to the landscape and I think that the landscape or the terrain itself has this memory underneath it. . . . I would like for the audience to place themselves in these images, replace this figure they see in the photographs with their own image, and how they imagine the photographs work."

To Move Mountains evokes the biblical scriptures around faith. In Matthew 17:20, Jesus tells his disciples, "If you have faith as small as a mustard seed, you will say to this mountain, 'Move from here to there,' and it will move; nothing will be impossible for you." *To Move Mountains* can be read as a critique of the ANC's failure to manifest their promise of a better life for all. South Africans believed that the ANC would deliver them from the pits of apartheid hell and that democracy will equal black freedom. However, as I have examined throughout this book, freedom for the black majority population remains illusive and has been captured/curtailed by the state's investment in neoliberal economic policies. Neoliberalism is sustained through older extractive practices that continue to depend on the disposability and fungibility of black African bodies. Thus, Modisakeng's evocation of the biblical scripture around faith is an indictment of the ANC's antiblackness/Africanness that manifests through performances of Afro-normativity.

In this video, the miner is represented as vulnerable and feminized. His body is under constant threat of being buried by the mountains of coal that surround him. The coal mine, like the sugarcane plantation examined in the section above, is a site of containment and death for black and blackened people. The white overalls, white collared shirt, and the trilby hat are not typical mine worker's clothing. From the back, the overalls look like couture dresses. Modisakeng uses costume to play with gender. Although the overalls are beautiful in their whiteness, they are also heavy and bulky, rendering the black body ambiguous. At first, the audience does not know whether this is a male or female miner. The whiteness of the overalls, shirt, and head gear contrasts sharply with the blackness of the environment. This contrast is further emphasized by the whitened feet of the black mine worker as they walk on the coal. The white costume weighs down the black body and limits its field of vision. The costume signifies the weight of whiteness (European histories of colonial exploitation that extend into the present) and the intimacies between white and black. The coal dust stains the white overalls and the black/ened body of the performer. The intimate connection between black and white evident across Modisakeng's works suggests to me the entanglements between whiteness and blackness, the coconstitutive ways in which blackness and whiteness are constructed. The production of whiteness through the exploitation of blackness implicates the making of whiteness in this larger theater of trauma. The black stains on the overalls can be read as a stain on white claims to innocence and white comfort in the postapartheid period.

The trilby hat that Modisakeng uses throughout his works resonates with the hat that Kganye uses in her project *Ke Lefa Laka: Heir-Story*. Whereas Kganye uses the hat to reference her grandfather, Modisakeng uses the hat as a prop to reference his father's generation. It evokes the memories of the many men who "moved from rural South Africa to cities where they sometimes adopted the white colonial gentleman's hat as a means to show they were members of urban society." The hat becomes a small and minor symbol of resistance and a form of self-fashioning through which men negotiated the shifts in their masculinity as they moved from the rural and the urban, from a space of dignity to one of death and fragmentation. In the context of coercive labor practices, where the laborer is dehumanized and rendered fungible, the hat, as well as costume, dress, adornment, and fashion, direct us to small and minor claims to subjecthood within the death-worlds of labor.

Modisakeng explores the dynamics of time as it shapes the Afro-normative nation's desire for progress and development. Afro-normative time rubs against the temporality of the new black/ened Others. In *To Move Mountains*, the miner wears blinkers, usually associated with limiting the peripheral vision of animals. The blinkers ensure a forward-looking gaze and is designed to strategically block anything that could possibly disrupt this movement in a forward direction. Modisakeng's use of the blinkers is a critique of the postapartheid nation's quest to forge ahead by strategically forgetting the primal violence through which South Africa has been formed. This linear narrative of progress and development depends on submerging the history of violence and violation that extends from the era of slavery to the present. The forward and backward movement of the body through the mine is a play with temporality and a strategic disruption of Afro-normative time. Whereas Afro-normative time is linear, progressive, and future-orientated, Modisakeng's notion of time is circular. Whereas Afro-normative time is the time of the black elite, Modisakeng's notion of time directs us to the temporality of the new black Others. The gravitational pull backward—his video ends at the beginning—emphasizes the ways in which the black/ened body exists in a loop where the past, the present, and the future bleed into one another, returning to the primal scenes of slavery and colonialism. It is impossible to think of black time in South Africa as homogenous. The black majority exists in an alternative temporal and spatial logic, directing us to the many overlapping and disjunctive textures of South African blackness. Thus, throughout his works Modisakeng queers Afro-normative nation-time and this emerges through the feminized figure of black male vulnerability.

Indeed, Modisakeng's critique around time relies on an aesthetic of male femininity. In his video art piece *Ga bose gangwe* (2014) (plates 17 and 18), Modisakeng riffs off the Setswana idiom *Phiri o rile ga bose gangwe*, loosely translated to mean "One must always think and plan for the future." In this video, a group of black/ened men are trapped within a time loop. The men, whose bodies appear to be stained black, are dressed in pleated white skirts that cover the lower halves of their bodies. The video begins with the men lying down on their backs in a circle. They slowly begin to rise, but fall down, pulled by a gravitational force. Some turn toward the camera and begin to rise again, a little higher this time, but once again they fall to the ground. They begin to rise a third time and fall flat on the ground. The performance repeats in a loop. The repetition of the performance creates an aesthetic of time as a loop, rubbing against the linear time of the nation, foreclosing the possibilities of a future. They represent the lives of those who have been "blackened," rendered abject and outside of history and nation-time (Scott 2010, 38). These are the bodies of the African migrant laborers and the new black Others who exist within the space-time of slow death. Modisakeng uses this aesthetic of blackening to queer the project of black authenticity, emphasizing that those who are black/ened have no future and exist outside of the historical frame.

Vulnerability and violation are passed down from black father to son. Modisakeng's body of work grapples with this inheritance. In *Lefa La Ntate*, a series of five photographs (plate 19), Modisakeng engages the ongoing legacy of coal mining and its impact on black masculinity. In this series of photos, Modisakeng, the artist and performer, is partially buried in a coal mine. Chunks of coal surround his body, glistening in the light. Coal dust sticks to and stains his skin, blackening the surface of his black body. Some photos are close-up shots of his shoulders and head and others are long shots capturing his entire body partially buried in coal. In some photos, his hands cover his face; in others, his hands hold his chest or are positioned on the sides of his body. In all photos, his black body is encased in coal, which threatens to swallow him alive. In this series of photos, Modisakeng captures the vulnerability of the black body within the coal mine and the weight of history that is passed down, generally foreclosing the possibilities of any futurity. The photos are claustrophobic and Modisakeng's black body blends into the blackened environment. He positions the black/ened body as part of the natural environment; in these photos, we do not know where the body begins and where it ends. This is a black male body that is permeable, malleable, and sticky, a body that is both vulnerable and one that bleeds into the blackened environment, disrupting the boundaries between body (subject) and object (coal). Under the deadly conditions of labor, the black/ened body is objectified, depersonalized, and reduced to units of labor. This is the black/ened body that the Afro-normative nation must violently abject in its quest for postapartheid mastery, rendering those who exist on the margins queer/nonnormative. Modisakeng states that his "work responds elementarily to the history of the black body within the (South) African context, which in most cases cannot be removed from the violence of the apartheid era and the early 1990s."[17]

Lefa La Ntate can be loosely translated to mean "legacy of my father or inheritance from my father."[18] If vulnerability and violation are passed down generationally—are the inheritance and/or legacy of Southern African blackness—then Modisakeng's aesthetic of male femininity disrupts the "patrilineal genealogical inheritance" (Gopinath 2005, 64) that secures heteronormative blackness in the postapartheid period. Through black male vulnerability he disrupts the ways in which "proper" gender, sexual, and racialized subjecthood is secured within the postapartheid contexts. According to Freud, the Oedipal complex "explains the consolidation of proper gender identification and heterosexual object choice in little boys, as masculine identification with the father is made while feminine identification with the mother is refused" (Gopinath 2005, 5). In *Black Skin, White Masks*, Frantz Fanon demonstrates how the Oedipal complex is inadequate to understand the development of proper gender identification within the colonial context. Within the colonial context, the colonizer occupies the positionality of paternal power (the symbolic father), disrupting the possibility of proper gender identification for the black boy-child because of the black father's "lack of access to social power" (5). Thus, the black father occupies a feminized positionality. For the "captive body" (Spillers 2003b) within the death-worlds of capital, normative gender identification is disrupted, the symbolic order is ruptured, and the body is reduced to "flesh," the site of racial-sexual difference (Musser 2018b; Nash 2014a). The trauma of coercive labor practices and their afterlives allows Modisakeng to engage gender in his work through performance. His disruption of the gender binary (male/female) and his play with masculinity and femininity is also influenced by his relationship to African spiritual practices as mediated by his mother. Responding to his play with gender, Modisakeng states: "In African spirituality, you don't possess gender . . . just spirit."[19] Importantly, Modisakeng's aesthetic of black male vulnerability is influenced by the maternal feminine, which must be violently expelled within Freud's Oedipal drama in order to secure normative gender identification for the (white) boy-child.

In chapter 1, I examined Kganye's mobilization of gender subversion in *Ke Lefa Laka: Heir-Story*. She uses gender subversion as a strategy to disrupt the "male-model" of migrancy, which invisibilizes African women's experiences and the impact of migration on the construction of black femininities. Through gender subversion she also offers an aesthetic of time that is elastic, rerouting the linear and forward gaze of the Afro-normative nation through her own reverse migration from the city to the rural areas after 1994. Throughout his aesthetic practice, Modisakeng plays with gender and offers an articulation of black male femininity that is a reminder of the history of violence and vulnerability that is the collective inheritance of those stained black and blackened. Importantly, through black male vulnerability he suspends Afro-normative nation-time in order to create an opening to imagine otherwise. This opening is not a guarantee of black futurity. Rather, this is an invitation to attend to the violence of the past in order to create alternative futurities not bound to the nation and national consciousness. Modisakeng's suspension of time depends on gender subversion. This is most evident in his video *Inzilo*.

According to the artist's website, *Inzilo* is an isiZulu word that means "mourning or fasting."[20] In African cultures, *Inzilo* refers to the "mourning attire" that a widow is required to wear. It symbolizes the loss of the husband, marks her separation from the rest of society, and inaugurates the mourning process. *Inzilo* is connected to *ukuzila*, the ritual practice of mourning the dead. The period of mourning can last from three months to two years and the widow is often required to observe the various steps associated with *ukuzila*. *Ukuzila* includes the widow wearing specific kinds of clothing that separate her from the rest of the family and community: covering her head, shaving her head, slaughtering animals (usually cows, sheep, or goats), isolating from community and restricting from participating in community events and social gatherings, and undertaking numerous purification rituals. During the period of mourning the widow is regarded as "impure and unlucky" (Magudu 2004, 143; Daber 2003; Ntshangase 2018). The widow embodies "ritual danger . . . expressed in terms of 'heat,' 'darkness,' and dirt'" (Ramphele 1996, 100). Her body is "both object and subject of mourning rituals. The individual suffering of a widow is made social, and her body becomes a metaphor for suffering" (99). *Ukuzila* entails the "withdrawal from normal routines" and the "correct behaviour" women must follow in order for the spirit of the deceased husband to join the ancestors (Carton 2006, 92). According to the social anthropologist Harriet Ngubane, if a widow "did not remove herself from society . . . she could become 'a sexual pervert, speak or sing when she should not, and be aggressive without any provocation'" (Ngubane quoted in Carton 2006, 95).

Widowhood signifies a state of liminality, and the widow is a site of contamination. Apart from wearing clothing that separates her from the community, her body is also smeared with "a mixture of herbs and ground charcoal" (Ramphele 1996, 100). During the mourning rituals, the "polluting aspects of the corpse are associated with women." The widow's body also becomes "the channel for the expulsion of the polluting elements" (Ramphele 1996, 103). Mokoena (2016, 5) writes that the word *Inzilo* encompasses "not just the loss occasioned by death but the *arrest of time* that is often extended to widows in mourning." Widows live in a state of reversals that further signify their liminal status; "these may include eating with her left hand, wearing shoes inside out, wearing one shoe, or eating out of a lid instead of a plate" (Ramphele 1996, 100). The widow represents the queer limits of African womanhood. She is physically and psychically marked as excessive and disruptive. Proscriptions around sexual conduct situate her body as a site of sexual excess and outside of reproductive femininity. The widow rubs against and sticks to Modisakeng's aesthetic of male femininity. Within patriarchal cultures, the feminine excess of the widow imbricates with the excesses of male femininity. This is what threads together Modisakeng's performances of male vulnerability across his interconnected bodies of work.

Inzilo (plates 20 and 21) begins with Modisakeng seated on a wooden chair with his arms raised to his sides. He wears a ballooning black skirt and a black trilby hat. Modisakeng's skin is blackened and shines against the stark white background. The movement of the camera creates an illusion of the performer being suspended in the space. Modisakeng disrupts the gender division enforced by *Inzilo*. The skirt is a signifier of the feminine and the hat is a signifier of the masculine. Through the vulnerability of his black/ened body he suspends gender division and queers the ritual of *Inzilo*. As the camera moves to create the illusion of being suspended in time and space, the artist slowly shifts his head to the right. He moves his fingers, and dust begins to fill the space by his hands. Shards of black/ened skin slough off his fingers and palms and fall onto the white ground. The video then cuts to an extreme close-up of his left hand. His fingernails are stained black. He picks off the layer of skin that sticks to him like a scab. It reveals his black/ened skin. The camera then cuts to a shot of his right hand where we see him also removing the flaky layer of skin. Then the camera cuts to a close-up of his feet. Dust and skin lie all around his feet on the floor. We then see his hands grabbing onto the shards of black/ened skin, now attaching them to his feet, rather than removing them from his body. In this scene where he reverses the action, we get the sense that he is caught up in a time loop. Finally, the video cuts to a long shot of the artist sitting, hunched over the chair, holding his black skirt. In a fluid motion, he rises from the chair and his skirt moves upward, releasing black dust and black/ened skin into the environment, staining the whitened ground.

Through his performance of *Inzilo*, Modisakeng queers the mourning ritual by using the liminal figure of the widow to attend to the violence of the past. His liminal body, suspended in time and between genders, is a site of contamination signified by the coal dust and the layers of thickened skin falling off and reattaching to his body. Is he performing this mourning ritual to honor his brother, who died in the death-worlds of the township in the early 1990s? Or is he performing this ritual to mourn the deaths of those who have died, and continue to die, within the death-worlds of Southern African mines? Throughout his work, the township and the mines imbricate. Both are sites of containment and regulation, sites of slow death for black bodies. Modisakeng demands that we mourn for all those black and black/ened workers who continue to die in order to keep the wheels of capital churning. The staining of the body black, as well as his aesthetic of ash, grittiness, and flaky skin, for instance, is indicative of the histories of exploitation that have contaminated and fragmented the body, rendered the black/ened body a site of excess and abjection. This is the history of blackness in Southern Africa that we need to attend to, a history of abjection that has been strategically erased in order to secure the postapartheid nation-state and its myth of mastery over historical experience. Black/ened bodies carry the stain of nonnormativity. By returning to the death-worlds of the mines, Modisakeng works through this history of abjection—this process of becoming black—through male vulnerability and the queer figure of the widow.

Similarly to Khan's aesthetics of slow death in *when the moon waxes red*, Modisakeng's work offers no redemptive narrative. At the end of Khan's video, the Afro-Indian female body is left in a watery grave, decaying and deteriorating. Through female vulnerability, Khan demands that we attend to the memories and histories of black/ened women who have been forgotten and erased from historical and national consciousness. Attending to these violent histories requires us to stop—"to bring time to a halt"—and to mourn as a practice of care and love for those whom the nation must strategically forget. By positioning Khan in relationship to Modisakeng, I read *Inzilo* as an invitation to mourn together across our differences of race, gender, sexuality, class, and region. During the mourning ritual, the African widow is required to be seated and covered. In his interpretation of the ritual, Modisakeng's liminal body—suspended between the past and present and male and female embodiment—stands up and reaches outward, shifting the mourning ritual as an embodiment of "personal loss to that of incorporating public loss" (Ramphele 1996, 99). As he stands, the dust and flaky skin—which stick to contaminating the body—are expelled outward, implicating everyone (black/white, male/female) in this larger history of violence and violation. The coal dust and the flaky skin stain the white ground, rendering visible the deathly intimacies between white and black. This is a call for whites to also deal with their ongoing role in the slow death of African life that began with the colonization of the region and continues today. The black stains on the whitened environment stain not just the normative and nativist parameters of Southern African blackness but also white comfort in the period after 1994. White comfort and innocence are imbricated with the Afro-normative nation's linear narrative of progress and development. For the postapartheid nation, a new beginning emerges through the forgetting of the past. To move forward, to move into national consciousness, the past must be strategically put to rest and buried. Khan and Modisakeng disrupt this imperative through their aesthetics of slow death. Their works are powerful reminders that the past continues to haunt the present, foreclosing the possibility of a future. They remind us that the black/ened body, constructed out of histories of coercive labor practices and intimately embedded within its afterlives, refuses to forget.

Through the vulnerable figures of the Afro-Indian female and black migrant mine laborer, Khan and Modisakeng suspend nation-time and bring to a halt the linear and progressive narrative of the Afro-normative nation. Across both works, vulnerability attaches to feminine and feminized black/ened bodies, directing us to the queerness of Afro-Indianness and the queerness of blackness. Both artists articulate a politics of (un)belonging through feminine vulnerability that reorients us toward one another, illuminating the deep intimacies between indentureship and the African migrant labor system. In chapter 3, we shift from the aesthetics of slow death to queer-kinship formations and the emergence of Afro-intimacies in unlikely spaces, small town and rural South Africa. Through an examination of Sabelo Mlangeni's photoseries and my own short film, *cane/cain*, I am interested in the emergence of forms of queer worldmaking in feminine and feminized spaces. The next chapter situates rural and small towns as feminine and feminized spaces where time slows down.

3

Afro-Intimacies

QUEER-KINSHIP FORMATIONS AND AFRICAN RURALITY

In this chapter, I want to dwell longer in and alongside the death-worlds of capital (the coal mines and sugarcane plantations) examined in the previous chapter. Whereas in the previous chapter, I examined Khan's and Modisakeng's aesthetics of slow death and their use of Afro-vulnerabilities to examine the trauma of indentureship and migrant labor, as well as their afterlives, this chapter examines the emergence of alternative life-forms alongside the death-worlds of capital. In this chapter, I examine forms of queer world-making in rural and small-town South Africa by juxtaposing Sabelo Mlangeni's photographic projects, *At Home* (2004–9), *Country Girls* (2003–9), and *Men Only* with my short film *cane/cain* (2011). *At Home* is a series of photographs that examine the long-term effects of male migration from rural areas to the cities. It brings into sharp focus those who are left behind—women, children, and the aged. Many of the photos in this series also focus on the rural landscape—expansive and tranquil, yet also bearing traces of underdevelopment and deterioration.

Mlangeni's photographs reveal an aesthetic of suspended time that situates rural areas and small towns as feminized spaces. Whereas *At Home* focuses on the effects of male migration, *Country Girls* explores gay life and queer world-making in the countryside. I conclude this section with an analysis of *Men Only*, a series of photos shot by Mlangeni in the George Goch Hostel, built in 1961 to house male migrant mine workers. In this series, Mlangeni inserts himself into this environment, offering nuanced representations of male-male intimacies that arise in spaces usually associated with violence, hypermasculinity, and criminality. *Country Girls* and *Men Only* offer complex articulations of intimacies between gay and straight-identified men to reveal queer-kinship formations and queer world-making practices that complicate how we understand the relationship between blackness and queerness in South Africa.

I then analyze *cane/cain*, a nonlinear film shot in the sugarcane plantations in Tongaat and Fordsburg, an urban area previously known as Johannesburg's Indian Quarter. The website "In Your Pocket Essential City Guides" describes Fordsburg: "The cultures and flavours of the Indian subcontinent are a defining feature of the multi-cultural suburb of Fordsburg, a downtown neighbourhood. The streets here are a bold and colourful collision of cultures, with an abundant and eclectic selection of street food that offers authentic tastes from across India and Pakistan as well as North Africa and the Middle East."[1] Indeed, the clash of cultures, smells, bodies, and aesthetics held within this space influenced *cane/cain*. Set against a series of xenophobic attacks in Johannesburg and surrounding areas in 2008, *cane/cain* explores an encounter between two men, Aben, an Afro-Indian business owner in Fordsburg who grew up in rural KwaZulu-Natal, and Tariq, a recent Pakistani immigrant, who sells freshly squeezed sugarcane juice as an informal trader in Fordsburg. Project *cane/cain* deliberately disrupts the ways in which the local and national press represented the xenophobic attacks as black-on-black violence. Xenophobic violence in South Africa is often represented as attacks between local South African blacks and Africans from the rest of the continent. Such eruptions of violence, which are deadly, have become a characteristic of the postapartheid milieu. The rise of xenophobic attacks against non–South African nationals, refugees, and other vulnerable populations from the rest of the continent and from South Asia reflects the ongoing economic crisis and underdevelopment in a country where the unemployment rates have systematically increased since the 1990s. The attacks reflect deeply embedded anxieties over who is the authentic national subject (autochthonous) of the postapartheid state and, therefore, who is truly entitled to enjoy the nation. The xenophobic attacks reveal the limits of South African nationalism, where those who are not native to South Africa are violently abjected.

The xenophobic attacks bring these two men, both rendered out of place differently in Johannesburg, into close proximity (bodily, psychically, and historically), which results in a brief sexual encounter between them. It reimagines the violent and traumatic history of the sugarcane plantations as a site of sexual erotic excess. Even though Tariq and Aben spend only one night together, the film uses this fleeting moment to explore and imagine the complex entanglements between an Afro-Indian man from the indentured class and a working class/working poor Pakistani immigrant. By reading *cane/cain* in relationship to Mlangeni's photoseries, I am interested in how these artforms work against and complicate simplistic identitarian categories (straight, gay, Indian, black, rural, and urban) to reveal forms of intimacies between men shaped within rural and small-town spaces. Whereas *Men Only* and *Country Girls* examine intraethnic relations between black African men, *cane/cain* examines intraethnic intimacies between two men historically from the Indian subcontinent, further complicating the category of the (Afro) Indian in South Africa. Through my queer curatorial practice of juxtaposing these two bodies of work, this chapter also expands on how we understand Afro-Indian/South Asian relations in contemporary South Africa.

Positioned together, these projects offer nuanced articulations of sexuality and same-sex intimacies alongside sites associated with trauma and social death. Importantly, these projects allow us to understand how within the "Zones of Black [and blackened] Death" emerge "new states of being for Black [and blackened] life forms" (Walcott 2021, 34). The forms of queer world-making I analyze in this chapter reveal forms of queer-kinship structures and intimacies as sites through which marginalized subjects negotiate the violence of unbelonging in postapartheid South Africa. Within and alongside these sites of slow death, Rinaldo Walcott notes that "Black life-forms survive by both mastering the conditions under which life proceeds and simultaneously deforming those conditions so that they might have access to selves beyond the degrading violence of everyday life" (34). I am interested in forms of queer world-making that emerge out of unlikely spaces: rural and small-town South Africa. Thus, this chapter disrupts the overdetermined relationship between the urban center and LGBTIQ+ politics, which folds into the Afro-normative nation's narrative of linear progress and development. This chapter explores how marginalized subjects create alternative forms of socialities, reframing how we think about queerness and embodiment. I am interested in kinship formations and forms of queer world-making that emerge within feminine and/or feminized spaces—the rural and the small town.

The shift from the urban center to the margins (rural and small towns) is important to my concept of *indenture aesthetics*. Rural and small-town South Africa exists in an alternative spatial and temporal framework that rubs against the narrative of newness associated with postapartheid South Africa. In the previous chapter, I examined Khan's and Modisakeng's invitations to suspend nation-time through their aesthetics of slow death. Khan's and Modisakeng's works foreclose the possibility of black futurity within the afterlife of colonial apartheid. In this chapter, I am interested in how rural and small-town South Africa disrupts Afro-normative time. I seek to understand what possibilities emerge when time slows down. How can such a temporal lag, a fracture within the neoliberal logics of Afro-normativity, open a space to understand the emergence of alternative life-forms within the ongoing context of slow death?

This chapter curates the aesthetic practices of two artists who grew up in rural South Africa. Sabelo Mlangeni was born in the Mpumalanga Province, in a town called Driefontein (Three-fountain). Mpumalanga borders the KwaZulu-Natal Province and the Kingdom of Eswatini, the last absolute monarchy in Africa. Mlangeni migrated to Johannesburg when he turned twenty-one, encountering the "big city" for the first time. In Driefontein, Mlangeni worked as an assistant "in the ramshackle studio of a village photographer, Mrs. C. S. Mavuso" (Madondo 2017, 56). Johannesburg disoriented him. He felt alienated and has referred to the city as a "non-home." Mlangeni discovered the Market Photo Workshop and enrolled for a thirteen-week introduction to photography course. Thus, Mlangeni turned to photography to develop a visual language to communicate his feelings of displacement and alienation in Johannesburg. From early on in his career as a photographer, Mlangeni has used the camera to develop an intimacy with those who live on the margins of society, those shadow figures who challenge notions of black freedom as routed through Afro-normativity. Although he is based in Johannesburg, Mlangeni is interested in rural and small-town South Africa, shifting his gaze (and lens) from the problematics of freedom within the urban (Johannesburg) to intimate and creative practices of freedom as exercised by men and gay, trans, and gender-nonconforming folk who live outside of the city.

In chapter 1, I examined my own movement from rural KwaZulu-Natal to Johannesburg. The displacement I encountered in the city informed my constant return to rural KwaZulu-Natal. The rural is central to my exploration of memory, history, desire, and pleasure in the afterlife of indentureship. I have always understood my queerness, in terms of sexuality and femininity, as part of a larger queer social world that emerges out of rural and small towns. Here, I mobilize queer to shift from the domain of sexuality to an understanding of nonnormativity more broadly. More specifically, I use the term *queer* to suggest that those racialized subjects who live in rural and small-town South Africa exist in an alternative temporal and spatial framework that rubs against the logics of Afro-normativity. The histories of displacement, relocation, and underdevelopment of rural and small-town South Africa have largely rendered these spaces zones of abjection and waste. I argue that these spaces are feminine and feminized spaces—spaces that must be submerged in order to secure the narrative of postapartheid freedoms. The femininization of these spaces is indicative of the ways in which normativity is elusive and belonging is largely rendered impossible for those black/ened subjects who continue to carve livable lives out of their abject positionality. I am interested in how new life-forms and queer-kinship structures emerge within such spaces and what they reveal about the relationship between pleasure, freedom, and the mundane. Rural and small towns are not associated with queer pleasures and/or queer freedoms. Furthermore, while Mlangeni's photoseries offers an archive of black gay world-making in small-town and rural South Africa, there is an absence of material on Afro-Indian (queer) world-making in this context. My creative work is a response to this absence.

Queering the Rural and Small-Town South Africa

In the *At Home* series, Mlangeni explores the long-term effects of male migrancy to cities and the ways in which labor migration has shaped rural life. *At Home* is an important series because it focuses on the effects of labor migration in rural South Africa, rather than the problematic relationship between the urban and black masculinity, which has been a recurring trope in cinema, television, and visual culture more broadly. In this series of black and white photos, Mlangeni captures those left behind—the young and the old—when men migrate to the cities to find work. The migration to cities did not sever these men's relationship to the rural. Rendered temporary and out of place within the city, black African urban immigrants maintained strong links to the rural. This series of images offers a sharp contrast to Mlangeni's series titled *Men Only*. The *At Home* series consists of a number of landscape photos of the rural environment, emphasizing its expansiveness and sublime beauty (plate 22). Some of the photos are empty of human life-forms, while others are portrait-style photos of women, children, and older men. Across this body of work, Mlangeni focuses on the mundane and rhythms of everyday life.

The exhibition catalogue notes: "For those 'left behind at home,' life is slow and seemingly empty; the landscape assumes unreal contours, and light and dust make everything look as if suspended in time. These places, where many urban immigrants have their roots, are portrayed as spaces of waiting, seen through the filter of memory. The villages possess a distinct tranquility and spaciousness even though there is poor sanitation, teenage pregnancy, lack of basic information and an increasing number of orphans."[2] Shot in black and white, with the majority also shot outdoors, the photos exude a sense of beauty and aesthetic appeal. Haunting and ethereal, the photos evoke the suspension between memory and nostalgia. There is a fullness to the frame of the images, capturing a sense of suspension between the past and the present, and official history and ancestral memory, routed through the vulnerable and feminized—women, children, and the aged. The empty rural landscapes direct us to the theft of human life, which was one of the main characteristics of colonialism and imperialism, stretching from the era of slavery to the present. Young, able-bodied men were stolen, recruited, and coerced into labor regimes that reduced them to replaceable units of labor, which fueled the capitalist economies of the world. Southern Africa is no different. Mlangeni's series offers a feminine and feminized representation of the rural, directing us to these larger histories and their legacies in contemporary South Africa.

In a photo from this series titled, *Portrait of a Family, Msibi* (2008), an older woman sits outdoors on a chair in front of a white cloth (plate 23). The white cloth provides a glaring backdrop to the photo. Shot outdoors, the white cloth is draped on a wire fence-like structure and is held up on the right by another woman, who appears middle-aged. The older woman (whom we would refer to as *gogo*, the Zulu word for grandmother) is impeccably dressed in a long skirt, blouse, and headwrap made from the same material. She wears a long-sleeved top under her blouse and a pair of black shoes. The sunlight is intense and bounces off the white makeshift backdrop, subduing the blackness of her face. She holds her hands together on her lap. Her feet rest on a scratchy patch of grass. She gazes directly into the camera, frowning in the sunlight. The woman who stands to the right, possibly a daughter or granddaughter, is dressed similarly, but wears lighter-colored clothing. The older woman's body is thin and frail and appears to be held tightly, whereas the younger woman is fuller and rounder. In this family portrait, men and children are absent. It implicates colonial-apartheid-era migrant labor practices in the disruption of the black African family structure and the creation of a context where women were left behind in the rural areas as men were forced to temporarily relocate to the cities. Importantly, this portrait's emphasis on the figure of the grandmother directs us to the burden placed on older women to take care of children, grandchildren, and sick, injured, and disabled husbands and sons, who return to the farms when their bodies can no longer provide the labor necessitated by capitalism. What does the absence of children in this portrait reveal about the gendered afterlives of colonial apartheid and black/ened futurity? When I first encountered this photo, I was struck by its similarity with the family photo I examined in the introduction, of my own great-grandmother seated outdoors, surrounded by her daughters and their children. Although the experiences of these two women cannot be conflated across time and space, I am interested in how in both photos, the notion of the family (the Afro-Indian family and the black African family) is routed through the figures of the grandmother in the afterlife of colonial apartheid. Shot in rural South Africa, both photos resonate aesthetically, enabling us to read tropes of blackening and its relationship to coercive labor regimes across these different migration routes.

In rural Africa, the term *feminization* has been employed by social scientists to understand the relationship between gender and poverty. Women's studies professor, Claire C. Robertson (1998) traces the relationship between African women and poverty to European colonialism and neocolonial modes of governance that have further impoverished the African continent, with particularly detrimental effects on women. She writes: "African women perform approximately 80 per cent of the routine farm labor on the continent, with high variations from place to place" (167). Robertson identifies the following as "important roots of the feminization of poverty in Africa": "Lack of access by women to education, well paid jobs, land, and capital; an unequal division of labor; and a pervasive male dominance that promotes all of the above, spread and reinforced by colonialism, international monopoly capitalism, and structural readjustment programs" (199). However, African women are not merely victims. She examines how communal/community efforts, led by both rural and urban African women, are leading the way to improve the lives of Africans within local and national contexts.

Other social science scholars have studied the feminization of migration in rural South Africa. In their study "Gendered Patterns of Migration in Rural South Africa" (2013, 528), focusing on the period after 1994, Camlin et al. note that "women were more likely to undertake any migration," and in the post-apartheid period, African women are more likely to migrate from one rural area to another. Historically, African men have been associated with urban migration. However, research indicates that "since the late 19th and early 20th centuries . . . women have migrated independently to and within South Africa" (Camlin et al. 2013, 529). Many African women who migrated to the cities worked as domestic laborers and in the informal sectors, "which evolved in tandem with the male migrant labor system" (529).[3]

At Home offers a complex narrative of the rural through the tropes of waiting and suspension. It is an articulation of placeness that rubs against the out-of-placeness historically associated with the city. However, Mlangeni's photos offer an articulation of placeness forged out of regimes of displacement and strategic underdevelopment. This is not an essentialized representation of ruralness most often routed through the white/European gaze. Importantly, these are feminized tropes that direct us to the familiar and the minor. There are many ways to read the catalogue's emphasis on waiting. The subjects in the photos could be waiting for their husbands, fathers, and sons to return during the off-seasons. However, for me, Mlangeni is also suggesting that these people living within rural South Africa are still waiting for freedom and the promises of the newness of the new South Africa. Excluded from the narrative of linear and progress development, these are the new black/ened Others.

The rural in South Africa is complicated and heterogenous, and experiences of rurality shift according to race and class. The rural has also become a contested site over the redistribution of land after 1994. The contestation often occurs between white Afrikaner Boers, a class of farmers who have for decades claimed ownership over the land and have controlled the agricultural industry, and local black African communities, held captive within these spaces as an exploited laboring force.[4] In KwaZulu-Natal, the ownership of many sugarcane plantations shifted from the hands of white settlers to Indians, many of whom are descendants of indentured laborers. Whether white or Indian owned, what remains constant is that black African men and women, from rural South Africa and neighboring countries, continue to provide the main labor source. In an online article titled "Farmers with New Land Reform Process" published on the *Global Citizen* website on October 6, 2020, Khanyi Mlaba writes: "Although they form the majority of the population, black South Africans currently own the least amount of land for farming and agriculture (4%), followed closely by Indian people (5%)—in comparison, white people own 72% of farms and agricultural holdings owned by individuals." Given the complex histories of migration, settlement, overlapping coercive labor practices, and colonial missionary interventions, rural South Africa is a complex space. In the anthology *Queering the Countryside: New Frontier in Queer Rural Studies* (Gray et al. 2016, 8), which focuses on rurality in the United States, the editors define the rural as an "astoundingly complex assemblage of peoples, places, and positionalities." This is true also for South Africa. Furthermore, rural and small towns are associated with slowness or backwardness (as compared to cities), and this attribute is also often used to describe rural and small-town inhabitants. Rurality is not "simply a name we give to sparsely populated regions, [it] is imagined to be a distinctive way of life complete with its own traditions, institutions, and worldviews" (1). Within the popular imaginary, rural areas and small towns evoke religious and gender-sexual conservatism as well as right-wing politics. These structures of conservatism could very easily map the rural as heteronormative. However, centering a racial analytic positions rural and small towns as femininized spaces that can reveal something different about South African blackness and the queer limits of Afro-normativity. This is my entryway into thinking through the relationship between gender, sexuality, and rurality in a context where queer world-making is routed through the urban. This chapter thus unsettles how the urban organizes our fantasies of (queer) freedom.

Sabelo Mlangeni and the Femme Aesthetic of Black-Queer World-Making in *Country Girls* and *Men Only*

In a portrait photo titled *Palisa* (2009), Palisa poses in front of a coal mine dump. She wears a chunky sweater, buttoned at the top, just reaching mid-thigh length. She poses with her right leg extended and her left hand positioned on her left hip. Palisa wears shiny, silky stockings, medium-high heeled shoes, and sunglasses. Her head tilts toward the camera, and her mouth is slightly opened as if she exhaled as the photo was shot. Palisa's stance and her attention to beauty and fashion are indicative of her pleasure in being photographed. Her shadow extends behind her and out of the photographic frame. She stands on a lawn in what appears to be a backyard. The landscape is dry and arid, and this aesthetic is heightened because this series, like many of Mlangeni's works, is shot in black and white. The tree to the left of the image has a couple of leaves still hanging on, indicating that this photo was shot in winter. The wire fencing behind Palisa provides a permeable boundary between the backyard and the mine, which rises toward the sky. The side of a car is visible to the right. The black-and-white aesthetic of the photo flattens out the image in a provocative way. Palisa's posture, stance, and her embodiment of pleasure rub against the coldness of the winter highveld and the history of the area—deeply embedded within the mining economy—that has constructed black bodies as out-of-place. Palisa's embodiment of beauty and pleasure disrupts the death-worlds of capital as represented by the mine dump behind her. The mountain behind her is a site of excess and abjection formed out of the waste by-product of mining. Palisa, gay, queer, and femme, slowly erodes the boundaries of authentic blackness, representing a different but interrelated kind of excessiveness

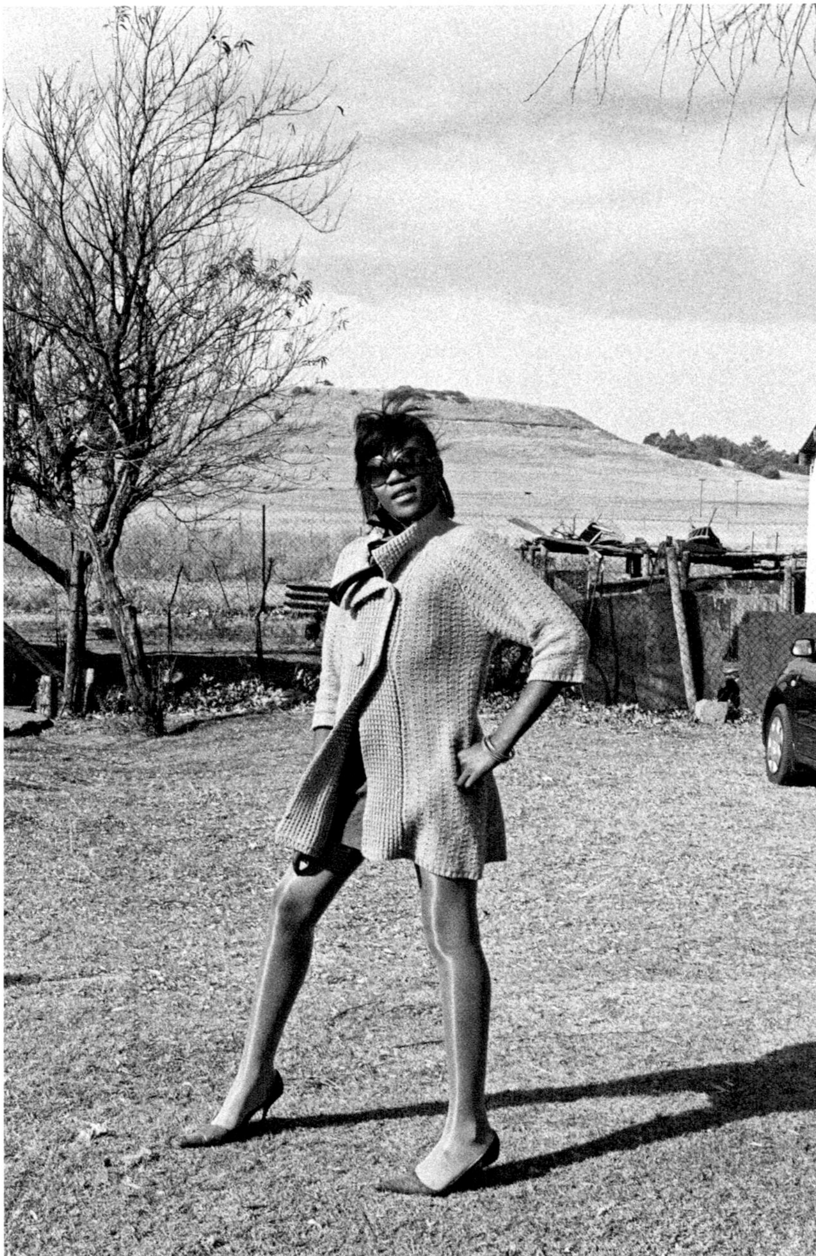

FIGURE 3.1. *Palisa* (2009). Image courtesy of the artist and blank projects, Cape Town. © Sabelo Mlangeni.

and abjection. Mlangeni's photos offer an articulation of claiming space and actively constructing and fashioning subjecthood in an unlikely area, a rural area not usually associated with black-queer world-making.

Mlangeni's photo series *Country Girls* focuses on rural areas and small towns like "Driefontein, Ermelo, Platrand, Piet Retief and Secunda—nodes of mining, agriculture, forestry, and coal-fed power stations" (Reid 2010, 3). The series, according to Graeme Reid, offers "an intimate portrait of gay life in the South African countryside." It focuses on forms of intimacy and self-fashioning that develop in "bleak environments where township life is rough and poor." The title of the series plays with the urban/rural divide and troubles the dominant idea that the urban/city is the place par excellence for the realization of a fully modern gay/queer identity. Reid captures this dynamic as follows: "Narratives of gay community formation are almost invariably city-based and tell a familiar story: the relative autonomy of city life, the loosening of family and kinship bonds and the wage labor economy free individuals to follow their personal desire and to explore more varied erotic lives" (3). Mlangeni questions the relationship between the city and black queer self-determination. *Country Girls*, like *Men Only*, complicates the categories "gay" and/or "queer" to reveal alternative kinship formations and forms of sociality that straddle the modern/traditional binary in sophisticated ways. The series juxtapose outdoor scenes, like the one described in the paragraph above, with intimate indoor scenes that focus on the daily rhythms of domestic life. The grittiness of domestic life and the different forms of labor constitutive of the everyday rub against the intimate portraits of the country girls, posing either on their own or with their lovers. This series focuses on the labor of creating livable lives and the practices of care and love between the girls and between the girls and their lovers that is framed through the ordinary. Mlangeni's series reveal the many ways in which black queers in rural areas create their own home-spaces as spaces of refuge, reconfiguring the everyday through alternative kinship formations.

The exhibition catalogue begins with two photos that invite the viewer into the home-space and the intimacies that constitute the everyday. In *Bafana Getting Ready for Work* (2009), a soft-focus photograph, we see Bafana standing with his back against the camera, wearing a stained towel around his waist. The photo captures Bafana in movement. It appears as if he is walking toward a door. In the frame of the photo, we see a couch with clothes and other materials strewn across it, a dresser on the right, and a table with pots and other kitchen objects. In another photo titled *Kgomotso, Palm Dove Lodge, Ermelo* (2008), Mlangeni photographs Kgomotso in a kitchen, standing with his hands in a bowl of soapy water. Kgomotso could be washing the dishes, or he could be

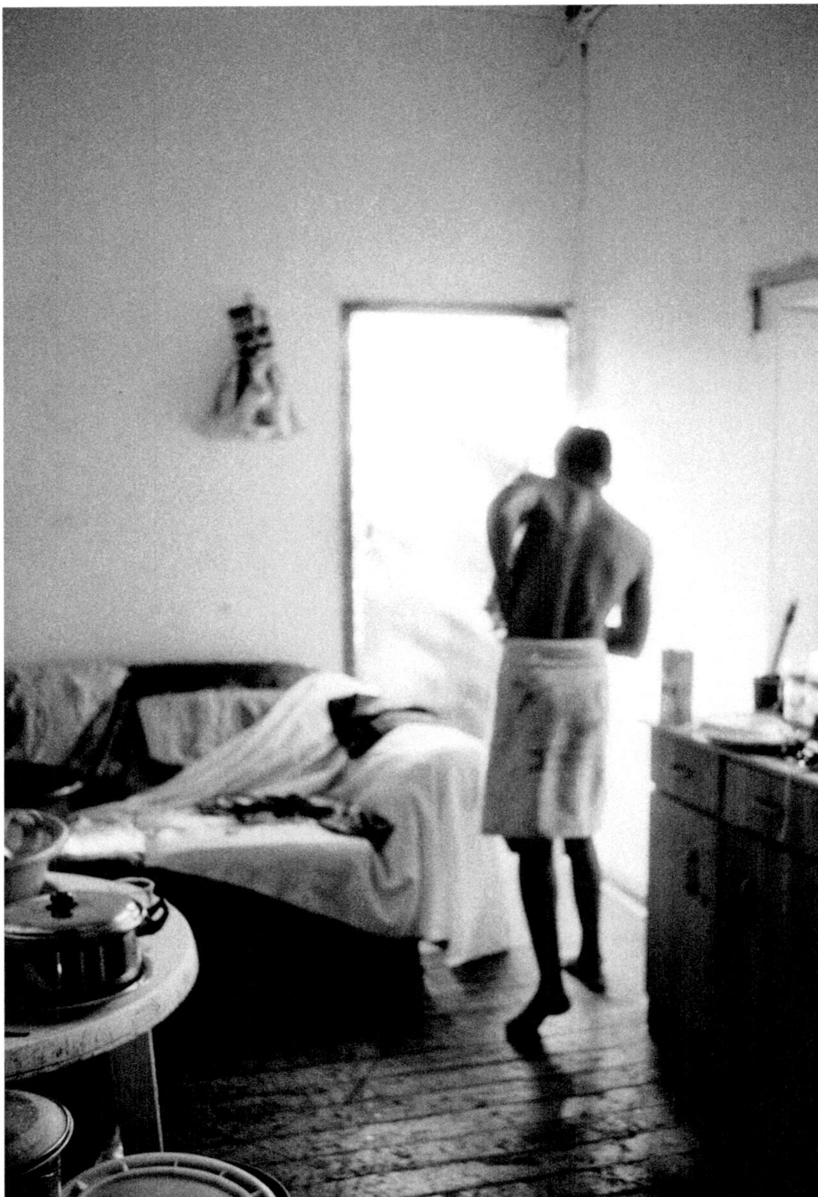

FIGURE 3.2. *Bafana getting ready for work* (2009). Image courtesy of the artist and blank projects. © Sabelo Mlangeni.

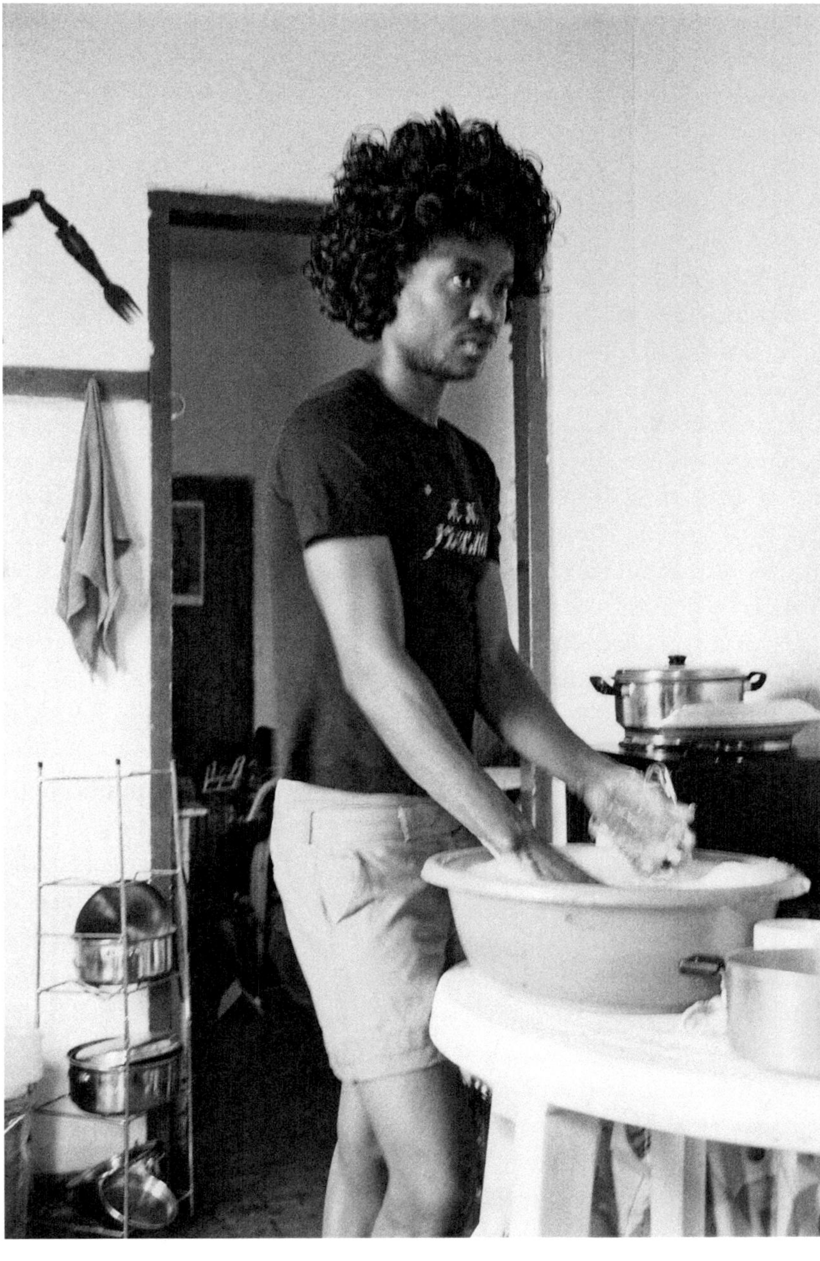

FIGURES 3.3. Kgomotso, *Palm Dove Lodge, Ermelo* (2008). Image courtesy of the artists and black projects, Cape Town. © Sabelo Mlangeni.

having a wash, meaning bathing or cleaning himself in the kitchen. The photo suggests the absence of running water and clearly demarcated living spaces associated with modern standards of living. By focusing on the interior of the home-space, Mlangeni "alludes to" the hardships of everyday life in rural and small-town South Africa, but his gaze is not voyeuristic. He does not glamorize or spectacularize poverty and marginalization. Rather, these two photographs have a soft aesthetic that I refer to as a *femme aesthetic*. It challenges the ways in which we have been conditioned to see and understand poverty in South Africa, especially as it relates to black spaces and black bodies.

In many of the photos, Mlangeni focuses on the "routines of everyday life" (Reid 2010). Thus, the labor of self-fashioning evident in the portrait titled *Palisa* brings into focus the labor of "personal grooming" in a context where running water and electricity—those aspects of modern living that we do not think about on an everyday basis—are largely absent. Indeed, this characterizes rural and small-town living and necessitates a different understanding of temporality. In his *At Home* series, Mlangeni offers a feminine aesthetic of waiting, which shifts to a femme aesthetic of suspension in *Country Girls*. In the two images I described above, the body is represented in suspended movement. It captures a moment or movement, a presentness, between the past and the future. Mlangeni's soft-focus photos of quotidian moments suspended in time direct us to a femme aesthetic of temporality.

However, the home-space is not only a space of lack. Mlangeni also photographs scenes of intimacy and joy. In an indoor group photo titled *Talent and His Girlfriends* (2009), we see Talent, in the background in soft-focus, styling his girlfriend's hair. The girlfriend is seated, and she is caught in a moment of laughter. The woman holds a baby against her chest. She looks downward at the baby, while the lady who is seated gazes at her looking at the baby. This photo captures many overlapping scenes of intimacy and joy. Whether his interlocutors are lounging on a sofa, seated on a chair smoking a cigarette, or lying on a bed contemplatively, Mlangeni captures his subjects in quiet and intimate moments that suggest an aesthetic of pleasure rather than waiting. Importantly, the mundane rhythm of domestic life opens the space to create alternative kinship structures that disrupt the relationship between family, blood, and belonging. The home-space is located as a "social hub" and figures as a safe space in a country generally hostile to black queers, particularly those who are femme, gender nonconforming, or engaged in cross-dressing.

The series eloquently shifts from intimate domestic scenes of everyday life to portrait photoshoots outdoors. Whereas the indoor scenes revealed the grittiness of everyday life in small-town South Africa, the outdoor portraits are clear

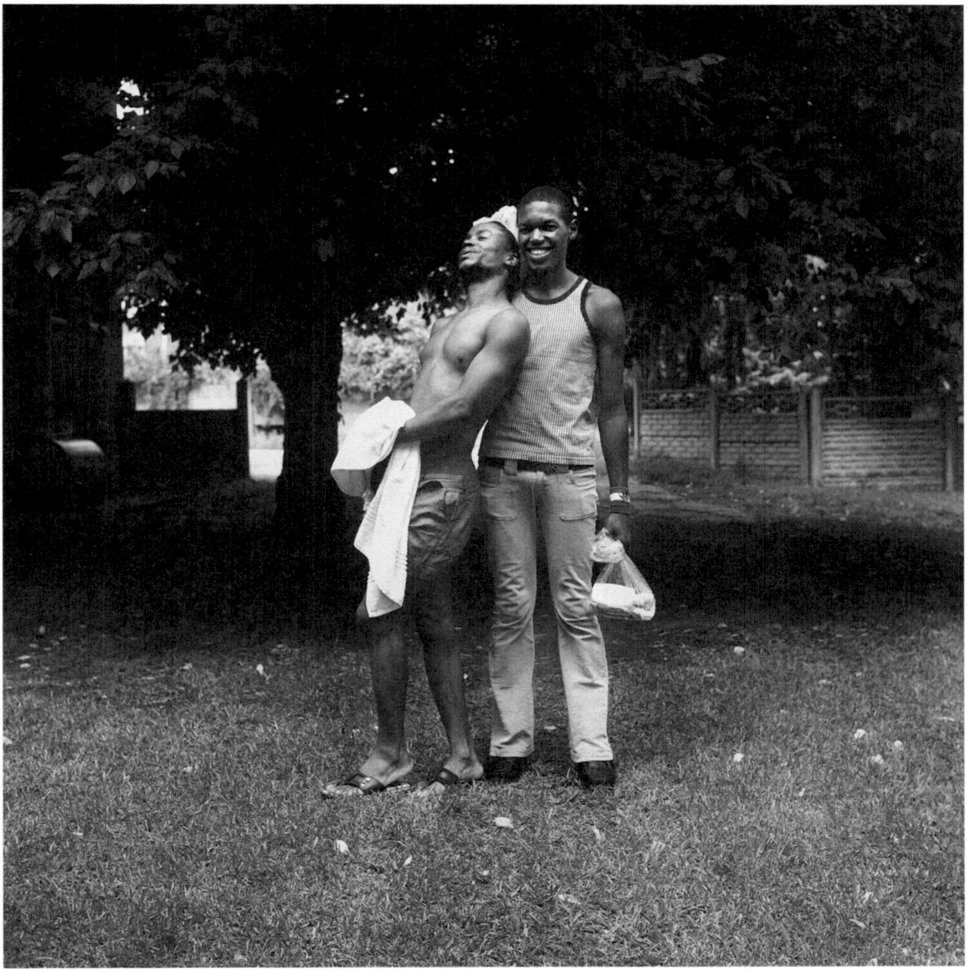

FIGURE 3.4. *Kgomotso and his three days date* (2008). Image courtesy of the artist and blank and space projects, Cape Town. © Sabelo Mlangeni.

and in focus. The portraits of the various ladies, posing playfully and sometimes confrontationally, direct us to their pleasure in being photographed. Some outdoor portraits capture scenes of intimacy between the girls and their boyfriends, referred to as "gents" (Reid 2010, 4). In *Kgomotso and His three days date* (2008), two men stand under a large tree. One of the men, wearing jeans and a vest and holding a plastic bag, gazes directly at the camera, smiling widely. To his left, another man, his date, leans into him, resting his shoulders against the other man's chest. Although the men face away from each other, their bodies fit together comfortably and intimately. The leaning man is shirtless, and the light reflects off his skin, sensually accentuating his toned muscles. The light that bounces off sensually from his skin resonates with the glow evident on Kgomotso's face, capturing a scene of joy and pleasure between these two black men. In another outdoor photo, *Couple Bheki and Sipho* (2009), two men sit under a tree on a white cloth. The hands and legs of others are evident in the photo. The two men, who are the focus of the photograph, lean into each other as they gaze directly into the camera. Dressed in pants and shirts, their bodies flow together, suggesting an intimacy and familiarity between them. The man seated on the left smiles softly, while the man on the right gazes directly, with his lips gently pursed. Mlangeni's photos capture a sense of joy, pleasure, and satisfaction.

Country Girls is important because Mlangeni emphasizes the importance of visibility and visuality in the making of black queer subjecthood. His body of work, like that of the visual activist Zanele Muholi, is concerned with constructing an archive of black queer visibility. Mlangeni's photos emphasize the ways in which his interlocutors are actively *imagining* and creating a future in the present, which I refer to as a *future-present*. The relationship between black (slow) death, indicative of the mine dump that is captured in the background of the photo titled *Palisa*, and black-queer world-making is evident throughout Mlangeni's project. However, the juxtapositioning of Palisa posing in front of the mine dump emphasizes her pleasure in being photographed (her posture and stance, dress and adornment, and attention to beauty as an everyday practice of resistance) as well as her desire to live a future in the present. Throughout this series, Mlangeni's interlocutors claim space and exercise their right to belong within unlikely spaces—rural and small-town South Africa—where the emergence of vibrant interconnected black queer cultures is largely rendered unimaginable. This is evident through the photographs, but most provocatively evoked in a photo titled *Piet Retief*.

In *Piet Retief*, Mlangeni photographs a group of ladies walking confidently on a residential street. The ladies are dressed casually, wearing T-shirts, short pants or jeans. In typical Mlangeni style, the photo captures the ladies in movement—they are walking toward the camera. The photograph is shot in soft-focus, where the image flattens out. The ladies do not stand out spectacularly from the environment. Rather, Mlangeni's femme aesthetic—where the background and the foreground, the environment and the subjects, bleed into one another—offers a critique of settler-colonial logics in South Africa, and their afterlives, that construct black/ened bodies as out-of-place. The town Piet Retief was named after the man Piet Retief, one of the Boer leaders of

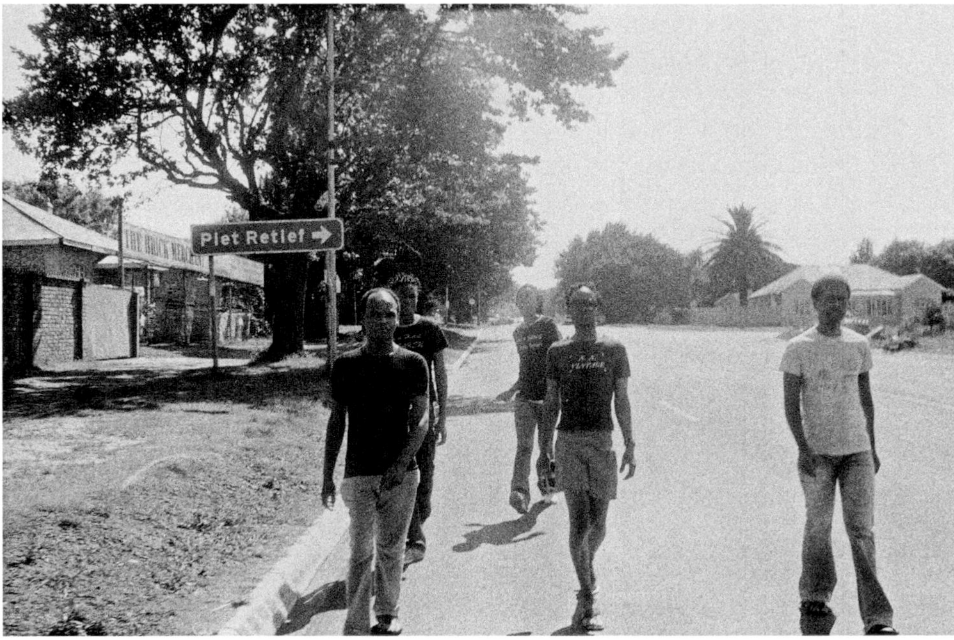

FIGURE 3.5. *Piet Retief* (2009). Image courtesy of the artist and blank projects, Cape Town. © Sabelo Mlangeni.

the Great Trek (1835–1840s). The Great Trek refers to the movement of approximately twelve to fourteen thousand Afrikaners from the Cape Colony to the interior of the country "in rebellion against the policies of the British government and the search for fresh pastureland."[5] It resulted in the defeat and displacement of African peoples throughout the interior and the settlement of Indigenous lands.

Thus, Mlangeni offers a critique of settler-colonial-apartheid policies and practices, which have strategically dislocated and continuously rendered black bodies out of place within these spaces. His critique is powerful because it emerges from the positionality of black queer folks who are most vulnerable and subject to regimes of everyday violence. It is undeniably a radical act for black queer (femme) men to craft their own modes of belonging and kinship structures in spaces that continue to render black people out-of-place. Through this series, Mlangeni's interlocutors offer complex articulations of freedom routed through visuality and visibility. Black queer studies scholar Xavier Livermon (2012a, 300) argues that "visibility refers not only to the act of seeing and being seen but also to processes through which individuals make themselves known in communities as queer subjects." Mlangeni's femme aesthetic of temporality functions as a site of reorientation, revealing black life-forms and queer world-making practices where joy, pleasure, and love rub against the grittiness of everyday life in rural South Africa.

Throughout *Country Girls* the quotidian is associated with a temporal lag, which allows us to understand the emergence of black queer life-forms within the context of slow death. *Country Girls* appears as a photo-essay in Graeme Reid's book *How to Be a Real Gay: Gay Identities in Small-Town South Africa* (2013b), which is the first monograph to examine black gay communities in small-town South Africa. What is evident throughout Mlangeni's photos are the ways in which black queer identities and sexual practices in small towns and rural areas replicate rather than disrupt the gender binary. There is a stark distinction between *ladies*, who, through self-fashioning and practices of beatification, embody hyperfemininity, and their *gents*, who embody hegemonic and normative notions of masculinity. Reid writes: "The dichotomy between masculine and feminine has a profound effect on processes of self-identification. Making a clear distinction between who is a lady and who is a gent—and the related idea that ladies can only be sisters to each other and only fall in love with a gent" (274).

Many of the interlocutors in Reid's study as well as in Mlangeni's photos are black gay hairdressers, men whose careful negotiation of the gender binary has enabled them to flourish in small towns. At the time of his research in 2013, Graeme notes that the hairdressing industry in small towns had been dominated by black gay men who present as ultrafeminine. Feminine gay hairdressers, because of their ability to create feminine beauty among their female clients, often achieve celebrity status in these small towns. Reid notes, "Gays are perceived to be particularly adept at producing femininity among female clients, precisely because they are constantly performing femininity themselves" (Reid 2013b, 275). Male femininity in this case functions on numerous levels. It is a form of self-identification and self-realization, a way of gaining acceptance within conservative communities, and a strategy of survival within, what FAKA (examined in the next chapter) describes as a cisheterotopic African society. Indeed, in this case, femininity is pivotal to the constructions of community, erotic relationships, and other forms of kinship structures.

By embodying and performing hyperfemininity, these ladies do not rupture the gender binary and thus do not directly "threaten hegemonic masculinity or undermine patriarchy" (Reid 2013b, 276). A functionalist reading of the gender binary in this context does not leave room for pleasure, desire, and joy that is evident throughout Mlangeni's photos. The performances of hyperfemininity, unstable and fluid, may not "threaten hegemonic masculinity," but they push against and challenge the association between blackness and compulsory heteronormativity. Through femme embodiment and the intimacies of everyday life, these black rural queer folks create social worlds that challenge categories and binaries of gender and sexuality, even as they creatively embody and play with these same categories. Male (hyper) femininity creates small and minor lines of flight away from the normative, slowly eroding the relationship between blackness and heterosexuality that secures the Afro-normative nation-state's narrative of linear progress and development. However, hyperfemininity, a positionality of vulnerability, does not provide refuge from various forms of violence generally associated with women and the feminine, like gender-based violence and high transmission rates of HIV.

Importantly, Mlangeni reveals the labor of black-queer world-making through the vulnerable bodies of the ladies. By employing a femme aesthetic of temporality, Mlangeni foregrounds the labor of creating visibility and the importance of visuality as subversive and disruptive. The creation of livable lives through cultural labor (performance, fashion, beauty, feminization, photography) is an active and ongoing creation of the "very liberation promised by the constitution and giving freedom its substantive meaning" (Livermon 2012a, 301).

The creation of queer-kinship formations and black queer social worlds in unlikely spaces is also evident in Mlangeni's series *Men Only*. In this series, Mlangeni focuses on the intimacies of everyday life (the pain, the pleasure, the joy, and the formation of queer-kinship structures) in a hostel, initially built to house migrant mineworkers. In the exhibition catalogue, Federica Angelucci (2009) writes: "Only men are allowed into this and other such hostels giving rise to a certain kind of curiosity about life inside. In the collective imaginary, they are places of violence, sexual abuse and illegal trafficking" (3). Mlangeni notes that "these imaginings . . . led me to photograph life in these buildings, going beyond the stereotypes and trying to capture the normality that exists in an abnormal, unnatural situation" (Mlangeni quoted in Angelucci 2009, 3). In this series of photos, Mlangeni focuses on the everyday—men cooking, bathing, ironing clothes, cutting hair, chatting, smoking together—to access how these displaced men refigure the normal in a context deeply embedded within the plantation and carceral spatial logics of colonial apartheid. The history of mining (see the previous chapter) and its reduction of black migrant workers to fungible units of labor haunt this space and provide context and depth to understand Mlangeni's concern with what everyday life looks and feels like for these men. In this series, Mlangeni's femme aesthetic of temporality directs us to the different forms of labor undertaken by these men to create domestic life

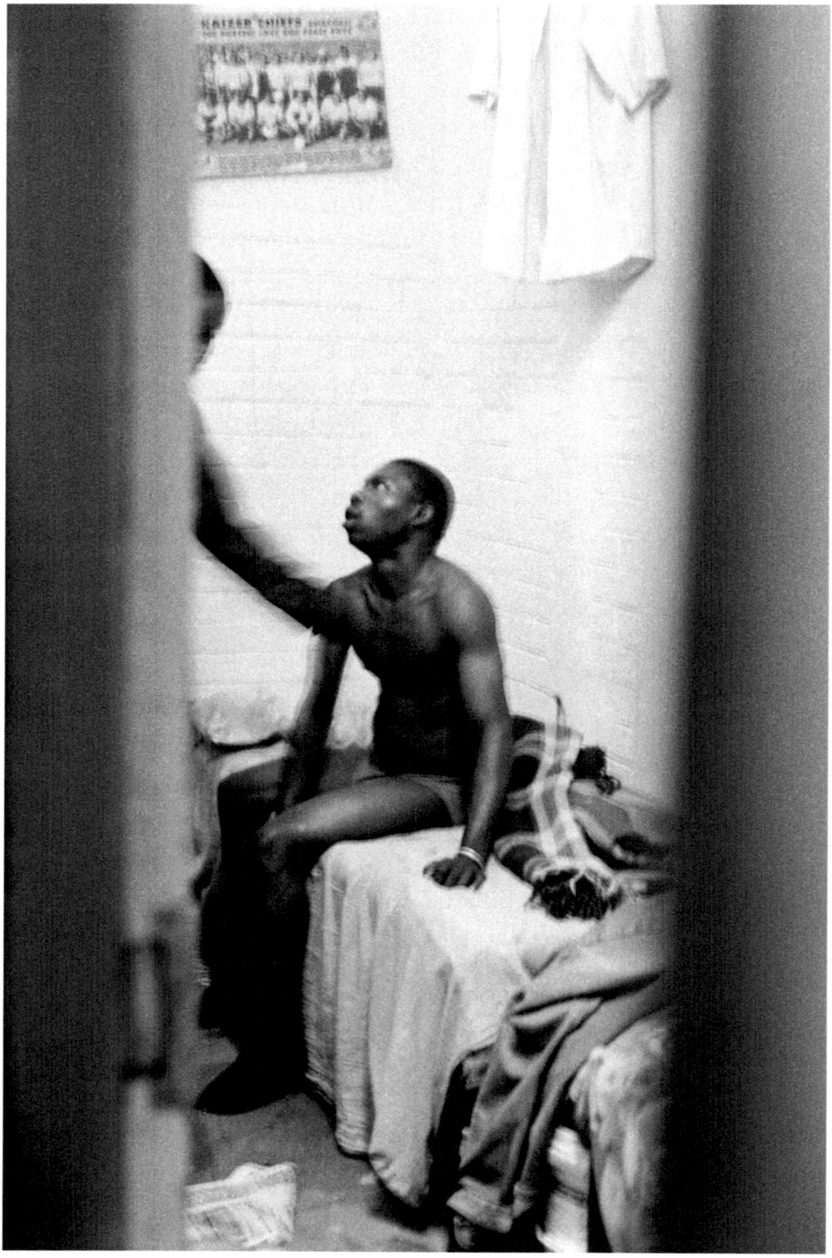

FIGURE 3.6. *Usbali Visits the Hostel* (2008). Image courtesy of the artist and blank projects, Cape Town. © Sabelo Mlangeni.

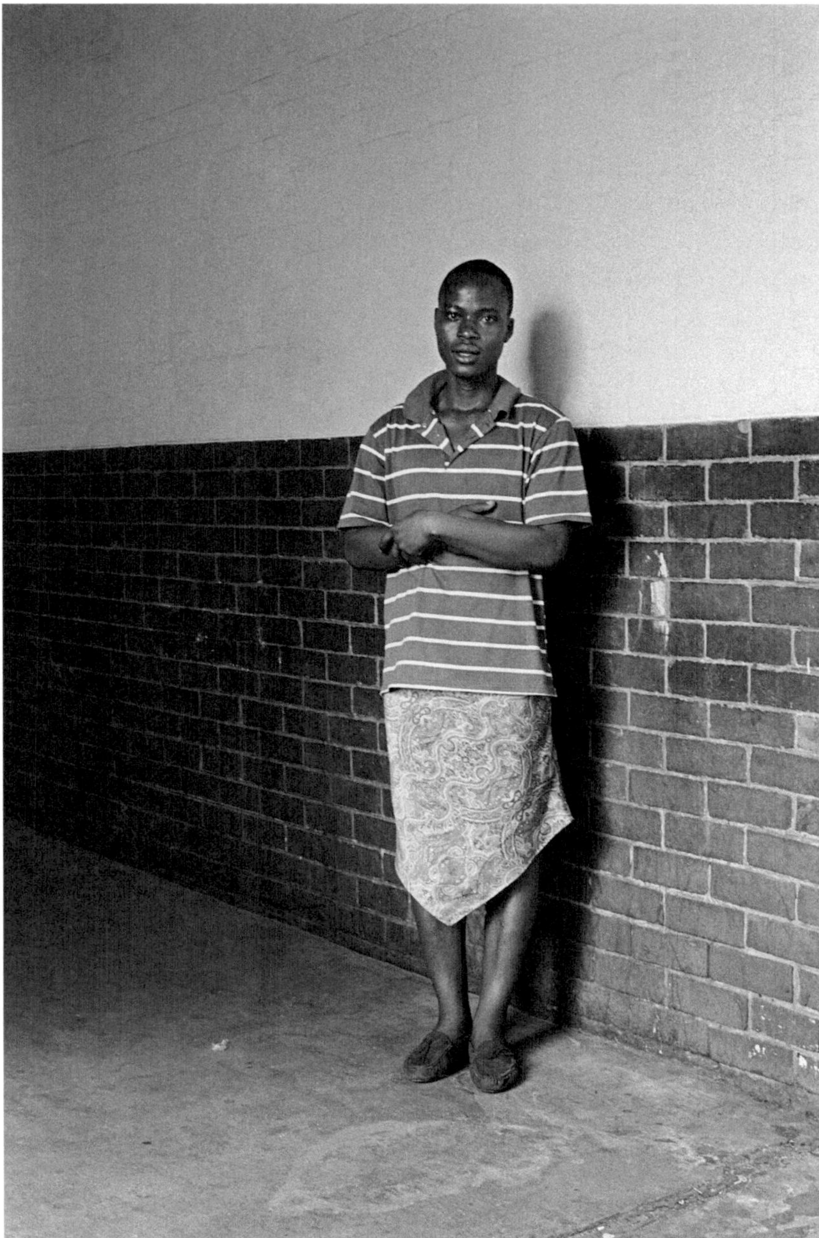

FIGURE 3.7. *Mshana* (2008). Image courtesy of the artist and blank projects, Cape Town. © Sabelo Mlangeni.

and queer-kinship formations. Similarly to *Country Girls*, Mlangeni captures small, intimate, and minor moments between men that direct us to how care, joy, and pleasure inform and shape the everyday.

In his recognizable style, Mlangeni captures portraits of men indoors and outdoors, as well as photos of men in the couple form or in groups. The photos reveal forms of homosocial bonding that disrupt the violent hypermasculinization of the mine worker, as evident in the media and popular culture. In a photo titled *Usbali Visits the Hostel*, Mlangeni captures a moment of intimacy between two men that is heightened through the photo's soft-focus. We see one man, wearing only underwear, sitting on a bed, positioned against a wall painted brick white. He looks up at another man, whose body is mostly obscured by what appears to be an open door. The man who stands reaches his hand toward the chest of the man who sits. It appears as if the hand touches the man who sits. The camera captures the image as they look at each other. In this photo, the meaning of this moment and the relationship between these men is ambiguous and left open to interpretation.

In the photo *Mshana*, Mlangeni captures a portrait of a young man standing against a wall, holding his arms across his lower chest. The young man wears a colored shirt, a skirt, and a pair of black shoes. Interestingly, Mlangeni reveals that what fascinated him about the hostel is that he noticed small enactments of freedom that have been curtailed because of narrow identitarian politics, a politics that have exacerbated the stigma of being called a homosexual. This has resulted in men rejecting all forms of male-male contact and intimacies, from touching to hugging or casually holding hands, in order to assert a masculine identity. In the hostels, he noticed that men did not have such concerns over male-male contact and dress. The man in *Mshana* wears a skirt not because he is gay but because this is a familiar and comfortable outfit. If he walked through the streets of Johannesburg in a skirt, the young man in this photo would be transgressing gender norms and expectations. However, within the space of the hostel, the skirt and forms of male-male intimacies are not transgressive or spectacular but part of the ordinary rhythms of everyday life.

Indeed, the evocation of male-male intimacies in *Men Only* is complex and layered and evokes the phenomenon of "mine marriages" between men in Southern Africa (van Onselen 1985; Moodie 1988; Achmat 1993; Epprecht 2013; Reid 2013b). Much of the earlier work explains the incidences of male-male homoerotic encounters within the context of the mining compounds as "situational homosexuality," which occurred in the absence of women and/or the fear that black urban women were vectors of venereal disease. However, Zackie Achmat (1993) challenges this functionalist approach, which leaves no space to understand how desire and pleasure could have structured these encounters within this context. An interview between Jan Note and Nongoloza, a prominent gang leader (engaged by van Onselen, Epprecht, Reid, and others), indicates that homoerotic practices were much more complex and nuanced than the flattening out of desire and pleasure through the framework of situational homosexuality. Nongoloza has become (in)famous for ordering "his men to have sex with each other or with boy servants rather than with women sometimes in the mid-1890s" (Epprecht 2013, 9). Apparently, this order was given to protect his gang members from sexually transmitted diseases carried by urban black women. In the interview, Nongoloza states: "Even when we were free on the hills South of Johannesburg, some of us had women and others had young men for sexual purposes" (quoted in Reid 2013b, 22, and Achmat 1993, 99). The fuller interview related to this incident complicates the situational homosexuality thesis. The south of Johannesburg would have been rural and undeveloped during the time Nongoloza evokes in this interview. More importantly, Nongoloza's statement evokes pleasure, desire, and autonomy in a context where same-sex practices among men and women were not positioned as deviant or transgressive.[6] In many contexts in Africa and the African diaspora, same-sex erotic relationships existed alongside heterosexual relationships.

Mlangeni's photos in this series and *Country Girls* also complicate the functionalist approach to male-male homoerotic expressions within heteronormative spaces. Mlangeni does this by offering complex articulations of male-male intimacies that may or may not be homosexual. The point is not to recuperate homosexuality to disrupt the ways in which Africa is imagined as heterosexual, but to understand forms of intimacies, pleasure, and joy that escape categorization and the identitarian logics that have sedimented to produce new forms of visibility and legibility around African LGBTIQ+ subjects. Indeed, these articulations of male-male intimacies rub against a larger politic of black queer visibility framed through a human rights discourse. Mlangeni's work enacts a temporal lag by resisting the seduction of contemporary LGBTIQ+ politics and its association with a modern/proper queer subjecthood. From the countryside to migrant hostels, Mlangeni uses a femme aesthetic of temporality to grapple with black life-forms and the formation of queer-kinship structures within and alongside spaces of slow death. His work powerfully evokes the queerness of blackness and the blackness of queerness in the afterlife of colonial apartheid. This is a queerness organized around the displaced, the disenfranchised, the feminine, and the feminized. It cuts across identitarian categories to reveal their limits and their function as a site of capture that continues to curtail black life possibilities. Mlangeni's focus on male-male intimacies provides a way to understand black/ened queer life-forms as "alternative modes of life," which exist "alongside the violence, subjection, exploitation, and racialization that define the modern human" (Weheliye 2014, 2).

Race, Space, and Sugar

The Aesthetics and Poetics of Sensuality in cane/cain

In this section, I return to the sugarcane plantations in rural KwaZulu-Natal (KZN) to examine the aesthetics and poetics of sensuality in my film *cane/cain*. Tongaat is a small rural space (that we refer to as a village) developed along the Indian Ocean and surrounded by sugarcane plantations. It is home to Tongaat-Hulett, which "focuses on cane growing, sugar milling and refining throughout the Southern African region."[7] The growth and development of the sugar industry in Natal is attributed to James Liege Hulett. Hulett, a "Natal planter, industrialist and politician, was born in England and came to South Africa in 1857 at the age of 19. Hulett pioneered the country's sugar industry when he founded the Hulett Company in 1892, which had extensive cane plantations and erected the first sugar mill in 1903."[8] To enter Tongaat today is to enter a different time and space. The richness of the environment, shaped by the tropical climate, rubs against the built environment in surrounding cities like Durban, for instance. Regular electricity cuts (referred to as load-shedding) and disruptions to water supplies initiate a different kind of everydayness that rubs against the promise of newness after 1994. These are exacerbated by the deterioration of roads, infrastructure, and local municipal services. The deterioration and impoverishment of these spaces indicate the precariousness of life in the absence of a future. Within this context, many of the small towns and rural areas have seen major streams of out-migration to cities like Johannesburg and Cape Town. Young adults usually migrate to the cities, leaving behind parents and grandparents. Many fear that their loved ones may not return because, for many, there is no reason to return. Rural KZN, like Mlangeni's representations of rural Mpumalanga, is a feminized place shaped by an alternative rhythm of everyday life. Indeed, for many of us who have lived in this space, time is organized cyclically, informed by planting, growing, and harvesting sugarcane. In *cane/cain*, I attempted to capture this alternative time-space through an aesthetic of the sugarcane plantation that is sensual and lush, where the sublime beauty of the sugarcane rubs against the gritty realities, the pain and pleasure, of everyday life. My own concern with an aesthetic of sensuality in *cane/cain* resonates with Mlangeni's femme aesthetic. Located within rural/small towns, *cane/cain* and Mlangeni's photoseries use different, but interrelated aesthetics to disrupt the spatial and temporal logics of Afro-normativity.

cane/cain was completed in 2011 and debuted at the Wits Arts and Literature Experience (WALE) in Johannesburg, the Durban International Film Festival (DIFF), and the Third South Asian San Francisco International Film Festival in the same year. *cane/cain* was my first foray into short filmmaking and emerged from my own desire to understand an Afro-Indian queer positionality in a country celebrated for its progressive LGBTIQ+ politics. Within the South African public sphere, Afro-Indian intimacies and erotics were largely absent within media and visual culture. This has historically been compounded by the idea that Indians are not artists, curators, and creators but rather doctors, accountants, engineers, and lawyers. When *cane/cain* first screened in Johannesburg in 2011, I spoke about my own desire to see Afro-Indian bodies on screen—this film began as a pedagogical practice in learning how to desire my own body and to position the Afro-Indian body as desirable. Madhumita Lahiri reflects on this when she writes that the film "serves as a vehicle both of identification, and through its narrative focus, of desire" (Lahiri 2018, 208). The film maps "xenophobic intolerance" onto "homoerotic intimacies" to engage questions of sexuality, national and diasporic belonging, historical trajectories of migration, and ethnic and racial conflict (Ebrahim 2017).

The idea for *cane/cain* emerged out of my ongoing engagement with the family photoarchive (explored more fully in chapter 2) and the sensuousness of the sugarcane plantations in oThongathi. I wanted to create a film—a moving-image narrative—that explored male-male intimacies between Indian men. I was certain from the beginning of the project that the film would include a sex scene between two Indian men and that it would attempt to deliberately eroticize the Afro-Indian male body. My desire was to represent the Afro-Indian male form as desirable and as a site/source of pleasure. From a young age, I was more interested in sexual pleasure and ecstasy than in gayness. This was informed by my mother's attention to beauty and sensuality as well as the Indian Evangelical church I attended with my mother and two sisters for years until I left the home-space for Johannesburg. For me, the Evangelical church was an erotic space, dedicated to a particular form of ecstasy, where the body and the spirit merge in moments that disrupt time and space in the individual and collective quest to attain salvation. I grew up in an Indian church from the 1980s to the early 2000s, informed and shaped by the colonial-apartheid-era policies of separate development, but devoid of the politics that shaped (and continue to shape) these social worlds. I have since come to understand that a church, which is consciously apolitical, is both irrelevant and dangerous.

It is undeniable that the church was a site of regulation and surveillance. As a young femme boy-child, I did not embody proper Christian masculinity. However, from what I remember, women and young-girls' dress, comportment, and performances were more violently and insidiously regulated. Within the church, I learned about bodily pleasure and sexual ecstasy. This was routed through the body and performances of the pastor. The pastor was a short, muscular man, always well dressed in tight shirts that accentuated his musculature, and also very aware of his attractiveness and masculine performance. I began to realize that his job, on a Sunday morning, was to take his congregation on a journey—through praise and worship singing, preaching, the casting out of demons, and the saving of souls—where the lucky few entered into an alternative state, one of ecstasy defined by the waving and clapping of hands, speaking in tongues, and falling over when filled with the spirit. The pastor built himself up to a frenzy every Sunday. Sweat poured down his face, creating dark circles around his arms, spit flying across the stage as he walked, ran, and jogged across the platform and the aisle. At times, he also changed his shirt in the middle of the sermon. Spending many hours closely observing his performances, I began to understand something about the body, pleasure, ecstasy, and the otherwise. For me, church services were an erotic experience that oftentimes culminated with me masturbating once I got home. Through the orgasm, I entered into the state of ecstasy that the church promised. In her study of Pentecostal worship leaders within the African American church, Alisha L. Jones writes: "They [worship leaders] tap into the Pentecostal and gospel music traditions to 'take people there,' that is, to happiness, to joy, to love-making, to heaven in sensually and sexually conservative religious spaces" (2020, 1). The affective structures of the church allowed me to imagine the potential of the body, my queer racialized body that was a site of abjection and shame, in a counterintuitive manner. I understood the power of pleasure as a (queer) world-making practice during social and political change.

In Johannesburg, confronted with a virulently racist and cisnormative queer culture, I began to spend a lot of time in Fordsburg, particularly late Saturday afternoons and evenings. I usually visited Fordsburg with my *sisters*, a term that reflects the familial arrangement of close gay friends. The space overwhelmed my senses and disrupted my understanding of Indianness. This was an urban, cosmopolitan Indianness that I was unfamiliar with. The smells of food and fragrances, the mix and movement of bodies, and the sounds and visual cultures of South Asia mediated through Bollywood were something I had never encountered growing up in a Christian family in rural KZN. Soon after my introduction to this space, I began to get my haircuts and my eyebrows threaded by Pakistani male beauticians. Although the home-space and my mother's attention to femininity continue to inform my own understanding of beauty and sensuality, I learned about beauty as a practice of self-care in Fordsburg from Pakistani men. Many of these men from South Asia (mainly from Pakistan, India, and Bangladesh) embodied and performed a different kind of masculinity that I was unfamiliar with but was drawn to. Many of the men were feminine in their attention to clothing and style, comportment, and in the way they related to one another. They moved through space differently, and as I became attuned to their bodies and embodiment, I noticed fleeting instances of male-male intimacies that disrupted the ways in which I imagined these men as heteronormative.

Indeed, within South Asian cultures, forms of male-male bonding and friendships, often referred to as *dostana*, are common and articulate local ideas of male-male intimacies that are also found within African culture.[9] Indeed, many spoke of their wives and children. Many had also married women from local Indian and black communities.[10] However, there was something queer about them, informed simultaneously by their (working) class and immigration status, as well as their open display of forms of intimacies between men. On a Saturday night, the atmosphere was saturated with the aromas of curries and tandooris and the sounds of Indian and Pakistani music. It was common to see men holding hands, hugging, kissing on cheeks, standing in close bodily proximity, rubbing each other's shoulders and thighs, and sharing intimate moments. These moments of male-male intimacy resonated with the traces of male-male intimacies I glimpsed in family photos from my grandfather's and father's generation. These moments/traces were not easily categorizable, and there was something pleasurable for me at that stage in how this form of queerness rubbed against what was expected of a proper gay male subject in postapartheid South Africa. I also learned that many of these men engaged in once-off or ongoing sexual relations with local South African men, even as they maintained heteronormative familial life. In casual conversations with friends and others, many reduced these same-sex encounters between South Asian immigrant men and local South African men as instances of situational homosexuality that arise out of economic needs. While there may be an element of truth to this, this functionalist reading is unable to account for forms of desire and pleasure that have historically informed local sensibilities and that translate differently within a diasporic context. Functionalist reductive readings also reinscribe limited and singular understandings of same-sex intimacies and practices in the era of LGBTIQ+ politics, informed by a human rights discourse.

Within the mainstream white queer scene in Johannesburg, I came to understand that black and Indian queer bodies were sites of fetishization and revulsion. Whiteness and its attachments to hypermasculinity and cisnormativity structured regimes of desire and determined which bodies were desirable and beautiful. This was also a context where, after 1994, homosexuality was positioned as a marker of the "success of constitutional democracy" but same-sex desire was simultaneously "cast as untraditional, as un-African and as un-Christian—a dangerous threat to the social fabric" (Livermon 2012a, 302). The ability for homosexuality to function as both representative of "democratic modernity" and a "threat . . . rests on the racialization of the queer body as white and the sexualization of the black body as straight" (302). In other words, the white queer body becomes the marker of freedom, whereas the black queer body is a threat to the imaginary of an authentic Africa and Africanness. How does the Afro-Indian figure within this racial-sexual configuration, which relies on the black-white racial binary? More important, does this binary provide space for a queer Afro-Indian positionality? How does an already queer black-white racial binary strategically erase any possibilities for conceptualizing and imagining queer Afro-Indianness? Within this configuration, the Afro-Indian queer positionality is an impossibility. I did not fully realize how my mother's impossible positionality as an Indian woman one generation removed from indentureship rubbed against my own positionality as a queer Afro-Indian subject.

I wanted *cane/cain* to do something else, to articulate a notion of queerness that emphasized the various layers that give meaning to embodiment, rather than being a film that routes queer freedom through constitutional protections. At a screening in Johannesburg in 2011, this troubled a group of attendees who spoke out that they expected the film to center LGBTIQ+ rights in the documentary tradition that focused on the Indian community, rather than a film that was deliberate in its eroticization of the Afro-Indian male body. To them, sexuality, pleasure, and the erotic are apolitical because they do not fall within the familiar narrative of what the political looks like in South Africa, informed by the grand spectacle of apartheid and struggle/liberation politics. However, an understanding of freedom, solely routed through the constitution and its emphasis on LGBTIQ+ rights through a human rights framework, dangerously abstracts and obscures the body and embodiment, desire, pleasure, and sex.

My engagement with the family photoarchive (examined in chapter 1) informed how I began to think about pleasure and how to read for pleasure within the archive. By working with this archive—touching, feeling, assembling, and disassembling—I recognized something pleasurable in my own engagement and understanding of how photography and visuality, more broadly, were being mobilized by these colonized subjects. The minor moments of touch evident across the photos in this archive resonated differently, queerly, for me. Could these traces of male-male intimacy speak to the embodied ways in which these men (and women) resisted their erasure and social death under the system of indentureship and its immediate afterlives? What was I, as the artist, to make of my own pleasure in recognizing these traces of intimacies? What could this mean for my project of queering the archive and reimagining Afro-Indian masculinity and race?

Across the literature in South Africa, the Indian is imagined as heteronormative, and when fleeting traces of same-sex intimacies appear within colonial records, they are positioned as an aberration. In the book *Essays on Indentured Indians in Natal*, a report on Reynolds Estate notes that indentured men sought medical treatment for "women's diseases," attributed to the "shortage of women and the inability of many males to find wives" (Bhana 1990, 147). The insinuation here is that men had sexual encounters/relations with other men, and "women's diseases" is code for sexually transmitted diseases. It is significant that this incident of male-male homoerotics is included in a section that outlines the harsh conditions of plantation life and the high rate of suicide. Reading against the grain—the logic of straightness that permeates these records and imaginings of the Afro-Indian—I am more interested in what this record reveals about the emergence of practices of care and survival between men that the colonial archive is unable to account for. This fleeting moment of male-male intimacy, routed through the pathological, tells us something else about the deadly conditions of indenture labor, where the body's relationship to the normative and what constitutes the normative is suspended. What does this record reveal about queer-kinship formations within the plantations and other sites of coercive labor practices, and what happens when these deviant practices inform how we understand the making of Afro-Indianness in Southern Africa?

In my family archive, the men in the oldest photos are unidentifiable. Were they brothers, cousins, neighbors, friends? Were they from the same village in India? Did they meet on board a ship? Scholarship on Indian indentureship in the Caribbean provides a lens through which I began thinking about these fleeting traces of intimacies between these men. It is undeniable that the journey across the *kala pani* from colonial India to Mauritius, South Africa, and the Caribbean resulted in intimate social formations between indentured men and women. Indo-Caribbean scholarship reveals that homosocial formations like *jahaji bai* (fraternal ship brother) and *jahaji bahin* (ship sisters) were common on indenture ships and resulted in what we would refer to as *queer-kinship formations* that emerged out of loss and natal alienation. Bonded by their common experiences of "mutual suffering during colonial transoceanic ship journeys," *jahaji bai* and *jahaji bahin* were social formations that suspended, if only temporarily, the organization of Indian colonial society through caste, language, and regional differences (Khan 2016, 251). Indeed, these "relationships replaced the bonds of family and caste aboard" and went on to determine racial-ethnic-cultural contours of Indian diasporic community formations in colonial spaces (251). These homosocial bonds, constructed through loss, are rescripted into narratives of survival, through which diasporic communities imagine themselves as heterosexual. In the South African case, Vahed and Desai (2010, 33–34) offer a very heteronormative reading of these intimacies, evoking the overdetermined political language of "comradeship" and "bonds of fraternity." Such language is indicative of a politics of respectability that informs the scholarship on the Indian in South Africa, which must submerge the queerness of indentureship and its afterlives.

Within the archival record, there are minimal recorded incidences of homoerotic practices among Indian indentured men on coolie ships. In the South African case, I have been unable to trace any such records. However, in the Indo-Caribbean case, there is one documented record of same-sex practices. This incident occurred in 1898 on board the British ship *Mersey* and refers to an "alleged act of sodomy" between Nobibux (male, twenty years; indenture no. 696) and Mohangu (male, twenty-two years; indenture no. 351). According to A. H. Alexander, immigration agent-general of British Guiana, Nobibux and Mohangu were caught in the act of committing sodomy by Rambocus, a Sirdar aboard the ship. It is alleged that the two men confessed to committing sodomy to both Alexander and the ship's captain. According to the record, Nobibux admitted to engaging in such "acts of beastliness" for the last ten years and it was determined that he influenced Mohangu (Khan 2016, 258). When questioned why they did this "wrong thing," a crime in colonial Britain and its colonies, the two confessed that they did it for *pleasure*.[11] An analytic that centers pleasure within such a violent context complicates any simplistic understanding of resistance and how those held captive within the deadly worlds of coercive labor practice mobilized their bodies as sites of resistance. I am interested in pleasure not only as a form of resistance but also as a site of queer worldmaking that can reframe how we understand power and relationality outside of identitarian categories like "gay," "straight," "queer," and such. What does pleasure reveal about embodied practices of freedom? This is fundamental to indenture aesthetics and a disruption to the performances of Afro-normativity. Thus *cane/cain* and *Queering the Archive: Brown Bodies in Ecstasy* are my ongoing attempts to understand embodiment, Afro-Indianness, and Afro-Indian intimacies by centering pleasure and the aesthetic.

cane/cain ties together three narratives of displacement and out-of-placeness that converge in Johannesburg but are deeply informed by the larger history of colonial apartheid. It positions Afro-Indian history in relationship to more recent, post-1994, migrations and settlement of South Asians across South Africa. I use the contested term *South Asian* here, to make a distinction between newer immigrants from the Indian subcontinent and the more settled (Afro) Indian communities in South Africa that emerged in the wake of indentured labor. However, it is important to note that within the South African racial and visual imaginary, South Asians and Indians are conflated into one category. The official 2011 census that places "South African Indians" at 2.7 percent of the population "excludes the migration of Indian nationals [and other nationals] from the subcontinent post-1994" (Rugunanan 2017, 54). Fordsburg was a strategic choice because this is a place of convergence that includes immigrants from other Global South countries and from across Africa. In South Africa, it is difficult to determine the actual number of immigrants because many are undocumented. Pragna Rugunanan writes:

> A significant number of migrants from the Global South make their way to Johannesburg and Fordsburg. Migrants from Sudan, Egypt, Morocco, Uganda, Kenya, Nigeria, Zimbabwe, Malawi, and Mozambique can be found in Fordsburg. From South Asia, there is a growing Pakistani, Indian, Nepalese and Bangladeshi migrant population, with new waves of Chinese migrants. Two waves of migrants are found in Fordsburg: in the period 1994–2000, the first wave of Indian and Pakistani traders appeared; and, post-2000, in the second period, a more heterogeneous group of nationalities and gender distribution, persuaded by the promise of political stability and economic opportunity made their way to South Africa. (59–60)

Set against the major xenophobic attacks in 2008, *cane/cain* unsettles the framing of these attacks within the local media and international press as black-on-black violence. Given the long history of anti-Indian sentiment, it was inevitable that the Indian and other Asian immigrant groups would become a target. In 2015:

> A resurgence of xenophobic violence swept across parts of Soweto, targeting specifically Somali, Pakistani and Bangladeshi traders. Renewed violence broke out in Gauteng and KwaZulu-Natal provinces in April 2015. The *Business Day* (2015) reported that "life in South Africa's townships is certainly no picnic for Pakistani, Bangladeshi, Chinese or Indian

> merchants." While these groups may not be as directly affected by mob violence as migrants from Somalia, Ethiopia, Zimbabwe or Malawi, they nevertheless remain vulnerable and live a precarious existence.[12] (Rugunanan 2017, 53–54)

Thus, *cane/cain* brings the histories of migration and displacement of Indian and South Asian communities into relationship with migrant histories and experiences from other African countries. It is important to note that *cane/cain* tackles a South Asian migrant experience from the working/lower class. This is a significantly different immigrant South Asian experience than that of the Guptas, for example, who were centrally involved with former president Jacob Zuma and accused of state "capture." Importantly, by bringing these groups into close proximately, *cane/cain* shows how they are familiar strangers, occupying a similar positionality of queerness.

For many Indian communities in KwaZulu-Natal, the rise in xenophobic attacks after 1994 is a reminder of the 1949 race riots that occurred in Durban. Indeed, much of the anti-Indian sentiment/discourse after 1994 replicates the very same tropes and stereotypes of the Indian that emerged in the late 1940s, which have overdetermined Afro-Indian relations since. The more recent xenophobic attacks must be considered within and alongside political and popular discourses that continue to position the Indian as "foreign-other," alien, and disruptive to black African sovereignty. During these xenophobic attacks, members from the Indian South African community were *misrecognized* as newer South Asian immigrants and asked to prove their South Africanness. South African migration studies scholars Loren B. Landau and Tanya Pampalone argue that "South Africa's entangled history of xenophobia reaches deep and wide throughout the making of the nation" (2018, 6).

The Sensual Aesthetics of Sugarcane

By bringing into conversation three different historical experiences of migration, *cane/cain* produces narrative and aesthetic tension through the form—assemblage, color, editing, nonlinear storytelling—which activates the sensual and sensorial parameters. Against this backdrop of violence, I wanted to use the aesthetic form to bring together different spatial and temporal moments, which rub against one another to produce various overlapping regimes of pain and pleasure. Through a sensual aesthetic, particularly related to the sugarcane plantations, I wanted *cane/cain* to activate a visceral response in the viewer routed through the sensual. Arnold Berleant (1964) describes the sensual as referring to "that experience of the sense which is confined to bodily pleasures... where the appeal is to the 'grosser' bodily sensations, particularly the sexual" (185). I was particularly interested in how interracial and intraethnic desires and bodily pleasures could enable us to understand the abject body as a counterintuitive archive of history. How does queer desire become a portal to unthink and re-imagine the terrain of history, memory, and power? In my creative practice, I am interested in the shift from desire to pleasure and how the hunger for the otherwise enables this shift to occur. What happens to our memories, histories, and archives when we experience bodily pleasure—sexual pleasure—with and for the Other, particularly the Other who occupies a similar positionality, yet one rendered invisible and incompatible through overlapping projects of racialization?

In *cane/cain*, Aben and Tariq are familiar strangers, and this is established early in the narrative when Aben stops by Tariq's stall to purchase a cup of fresh sugarcane juice. The juice is extracted from the sugarcane stalks as Aben (the customer) waits. On this particular day, tensions are high and Tariq's precarious position as an outsider is revealed in a brief but violent interaction between himself and another customer, who performs and sounds like a local Indian man. In this interaction, Tariq is berated by this customer because he gets the order wrong. The customer calls Tariq a "bloody idiot" and accuses him of being "all over this place" and "fucking everything up." Soon after, Aben, from the safety and security of his shop, witnesses Tariq being attacked by a mob who destroy his informal set up and beat him up. Aben goes out into the street to help Tariq. The viewer does not see the angry mob; rather, we only hear them. It is important to note that the mob would have consisted of local black Africans who are poor, destitute, and desperate, who are often ignited by the political elite to attack the foreigner.[13] Aben takes Tariq to his home and cleans his wounds. This act of care leads to a sexual encounter between these two men after a brief conversation that establishes points of intimacies between them even though they are situated differently in terms of migration history, citizenship status, language, and nationality.

Throughout the film, spoken dialogue is deliberately sparse, leaving the audience to connect the different unfolding events through an excessive mise-en-scene. Lahiri (2018) argues that the film is "markedly melodramatic" (295–96) but marks a shift: the "melodramatic convention of saying too much, associated with the dramatic use of dialogue and the excessively explicit unfolding of the film's plot *cane/cain*—with no opening titled credits, and very little dialogue—speaks to issues of sexuality and xenophobia... through characters who say almost nothing." Ebrahim (2017) writes: "Particularly noteworthy... is the density of its soundscape in contrast to its sparsity of dialogue." She goes on to argue that the film "replaces verbal narration . . . with an excess of mise-en-scène and non-dialogue sound." Indeed, the film eschews spoken language as one of the privileged ways that structure the "will to know" by displacing language onto an *aesthetics of excess* informed by the recurring trope of sugarcane. It gestures toward the sensual and sensorial regimes beyond both spoken dialogue and the visual. While making *cane/cain*, I was aware that this was the first South African film to represent an explicit sex scene, which included kissing, touching, and fucking, between two men (mis)recognized as Indian within the South African racial imaginary. Soon after its release, the film was described as an "Indian homosexual film." Labeling the film Indian flattens out the heterogeneity of experiences and their manifestations in South Africa that this film seeks to explore through queer desires. The sensual aesthetic of *cane/cain* functions on two levels. First, it sticks to and rubs against the various bodies, queering while eroticizing them. Second, by foregrounding its "sensuous materiality" it elicits a "sensuous mode of relation" with the audience (Amin et al. 2017, 228).

The fragmented narrative of *cane/cain* begins and ends in the sugarcane plantations of KwaZulu-Natal. The film opens with a close-up shot of sugarcane gently swaying in the breeze. We hear children laughing and birds chirping. It is significant that the film opens by juxtaposing the lush green sugarcane stalks with sound. This immediately attunes the audience to the sensorial regimes beyond the visual. The opening scene of the film introduces us to two young boys running into a sugarcane plantation, capturing the playful innocence of youth. As the two boys—one the protagonist of the film, Aben, and the other his childhood friend—play in the field, the film cuts to another close-up shot of sugarcane, and we hear what appears to be a kiss, a buckle and zipper opening, and then we see two bodies lying in a patch of grass and reed, contrasting the brownness of Aben's upper torso and the lush green of the sugarcane. The next series of cuts in the narrative to the sugarcane plantations occurs just before and after the xenophobic attack against Tariq. From inside his store, Aben watches Tariq as he switches the sugarcane-crushing machine on. As the machine begins to swirl into life, the camera zooms into the rotating mechanism of the machine as Tariq pushes fresh stalks of cane into the crusher to extract the juice that he sells. As the juice flows down the lip of the machine into a cup, the film cuts to a scene in the sugarcane plantations. In a close-up shot, we see a black man, a plantation laborer, sharpening a machete. The sound of metal rubbing against metal rubs against the sounds of insects emerging out of the plantations. We see a man chopping cane. The burnt cane stalks offer a stark contrast with the lush green sugarcane fields that have not been burnt yet. This scene then ends and cuts to a scene of Tariq crushing the cane. In the distance, we hear a crowd approaching as Aben watches this scene unfold from the safety of his store.

After the attack, Aben holds Tariq, injured and bleeding, safely in his arms. The film cuts to an intimate scene between Aben and his childhood friend, whose face is streaked with tears. The scene of violence—the xenophobic attacks—transports Aben to a different time and space, a different scene of violence that is never resolved in the film. We see Aben gently kiss the forehead of his childhood friend, drawing him into an intimate hug. The film then cuts to a wide shot of a majestic tree standing alone in the middle of the cane field and then to a shot of the sun setting over the fields. The next cut to the cane field occurs after Aben and Tariq have a sexual encounter. As Tariq ejaculates while on top of Aben, Aben closes his eyes, and we are transported to the sugarcane fields of his younger days. He runs through the lush green fields and the brown-blackened burnt stalks before encountering a scene of violence that ends the film. He discovers a rope hanging from a tree. He begins to retreat in slow motion. The audience is not allowed to see what hangs at the end of the rope as the film comes to an end. The title of the film appears after this last scene, followed by a shot of burning cane superimposed on an image of Tariq and Aben in a Christ-like position.

In this film, the sensual aesthetics of cane connect the three key narrative themes of homoerotic intimacy, overlapping migration routes from the Indian subcontinent, and xenophobia. Throughout the film, the main character's desires are ignited through the sensual aesthetics of cane. The sugarcane plantations are figured as sites of both pain and pleasure. For Aben and his childhood friend, the sugarcane plantations represent both playful innocence and erotic awakening. But as the narrative progresses, the representation of the cane fields shifts from pleasure, play, and discovery to a site of violence, pain, and trauma. Through the intercutting in the film, pain and pleasure intermingle and coexist. However, even as the film marks these moments differently, the sensual aesthetics of the cane remain constant, positioning sugarcane as the site of entanglement between bodies, spaces, history, and memories. Throughout the film, sugarcane ignites Aben's memories, transporting him and the audience to a different time and space. Ebrahim (2021, 153) captures this movement and its significance in the film as follows: "In *cane/cain*, the life cycle of the sugarcane marks its own migration—from the sugarcane plant to the juice and from the coasts of KwaZulu-Natal [KZN] to the urban 'ghetto' of Fordsburg in Johannesburg. This trajectory parallels both the increasing domestic migration of Indian South Africans from [KZN] to the economic hub of Johannesburg and its surrounding areas, as well as the increasing social mobility from indentured labor to professional occupations and a more affluent lifestyle."

Furthermore, the sugarcane connects Aben to Tariq by foregrounding the intimacies between these two men not based on formations of kin and/or community through notions of blood and belonging. Before Aben and Tariq have sex, the two men have a brief conversation where Aben's great-grandparent's desires for a better life, which probably propelled their entry into the indentured system, imbricates with Tariq's desires to provide a better life for his wife and child. Here, Aben's ancestral legacy of indentured labor on colonial plantations in KwaZulu-Natal merges with Tariq's post-1994 migration to Johannesburg and his labor as an informal vendor selling sugarcane juice. The logics of labor and capital that drove indenture migration and the sugar industry during the colonial era are the same logics that determine labor, capital, and migration in the neoliberal postapartheid period. Regimes of labor and capital continue to produce some populations as surplus and disposable, rendering them more vulnerable to state regulation and xenophobic violence. Here, sugarcane sutures these temporal and spatial geohistories; this brief conversation ends with Tariq stating, "So, we're not that different after all," securing "a tenuous moment of homosocial and homoethnic bonding" (Ebrahim 152).

The sensual aesthetics of cane allows Aben and Tariq to momentarily suspend their deep differences in order to rescript their bodies into sites of counterintuitive pleasure. Their bodies join in coitus as an act of care, a mode of *feeling* and *feeling for*. Across their embodied differences—history, migration, racialization, sexuality—they reach outward toward each other and use their differently abjectified bodies to connect across geohistories (colonial-era indenture migration and post-1994 neoliberal migration), nationalities, language, racial/ethnic formations, and gender and sexual logics that are designed to obscure our commonalities. Thus, the excessive sensual aesthetics of cane becomes a signifier of desire, which activates the sensorial and sensual regimes. The sex scene between Tariq and Aben is inaugurated by a mirror scene where Aben stands behind Tariq as they both gaze into the mirror, looking at and desiring each other's bodies across various regimes of difference. Aben stands behind Tariq, touching his skin and kissing his neck as their bodies become entangled within a complex dialectic of pleasure and pain. The mirror scene progresses to a sex scene on the bed that emphasizes touch and care. This act of touching, caring, holding—bodies coming together in pain and pleasure—allows these two familiar strangers to "invent and sustain new ways of being together" (Macharia 2019, 52). The film ends with a return to the sugarcane plantations, situating the rural as a site of queer world-making.

The rural signals an alternative spatial and temporal logic where the sensual aesthetics of cane—deeply embedded within the histories of overlapping coercive labor systems—binds us, black, African, and Afro-Indian, together across differences. Forms of queer world-making within rural spaces reveal alternative kinship structures and the pursuit of freedom dreams that erodes the hierarchies and binaries that structure the (un)freedoms of the postapartheid.

The term *xenophobia* is derived from the Greek word *xenos*, which means "stranger" or "foreigner," and *phobia* meaning "fear," and is simply defined as the fear of those who are perceived to be strangers/foreigners. In *cane/cain*, the sensual aesthetics of sugarcane generates its own queer (and) affective passions and desires that disrupt the hierarchies and binaries that produce the stranger/foreigner, by revealing, through touch, our deep intimacies, emphasizing our desire to "generate new kinds of bonds" through touch. The narrative structure of *cane/cain*, which begins and ends in the cane fields, offers an aesthetic grammar of temporality that is cyclical and repetitive. This temporality is shaped by the sensual aesthetic of the sugarcane plantations, constantly returning the viewer to the rural. Indeed, this sensual aesthetic of the sugarcane informs the feminization of the rural. The shots of the sugarcane plantations resonate with Mlangeni's landscape shots of the rural. The only people who inhabit the sugarcane plantations in *cane/cain* are two young boys and the black African plantation workers, who themselves occupy a feminized positionality. Whereas Mlangeni examines the temporality of the rural through the figure of women and small children who are waiting—waiting for their sons, husbands, and fathers, and simultaneously waiting for freedom—the sugarcane plantation, an iteration of the rural, is also a space characterized by a temporal lag.

Mlangeni's series *Country Girls* evokes the formation of life-forms and kinship structures within and alongside spaces associated with slow death. He unearths the various ways his interlocutors consciously craft livable lives through gender-sexual-erotic arrangements that challenge these spaces as antiblack and antiqueer. In *cane/cain*, I wanted to capture the beauty, sensuality, and erotics of the sugarcane plantation as it folds into the home-space of a rural Afro-Indian family in the afterlife of indentureship. These overlapping spaces have always been feminine and feminized for me because they are associated with my mother (the maternal feminine) and the feminization of the Indian indentured male body. I also wanted to articulate a different trajectory of queerness and a different understanding of embodiment and sexuality that emerge out of the sugarcane plantation, a site of overlapping coercive labor practices that continue to construct black/ened life-forms in contemporary South Africa.

The black African workers, consisting of men from local rural areas and immigrants from surrounding countries like Zimbabwe and elsewhere, continue to grow and harvest the cane using mostly manual methods. They exist outside the time-space of Afro-normativity and are still waiting for freedom to arrive. Their everyday lives have not changed since the era of colonial apartheid; they belong to the new black/ened Others who continue to live on the edges of society, haunting the linear and progressive narrative of the postapartheid era.

To dwell in the sugarcane plantations is to dwell both in the afterlife of indenture and the afterlife of colonial apartheid. It is to reckon with the ways in which performances of labor resonate across time and space, suturing different spatial and temporal geohistories to one another while emphasizing how our differently racialized and ethnicized bodies stick to one another and desire one another across our differences. To dwell in the sensual aesthetics of cane is to *feel* and to *feel for* the otherwise before language merges with the visual regimes to shape our understanding of the world as it determines our relations across structures of race, ethnicity, region, gender, and sexuality. To enter the rural is to step into a different time and space. To attune one's body and senses to the rural is to grapple with life-forms constantly creating and re-creating, imagining and reimagining livable lives "beyond the degrading violence of the everyday" (Walcott 2021, 34). From the rural and small towns in Mpumalanga, the mine workers' hostels, the sugarcane plantations in KZN, and Fordsburg, this chapter has examined practices of care and the emergence of pleasure in unlikely spaces. Pleasure can enable us to work across difference. It directs us to the everyday and an experience of the ordinary defined by "gathering into a livable, pleasurable social. We gather to practice freedom as we work across difference" (Macharia 2017).

In the next chapter, I shift from forms of queer world-making in spaces associated with slow death to two bodily sites, the anus and the yoni. The next chapter examines the performance and aesthetic art practices of the black queer and femme duo FAKA in relationship to Reshma Chhiba's multimedia and multisited project *The Two Talking Yonis*. The (black queer) anus and the (Afro-Indian) yoni are spaces associated with feminine/feminized and female excess and deviance. In chapter 4, I am interested in the emergence of forms of feminist-queer world-making when abjection and the erotic merge and rub against each other. For different but overlapping reasons, FAKA and Chhiba are positioned by the logics of Afro-normativity as un-African, and they both use sex as art to explode and expand our understanding of Southern African blackness.

4

Afro-Transgressions

QUEER FEMININITIES AND SOUTH AFRICAN SEX PUBLICS

In 2013, *The Two Talking Yonis*, a multisited solo exhibition by Reshma Chhiba in conversation with Nontobeko Ntombela, opened simultaneously at three galleries in Johannesburg. The most spectacular part of this exhibition was a twelve-meter walk-in yoni made from red velvet material (plate 24). It included a protruding tongue and pubic hair around the opening created from black acrylic wool. Although I offer a more detailed description and analysis of Chhiba's installation in the introduction, it is worth reminding the reader that when visitors walked into the yoni, they encountered a screeching scream and laughter, machetes hanging from the roof, and a portrait photo of the Indian goddess Kali, whose tongue sticks out disrespectfully, emphasizing her transgressive and abject nature.

Two years later, in 2015, FAKA, a black queer/femme performance duo consisting of Fela Gucci (Thato Ramaisa) and Desire Marea (Buyani Duma), performed *Bottom's Revenge* at the Berlin Biennale. This was a performance of black queer sex set in an anus. The multimedia performance included the two artists performing sex in a bathtub filled with a brown liquid (to represent the anus and feces), video footage of a camera moving through a digestive system, the sounds of digestion, and footage of Ugandan minister Martin Ssempa's "eat the poo-poo" lecture.

In this chapter, I focus on two spaces associated with female and feminine/feminized excess and deviance, the yoni and the anus. I examine Chhiba and FAKA's use of these spaces as sites of critique and forms of queer and feminist world-making. The artists also dwell, literally and symbolically, on different manifestations of abjection. Chhiba's art is influenced by the figure of the Indian goddess Kali and her association with female/feminine excess and abjection. Chhiba (2013) writes, "Kali is . . . the embodiment of the wild, untamed side of human nature. She is . . . represented as semi-naked and wears a girdle of human arms as her skirt and a necklace of human skulls or heads. Her hair is unbound and disheveled; her outstretched tongue drips with blood, evident in her aggressive temperament and suggestive of her erotic sexuality as a goddess" (3).

Whereas Chhiba's aesthetic practice draws on Kali, FAKA is interested in the deviant positionality of male femininity and anal erotics. Through these positionalities of abjection, FAKA articulates a broader politics of bottomhood as indicated by their name. *Faka* is a Zulu word, translated by the duo to mean "enter, penetrate, occupy." They write, "We chose this name because it is our intention to penetrate and communicate silenced themes in the spectrum of black queer identity. . . . *FAKA*, in the context of sexual intercourse, is an order given to the perpetrator to penetrate. Our ownership of a term linked to the assumption of passivity is a protest to empower the most shamed identities. It is the 'bottom's revenge'" (Marea and Gucci 2016, 10). I am interested in what happens when abjection and erotics rub against each other, especially in relationship to Chhiba's and FAKA's critiques around normative racial formations and the violence of heteropatriarchy and cisnormativity in South Africa.

This chapter enacts my queer curatorial practice by bringing into conversation two artists (Chhiba and FAKA) who occupy different and at times opposing positionalities. However, this method of curation informs my notion of indenture aesthetics, dedicated to creating/curating a counterarchive against the logics of Afro-normativity. In this book, I have focused mainly on Afro-Indian artists—Indian South African artists who are of indentured origin. However, in this chapter, I include Reshma Chhiba, an artist from a trader-class family. How do we account for Chhiba's passenger Indian heritage in a book that critiques the ways in which Indianness in South Africa has been historically conflated with that of the passenger Indian, erasing the experience of indentureship and its afterlives? Importantly, my notion of *indenture aesthetics* is not reducible to *indenture history*. Chhiba disidentifies with the hegemonic narrative of the passenger Indian and employs a politics of disrespectability, routed through the figure of Kali, to unsettle the ways in which this hegemonic narrative articulates a race-gender-sexual-diaspora politics that situates the Indian over the black African and the Afro-Indian. Thus, my notion of indenture aesthetics is open, supple, and inclusive. It is invested in how the new black/ened Others eschew performances of Afro-normativity to articulate a radical politics of (dis)belonging that provides a blueprint to think and feel outside of sedimented racial categories. This is what draws me to Chhiba's work. Thus, the concept of indenture aesthetics has the potential to frame the aesthetic practices of artists beyond the Afro-Indian and black African relationalities curated and imagined in this book.

The Two Talking Yonis emerged out of a series of conversations between Chhiba and Ntombela, a curator based in Johannesburg. Most of their conversations addressed Chhiba's "placement within the discourse of contemporary art in South Africa" (Chhiba and Ntombela 2019, 31). They write: "These intense moments often pointed us to issues of gendering, ethnicization and racialization . . . that . . . were framing Chhiba's work in problematic ways. Such was the stereotyping that had to do with her being a South African woman artist of Indian ancestry . . . some of the readings and reviews often reduced and simplified the work too hastily, overlooking the irony and sophistication of the aesthetic and symbolism that Chhiba's work employs" (31). From its inception, *The Two Talking Yonis* was an Afro-Indian project that emerges out of an ethical relationality crafted between an Indian and a black African woman.

Whereas Chhiba is of Indian origin, who grew up in the suburbs of Johannesburg, Gucci and Marea are black African artists. Fela Gucci was raised in Katlehong, a township on the East Rand of Johannesburg. According to Gucci, Katlehong "is like any other township in South Africa where poverty is rife but people still dream and thrive" (Gucci quoted in Meslani n.d.). Raised by his grandmother after the death of his parents at a young age, Gucci writes: "I carry her [his grandmother's] strength and teachings with me, and they have given me the tools to navigate life today" (Gucci quoted in Meslani n.d.). Whereas Gucci was raised in a township in Johannesburg, Desire Marea grew up in Amandawe, a rural town in KwaZulu-Natal's South Coast. As a rural space, Amandawe is not well known, and according to Marea, "Nobody really knows anyone from there, if they know the place at all." In this statement,

Marea reflects on the erasure and invizibilization of rural and small towns within the South African imaginary. He writes: "Existing in that condition of perceived invisibility fuelled my curiosity about worlds beyond the one I existed in. . . . Any fear of being in a foreign or strange place seemed significantly smaller than my dream to be seen and heard, so I left. Luckily, I come from a supportive and loving home, so I will never lose connection to the world I grew up in" (Marea quoted in Meslani, n.d.). What is important here is that Gucci and Marea reframe our understanding of township, rural, and small-town life from one of lack, poverty, and destitution. Indeed, these spaces ignite "freedom dreams" and propel the queer world-making that rubs against hegemonic understandings of queer liberation and postapartheid freedoms. Across the various chapters, *Indenture Aesthetics* demonstrates how the intimacies of the everyday, as they manifest within these spaces, offer alternative visions of space and time that provide a break within the performances of Afronormativity. This break allows us to sense, feel, touch, and envision embodied practices of freedom otherwise.

This chapter focuses on FAKA's and Chhiba's use of transgressive feminine excess as interventions into South African discourses around the question of sex. I argue that for FAKA and Chhiba, their "question of sex" is not "exclusively concerned with sexual acts or object choice" (Snorton 2017, 4) but instead functions as a critique of how the regulation of gender and sexuality is "used to police both national and racial authenticity" (Hoad 2007, 2). Through performances of sex and the embodiment of a radical femme aesthetic, FAKA is invested in creating inclusive queer social worlds that offer a safe space—a refuge—for those who are queer, trans, femme, and/or gender-nonconforming, from the violence of the everyday. Their objective is to dismantle the "internalized heteronormative righteousness that has contaminated our community with its hierarchy of male privilege" (Marea and Gucci 2016, 10). They are dedicated to a project of queer world-making from the bottom, from the positionality of those most vulnerable within society. Through male femininity, they productively disturb the parameters of black African heteromasculinity and homonormative performances of (black) queer masculinity. FAKA's objective is to occupy, penetrate, and disrupt femmephobic spaces (nightclub spaces, township, urban, and rural spaces) that reinscribe cishetero and homonormative performances of masculinity. Working across genres, FAKA is committed to "amplify[ing] the voices of the country's LGBTQ+ scene" (Davidson 2019). They regularly host an inclusive club night called "Cunty Power." *Cunty* signifies ultrafemininity within ballroom culture. It is also a term of female/feminine disparagement. Through the abject positionality of male femininity and feminine excess, FAKA reimagines blackness away from the violence of the normative, disrupting the binaries (male/female, masculine/feminine, man/woman, authentic/inauthentic) and hierarchies that maintain the boundaries of the Afro-normative.

FAKA's notion of Cunty Power resonates with Chhiba's creation of "yonic spaces." Chhiba's yonic spaces transform the yoni into a "space of power and defiance."[1] She resituates the yoni as a site of creative feminine energy and female sexual pleasure that is disruptive of heteropatriarchy and women's biopolitical regulation within culture and society. It is significant that her critique of normative blackness and heteropatriarchy manifests through the figure of Kali. Kali is associated both with abjection and female/feminine erotic excess and deviance. In Hindu mythology, she is associated with "death, disease, and decay," and she is "worshiped by low-caste people in uncivilized and wild places" (Oleszkiewicz-Peralba 2015, 56).

It is undeniable that the question of sex has historically shaped and determined the contours of South African society and has been foundational to imaginaries of race and racial differences. Indeed, postapartheid freedoms are intimately attached to the domain of sexuality and discourses around sex. This chapter first contextualizes FAKA's and Chhiba's use of *sex-as-art* as an intervention into discourses informing the relationship between sex and freedom in South Africa. Second, I examine FAKA's performances of sex at the German Biennale in 2015 titled *Bottom's Revenge* and a live performance of sex in 2016 for the group exhibition *Sex* (curated by Lerato Bereng). I trace how FAKA's performances of sex shift from a critique of the disavowal of same-sex desire and erotics to their investment in radically reimagining blackness through embodied knowledge. I then examine Chhiba's Afro-Indian aesthetics, focusing on her portrait, *I Am Kali, I Am Black*, and her representations of sex between Kali and the Indian god Shiva. FAKA's and Chhiba's artworks attest to their constant negotiation of their outsider positionality within the logics of Afro-normativity, which positions them both as un-African and inauthentic.

Sex and South African Publics

During colonial apartheid, the state regulated the domain of sexuality and sex. The apartheid state came into power in 1948 on the promise of protecting white women from black men, whose sexuality was constructed as criminal, deviant, and aggressive. Racial segregation, through the official system of apartheid, manifested through anxieties over interracial sex. Thus, some of the most enduring and damaging apartheid-era policies were the antimiscegenation laws, which prohibited marriage between whites and non-whites. These lasted until the mid-1980s. However, the regulation of African Indigenous sexualities can be traced to the era of colonialism. Scholars of gender and sexuality in Africa have examined the ways in which colonial modernity anxiously embarked on a project to produce proper African subjects/bodies through heterosexuality, in the process queering Indigenous articulations of gender, sexuality, and the body. These processes reshaped African erotic autonomy, subjectivity, and intimacies (Macharia 2019). Scholars like Signe Arnfred (2004), Brenna Munro (2012), and T. J. Tallie (2019) have examined how colonialism imposed gender binaries and hierarchies onto African modes of being. Munro (2012, xiii) argues that while colonial rule attempted to "eradicate indigenous social formations that were deemed deviant, from polygamy to 'female husbands,'" it also enabled the emergence of "unruly new sexual cultures . . . in cities, industries, and institutions of a changing Africa." Colonialism's intervention into the intimacies of everyday African life constructed new sexual identities and reshaped what constituted sex by producing "new sexual taboos" that regulated desire and sex across the racial divide and criminalized homosexuality. According to scholars Zethu Matebeni and Jabu Pereira (2014, 7), many of the laws used to regulate and marginalize gender and sexual nonnormative Africans in postcolonial Africa are in fact colonial-era laws that "introduced penal codes, commonly known as sodomy laws that criminalize so-called 'unnatural' sexual acts." Colonialism's mandate, as Frantz Fanon (2001) argues, was a systematic process of distortion, destruction, and negation of the Black/African/colonized body. In 2004, Africanist scholar Signe Arnfred argued that it is time to "re-think . . . sexualities in Africa: The thinking beyond the conceptual structure of colonial and even post-colonial European imaginaries, which have oscillated between notions of the exotic, the noble and the depraved savage consistently, however, constructing Africans and African sexuality as something 'other.' This 'other' thing . . . functions to co-construct that which is European/Western as modern, rational and civilized" (7). With the end of apartheid, the domain of sex and sexuality has received renewed attention to become an important signifier of the *newness* of the new nation. Sex and sexual freedom now differentiate this era of freedoms from the era of unfreedoms associated with colonial apartheid. Deborah Posel (2005, 135) argues that issues of sexuality are now framed within a discourse of "empowerment and rights-speak." Yet it is undeniable that the relationship between sex and freedom is fraught with many contradictions. South African scholars have examined the contradictions that shape postapartheid freedoms related to the HIV/AIDS crisis (Posel 2005; Hoad 2007), violent masculinities (Morrell 1998; Ratele 2006, 2015; Ellapen 2007,

2018), and gender-based violence like rape, which continues to disproportionately affect black women, children, and lesbians mainly from rural, township, and semiurban spaces (Posel 2005; Hassim 2009; Gqola 2007, 2009, 2015). Since 1994, this social reality, "sex as menace, sex as death," rubs against the "imaginary of sex as freedom, as the symbol of a virulent lease on life" (Posel 2005, 135).

In 2016, Lerato Bereng curated the exhibition *Sex* to examine the relationship between sex and freedom and the increased visibility of sexual cultures in contemporary Africa. In her curatorial statement, she writes:

> Sexually speaking, the start of this decade was marked by Jacob Zuma's statement during his rape trial that he had showered after sex with an HIV-positive woman. Another milestone . . . was a wave of nationalism with the hosting of the 2010 World Cup. . . . In this time of jubilation and hedonistic indulgence, sex seemed to be on many minds. 2010 was the year that *Mapona Vol 1* was produced, the first all-black South African porn film. The film . . . "sought to promote safe sex and combat HIV." In the same year, a nationwide debate around the temporary legalization of prostitution ahead of the hosting of the World Cup ensued. AWB leader Eugene Terreblanche was murdered, and the circumstances surrounding his death were allegedly said to have homoerotic undertones. (Bereng 2016)

Bereng invited artists to respond to sex as a question, imagining the exhibition as "a kaleidoscope of positions unearthing sexual narratives" from the continent. Bereng's objective was clear: she "did not want the show to treat sex as an academic paper but for it to explore the act of sex and everything that comes with it—both the fun and the serious aspects" (Katlego 2016). In this statement, Bereng critiques how industries and institutions that deal in sex (the state, academia, and medical and legal institutions, for example) produce discourses and knowledge about sexuality that are inherently antierotic. In this exhibition, Bereng disrupts the boundaries between those who theorize sexuality, those who use aesthetic practices to imagine sex and sexuality, and those who sell sex in the more traditional sense of understanding sex work as prostitution. In her review of the exhibition, Mary Corrigall (2016) writes: "The exhibition offers stimulation for the body, not just the mind (the art setting usually demands that you think about the works rather than respond to them physically)." While the exhibition offered some nuanced representations of (black) queer sex, Jessie Cohen (2016) writes that the exhibition failed "to navigate heterosexuality through innovative representations." Although Bereng's interventions into African sex publics, routed through South Africa, are daring and innovative, the exhibition did not offer any representation of African sex and sexuality outside of the black-white racial binary. The exclusion of Afro-Indian artists, for instance, reinforces the notion of the Afro-Indian as outside of the parameters of the South African nation and as having nothing significant to contribute to the discussion concerning race, gender, and sexuality. Furthermore, Bereng maps a sexual timeline onto the timeline of the nation, invariably reinscribing "historicity, linearity, and nationalism" (Stallings 2015, xv). This chapter complicates and unsettles this imperative by focusing on FAKA and Chhiba, who trouble the parameters of the nation and the nation-state's investment in black normativity and authenticity through the aesthetic of sex-as-art.

Marea and Gucci contributed a live performance art piece. In this chapter, I am interested in how FAKA and Chhiba mobilize "sex talk" as a strategy to illuminate the conditions under which women and queers create livable lives against and alongside the postapartheid/postcolonial African state's anxious construction of a normative African subject. In the introduction, I examined how "ruling masculinity" mobilizes political talk to reinscribe the relationship between the black norm and the proper African body. Indigenous studies scholar Billy-Ray Belcourt (2017, 182) argues that "the genre and form of political talk . . . stomp some of us into the rut of social death," whereas "sex talk" has the potential to reveal the "tumult of everyday life," the contradictions of postcolonial/postapartheid freedoms, and the messiness of the everyday in the afterlife of colonial apartheid history. Whereas political talk functions as a regime of biopolitical regulation and surveillance, emerging from the political elite and informing Afro-normative respectability politics, I am interested in forms of sex talk that emerge from the positionality of the new black/ened Others. I understand sex talk as a strategy for creating livable lives through erotic autonomy in the ongoing pursuit of freedom. For FAKA, sex talk reveals the importance of embracing "states of fragility" and vulnerability through their politics of bottomhood. For Chhiba, sex talk reroutes the abject and transgressive feminine energy associated with Kali into a form of feminist world-making that disrupts the violence of heteropatriarchy while simultaneously eroding the boundaries of Afro-normative blackness.

Within feminist and queer studies, sex and sexuality are contested terrain. In the early 1980s, the divide between sex-positive and sex-negative feminists was animated at the Barnard conference in New York City titled *The Scholar and the Feminist IX*. Sex-negative feminists, also associated with the antipornography movement, conflated sexual "positions of domination or subordination" with positions of gender (Butler 1994, 7). Male/men were viewed as active/penetrators, whereas female/women were positioned as passive/penetrated.

Within this view of sex, the sex act, where men are positioned as dominating, and women are positioned as being dominated, reproduced social inequality between the genders and exacerbated the subordination of women. In this reading, women can only be perceived as victims and vulnerable. Sex-positive feminists "drew on strong feminist traditions of promoting sexual freedom for women." They also "consistently refused the assimilation of all sexuality to coercive models of domination, and refused as well the assimilation of models of domination to socially fixed positions of gender within a totalizing map of patriarchal domination" (Butler 1994, 7). Indeed, South African feminist Patricia McFadden (2003), drawing on Audre Lorde's notion of the erotic as power, argues that women's sexual pleasure and erotic autonomy should inform women's "fundamental right to a safe and wholesome lifestyle," and be "a political resource in transforming our various social spaces and ourselves."

Queer and feminist studies scholars have also argued that sex can critique regimes of the normal (Bersani 1987; Rubin 1993; Warner 1999; Nguyen 2014). FAKA's and Chhiba's aesthetics of sex—sex-as-art—*fuck* with the racial-gender-sexual-erotic binaries and hierarchies of Afro-normativity. In this chapter, I situate the anus (FAKA) and the yoni (Chhiba) as bottom spaces. Together, they articulate a queer-feminist politics of bottomhood. Drawing on queer-of-color theorist Hoang Tan Nguyen, I understand bottomhood not as a "fixed role, an identity, or a physical act" but as a "position—sexual, social, affective, political, aesthetic—[that] facilitates a more expansive horizon for forging political alliances" (2014, 3).

Sex and the Profane

FAKA and the Politics of African Anality

FAKA emerged on the South African art scene in 2015 and has since acquired an international following, attesting to the importance and impact of their work. Through performance art and aesthetic practices that include photography, sound art, and music, Thato Ramaisa and Buyani Duma reimagine themselves as Fela Gucci and Desire Marea. When FAKA emerged in 2015, their intention was to intervene in current debates on gender and sexuality in South Africa and, more broadly, in Africa. FAKA introduced their feminist queer praxis to South African publics through their multimedia live art performance titled *#Wait Lorraine: A Wemmer Pan-African Introduction to Siyakaka Feminism* (2015) in Johannesburg. Translated by the duo, *Siyakaka* means "We're shitting all over you," emphasizing their use of abjection—in this case, human feces—as a disruptive aesthetic strategy. In a different context, I argue that *Siyakaka* feminism is an African queer-feminist framework that is organized around deviance and transgression. I situate FAKA's uses of "abjection and deviance . . . as both an aesthetic and philosophy of unbecoming normatively human [that] reveals what a contemporary antiracist, anticlassist, antihomophobic, and anti-trans-phobic feminism can look like from FAKA's unique perspective on the black (queer) experience" (Ellapen 2021a, 116). *Siyakaka* feminism is an African decolonial praxis where the erotic and the abject imbricate to unhinge the African body from its colonial and neocolonial attachments. For FAKA, the regulation of black and African gender, sexuality, and erotics directs the incomplete project of freedom; total freedom can only be achieved once the colonized body is free from all structures of surveillance and a(o)bjectification. FAKA's performances of male femininity are important. Male femininity, a form of embodied vulnerability and a feminized orientation toward the world, disrupts the time-space of Afro-normativity and its authentic national subject, which is imagined as cisheteronormative. Thus, FAKA's body politic is a powerful reminder that the black body is not just an archive of historical experience, but also one that already inhabits and imagines a future in a context where the logics of Afro-normativity foreclose this possibility for the black (queer) subject.

Through the aesthetic realm, FAKA plays with the idea that the black body is always already excessive, already abject. Black studies scholar Darieck Scott argues that abjection describes the "historical experiences of people in the African diaspora" (2010, 4–5), and by extension, in Africa, and he reminds us that "blackness [and Africanness] is constituted by a history of abjection, and *is* itself a form of abjection" (4–5). Thus, abjection informs the ways in which (deviant and transgressive) racial and sexual logics coalesce around blackness and Africanness. In his study of "extravagant abjection," Scott turns to the site of abjection—the abjection of blackness and the abjection of black sexuality—to formulate a theory of black power. For Scott and other Black and African anal theorists like Jennifer Nash, for instance, the bottom functions as a "site of black pain" and one of "complex black pleasures" (Nash 2014b, 445).

I first encountered FAKA through their portrait photographs. In their photography, their aesthetics of male femininity is structured around an excessiveness coded through costume and fashion, adornment, make up, and comportment. *Siyakaka* feminism is an unapologetic celebration of the *black male feminine body*. As a manifesto that foregrounds the body, it insists that freedom is only possible through bodily and erotic autonomy.[2] Through aesthetics and appearance, FAKA's bodies become subversive sites of resistance and reconstitution. Their style is characterized by their use of make up to accentuate the fullness of their lips, the contours of their eyes and nose, and their cheekbones. Their heads are always covered with either long, curly weaves, natural hair, or fashionable hats. Their clothing ranges from high couture fashion found on the runways of Paris or Milan to cheap, mass-produced outfits from malls in Johannesburg catering to the working class. Their bodies are canvases that are politicized through their performances of black male femininity. Feminine beauty and fashion, represented through an "aesthetics of excess," to evoke Jillian Hernandez (2020), transform the abjection and deviance of their black femme bodies into subversive sites of beauty.

Thus, FAKA's attention to beauty and fashion resonates with my mother's attention to beauty and fashion in her portrait photos taken in the immediate afterlife of indentureship, as well as Kganye's mother's attention to fashion in her vernacular photos taken in Soweto, and the dead Afro-Indian woman, adorned in an Indian sari, in Khan's project, *when the moon waxes red*. Beauty, fashion, and adornment are key tropes of indenture aesthetics. Feminine beauty rubs against the grittiness of everyday life for those ejected and rendered invisible by Afro-normativity. Beauty and fashion are indicative of the complex ways these disenfranchised subjects understand the body as a site of resistance and reconstitution. Madison Moore argues that "fabulousness . . . allows marginalized people and social outcasts to regain their humanity and creativity, not to boast about power and influence" (2018, vii). They write: "Fabulousness may look great on the outside, and beautiful eccentrics may seem confident and well put together, but underneath the surface lurks a story of survival, and resistance, even if that story is still being written. The watershed moment of fabulousness occurs when marginalized people and other social outcasts . . . [take] the risk to live exactly the way they see fit" (4–5).

Desire Marea writes: "We don't owe anybody an apology. We will do what we want. Nobody will police our bodies (2016b). Through *Siyakaka* feminism, FAKA examines their "complex black experiences." They write: "The themes we explore are mostly focused on the politics of our *bodies* because our *bodies* are a way of confronting the root of our displacement in the world. Our queer identity is an irrevocable layer of our blackness that we cannot ignore either, because it has pushed us further away from being accepted into society. Hence, we have to re-imagine equally radical ways of existing truthfully" (Shezi 2015).

Visibility also shapes their art practice and politics of disruption (plates 25 and 26). Their first photographs to appear on social media platforms emphasized their playful yet critical project of reimaging and refiguring black masculinity. In a photo shoot for *Cakeboy Magazine* (2016), Gucci and Marea wear silk slips and silk head coverings while standing side by side gazing directly into the camera. Gucci's hand rests slightly on Marea's right shoulder. Their bare, athletic/toned chests glisten in the light, emphasizing their masculine yet feminine bodies. The shine on their skin merges with the shine of their silk slips, foregrounding a version of soft masculinity—a male feminine aesthetic—emphasizing their femme and gender-nonconforming identities. FAKA mobilizes the photographic medium to disrupt the cisheterotopias that attach to the imaginary of the proper masculine subject. These photos represent their mandate of disruption and penetration through feminine excess and are examples of their mandate to use their bodies as sites of intervention in the current debates and discourses around gender and sexual politics in Africa.

FAKA is an act of protest and a mode of empowerment that rescripts the abjection of passivity/bottomhood/femininity into a site of pleasure and ecstasy. FAKA is their ultimate revenge—the "bottom's revenge"—on a system/structure that disavows the feminine, a form of energy that is a "resource within each of us" and is "a source of power and information" when mobilized by the most vulnerable in society (Lorde 2007a, 53–59). Importantly, FAKA's attention to male femininity and the politics of bottomhood disrupts, exceeds, and plays with a visual economy that overdetermines blackness. Their starting point is the excessiveness of blackness—an excess that reveals the limits of the category "Human." Through the abject—in this case, feces and male femininity—they spectacularize blackness, shifting the "visual regimes of colonial [apartheid] modernity" to an anal economy that plays with the sedimented truth of the black body in the modern world. They embrace the abject as the truth of blackness to imagine the otherwise. In his work on bottomhood, Nguyen argues that the shift "from opticality to tactility is consonant with a transfer of value from a phallic economy of visible evidence to an anal economy of felt receptivity" (2014, 113). Indeed, through the positionality of the anus, FAKA activates a politic that emphasizes queer-femme embodiment as a route to feeling across various structures of difference.

Below, I examine FAKA's live performance art piece *Bottom's Revenge* and their re-creation of sex scenes for the exhibition *Sex*, moving from their live performances of black queer-femme sex to their short stories. I examine how they use sex and nonnormative pleasures to reimagine black identity—more specifically, the black masculine—as a praxis of care and survival. In an interview, Gucci (2016) states that their whole project, the project of *Siyakaka* feminism, "*is a reimagined existence for all black people*" (my emphasis) (Marea 2016b). FAKA's mandate is to mobilize the bottom positionality—one associated with passivity—to foreground "sexual fluidity and othered masculinities," contesting hegemonic and mainstream representations of black masculinity. *Siyakaka* feminism is a critique of "society's power structure" from the positionality of male femininity" (Manete 2018). Within heteropatriarchal cultures, male femininity is a site of abjection and is often violently regulated.

FAKA has described *Bottom's Revenge* as "a cleansing ritual that involves the purging of anal denialism and queer erasure" (2016). *Bottom's Revenge* is a performance of black queer sex and pleasure in an anus. The performance unfolds in three acts. The multimedia performance art piece begins with footage of Martin Ssempa's "Eat Da Poo Poo" lecture. Ssempa, a Ugandan pastor and chair of Uganda's Pastors' Task Force against Homosexuality, states that their objective is to introduce legislation so that "homosexuality and sodomy never see the light of day in Uganda." It is significant that FAKA begins their performance with this footage, as it situates their performance within current debates concerning homosexuality and same-sex practices on the continent. Ssempa's lecture focuses on gay sex acts and positions sex acts like analingus (rimming) and fisting as deviant and transgressive. In the video footage, Ssempa is seen demonstrating to the audience the act of fisting while stating that gay sex involves the consumption of "poo poo" (feces). As part of his sermons, Ssempa screened Euro-American gay pornography to teach his audiences about gay sex while reiterating the hegemonic position that homosexuality and gay sex acts are un-African and a Western contamination. As the footage ends, Gucci and Marea, dressed in silk slips, enter the stage and step into a bathtub, which is filled with a brown viscous liquid. The artists disrobe and immerse themselves in the liquid. Their performance becomes increasingly erotic as they sensually touch and rhythmically move together. As the two artists touch each other, covering their bodies with the brown liquid, the internal organs of a digestive tract are projected onto the screen. The camera moves through the tract, creating the illusion that the bathtub, with the two performers, is moving through the digestive system. The soundscape emulates the sounds of digesting food as it passes through the intestines. In the final act, the performance ends with the duo *performing sex*; Gucci is on his back in the tub with his legs raised, and Marea perches on top of them. If the bathtub represents the anus, the brown liquid represents human feces, the ultimate form of abjection. In this context, the use of feces is a powerful metaphor for blackening.

Bottom's Revenge, like their performance of *#WaitLorraine*, positions sex talk against political talk; sex talk is FAKA's method to disrupt how the African body is captured within a heteropatriarchal order of things. Ssempa's sermons are indicative of how the "policing of sexual behavior" stabilizes the power of the state over its citizens (Currier 2018, 8). Ssempa's lectures/sermons focus on specific sex acts—like analingus and fisting—to separate the authentic and normative African subject from the inauthentic and queer. African queer studies scholars Matebeni and Pereira remind us that "The language of religion, culture and tradition is often used to speak against sexual and gender diversity in the continent. Within this problematic framework, Africans are and can only be reproductive heterosexuals" (2014, 7). Ssempa focuses on sexual practices to reiterate how proper African bodies achieve legibility through specific sex acts. The authentic African body is designed to engage in proper sex acts where the penis (associated with masculinity and power) is inserted into the vagina (associated with women and passivity). They code normative and authentic Africanness through normative sex acts (active male/passive female), reinforcing racial-gender-sexual binaries and hierarchies. According to this logic, the authentic African (masculine) subject is rendered legible through the penis/phallus, whereas the anus and anal penetration are associated with the loss of power and authenticity and coded as a site of disruption. Ssempa, as well as Jacob Zuma, reflects the hegemonic position in Africa where blackness and Africanness are rendered legible through heteronormativity.

Bottom's Revenge demonstrates how African same-sex desire is produced as waste, filth, and excess, that which is coded as the abject. Indeed, feces is one of the most abject of human bodily excretions. However, they disrupt this association between the black queer/femme body and abjection through pleasure and ecstasy in abjection. In this performance, abjection (feces, waste) merges with transgressive erotics (same-sex practices and pleasures) as a praxis of disruption and regeneration.

For the exhibition *Sex,* FAKA recreated a performance space where abjection (sweat, cum, male femininity) merged with transgressive erotics (masturbation, gay pornography, same-sex pleasures). For this performance, FAKA recreated sex scenes from *The Factory*, a men-only sex club in Johannesburg. Their allocated space in the gallery was designed to re-create the atmosphere of a sex club: their performance occurs in a darkened corner, where they have positioned two beds next to each other in front of a TV screen playing gay pornography. A crowd gathers around them, and many are shocked to discover two naked black men viewing gay pornography as they masturbate in this public space. As they touch themselves sensually, gyrating their hips and buttocks erotically, sweating, and eventually ejaculating, they transform their black (queer) bodies into sites of pleasure and ecstasy. FAKA's live performances of sex position the black body as a spectacle of sexual excess, *reorganizing blackness as transgressive erotics*.

In an online article written for *okayafrica*, published on May 31, 2016, writer Tseliso Monaheng offers a description of this performance: "So there they were, the FAKA collective, queening atop makeshift bed structures, naked and ripped and muscular, sweating while they performed the act of sex—not on each other, though that would've been so ill!" After they ejaculated, Monaheng captures the audience reactions: the "comments; the shocked looks on people's faces." This description emphasizes the "funkiness" of their performance; sweat coagulating with cum on their lean muscular, yet feminine bodies is a site of both revulsion and attraction. FAKA plays with the pain/pleasure dichotomy. They articulate an embodied politic that refigures blackness as a site of complex pleasures routed through transgression and abjection. Their performance drew the attention of visitors, and a crowd soon gathered around them. The audience gazed at them with wonder and surprise; some were visibly uncomfortable, while others displayed curiosity about the performances of gay sex and pleasure in the space of the gallery.

FAKA's ejaculation in this performance piece is significant. This is the *cum* of queer futurity rather than the ejaculate of a reproductive present. Since progress and futurity are marked by reproduction, their queer feminine *cum* signifies failure. It is both visual and visceral, but this is not the "money shot" of cisgender male pleasure and mastery over female/feminine bodies. Their performances of queer sex and pleasure that culminate in the act of *cumming* activate the senses beyond the visual organization of the gallery. The smell, texture, color, and the state of cumming shift their bodies from the "space of the sensual toward movement into the space of the chaotic" (King 2019, 147), which I understand as another affective and sensual regime that can be described as a state of ecstasy. FAKA positions the black queer-femme body in ecstasy as an important political mandate to reimagine black sexuality and forms of relationalities between black men outside of limited identitarian categories. FAKA's cum, coded as nonreproductive and therefore associated with anality (waste), represents *queer futurity* rather than the ejaculate of a *reproductive present*.

Sex talk is a method employed by FAKA to situate embodied knowledge as an important political call to reimage black (men's) sexuality and pleasure away from a heteropatriarchal context that guarantees black death (literal and social). They disrupt the authentic/normative/nativist parameters of South African blackness by displacing the penis/phallus for the anus/bottom. Their relationship between anal erotics and "felt receptivity" creates lines of flight away from discourses of mastery, newness, and neoliberal individuality toward an alternative architecture of blackness that emphasizes a queer-feminist politics of ethical relationality. In the next section, I examine two short stories written by Desire Marea in order to understand how FAKA's performances of sex provide new ways of imagining male-male intimacies and blackness away from the violence of the norm.

Sex, Relationality, and New Architectures of Blackness

In a story titled "Thabiso: Gay CBD and the Complexities of Nivea-ness," Marea writes about a failed sexual encounter between themselves and Thabiso, described as a stranger in their bed (Marea and Gucci 2017). The story begins and moves through the different layers of failure that mark this sexual encounter. First, Thabiso fails to maintain an erection in order to successfully penetrate Marea. Since Thabiso is unable to fulfill the role of the top in this sexual encounter, they decide to invert positions and Marea shifts from the bottom position to the top. However, once Marea has penetrated Thabiso he lasts only three seconds, and since this sexual encounter did not stand up to the "pornographic positions" and sexual fantasies promised in their WhatsApp conversation, this encounter is coded as a failure (Marea and Gucci 2017). It is now 3 a.m. and Marea longs to process this failed encounter in the privacy and safety of their home. Afraid that Thabiso's failure (emasculation) may result in violence, Marea asks him to leave, revealing his own "violating sexual experiences" (Marea and Gucci 2017). However, Thabiso is reluctant to leave and Marea is exasperated that once again he is stuck with a stranger in his bed. Marea's anxiety dissipates when Thabiso reveals his own experience with sexual violation at the age of nineteen. Thabiso's experience of being gang raped by his boyfriend and others positions both Thabiso and Marea within the terrain of vulnerability. Instead of their failed sexual encounter reflecting a disconnect between them, it opens up the possibility of crafting counterintuitive relationalities based on their shared affect of displacement and shame. Marea writes that stories of violation, sexual abuse, and rape "are not necessarily the things we discuss during/after (a failed attempt) at meaningless sex" (Marea and Gucci 2017). In this moment of failure, Thabiso embraces this position of vulnerability and uses this as an opportunity to unmask himself to reveal a complex black subjectivity.

Marea uses the term *Niveaness* to describe black men's desire for assimilation and recognition within mainstream queer culture. Their idea of Niveaness draws from the discourses about black masculinity produced by the advertising campaigns for Nivea, a popular lotion marketed to the middle class across the racial spectrum in South Africa. The association between a lotion (a skin care product) and hegemonic black masculinity is significant. In South African Nivea adverts, black men are represented through tropes of hypermasculinity (hard, muscular, impenetrable), heteronormativity, cleanliness, and reproductive futurity. This version of black (hyper)masculinity has also permeated queer cultures and has become fetishized and desired by queer men. These tropes of masculinity stand in sharp contrast to FAKA's embodied masculinity, which emphasizes femininity, vulnerability, and fluidity. Niveaness also reflects a class positionality. Nivea's black men are middle to upper-middle-class and socially mobile, fitting into the ethos of the cosmopolitan neoliberal subject. Whereas FAKA is interested in the abject—feces, waste, residue, and ash, for instance—Nivea's black men are clean, sanitized, sterile, freshly showered, shiny, sexy, and cosmopolitan. Thus, the shine that emanates from FAKA's bodies, evident in their photographs, rubs against the shine of Nivea masculinity, an assimilationist black masculinity. FAKA's shine signifies filth and abjection, the waste, by-products, of a cisnormative privileging society. For Marea, the Nivea aesthetic of manhood is an embodiment of "whiteness," where whiteness signifies power, social and economic mobility, and the desire for postcolonial respectability that echoes the logics of neoliberal capital. For Marea, Niveaness is a mask that black (queer) men are "pressured to portray in public." It is a mask that disavows vulnerability and those who embody vulnerability, coded as failed masculinity. Niveaness is privileged in queer nightlife cultures in South Africa where it displaces the femme/trans/gender nonconforming subject by privileging those who are "straight-acting" and homonormative.

Niveaness functions as a mask for black cisgender normative men (both heterosexual and homosexual). Those who do not live up to the expectations of "Nivea-ness" operate through a complex terrain of shame and vulnerability. Niveaness manages public performances of black (queer) masculinity and violently shapes the terrain of desire and pleasure. Marea writes: "You cannot even dance if you want dick when the dick wants nothing but the *straight-acting* serenity of post-mig33 nivea-ness, dipping its tongue into the neck of a Savannah bottle there by the corner" (Marea and Gucci 2017).

FAKA intuitively understands how the mask polices gender identity and sexual subjectivity and exacerbates gender violence, where straight (acting) men feel entitled to violate the bodies of those who are perceived to be embodying "failed" masculinity. Marea writes that this mask "limits the way we love" and our capacity to create intimate attachments. It alienates us from ourselves, our bodies, and from one another.

> Imagine if you want to talk, if you wanted to be nothing but yourself, to be transparent about the things that bother you: your poverty, your strained love life, the residual trauma of growing up gay in an anti-gay

world, the trauma of not being able to interrogate your own experience of sexual violence because misogynoir has become an integral part of your existence, a mere gaze that polices your horny, gyrating femme body into undesirable sub-human spaces where "tops" can force themselves into your anus even when you have said no because what else could you be asking for? You are gay. Gays love sex (Marea and Gucci 2017).

In the second story, titled "Sisqo: The Complexities of Soccer Player Dick," Marea recounts a sexual encounter with a black soccer player he met on an online dating app (Marea and Gucci 2017). At the beginning of this narrative, the writer fetishizes the soccer player, describing him as a "real man," expressing desire for "soccer player dick." The dick was not only easily available to him (Sisqo contacted Marea on an online app and delivered his dick to Marea), but it also promised a particular kind of masculine performance of sex and pleasure for Marea. Marea does not shy away from the contradictions of desire and pleasure. Marea writes that Sisqo was a soccer player who "did not make it to the first team," framing this story around failure. However, Sisqo's failure to achieve star status did not detract from the fact that he has a "dick in his sweatpants." In the apartment, Marea discovers that Sisqo is a "straight" man who is curious about gay sex and that this is "his first interaction with a homosexual man" (Marea and Gucci 2017). Marea unpacks for Sisqo the complexities of desire and identity and the limits of our vocabulary to render our bodily desires legible, especially those that disrupt categories like "heterosexual" and "homosexual." Marea and Sisqo have sex; Sisqo fucks/penetrates Marea.

Through this story, Marea revels in the messiness of desire and pleasure, especially when they rub against the politics of his queerness that is based on dismantling the binaristic logics of masculine/feminine, male/female, top/bottom, heterosexual/homosexual. For Marea, fucking is about creating human connections that are not governed by identitarian logics; sex is not only about fucking in order to validate their humanity as a black queer subject but also about the pleasure of creating physical and intimate contact with another human being, even if it is just for a night. Sex is a practice of humanization in a context where black queer men, particularly those who are femme and gender-nonconforming, are strategically excluded from the domain of pleasure and desire within a cisnormative and racist queer culture.

In this story, the generative potential of sex shifts from the private to the public domains. Marea writes that the power of finding pleasure with the "dick of a stranger" is the affective connections it creates the next day when they navigate the city, "walking among the millions in the street" (Marea and Gucci

2017). The lingering sensation after being anally penetrated (having a "burning anus") produces a larger sense of belonging and connection with the masses moving through Johannesburg. Through the negative affects associated with anal erotics, Marea crafts counterintuitive relationalities and modes of belonging that circumvent neoliberalism's emphasis on linear progress, upward social mobility, and individuality.

In both stories, Thabiso's and Sisqo's unmasking shifts the meanings of these sexual encounters for both participants. Unmasking renders them—their bodies and psyches—vulnerable to each other. This vulnerability, which requires the suspension of "heteronormative righteousness," allows for the construction of new forms of relationalities between black men, irrespective of sexual orientation. FAKA's stories reveal that the disruption of heteronormativity can generate new communities and forms of socialities that reconfigure the meanings of blackness itself. The history of colonial apartheid and the violence of heteropatriarchy have rendered the black subject unlovable and "blackness itself" as unlovable. Similarly to Black and African diasporic thinkers like Frantz Fanon, bell hooks, Marlon Riggs, and James Baldwin, FAKA positions love as pivotal to the liberatory politics of our time.

For FAKA, sex (which brings bodies together in pleasure, ecstasy, pain, vulnerability, exposure, mastery) is the ethical relationship that defines our current moment. Organizing their performances around pleasure and ecstasy rather than pain and injury, FAKA desires a different body-to-body relationality that emphasizes touch, feeling, and sensuality. FAKA imagines a different body-to-body relationality between black men that disrupts the relationship between blackness and death. The question of sex, especially the question of how black (gay) men fuck, is an important one in a context where the black masculine is objectified—reduced—as the hard black dick. FAKA offers a way to think through black sexuality and fucking as an ethical practice between black men that circumvents heteropatriarchy as the only form of legibility for black male subjectivity in an antiblack world. For FAKA, sex and the erotic, as well as their aesthetics of fabulousness, are sources of power that are central to their project of humanization and their politics of survival. In their stories, male-feminine power and anal erotics produce horizontal relationalities connecting their desire for intimacies with those that have been rendered disposable by the neoliberal state.

In their performance of *Bottom's Revenge*, their staging of black queer sex and erotics for the exhibition *Sex*, and through story-telling, FAKA mobilizes abjection—feces, sweat, anal erotics—to queer the project of black authenticity. Their aesthetics of waste and excess—intimately sutured to gender and sexual non-normative bodies—viscerally demonstrates the ways in which blackening functions in the post-apartheid period to separate the new black/ened Others from the authentic black subject. Through their sophisticated art practice, FAKA draws on the queer world-making potential of the positionality of being blackened in order to reimage a radical politics of relationality that disrupts the ways in which identitarian categories organize post-apartheid modes of belonging. Blackening in FAKA's art practice, similar to that of other artists examined in this book, troubles the very boundaries of South African blackness and the linear and progress narrative of development associated with the postapartheid, to articulate a deviant politic of unbelonging as a black political strategy of imagining otherwise.

Sex and the Sacred

Reshma Chhiba's Kalis and the Subversive Power of the Yoni

In *The Two Talking Yonis*, Reshma Chhiba mobilizes the racial, gender, and sexual excesses associated with Kali as a disruptive aesthetic strategy. In this project, the abject and the erotic (transgressive and deviant) bleed into each other. She simultaneously critiques the a(o)bjectification of women within heteropatriarchal society and the abject positionality of the Indian in postapartheid South Africa. Kali's association with blood, corpses, and the cremation grounds positions her on the peripheries of Hindu society. Her ferocious behavior on the battlefield and her dominating sexuality threaten to *disrupt* the stability of the cosmos. Kali is associated with bodily and libidinal excess that cannot be contained within the overdetermined identity categories of Indian, female, woman, mother, reproducer, destroyer, and recreator. Kali defies categorization; disrupts binary formations such as masculine/feminine, creator/destroyer, male/female, and life/death; and represents the excesses of female sexuality; Kali's feminine energy, coded as transgressive and disruptive, is most threatening to heteropatriarchy. Kali's association with excess renders her dangerous. However, the negative and the nonnormative excesses associated with Kali signify the potential for regeneration. For all intents and purposes, Kali resists capture within the "order of things," and by embracing her excess and abjection, Chhiba offers a sophisticated critique of how normative formations of race, gender, and sexuality imbricate with the postapartheid nation's project of heteronormativity (plate 27).

Tracy Murinik (2019) offers three originary narratives of the goddess Kali. In the first, Kali is the manifestation of the goddess Durga's rage. Kali manifests out of Durga's forehead on the battlefield against two demons. In this story, Kali destroys the demon god Raktabija and devours his clones, which appear from drops of his blood. The uncontrollable Kali dances on the corpses of the slain. In another origin story from the *Linga Purana*, Kali manifests when Shiva and the goddess Parvati merge. Shiva is associated with destruction, whereas Parvati is associated with fertility, love and devotion. Kali manifests from the merging of Shiva and Parvati because Parvati dutifully agrees to destroy the demon Daruka, who can only be killed by a woman. In this narrative, Kali is overwhelmed by her destructive nature and can only transform back into Parvati after Shiva's intervention. In a third narrative, also featuring Parvati and Shiva, Parvati is offended that Shiva refers to her as Kali, the "black one" (Murinik 2019, 83). Shamed by this, Parvati appeals to the gods "to lose her dark complexion" and become Gauri, the golden one" (83). Her dark skin becomes Kausiki, who manifests as Kali when enraged. These origin stories position Kali in binary relations to their masculine/male counterparts, where Kali's autonomy and pleasure are circumscribed and determined by the male/masculine god.

Chhiba's Kalis mark a significant shift from such origin mythologies. She explodes narratives of authenticity. The artist resists Hindu mythological interpretations where Kali only manifests when called upon by the masculine/male form to service his needs, reinscribing male/female and masculine/feminine as binary oppositions and a relation of masculine mastery over feminine submission. For Chhiba, Kali is the space where the masculine and feminine already exist as one form and are inseparable from each other. Through Kali's abject and transgressive erotics, boundaries, binaries, and hierarchies disintegrate. Kali's association with funk—decay, death, smell, bodily fluids like blood—and deviant sexuality is disorientating, disrupting the boundaries between the human and the nonhuman, the sacred and the profane, male and female, black and Indian.

Hinduism, like many African religious practices, recognizes and reveres male and female, masculine and feminine forms of the divine and is often positioned as "unique among contemporary world religions in its living practice of goddess veneration" (Diesel 1998, 74). Kali is associated with Siva, the Hindu god of destruction and restoration, and in representations of Kali and Siva, which are most often representations of the goddess and god engaged in the act of sex, Kali is usually represented as the dominant participant. She sits over the prostrate body of Siva with a sword in one hand. In Hindu mythology, Kali has traditionally been employed as "a symbol of female defiance" against heteropatriarchy in Hindu culture and society, and images of the goddess have been employed by artists of South Asian/Indian origin "as a means to symbolize female power and assert female sexuality" (Chhiba 2013, 3–7).

I Am Kali, I Am Black

Indian Blackness and the Making of Afro-Indianness

Deep within the twelve-meter walk-in yoni, visitors encountered a provocative self-portrait of the artist titled *I Am Kali, I Am Black*. This is also a portrait, Chhiba's Afro-Indian interpretation, of the goddess Kali. Kali is often represented as black or blue/black, and her name means "black or darkened color," pointing to the overdetermined association between women's sexuality and danger in heteropatriarchal societies. In a close-up shot, Chhiba stands in front of a white background gazing directly and defiantly into the camera. Her face is framed by her disheveled hair. Referencing Kali's deviant and aggressive nature, the artist's tongue protrudes from her mouth, pointing downward in a disrespectful manner. The right half of Chhiba's face is blackened out, while the left half is well-lit. In this portrait, Chhiba and Kali merge even as she plays with Kali's dual nature that resists and disrupts binaries and hierarchies.

Chhiba, a Kali worshipper, argues that her deployment of Kali is not culturally, religiously, or ethnically specific. According to Chhiba, Kali is the ultimate form of feminine energy and defiance. She represents all women who disrupt the violence of patriarchy through everyday practices of resistance. Provocatively, Chhiba writes that Kali is "*Indian in her blackness and black in her Indianness*" (my emphasis, Chhiba 2017, 48). Here, Chhiba complicates the racial categories of Indian and black as they have been constructed as oppositional categories through the long history of colonial apartheid. By evoking Kali's blackness, Chhiba also evokes Indian blackness and what Vanita Reddy (2021, 99) refers to as the "colorism hierarchy" in India. Kali's blackness allows us to read blackness across the Indian Ocean differently, articulating a South/South trajectory that complicates how we understand Southern African blackness, particularly when Kali's blackness manifests in South Africa as an iteration of South African blackness.

In India, South Indians, usually from the state of Tamil Nadu, are associated with dark skin (Reddy 2021, 99–100). Indian blackness, associated with the South and the Dravidians, rubs against Indian whiteness, associated with North Indians and the Aryan race. The dark-skinned Dravidians are associated with impurity and dirt, whereas the light-skinned Aryans are associated with cleanliness and authentic Indianness. Light skin glows, whereas dark skin is a signifier of impurity and contamination. Colorism largely determines notions of beauty in India. Lighter skin is valued, whereas darker skin, particularly for women, is a site of shame. Importantly, "South Indians, in particular, are routinely racialized as black in India's colorism hierarchy, and are disproportionately affected by colorism's economic, social, and cultural harms." According to Reddy (2021), "Even while the racialization of (South) Indian Blackness is distinct from that of African Blackness, the racial category 'Black' positions South Indians as further away from the Aryan beauty myth and, thus, further away from aspirational whiteness" (100). Complicating the notion that colonialism is to blame for the violence of colorism in contemporary Indian society, Reddy (2021) argues that "colonial whiteness . . . [does] not fully consider how colonial racial hierarchies historically reinforced pre-existing caste, color, and regional hierarchies on the subcontinent" (100). Furthermore, it is important to consider how notions of Indian whiteness and Indian blackness and the values attached to the color of skin manifest diasporically, particularly among diasporic populations formed out of the Indian indenture labor migration. How does Indian blackness manifest within a racially segregated society like South Africa? What happens when Indian blackness rubs against South African blackness? This remains unexamined in the literature on race in South Africa.

In South Africa, Indians were strategically racialized to occupy the space between the white settler population (at the top of the racial hierarchy) and the black African population (at the bottom of the racial hierarchy). Antiblack racism was a common feature among anticolonial fighters. Gandhi, for instance, "regularly used the racial slur 'kaffir' to refer to Black Africans" (Reddy 2021, 100). Gandhi's early politics have been critiqued.[3] He believed that the rights of Indians must be fought separately from those of coloureds and black Africans. Even though the antiapartheid struggle forged a common political language routed through Biko's Black Consciousness, histories of racial segregation and antagonisms between Indians and black Africans exacerbated the incommensurability between blackness and Indianness. Colonial apartheid created a context where whiteness was valued, and blackness was a site of shame and downward social mobility. This still resonates strongly in post-apartheid society. Furthermore, within Indian South African communities, colorism replicates and resonates strongly with the colonial-apartheid racial ordering/hierarchy. Within this heterogenous community, Indian blackness positions one closer to black Africanness. Indian whiteness attaches dangerously to white settler-colonial power through the impossible desire for assimilation. Indian aspirations for social mobility were (are) based on the abjection of blackness—both black Africanness and black Indianness.

In the portrait *I Am Kali, I Am Black*, Chhiba restores Kali's dark skin, which was disavowed in one of the originary narratives of the goddess. By resituating Kali within the complex terrain of blackness, she provocatively disidentifies with Indian whiteness. This is a disidentification with the class and racial-gender-sexual politics of the trader-class Indian. By evoking Indian blackness, she simultaneously critiques the nativist and normative underpinnings of Afro-normative blackness. In this portrait, where Kali and Chhiba, light and dark, masculine and feminine, Indian blackness and South African blackness rub against each other, Chhiba uses the aesthetic realm to articulate the complexities of Afro-Indianness. In this context, Atlantic Blackness rubs against an Indian Ocean manifestation of blackness to reroute how we think about South African blackness. Through her articulation of Afro-Indianness, Chhiba reorients us toward complex and imbricated formations of blackness that weave together Afro-Indianness and black Africanness. Importantly, in my analysis of Khan's project *when the moon waxes red*, Afro-Indianness is mainly rendered legible through Atlantic Blackness (Khan evokes transatlantic slavery). For Chhiba, Afro-Indianness emerges through the entanglements between Indian blackness (evoked through the figure of Kali) and black Africanness. Khan and Chhiba offer two different but interrelated articulations of Afro-Indianness. Positioning Khan's Afro-Indianness in relationship to Chhiba's Afro-Indianness demonstrates how Afro-Indianness itself is a complex articulation of Southern African blackness, where Atlantic Blackness and Indian Ocean blackness merge.

From Kali's Blackness to Kali's Yoni

Chhiba's Kalis shift from her destructive nature, represented by her dark/blackened skin (which must be violently disavowed), to her yoni, the site of regenerative feminine energy. Chhiba's yonis queer normative Indian/Hindu ideas of Kali. The term *queer* points to Kali's nonnormative nature. Positioning the "yonic space" as queer emphasizes the point where binaries and hierarchies collapse; Kali, in all her excesses, is the point where one loses oneself, and it is in the process of losing oneself—the point beyond beyondness—that one derives the most pleasure. Through this process, binaries and hierarchies unravel, and we enter a generative and creative space where the excessive nature of Kali shifts beyond women as "Other" as the "excess . . . that constitutes 'men' and 'humanity'" (Khan 2019a, 56). Chhiba's Kali resists and critiques Western identity categories. Drawing on the abject and the transgressive, she emphasizes the pleasure of destruction and re-creation as ongoing cyclical processes that resist fixity, binaries, and hierarchies.

In her series of paintings, Chhiba's Kalis are disembodied, gushing menstrual blood from their yonis, while using their male counterparts solely for sexual pleasure. Indeed, Shiva is represented as vulnerable and is feminized in these representations. Kali's bodily excesses—from menstrual blood, blackened skin, and her association with death, decay, graveyards, severed skulls, and aggressive performances of sex—are indicative of Kali's funkiness. Her paintings and the large installation are simultaneously sonic, haptic, and affective. My understanding of funk draws on Black studies scholars like L. H. Stallings (2015) and Rinaldo Walcott (2021). Stallings (2015, 4) offers an "etymological triad for *funk*" that includes "nonvisual sensory perception (smell/odor), embodied movement (dance and sex), and force (mood and will)" (4). Stallings's notion of funk fractures Western notions of eros and the human by directing us to what exists, what has always existed, beyond Western categories and knowledge systems. Funk is about the body (corporeality) and the creative and improvisational ways in which African people and their descendants have exceeded and exploded categories of being and regimes of capture designed to demarcate the boundaries between the human and the not-so-human. Funk, according to Stallings, is not a "reactionary mechanism." She writes: "I see it as imperiocorporeal cognition or imperiocorporeal perception—a simultaneous creation of new knowledge and an acquisition of knowledge through the body to counter imperialist or colonial appropriation of bodies and cultures. Funk is force, not power" (5).

Chhiba's articulations of Kali offer a provocative entry into sexual cultures in South Africa beyond the black-white racial binary. Indeed, Chhiba's articulation of Afro-Indian blackness extends beyond the colonial-apartheid project of race-making. It is a blackness—a funky blackness—that refuses capture within an order of things. Chhiba's renderings of Kali emphasize pleasure in abjection and excess. In her paintings depicting the sexual union between Kali and Shiva, Kali is the dominant sex partner, emphasizing Kali's autonomy and power rather than Shiva's. In these paintings, menstrual blood, which signifies transgression, abjection, and danger within heteropatriarchal societies because of its threat of contamination and emasculation, operates as a signifier of Kali's disruptive feminine energy. Chhiba's "yonic spaces" are disorientating and disruptive, the ultimate space of losing oneself, where either/or binaries unravel. This is a space where Kali's pleasure overrides Shiva's association with heteropatriarchal power, which exploits and abjects the feminine. Dwelling in the transgressive and the abject, Chhiba's "yonic space" transforms Kali's feminine energy into a force field where binaries (either/or) and hierarchies disintegrate, offering us glimpses of a future that is yet to arrive. For Chhiba, the "yonic space" functions as a critique of national and diasporic investments in heteropatriarchy. The abjection of her "yonic space" "reorients our thinking about sexuality, gender, and agency" (Stallings 2015, 2) away from the new configuration of the authentic national subject in the postapartheid period. Chhiba's Kalis engage in nonreproductive sex, where pleasure overrides procreation, emphasizing the role of pleasure in the creation of possible queer futures outside of linear progressive narratives that rely on blood and reproduction to produce heteronormative presents.

In these paintings, Chhiba demonstrates the ways in which "funk and fuck" are intertwined, and it is this imbrication that is disorientating and disruptive. In many paintings, Chibba's Kalis are decapitated. The painting *Sublime Essence* (2013) (plate 28) represents a decapitated Kali squatting on the ground, exposing her yoni. Menstrual blood rushes out from the canvas toward the spectator while Kali squats in her blood. In another painting titled *The One Who Is All That Has Been* (2013) (plate 29), a decapitated woman stands upright with her hands behind her back. Her yoni is framed in an inverted triangle. The red blood that gushes out of the yoni in the previous painting now moves up and emerges out of the neck. Kali's menstrual blood is so powerful that it threatens the destruction not just of the cosmos but of Kali herself. In a third painting, titled *Ultimate Reality* (2013) (plate 30), Kali and Shiva embrace postcoital bliss. Kali lays over Shiva, his hand on her hip and his leg bent, their faces touching intimately. What is striking about this image is that hovering over this scene of sexual pleasure is an image of a decapitated Kali, holding a sickle in one hand and her severed head in the other hand. Like the images discussed above, blood flows upward and gushes out of the neck onto the hand holding Kali's severed head.

It is significant that in many of the artist's depictions of Kali, she holds her decapitated head in her hands. This violent act of decapitation, which separates the head from the body, can be read as a critique of the ways in which Indian heteropatriarchy and Western modernity merge to produce the category "woman" while maintaining the separation between mind/body, rational/irrational, male/female, and masculine/feminine. Across patriarchal cultures and traditions in the East and West, women represent the body and the excesses associated with the body. Women occupy the terrain of negative effects (waste, excess, irrational, hysterical, submissive), whereas men are associated with the intellect/mind, control, rationality, and domination. Chhiba's depictions of sex between Kali and Shiva disrupt the binary logics that maintain the distinctions between male/female, man/woman, and human/divine.

In *Ultimate Reality*, where a decapitated Kali holds her head in her left hand over the bodies of a couple who have just had sex, Chhiba points to the disruptive force of female pleasure (yonic pleasure). Chhiba's decapitated Kalis are significant, emphasizing why female pleasure is so disruptive to heteropatriarchy. In my readings of Chhiba's Kalis, female pleasure is a source of feminine energy that explodes the category of "woman" itself, pointing to its ontological origins in Western imperialism. African feminist Oyèrónkẹ́ Oyěwùmís (1997) critiques the violence embedded in "Western philosophical, conceptual, and linguistic traditions" that assume the universality of human bodies, where gender is mobilized as a technique of power to capture bodies within the Western order of things. This reproduces gender binaries, reinforcing Western notions of the category "man." Embracing the excesses—negative affects—that construct woman as the other to man in Western conceptualizations of the Human, Chhiba disrupts how the category "woman" is always overdetermined in its relationship to the category "man" in the West and in diasporic contexts. Kali's transgressive erotics are uncontainable within any human form, disrupting not just the male/female binary, but the category "human" itself. The force produced by Kali's pleasure emphasizes the relationship between nonnormative erotics and "unbecoming human," a process that disrupts the Western order of things that maintains the gender binary.

The imbrication of funk and fuck in her paintings disrupts the binary logics of mind/body, artist/curator, and black/Indian. Instead, Chhiba emphasizes both/and at the same time—male and female, masculine and feminine, mind and body, Afro-Indian and black (Khan 2019b). In Indian culture, even though Kali appears to be independent, she is represented in binary opposition to the masculine and oftentimes requires the masculine form to appease her destructive, aggressive, and bloodthirsty nature. Religious Kali manifests within the patriarchal logics of Indian customs and traditions, where female sexuality is destructive and must come under the control of the male/masculine. Chhiba's aesthetic pleasure in funk—menstrual blood, decay, corpses, transgressive pleasures—disturbs these binaries, turning to sex and the imagination to "undo the coloniality of being/truth/freedom" (Wynter 2003).

In her creation and re-creation of Kali, Chhiba disrupts Kali's deadly association with abjection, transgression, and erotics by rescripting Kali's feminine energy into a site that enables the emergence of new socialities. Through the excesses of feminine pleasure, Chhiba's "yonic spaces" generate and regenerate social worlds characterized by "(un)becoming (normatively) human" (Ellapen 2021a, 142), not governed by the logics of binaries and hierarchies. Indeed, Kali is dangerous to heteropatriarchy because she is the ultimate form of pleasure, where difference (gender, race, ethnicity, bodily) disintegrates and where it becomes possible to imagine humanity outside of the limits of identitarian logics. Kali is funk, Kali is force; Kali is everything and nothing at the same time. Chhiba's Kalis represent the abject excesses of the universe where everything (black, Indian, African, masculine, feminine, body/mind) is absorbed into the great expansiveness that is Kali as she takes on the labor of destroying heteropatriarchy in order to regenerate new social worlds.

Chhiba's Feminist Futurity and the Notion of Home

Even though Chhiba's artwork is spectacular in its size and representation of the yoni, it is informed by the intimacies of the home-space. The home-space is a recurring trope throughout this book, and we have encountered it across various spaces—the home-space of the Indian family in the afterlife of indentureship, the home-space of the black African family in the township, as well as the male-male intimacies produced within the home-space in rural areas and within the mine-housing complex. *Indenture Aesthetics* is shaped and informed by the home-space and the various feminine and feminized articulations of black/ened life that emerge from within this space. It is a site of pain and pleasure where sexuality, sensuality, and beauty imbricate within and through the body. Chhiba rescripts the home-space counterintuitively to mine the possibilities of a feminist futurity situated within the stasis of home. *The Two Talking Yonis* is a response to the heteropatriarchal strivings of the Indian diasporic family that echoes the heteropatriarchal foundations of the nation. Chhiba's sense of South African Indianness is determined by her family's experience of migration, which differs from Indian indenture and "passenger" Indian migrations of the late nineteenth century. Chhiba's interest in the counterintuitive and disruptive feminine energy of Kali began with her grandmother Ajima, who traveled across the *kali pani* from Gujarat, India, with her seven-year-old son in the 1950s. Ajima embarked on this journey alone; her husband and his father were already in South Africa. Ajima waited until they had established themselves as shopkeepers before she joined them in this new country. Like other immigrant women during this time period, Ajima found herself constrained within the heteropatriarchal family. However, she resisted her erasure and silence by finding pleasure within the domestic arena in counterintuitive ways.

Chhiba draws on Ajima's defiance against the heteropatriarchal family, enacted through minor acts that can be easily rendered inconsequential in a country that is organized around the spectacle of the political. For instance, Ajima refused to communicate in English. She rejected the colonial language and communicated only in Gujarati and Fanakalo, an African pidgin language. Distinct forms of Fanakalo developed within urban and rural spaces. Although its origins are difficult to determine, linguistic scholars like Rajend Mesthrie (2019, 13) estimate that "the language has been in existence for at least two centuries" (see also Mesthrie 1989). Studies conducted in the early twentieth century positioned Fanakalo as originating with Indian indentured workers. But this theory has been contested. What is important to note, though, is that in Natal, Fanakalo "stabilized with the arrival of large numbers of indentured workers" (Mesthrie 2019, 14) and, by some accounts, it was the main mode of communication between Indians and the Zulus (Cole 1953). Even though in contemporary South Africa, Fanakalo is associated with the mines and became the *lingua franca* among mine workers, scholars agree that Fanakalo did not originate within the mining context, nor did it originate on the sugarcane plantations of Natal.

However, scholars like David Brown (1988) write: "The entire process of becoming a miner was bound up with the learning of Fanakalo" (quoted in Mesthrie 2019, 16). In mines, Fanakalo "proved a viable means of enabling work to be performed by black African miners." It was also taught to white miners "with an emphasis on instructing workers under them" (Mesthrie 2019, 16–17). For trader-class Indian families setting up business in the interior of the country, mainly serving the white colonial communities and black African displaced communities, the use of Fanakalo makes sense. However, as a main mode of communication between Indians and local black African communities, I am interested in how the use of this language also structured and sedimented the uneven power relationship between the trader-class Indian and local black Africans. My sense is that the language was mobilized similarly to the ways in which white mine workers were trained to use it as a mode of instruction and direction, replicating the relationship where the Indian is positioned above the black African. Even though Ajima may have rejected the colonial language (English) as a small act of resistance, her use of Fanakalo could have replicated the colonial-apartheid logic of domination through language use. Importantly, Mesthrie demonstrates how this language has developed in the mines to become relevant in contemporary South African struggles over justice and inequality. In the aftermath of the Marikana Massacre in 2012, Mesthrie (2019) writes, "Fanakalo has come to prominence as the language preferred by the strikers for mass meetings and negotiations with management" (13).

For all intents and purposes, Ajima embodied the dutiful and sacrificial Indian wife, who is often symbolized through the overdetermined figure of the

Indian goddess Sita. Sita is venerated in Hindu culture because she is represented as respectful, dutiful, and sacrificial. However, Sita's identity and sexual autonomy are circumscribed within the confines of the heteropatriarchal family. Instead of positioning Ajima solely through the oppressive gaze of domestic patriarchy, which inevitably reduces Ajima to the biopolitical, Chhiba emphasizes Ajima's pleasure in raising a large family, positioning this as a future-orientated act of defiance. Chhiba and Ntombela (2019) write that Ajima produced "a trail of female warriors in her shadow, of more Kalis to come" (2).

Chhiba's conjuring of Ajima, who simultaneously represents Kali, queers her biopolitical function within the Indian family. Ajima's counterintuitive pleasure is queer as it is both disruptive and generative. Ajima's pleasure arises from unhinging her reproductive capacities from the biopolitical and instead positions it as a way of producing alternative lines of flight that are future-oriented. Even though Ajima's reproductive capacities fulfill the logic of diasporic domesticity, she imagines and inhabits a future in the present—a future-present—that is engaged with the material realities of the present. Emphasizing nonnormative pleasure, Chhiba makes the discursive shift from the sacrificial Sita to the sexually aggressive and disruptive Kali.

Chhiba, like many of the artists examined in this book, dwells on the generative potential of the counterintuitive. Ajima's quotidian, mundane, and quiet acts capture moments of defiance. By focusing on the quiet and the quotidian, Chhiba's narrative of Ajima emphasizes "instances of rupture and refusal" (Campt 2017, 5) that are redirected through the transgressive feminine energy of Kali. The intimacy of the domestic space generates an affective force field that disrupts both temporal and spatial logics that subtend formations of family and nation. The artist's intimacy with both her grandmother and Kali generates a reading and deciphering practice that renders legible "alternative accounts" of subjects whose stories, histories, and lives are easily lost within official archives of the nation and diaspora. Chhiba's affect shifts from the intimacies of the domestic to the public, where her multimedia aesthetic practices create affective and haptic attachments with the audience, disrupting normative social categories that are locked within identitarian logics. I reframe Ajima's life story not within the biopolitical logics of family, kin, and nation but through the lens of a "Black feminist futurity," emphasizing the labor of living and surviving in a way that disrupts and refuses "the regulatory regime from which [she] could not be removed" (Campt 2017, 33).

According to the artist, Ajima embodied Kali's energy, and *The Two Talking Yonis* emerged out of an imaginary conversation she had with her grandmother.

This act of conjuring her grandmother through performance is itself a queer act of refusal that counters the politics of invisibility and illegibility through the aesthetic and the imagination. Like many other black/ened women, Ajima's existence within official archives is largely absent. Chhiba positions the domestic space as a counterintuitive archive (like photo albums, oral traditions/narratives, and memories), transforming the intimacies of the home-space into spectacular installations and artworks. She uses the spectacular to critique grand narratives of freedom that are largely out of reach for most of the South African population, particularly racialized women. Her practice speaks to the power of the feminist imagination in producing alternative structures of freedom by centering feminine energy, pleasure, and erotics. Ajima embodies Kali; Kali and Ajima merge in the artist's imagination; Kali and Chhiba are also one. Chhiba and Ntombela write (2019): "The embodiment of Kali is more complex. It is not simply about pushing against a system in aggressive ways. It is the ability to overcome, to transform, and to move beyond the space of difficulty" (2). Ajima's strength and determination produce a "yonic space," a space that positions feminine energy as disruptive of both heteropatriarchy and binary relations of race and gender. Chhiba's aesthetic and performance practice is influenced by Ajima's/Kali's feminine energy.

Throughout this book, we have encountered the figure of the grandmother. The grandmother is an important trope in my concept of indenture aesthetics. She is a queer figure who represents the limits of reproductive futurity, and her status within both the Afro-Indian and black African home-spaces positions her outside the temporal and spatial logics of the normative. She represents the limits of progress and development. She is simultaneously transgressive and valued. It is, therefore, significant that the grandmother, an iteration of the maternal feminine, emerges as the route to crafting alternative social worlds. Indeed, *Indenture Aesthetics* argues that the Afro-Indian positionality, as a site of reorientation, emerges through the feminine. The feminine is also the site through which we can reimagine Afro-Indian intimacies and South African blackness. Chhiba's Ajima resonates with Gucci's grandmother. Gucci embodies his grandmother's strength in his pursuit of queer world-making in a context characterized by structural and everyday violence and erasure. The grandmother also emerges in my discussion of Kganye's photomontages, where she functions as a memory-keeper (chapter 1); she manifests as the widow in my analysis of Modisakeng's performance *Inzilo*; she is the silent figure who emerges in Khan's dreamworld, which informs her project *when the moon waxes red*; and the grandmother is also the focus of one of Mlangeni's most provocative images in his series, *At Home*, which evokes the rural as a feminized space of waiting and suspension, where men have left behind wives, grandmothers, and children as they become entangled within the death-worlds of capital. These different, but imbricated manifestations of the grandmother coalesce around the figure of my great-grandmother examined in the introduction. In the family portrait photo, my great-grandmother is at the center of the frame: this old, tired, disabled, indentured woman—the most vulnerable and violated figure within this system of coercive labor—is at the end of her life cycle. She represents the soot (to evoke the grittiness of the black/ened body as routed through Modisakeng's performance art), the by-product of a violent capitalist system. However, I am drawn to her gritty, dirty, hard, and black/ened femininity, which creates lines of flight through which we can imagine the otherwise. She, like the other iterations of the feminine, the feminized, and the vulnerable examined across these chapters, informs *Indenture Aesthetics'* politics of (dis)belonging.

FAKA's and Chhiba's aesthetic practices take us on a journey from the *anus* to the *yoni*, two transgressive sites within heteropatriarchal and cisnormative cultures. Through performance art, they rescript that which is coded as dirty, transgressive, and disruptive into world unmaking and remaking practices. Their performances of sex-as-art move between the profane and the sacred, opening an alternative worldview through which it may be possible to write a new "coalitional politics by affirming an ethical mode of relationality" (Nguyen 2014, 2). Their use of abjection as a form of social, political, and cultural critique is intimately connected to the rise of new social movements in South Africa where human feces have been mobilized as a form of protest. In 2013, for instance, "poo protestors" flung feces at Western Cape Premier Helen Zille, as well as on a major highway, the steps of the Western Cape Legislature, and in the international airport in Cape Town. Steven Robins (2013, n.p.) writes that these "sanitation activists ranging from ANC Youth League militants to Social Justice Coalition Activists [had] the more difficult task of trying to convince the *political elite* and *middle class* that the stench and dangerous e-coli levels in some of the informal settlements in Cape Town constitute a health hazard that needs to be addressed with urgency." Human waste was also deployed in 2015 when student activist Chumani Maxwele hurled feces at a statue of Cecil John Rhodes. The incident occurred on March 9 when Maxwele picked up a bucket of human feces that was lying alongside a street and took it with him to the University of Cape Town campus in a taxi. Before throwing the bucket of feces onto the statue of Rhodes, he shouted into a gathering crowd, "Where are *our* heroes and ancestors?" Maxwele's actions led to widespread protests across South African universities and have reawakened calls for a radical transformation in faculty hires, student admissions, the decolonization of the curriculum, and the elimination of fees in order to begin the work of correcting the economic, social, and cultural imbalances in the present, caused by the long-enduring legacy of colonial apartheid and its afterlives.

FAKA's and Chhiba's use of bodily abjection and sexual transgressive practices (black queer sex and Kali's dominating sexuality) imbricate with a wider "politics of deviance" (Cohen 2005) as exemplified by Maxwele's use of human feces to confront the violence of everyday life shaped by structural inequality in the country, which has been exacerbated by the state's neoliberal policies after 1994. The rise of new social movements emphasizes the impatience of many "with the enduring colonial and apartheid logics of South African society" (Gillespie and Naidoo 2019, 193). At their conception, the Rhodes Must Fall and Fees Must Fall student movements were grounded in queer and feminist politics, emphasizing the language of intersectionality and a larger tradition of Black Radicalism.[4] It is evident that a deeper intersectional understanding of race and class that emerges from the position of the deviant and the transgressive can lead to new frameworks for the analysis of power and freedom in South Africa. Across South African townships and university campuses, the demands of the past (which promised life) and the fear of the future (death) collide in the present, disrupting the progressive linear narrative of the postapartheid nation. It is, therefore, significant that Chhiba's and FAKA's critiques emerge from the space of abjection and transgression as a disruption to modalities of power and the politics of Afro-normative respectability. Their uses of transgression, deviance, and waste are disorientating and *stain* South African blackness. This implicates the postapartheid state, which is imagined as black, in the biopolitical management of black/ened life. Their politics of deviance reminds us that a truly transformative society can only emerge when we center the lives and experiences of those who are most marginalized in society: those positioned at the bottom.

Coda

AFRO-QUEER DIASPORIC FEMININITIES AND EMERGENT IMAGINARIES OF FREEDOM

Throughout this book, I have been tentative about using diaspora as a framework to understand the specificities of the Afro-Indian experience in South Africa. I have been attentive to the ways in which the Afro-Indian positionality, as a site of reorientation, can gesture toward a radical politics of relationality that escapes both nation and diaspora. Indeed, Afro-Indianness, as formed within the long history of coercive labor practices in Southern Africa that stretches back to the era of slavery in the Cape, disrupts any easy affinity with contemporary discourses concerning diaspora, particularly the consolidation of the category "South Asian" within the US academy and the way this term has traveled globally. If *Indenture Aesthetics* is invested in *unthinking the nation*, this project is also committed to *unthinking diaspora*. Indeed, the Afro-Indian is not South Asian, a North American geopolitical term that erases the specificity of indentureship and the logics of colonial-apartheid racialization.

As I was completing an earlier version of this book, I encountered the aesthetic practices of a younger generation of Afro-Indians organizing under the label Kutti Collective. Individually and together, their art practices gesture toward new possibilities for thinking through Afro-Indianness in South Africa. The members of the collective have organized themselves outside of the established art organization, recognizing the ways in which the Afro-Indian, within the contemporary South African art world, continues to occupy a contested space. Unlike an earlier generation of Afro-Indian artists examined through this book, the Kutti Collective is deliberate in their use of the descriptors *South Asian* and *desi*, terms that have been contested by an earlier generation of Indian South African political activists and artists. The Kutti Collective's use of these terms could indicate a generational shift, but for me, it also reveals something about Afro-normativity as it informs regimes of racialized belonging and unbelonging. These terms may be gaining currency among a younger generation of Afro-Indians who are seeking transnational modes of identification and affiliation. This coda offers some thoughts on these new developments and how it extends our understanding of Afro-Indianness, gesturing toward new forms of Afro-Indian relations. Although the members of the Kutti Collective mobilize terms like *South Asian* and *desi*, associated with the Global North, they are also actively engaged in projects with black African and coloured creatives in South Africa. I specifically focus on the femme and gender-nonconforming artist Githan Coopoo.

Diaspora, Afro-Indianness, and Kutti Journeys

The term *diaspora* as a descriptor has been contested by both artists of Indian origin and Indian South African political activists who have historically identified with Black Consciousness. For instance, in 2003, Fatima Meer, a political activist and a sociologist, argued at an International Indian Diaspora conference that "South Africans of Indian origin had fought for acceptance too long and too hard to so easily abandon the *South African* as the primary signifier of cultural identity" (Meer quoted in Rastogi 2008, 1). As a member of the ANC, Meer supported the creation of a nonracial South Africa, where categories of "race" and "ethnicity" were viewed as appendages of apartheid. Evoking the ANC's identification as a nonracial organization, she negotiated her belonging and claims to the democratic nation by rejecting "Indianness" as the preeminent vector of her identity. However, the term *South African* is itself contested. On the one hand, South Africa is positioned as nonracial because of the ANC's identity as an explicitly nonracial organization. On the other hand, South

Africa is imagined as a black nation, where the boundaries of postapartheid blackness coalesce around performances of authenticity and nativism. Within this new configuration of South African blackness, Afro-Indianness marks its queer limits. Meer's rejection of diaspora is itself a performance of belonging, a deep desire to belong to a nation unable to reciprocate this desire. Many of the Afro-Indian artists I examined have also articulated an uncomfortable relationship with diaspora and have strong attachments to the category "black" while recognizing how it has shifted in contemporary South Africa. Indeed, individually and collectively, as curated in this book, Afro-Indian artists grapple with the relationship between blackness and Afro-Indianness, reminding us that the Afro-Indian is not outside of South African blackness.

Studies of the Indian diaspora often focus on North American South Asian diasporic communities, failing to account for the two historical moments out of which Indian diasporic communities are formed. Vijay Mishra (2002, 235) distinguishes between an "old Indian diaspora of plantation labor" and the Global North South Asian diasporas that formed out of "late modern capital." This is largely a post-1960s diaspora characterized by "the movement of economic migrants (but also refugees) into the metropolitan centers of the former empire as well as the New World and Australia" (235). The United States particularly attracted a professional class, primarily "consisting of doctors and scientists." The category "South Asian" emerges out of an area studies model and is unable to account for Indian indentureship, its entanglement with other coercive labor practices, and its deep intimacy with transatlantic slavery. Indeed, indentureship disrupts the area studies model and the category "South Asian," which is unable to account for colonial histories of migration and coercive labor practices, forms of race and racialization, and their afterlives in the wake of postcolonial nation-state formations and globalization. Thus, the Afro-Indian is not South Asian.

In a transnational world, the term *South Asian* has traveled from the Global North to the Global South through the movement of technologies, bodies, and cultural production. Even as we examine what purchase this term has for a new generation of Indian South Africans in crafting forms of identification and new modes of affiliation, we must also be conscious of how an uncritical use of this term to describe all movements away from the Indian subcontinent can manifest as an imperial gesture that flattens out the differences between the old and new Indian diasporas and the different modes of racialization across the Atlantic and Indian Ocean Worlds. Indeed, the modes of racialization through which the Afro-Indian is produced in Southern Africa renders us—the Afro-Indian and the North American South Asian—*familiar strangers* (Hall 2017).

Across the old and new Indian diasporas, scholars argue that it is important to recognize how these diasporic communities "function in tandem with different national agendas" (Gopinath 2005, 8). For Meer, diaspora is incompatible with the imaginary of a new South Africa founded on a nonracist future. Diasporic identification disrupts the deep desire for belonging that has historically shaped Indian claims to South Africanness. As an analytic, diaspora can productively unsettle this desire for belonging to the nation while disrupting the "ethnic absolutism" (Gilroy 1993) that underlies both formations of nation and diaspora. Routed through Indian indentureship, Afro-Indianness disrupts the geopolitical category "South Asian" and requires an alternative understanding of the shifting and multiple geographies of Indianness, Africanness, and blackness.[1]

My understanding of the term *diaspora* is indebted to Black cultural studies that situate diaspora as a site of difference and hybridity. For Stuart Hall, diasporic subjecthood is characterized by "heterogeneity and diversity." Diasporic identities "are constantly reproducing themselves anew, through transformation and difference" (1996, 244). This theorization of diaspora challenges its essentialist and purist iterations, often framed around "homeland, exile, return," figuring "diaspora for its potential to foreground notions of impurity and inauthenticity that resoundingly reject the ethnic and religious absolutism at the center of nationalist projects" (Gopinath 2005, 7). I am also influenced by queer diaspora studies scholars like Gayatri Gopinath, who disrupt the heteropatriarchal nature of diaspora through a queer diaspora framework. Gopinath (11) argues that "suturing 'queer' to 'diaspora' . . . recuperates those desires, practices, and subjectivities that are rendered impossible and unimaginable within conventional diasporic and nationalist imaginaries." According to Gopinath (11), one way to challenge "nationalist ideologies" of purity, authenticity, and normativity is to restore the "impure, inauthentic and nonreproductive potential of the notion of diaspora." In Gopinath's (2018, 6) later work, she extends her theorization of queer diaspora "as both a spatial and a temporal category: spatial in that it challenges the *heteronormative* and *patrilineal* underpinnings of conventional articulations of diaspora and nation, and temporal in that it reorients the traditional backward glance of conventional articulations of diaspora, often predicated on a desire to return to lost origins" (my emphasis).

Influenced by Gopinath's coupling of queer and diaspora, in this coda, I am interested in routing diaspora through the feminine and the feminized. Gopinath teaches us that "If diaspora needs queerness in order to rescue it from its genealogical implications, queerness also needs diaspora in order to make it more supple in relation to questions of race, colonialism, migration, and globalization" (2005, 11). What happens if we route our understanding of diaspora through the positionality of the feminine and the feminized, the violated and the vulnerable, the disrespectable and abject? How can we rethink diaspora as a site of *ethical relationality*, committed to the radical project of imagining our entangled pasts, presents, and futures otherwise? This coda offers some speculative thoughts by foregrounding the Kutti Collective's turn to transgressive feminine energy as a productive site to think through emergent imaginaries of freedom within and alongside performances of the Afro-normative that secures black authenticity.

Kutti, pronounced as "cu-tee," is a derogatory slang word from Hindi and Punjabi that means bitch/female dog. Kutti is a term of female disparagement and echoes FAKA's use of the term cunty. Kutti is indicative of the collective's politic of disrespectability, which they use as a mode of critique and a site of queer world-making. The Kutti Collective is "a South African Indian Art Collective" and is made up of "non-binary and LGBTQ+ identifying artists" who are invested in "*reclaiming [their] minds, bodies, and identities within cultural, public and social structures*" (my emphasis) (Saaiq'a 2020). The collective's objective is to dismantle structures of colonialism and patriarchy, which have distorted (our)their identities, bodies, and desires. Kutti is a derogatory term used to regulate women's bodies, desires, and pleasures. It marks the boundaries between proper and improper/deviant womanhood. The term *bitch* is often used to refer to women with "loose" morals, women whose sexual and erotic autonomy challenge the patriarchal foundations of society and family. The word *kutti/bitch* is "used to degrade and vilify" and is mobilized as a weapon to "project shame and insufficiency" on women and LGBTQ+ identifying folk (Saaiq'a 2020). The collective directs their critique through the aesthetic and performative realm at "mainstream society, family structures, our cultural and religious backgrounds, patriarchy and institutional racism, [and] the art industry." This is a collective endeavor to challenge the demand from various institutional structures to "submit and conform."

Kutti directs us to that which refuses to be captured within the heteropatriarchal "order of things." Kutti is indicative of the *wild* (Halberstam 2020) and the *wayward* (Hartman 2019), those excess and nonnormative desires, pleasures, sexualities, emotions, race/ethnicity, and bodies, which the collective harnesses into a praxis of world-making, directing us to other modes of being—other ways of moving and inhabiting the world—emphasizing quotidian practices of freedom-making. Attention to waywardness as a method holds the key to understanding the "utopian longings and the promise of a future world" as exemplified by the journeys of those who "[refuse] to be governed" (Hartman 2019, xv).

The resignification of kutti is important; it is an articulation of a politics of deviance that is invested in reclaiming power and agency by subverting its original meanings. The act of reclaiming and subverting a derogatory term that is weaponized against those who are marginalized is itself an act of queer/ing. At this stage, the Kutti Collective consists of nine artists working across various media including film, photography, performance art, jewelry making, and painting. The collective is made up of Kate'Lyn Chetty (@katelyn_portfolio), Youlendree Appasamy, Alka Dass (@alka_the_artist), Tyra Naidoo, Githan Coopoo (@githancoopoo), Talia Ramkilawan, Tazme Pillay (@iamtazme), Akshar Maganbeharie (@akshartbh), and Saaiq'a (@acollaredwomxn). The collective is the first transregional Afro-Indian collective that brings together artists from Durban and its surrounding areas, Johannesburg, and Cape Town. Their individual works emerge out of their positionalities of displacement within the South African art industry and within heteronormative structures while pushing against the limits of the category "Indian" in South Africa. Their mobilization of the term *Indian* recognizes it as a constructed racial category that is slippery and emergent. Coopoo and Saaiq'a, for instance, belong to both Indian and coloured communities. By gesturing toward the imbrication between Indian and coloured, they reveal the myth of the fixity of race while using their bodies to trouble the visual regimes of colonial-apartheid modernity that underpin how we understand race in South Africa. They reveal race and new ethnicities as always emergent, gesturing toward longer, yet strategically obscured, histories of intimacies between racial groups in South Africa. Thus, even though the collective organizes around the category "Indian," they redirect Indianness away from its (hetero)normative and racial/ethnic essentialist parameters. The Kutti Collective, like the works of Khan, Chhiba, and myself, queers the category "Indian," not as an act of claiming to belong to the nation but as one that pushes against the performances of Afro-normativity that render the Indian always foreign/alien Other. It is important to note that most members of the collective are of indenture origin, and the return to the indenture experience is significant within their aesthetic practices. These works mark what Stuart Hall, in a different context, referred to as the "end of the innocent notion of the essential [Indian] subject" (Hall 1996).

Through their art practice, they are invested in "redefining our histories" even as they create/curate alternative structures of belonging and relationalities that are transnational, cutting through and across differences of race, ethnicity, gender, sexuality, and region. This is a project of creating/curating new ways of seeing/feeling Afro-Indianness, while also archiving the Indian experience in a context where this has been severely neglected within the South African art industry and academic institutions. They write: "As Kuttis, we are building community, increasing visibility, and transforming representation for people of color and Indians; actively archiving our history and lives while redefining our identities even as they challenge social norms. We are simultaneously reflecting and engaging with our identities through our past and present experiences and traumas. But we are also ultimately transcending what that expected 'Indian' experience is, or what it should look like, through our art and our lives" (Saaiq'a 2020). Through the transgressive feminine energies associated with the term *kutti*, the collective resignifies the terms *desi* and *South Asian*. In the North American context, *desi* refers to people from South Asia, mainly of Indian, Pakistani, or Bangladeshi origin. *Desi* is a loaded term that signals purity, autochthony/indigeneity, and land (*desh*). Indeed, the relationship between *desi* and land suggests that *desi* signals not just authenticity and origins but also nativist claims to belonging. Indeed, as a post-1964 formation, *desi* is also a loaded term in terms of caste, class, colorism, and attachments to Hindu nationalism. However, the collective's use of the term *desi* is routed through kutti (transgressive and disrespectable female/femininity), queering the ways in which *desi* functions as a form of authentic diasporic South Asianness formed within the North American context. Thus, I argue that the Kutti Collective's use of the term *desi* emphasizes the *inauthentic* positionality of the Afro-Indian within this larger category of the "South Asian." The Kutti Collective offers an articulation of Afro-Indian *desi-ness* that engages the entangled field of racial formations in South Africa relationality (South African Indianness, blackness, and colouredness), while gesturing toward alternative ways to understand the queer geographies of Indianness (created out of colonial-era labor migrations like indentured labor migration) in relationship to South Asianness. I read their resignification of *desi*—Afro-Indian *desi-ness*—as an articulation of a radical politics of (un)belonging that explodes the boundaries of the South African nation while complicating the homogenizing global trajectories of the term *South Asian*. The collective's kutti journeys are not informed by a desire to return to lost origins that figure as authentic and timeless or to restore an authentic Indian subject positionality. Through their kutti journeys, they work through their out-of-placeness as a critical praxis of constantly creating/curating new relationalities and possibilities that do not rely on modes of belonging through mythical narratives shaped by blood, land, and belonging.

Sensual Excesses and Femme Diasporic Intimacies

Githan Coopoo's aesthetic practice is informed by the negative effects of vulnerability, failure, and the abjection of male femininity within a cisnormative-striving society. This is evident in their jewelry-making practice and their attention to beauty as an aesthetic and embodied practice of constantly making and unmaking selfhood. Beauty, and the quest to be beautiful, is a recurring trope throughout this book and is central to my concept of indenture aesthetics. This section also speculates on what happens when femininity—associated with vulnerability, failure, and abjection—attaches to diaspora. I am interested in how queer-diasporic femininities reorient the relationship between the nation and its new black/ened Others by reframing the terms that give substance to the abstract notions of nation, community, and diaspora by disrupting their relationship to notions of blood, kinship, belonging, nativism, and normativity. Coopoo's aesthetic and performative art practice resonates with that of the black queer/femme/gender-nonconforming duo FAKA. Like FAKA, Coopoo's work is organized around the negative effects associated with the feminine, the deviant, and the transgressive. Coopoo embraces vulnerability and failure as a praxis of reimaging racialized masculinity, while creating a new set of relationalities that reorient us toward a "new politics of freedom" that returns to the body as a site of decolonial possibilities.

Githan Coopoo is a young, emerging artist who identifies as femme and gender-nonconforming. Through his aesthetic art practice, Coopoo is interested in "queering the archive and unpacking the performative nature of dress" (Hlalethwa 2020). In their work, Coopoo gestures toward the home-space as a counterintuitive archive; indeed, their interest mines the home-space for its alternative possibilities to reimagine queerness. For Coopoo, to queer the archive is to probe and slowly erode the heteropatriarchal nature of the home-space. Through dress/fashion and jewelry, Coopoo emphasizes the performative nature of gender and the ways in which clothing and jewelry have been gendered (for either male- or female-presenting bodies) within global fashion markets that are implicated in maintaining the gender binary. Coopoo returns to the site of the home-space, the intimacies of the family constructed under the violent regimes of colonialism and apartheid. Coopoo writes that they were raised to be aware of their Indian and coloured South African heritages. However, within these communities and within South African history more broadly, there is little acknowledgment or visibility around queerness and gender nonconformity. Thus, Coopoo is interested in the engagement between the queer/queered body and objects that are refigured through their jewelry-making practice. Thus, similar to the aesthetic and performative art practices like FAKA and my own, Coopoo is invested in queering family narratives through dress, performance, and adornment as a praxis of unhinging the African body from its overdetermined heterosexualization.

In 2018, Coopoo released their first jewelry line, called the *Byzantine Collection* (plates 31–33). This series of hand-crafted jewelry is made from clay, a medium that the artist describes as "uncomplicated and universally timeless" (Coopoo 2018). Indeed, clay is Coopoo's preferred medium in their jewelry-making practice. In an interview with Vaid-Menon, Coopoo writes that the collection draws on their love for "Greek Mythology, Ancient Egypt and varied religious iconography" (Coopoo 2018). While the archival evidence indicates a plethora of sexual practices and same-sex intimacies within these ancient civilizations and religious practices, this has become obscured in the modern world. Thus, through jewelry Coopoo reclaims by queering these "symbols and motifs for [their] community." The *Byzantine Collection* is also a homage to their parents' love and romance. Coopoo reveals that their parents met at the University of Cape Town, which at that time was a whites-only university. The institution required students of color to obtain special permission to register for classes, and one of the elective courses that they were allowed to take was Greek and Roman language and philosophy. Determined to undermine the system, their parents forged a love for each other that Coopoo recognizes as important to their constitution. The *Byzantine Collection* is influenced by found objects, working with an aesthetic that emphasizes "the broken, imperfect and fallible." Coopoo writes, "I wanted to create a collection that looked like they had come from societies long gone, that had been worn and damaged, but still retained an uncomplicated beauty. I make everything by hand myself, and usually only once, so each piece is truly unique" (Coopoo 2018). Coopoo's interest in the broken, imperfect, and fallible directs us away from systems of mastery, dominance, and violence associated with imperial logics, both ancient and contemporary. Coopoo crafts new objects influenced by the fragments, residues, and that which remains after empires collapse and deterioration. They direct us to fecund possibilities of states of fragility and vulnerability in crafting new and alternative social worlds.

For the *Byzantine Collection*, Coopoo launched an advertising campaign that they offer as a "love letter to the Desi community in South Africa" (Coopoo 2018). For the campaign, Coopoo queers the home-space, positioning it as an alternative archive of the Indian experience in South Africa. The home-space shapes their queer aesthetic; the props and staging come from their parents' home and the clothes and garments worn by the models are from their father's personal collection. The campaign consists of several portrait photos of Afro-

Indian men wearing Coopoo's jewelry and dressed in men's clothes from the 1970s. The photos resonate with old family pics and point to Coopoo's engagement with family albums/archives as a project of queering the archive. The colors, tones, textures, and mood of the images mark a return to the home-space and are imbued with nostalgia and longing. I understand the nostalgia and longing, as expressed in these photographs, not as a longing for belonging to constructs like family and nation but as a visual exploration of Afro-Indian queer embodiment through the sensual parameters of touch, affect, and feminine erotics. Coopoo's choice of dress, adornment, and staging resonates strongly with Lebohang Kganye's project *Ke Lefa Laka: Her-Story* examined in chapter 2, where the artist restages photographs from her mother's album, dressed in clothes worn by her mother when she was approximately the same age.

Coopoo writes that *Queering the Archive: Brown Bodies in Ecstasy* influenced the aesthetics of their campaign. "I wanted to capture images that resemble traditional photographs from Desi families in South Africa from the '40s and '50s. I was inspired by an exhibition by South African artist Jordache A. Ellapen, who looked at an archive of photographs of an Indian family that lived in Durban. The images were beautiful—so timeless and elegant" (Coopoo 2018). Interestingly, Coopoo's return to the home-space echoes my argument that for Afro-Indian queer subjects, who exist liminally between the black-white racial binary, the home-space offers counterintuitive feminist and queer possibilities. These emerge out of the regimes of impossibility that the Afro-Indian occupies within the majoritarian South African public sphere.

It is evident that the sensual and erotic contours of Coopoo's project were informed within the home-space. Whereas I examine my relationship to sensuality through my mother's photoarchive, Coopoo directs us to the figure of the father as a site of feminist queer and sensual possibilities. They thus queers the figure of the father. This is important because, across the chapters in this book, the focus has been on the figure of the mother (the maternal feminine) and the grandmother. Coopoo's project is a form of memory-work that emerges out of the effect of displacement within South African publics. Coopoo demonstrates the important labor of "making queer use of racialized and gendered labor constructs and heteronormative familial relations" (Ellison 2019, 14) as a praxis of creating livable lives. Indeed, for queer, femme, and gender-nonconforming subjects of color, negotiating a racist public sphere, the home-space becomes a site of possibility. Coopoo's aesthetic practice is indicative of the role the aesthetics play in mining the normative for queer and feminist possibilities. In the series of photographs Coopoo produced for their jewelry campaign, their desire for the otherwise is entangled with their parents' political desires to disrupt the apartheid state's management of black/ened life, emphasizing the sensuous nature of the political even as they forge a new visual language and aesthetic in the contemporary moment.

Coopoo's interest in fragments, fragility, and brokenness in their jewelry-making reflects their own struggle with mental health issues and their HIV-positive diagnosis (plate 34). Coopoo prefers clay as their privileged medium because it mirrors their own "delicate nature" (Hlalethwa 2020). Clay, like the human body, is "fragile, sensitive, porous, broken and subject to the elements that are beyond our control." The fragile nature of clay allows them to reckon with their own "sensitivity and vulnerability." As a mode of survival, they write, "There was a day when I realized that it wasn't okay for me to try to fix myself while being happy and willing to let my work break" (Hlalethwa 2020). Coopoo's chosen medium, clay, is a metaphor for the ways in which emotions attach to and soften the surface of the body, reorientating the body differently to the world. For Coopoo, clay jewelry directs us to the brokenness and fragility of being. "It's about feeling and wearing the weight of your emotions" (Hlalethwa 2020). As examined throughout this book, vulnerability moves beyond the desire to willingly abdicate regimes of mastery. Vulnerability is the desire to actively create different forms of relationalities that circumvent the binaries and hierarchies of being. Vulnerability opens up a space to understanding forms of belonging outside of social constructs like nation, family, and community that depend on the biopolitical logics of blood and belonging. According to Sara Ahmed (2004, 69), "vulnerability involves a particular kind of bodily relation to the world." Through the positionality of bodily vulnerability, Coopoo, like many of the other artists examined in this book, provides an alternative template to forge ethical relationalities across our regimes of difference. Coopoo's emphasis on fragility, brokenness, and the porousness of the body and of being requires a different conceptualization of time and space. This rubs against the time-space of the Afro-normative nation that is invested in a linear and progress narrative of development. Whereas Modisakeng in chapter 2 was invested in bringing time to a halt and Kganye in chapter 1 offers an aesthetic of time as a loop, Coopoo offers an articulation of time as porous, fragile, and broken.

Queer of Color Creatives and Femme Power

Femininity, especially male femininity, is dangerous, disruptive, and a site of abjection within both hetero- and homonormative constructs of kin and community. Ellison (2019, 8) argues that "queer femininity . . . disorganizes and confounds the categories we often use to make sense of the world." Queer femininity directs us to lines of flight away from the violence of the normative as a critique of structures of power "through which subjects and identity categories are constructed" (8). Apart from their collaboration with Alok Vaid-Menon, Coopoo also collaborated with FAKA on their music video *Queenie* (2018). I offer an examination of this music video because it demonstrates how femininity—male femininity—is used by black and brown artists as a praxis of crafting livable lives and alternative social worlds in a context defined by antiblack-brown-queer-femme-gender-nonconforming-trans violence. *Queenie* speaks to the power of queer femininity to create a new set of relationalities that reveals what a decolonial South Africa could look and feel like as it emerges from the positionality of failure, vulnerability, and fragility.

Queenie opens with an interior close-up shot that slowly zooms out to reveal a wooden display cabinet. The video immediately takes us into the intimacies of the home-space. Portrait photos of FAKA and their friends are displayed on the cabinet and the walls, among other household objects like fancy plates and jars. This cabinet display resonates with the dining-room furniture one would find in their grandparents' or parents' home, where prized possessions are put on display. Interestingly, the photos of FAKA and their friends dressed in gender-nonconforming fashion position the home-space both as a site of regulation and surveillance and as one full of possibilities for the black and black/ened queer subject. One of the creatives reveals that one day they told their parents that they are a *stabane*, an isiZulu vernacular term that describes an intersex person. Amanda Lock Swarr (2009, 525), scholar of gender and sexuality in South Africa, writes, "To be called *stabane* is to be seen as having both a penis and a vagina." She also points out that those people labeled as *stabane* "rarely have intersexed bodies" (525) (Hlalethwa 2020). Instead, the use of the term *stabane* "exposes the complications and violence the concept evokes in the lives of those labelled as such. As well as highlighting the instabilities of sex—femaleness and maleness—in South Africa more broadly" (525). To begin the video by evoking the term *stabane* directs us to FAKA's politics of disruption, their politics of rendering male/female, penis/vagina, masculine/feminine binaries and hierarchical logics of sex and gender unstable, in flux, and constantly in a state of becoming. *Stabane* directs us to the performer's male femininity, a form of transgressive and disruptive femininity.

The video shifts between indoor and outdoor spaces. In the second scene, Desire Marea and Fela Gucci, dressed in long wavy wigs, baggy pants, and white blouses, arrive in a school gymnasium for a photoshoot. They proceed to dance and gyrate across the gymnasium, posing and performing as they are being photographed. In the next scene, FAKA and a group of other black and black/ened creatives are outdoors playing basketball. Dressed in feminine athletic wear, they bounce the ball, dribble, and pass the ball to one another, with many shots focusing on them shooting the ball into the hoop. Through the positionality of feminine masculinity, these scenes disrupt the cisheteronormative imaginaries of postapartheid space. Through play and pleasure, the queer creatives, marginalized within a cisnormative privileging society, actively produce and refigure the meanings of space, unhinging South African urban geographies from a cisnormative gaze that positions such bodies as out of place.

The next scene takes us back into the interior of the home. We are now introduced to a broader group of black, Afro-Indian, and coloured queer, femme, and gender-nonconforming creatives dancing, gyrating, and vogueing against the warmth of the wooden paneled walls, a Christmas tree that is lighted, and a stack of presents. The creatives are dressed to defy gender norms, embody and celebrate their positionalities as trans, femme, and gender-nonconforming. This is the first time that Coopoo appears in the video; it becomes increasingly visible that all the other creatives are wearing his clay jewelry. They all gather around the table loaded with festive food and drinks as they engage in celebrating this occasion. As they sit at the table, they continue to dance and vogue, queering the normative nature of this family holiday by centering their pleasures as nonnormative gender and sexual beings. Fela Gucci, dressed in a faux fur hat and a red outfit, sits at the head of the table, positioned as the (half) mother of the House of FAKA. Food is passed along and shared among this queer family. After eating and drinking, presents are distributed as the group continues to dance and vogue. The video then cuts to an outdoor scene with the creatives dressed in ballroom outfits. The last scene is an indoor club scene, taking us into the sensual and erotic atmosphere of FAKA's inclusive club night called Cunty Power. Here we see black, Afro-Indian, coloured, and white queers (lesbians, gays, trans, and gender-nonconforming, across the racial spectrum) dancing together, actively enacting joy, pleasure, and ecstasy from their femme positionalities. *Cunty* is a ballroom term used by the community to signify *ultra-femininity*. In FAKA's oeuvre of aesthetic and performative art practice, the feminine-erotic, associated with abjection and transgression, maps out an alternative Afro-diasporic genealogy that circumvents the logics of blood and belonging. FAKA and the queer creatives in this video, as well as the participants in the #FEMMEINPUBLIC Project, direct us to the labor of producing space as an everyday praxis of survival. Drawing on McKittrick (2006), Livermon writes: "Blacks in Afrodiasporic Space experience geography as an interplay between geographies of domination and their own experiences of space" (Livermon 2020, 78). FAKA's refiguring of Afro-diasporic space through the black and Afro-Indian femme and gender-nonconforming subject positionality "unfolds beyond the white-black hierarchy" to disrupt the intimacies between white and black heteropatriarchal supremacy as they unfold together in postapartheid South Africa. FAKA's Afro-diasporic spaces "create circuits of possibilities that engage affinities between colonized populations," emphasizing their larger mandate of using the femme positionality to disrupt the identitarian categories that lock us within the hierarchical and binary order of things designed to position us as strangers (71).

Throughout the video, the music and the visuals are intercut with personal narratives of coming out, first sexual experiences, the violence of capture within binary ideas of sexuality (straight/gay), and the displeasure of not being able to discover one's sexuality for oneself. The different creatives in this video render themselves vulnerable to one another and the audience, crafting sites of queer pleasure and alternative forms of kinship structures within heteronormative spaces that regulate nonnormative bodies, such as the volleyball court. In the dining room scene, the close-up shots focus on Coopoo's clay earrings worn by the creatives in this scene. In a video narrative that juxtaposes the precarity and the violence of the everyday lived experiences of queer and gender-nonconforming folk of color, their use of Coopoo's clay earrings resonates with the artist's objective of using clay as a medium that allows the wearer to feel the weight of their emotions. The recognition of a common emotion weight is indicative of the desire for a different bodily relation to one another and to the world. The video reveals the uses of states of vulnerability and fragility as a praxis of reimagining our relations across deep structures of difference.

I end this book by gesturing toward the important political work engaged by queer, womxn, trans, femme, and gender-nonconforming creatives of color who, through the aesthetic and performance art realms, are radically reimagining South African society by deliberately disrupting and disavowing the binaries and hierarchies of race, ethnicity, sex, gender, sexuality, and erotics. Against performances of Afro-normativity, a younger generation of creatives is directing us to their desires for new imaginaries and vernaculars of freedom that resist capture into the new "order of things" in postapartheid South Africa. I conclude this book by gesturing toward new creative practices that embrace vulnerability, fragility, abjection, transgressive sexual practices, pleasure, and desires as disruptive strategies, asking us to reimagine our worlds alongside the violence of domination and mastery. Throughout this book, I have examined how artists use their black/ened bodies as forms of embodied knowledge, revealing that freedom is about bodily autonomy and an ongoing praxis that centers the quotidian. We have encountered black/ened subjects who are actively crafting alternative vernaculars through "a corporeal language of seepage and excess" (Pather and Boulle 2019, 1). Throughout this book, excess rubs against respectability politics, directing us to practices of world-making designed to deliberately disrupt normative regimes of power. Seepage and excess create lines of flight away from the nation to enable the possibilities to imagine the otherwise. *Indenture Aesthetics* foregrounds the feminine, the feminized, and the vulnerable as a praxis of reckoning with our entangled pasts, presents, and futures and reimagining the landscape of coalition-building across regimes of difference. We have encountered artists dedicated to crafting emergent new political vocabularies and vernaculars of freedom that are indicative of nonstateist forms of belonging. Macharia writes: "New languages untethered to the state can help us imagine how we want to live with each other" (Macharia 2016).

In conclusion, I invite you, the reader, to consider what shapes and informs your own kutti journeys of becoming—kutti journeys that require the willing abdication of our individual and collective desires for mastery and domination. To map out our own kutti journeys of (be)cumming, we must also recognize the violence and regulation embedded within the sophisticated languages we have collectively developed around social justice, equity, and diversity, which continue to demarcate the boundaries of a proper vulnerable subject from those rendered improper. Informed and curtailed by a political correctness that maps onto respectability politics and oppression olympics, institutional structures agitating for social change can, at best, only offer cosmetic solutions that conceal larger structural commitments to difference as a site of rendering us *unintelligible* to one another. *Indenture Aesthetics* has demonstrated that the positionalities of the vulnerable, the feminized, and the feminine enable us to gesture outward, to reach for, to touch, to feel (for), to embrace the Other (wise)—as we collectively yearn for a new world and for other ways of being (together across difference). This is urgent in a global context characterized by the rise of fascism, the solidification of ethnonationalism and its attendant violent binaries and hierarchies, the increase in global anti-immigrant sentiment and xenophobia, violence against those black/ened, together with the ongoing genocide of Indigenous peoples, and the contamination and erosion of our natural environments for the purposes of racial capital. We are in a moment that necessitates a reckoning with how we relate to one another across our regimes of differences and how we relate to our environment and animal kin. FAKA's and Coopoo's work directs us to states of fragility and vulnerability as possible routes out of the muck we collectively find ourselves stuck in. They remind us that we, human beings, are fragile, sensitive, and porous, that we are connected to one another and to the environment even if our collective myths of mastery and superiority have blinded us to the fact that our survival requires us to collectively invest in and design new modes of relations. The artists examined in this book, and my queer curatorial mandate, are engaged in creating and imagining new forms of relationalities, pushing against the (un) freedoms associated with the postapartheid, slowly but systematically eroding this thing we have come to call the nation. The nation is designed to ensure the death (literal and social) of those it continues to blacken. *The need to unthink the nation is urgent.* Desire for nation, community, and belonging informed by such structures is insufficient; desire must shift to hunger for the Other/wise as an embodied and quotidian praxis of collective survival. Throughout the chapters, we get glimpses of what our decolonial presents and futures could entail. I reserve the last words for Frantz Fanon: "Why not the simple attempt to touch the other, to feel the other, to explain the other to myself?" (1986, 231).

Notes

PREFACE

Some sections of this book have previously been published as articles. Sections of chapter 1 have appeared in "The Brown Photo Album: An Archive of Feminist Futurity." An early analysis of Sharlene Khan's project *when the moon waxes red* was published in 2017 as "when the moon waxes red: Afro-Asian Feminist Intimacies and the Aesthetics of Indenture." I have also previously published two articles on FAKA titled "*Siyakaka* Feminism: African Anality and the Politics of Deviance in FAKA's Performance Art Praxis" and "Performing Blackness as Transgressive Erotics: African Futurities and Black Queer Sex in South African Live Art." All previously published work has been reimagined and significantly rewritten for this book.

1. https://theconversation.com/young-people-and-women-bear-the-brunt-of-south-africas-worrying-jobless-rate-167003.

2. Shandu and Ngema's discourse around the Indian begs the question of whether they also perceive whites as a foreign minority that have overstayed their welcome. The simple answer is no. I have not been able to identify any comments from either Shandu or Ngema to suggest that their opinion of the Indians also extends to the white settler community.

3. Ngema, quoted in Vahed and Desai, "Identity and Belonging." 3.

INTRODUCTION

Epigraph 1: Fanon 1986, 232.

1. https://www.concourt.org.za/index.php/about-us/role.

2. My notion of reorientation is influenced by Sara Ahmed's notion of orientation and what happens when we reorient ourselves, our bodies, toward those whom we have been trained to distance through the project of racialization. My use of reorientation understands its urgency in a context where we need one another to "help us find our way" (Ahmed 2006) out of the deadly trap of Afro-normativity, even as we create and recreate the "grounds on which we can gather" informed by difference.

3. The anthropologist Thomas Blom Hansen makes a similar argument based on class positionality in Hansen 2006.

4. For more on coloured identities, see Erasmus 2000; Ahluwalia and Zegeye 2003; Adhikari 2005, 2009; and Palmer 2015.

5. Even though the enslavement of Indigenous peoples was technically illegal, on plantations enslaved peoples of African and Asian descent/phenotype worked alongside Indigenous populations. Gradually, the enslaved population in the Cape became a mixed-race population, representing the entanglements between various coercive labor routes across the Indian Ocean and the African continent.

6. In the Indian Ocean World, Mauritius, a slave-holding colony, was the first island to introduce Indian indentured labor after the abolition of slavery by the British.

7. Although coal mining was not popular among indentured laborers, between "1903 and 1913, they made up 40% of the labour force" on coal mines (Beal 1990, 61). On some estates, like the Reunion Estate, indentured workers and African laborers worked side by side (Meer et al. 1980, 135).

8. In colonial Natal, the illicit trade and access to alcohol became a contentious issue (Tallie 2019). Natives were prohibited from consuming alcohol, whereas it was available to both whites and Indians, who illicitly traded with Africans. Yet Africans displaced their anxieties over the social ills caused by alcohol onto the Indian rather than white colonists.

9. See Ramsamy 2007, 470. One of the most significant coalitions, known as the "Doctor's Pact," was signed in 1947. The Doctor's Pact was described as a "joint declaration of cooperation between the African and Indian populations in fighting racism." The "Doctor's Pact" was signed between Dr. Xuma (ANC), Dr. Naicker (Natal Indian Congress, NIC), and Dr. Dadoo (NIC). With the formation of the ANC in 1912, the struggle was understood to be "a racial one, and their [founding members of the ANC] approach was predicated on a primary need for the unity of the African people." Given the historical context of early colonial Southern Africa, it was obvious that political interests that later gave rise to political parties were organized according to racial/ethnic affiliations. The Natal Indian Congress (NIC), like the ANC, was formed along racial lines. Although the ANC only embraced nonracialism in various forms from the 1960s to the 1980s, their commitment to African-Indian solidarity against racial oppression can be traced to 1947. In 1969, the ANC shifted its position from being exclusively black African by partially opening up its membership to coloureds, Indians, and whites. However, full membership, with all privileges, was only granted to non-black Africans in 1985.

10. Apartheid criteria for evaluating race and determining racial groups was at best arbitrary and shifting. The state was invested in a system where categories of race were "powerfully rooted in the material realities of everyday life" (Posel 2001, 109). The process of determining a person's race included "both appearance [the visual] . . . social habits [cultural]" (Posel 108), and class position (economic).

11. See also Breckenridge 2014, 225–40, and Posel 2001 for insight into the Population Registration Act's origins and role in determining racial difference.

12. The Population Registration Act of 1950 paved the way for other apartheid-era legislation like the Group Areas Act of 1950, which set the stage for the segregation and reloca-

tion/displacement of people according to assigned racial groups. These worked in tandem with the Prohibition of Mixed Marriages Act of 1949 and the Immorality Acts of 1927 and 1950, designed to cultivate "racial purity through social segregation" (Erasmus 2017, 93).

13. Fleming quoted in Eligon 2020.

14. The following sources illuminate these debates and what is at stake: Polak 1909 and Tinker 1974 described the system as one of "temporary slavery"; see also Mohabir 2010; Carter 1997, 2006; and Young 2017's chapter "Slow Death."

15. I use the term *Indigenous* to refer to the KhoiSan people, the first peoples of Southern Africa, consistent with how the term is deployed in South Africa after 1994.

16. Also see Persad et al. 2024.

17. My notion of indenture as a *hinge* intersects with and departs from the use of indenture as a hinge in Islam, Parsard, and Quadir 2024. In "Indenture, Iteration" the authors "rearticulate indenture as a hinge—an iterative set of forms, structures, and knowledges—rather than consigning ourselves to the prevalent conclusion that indenture as a system is merely a 'buffer' between the seeming past of slavery and the future of so-called 'free' labor" (2). In my use, indenture as a hinge illuminates overlapping regimes of racialized labor, similarly disrupting the binary unfree/free labor. I extend this notion of indenture as a hinge to also argue for resituating indentureship as formative to the racialization of the Afro-Indian in South Africa.

18. BC is part of a longer trajectory of intellectual work by both "Black South Africans and Blacks from elsewhere" (Collis-Buthelezi 2017, 15). In "The Case for Black Studies in South Africa," Collis-Buthelezi traces the study of the South African black experience by black people to multiple genres of texts, including periodicals and pamphlets, that go back to the early 1900s. These include the work of Sol T. Plaatje, particularly his book *Native Life in South Africa* (1916). Marcus Garvey's influence on black life and political organizing should also be included. Scholars like Hill and Pirio (2014, 209) note that the "Garvey movement developed in South Africa after the First World War into a potent expression of mass-based African nationalism." The establishment of the Institute for Black Research (IBR) by Fatima Meer in Durban in 1972 as well as the Institute of Black Studies (1975) directs us to the multiple ways in which blackness emerged as a critical site of analysis. The primary aim of the IBR was to teach "Black people to research and write" (Hassim 2019, 47). Black students worked with Meer as research assistants, and their desire to craft an alternative "language for race" informed the shift in Meer's work. She shifted to using the category "black" as a new framework to understand the conditions of displacement and disenfranchisement experienced by black African, Indian, and coloured communities as a result of the Group Areas Act (47). Meer and her students were actively involved in the BCM, and together they contributed to understanding blackness more capaciously.

19. Ashwin Desai writes that the "story of young Indians who sought to break the mould of racialized politics has not really been told, none more so than the Indian women activists of BCM" (Desai 2015, 39).

20. "Non-racialism has been the ANC's official ideological force to promote reconciliation and nation-building" and is often positioned by the politically initiated as "the politically correct orthodoxy" (Ndebele 2002, 133). Alliances developed between the

ANC and other political parties like the Natal Indian Congress and the Transvaal Indian Congress in the late 1940s and 1950s informed discourses of nonracialism. These alliances challenged state-mandated racism but did little to question the constructed nature of race. Also see Everatt, *The Origins of Non-Racialism*.

21. https://www.businessinsa.com/bee/.

22. Tenderpreneurs, according to Southall, are "social actors who use their political connections with individuals within the state to obtain contracts which, in a properly competitive situation, they would be denied" (2016, xiv).

23. Many scholars have written about the 2012 Marikana Massacre, where South African police opened fire on striking mine workers, killing thirty-four men. This massacre by the postapartheid state repeated the violence of the apartheid state. However, "this time it was predominantly black policemen, with black senior officers working for black politicians, who were doing the shooting." In this context, "white and black business interests coincided with that of the neoliberal state to crush a strike of poorly paid workers" (Desai 2015, 48). The Marikana Massacre revealed explicitly the elite underpinnings of the ANC and sanctioned formations of postapartheid blackness.

24. The Equality Clause rendered it illegal by the state to "Unfairly discriminate directly or indirectly against anyone on one or more grounds, including race, gender, sex, pregnancy, marital status, ethnic and social origin, colour, sexual orientation, age, disability, religion, conscience, belief, culture, language, and birth."

25. Ditsie was the first person to ever argue for the protection of lesbians and gays before the United Nations Conference on Women in 1995. Nkoli and Ditsie organized the first Gay Pride March in Johannesburg. Although Nkoli and Ditsie remained friends throughout his short life, Ditsie left GLOW because of its inability to recognize that lesbians were also women and black, and that the violence experienced by black (lesbian) women was different from that of black (queer) men.

26. See also the documentary film *Simon and I* (2002), directed by Beverly Ditsie and Nicky Newman.

27. *Indenture Aesthetics* is in conversation with Sharma's book *Home Rule*, as well as Mamdani's book *Neither Settler nor Native*.

28. During the antiapartheid struggle, culture (and cultural production) by the disenfranchised black population was viewed as a *weapon of the struggle*. In "Preparing Ourselves for Freedom" (1991, 187–88) Albie Sachs argues that artistic expression should disrupt the "multiple ghettos of the apartheid imagination" and that art should be central to the emergence of a "new consciousness." For Sachs, the "cultural imagination" must be freed from the constraints of protest art in order to "grasp the rich texture of the free and united South Africa that we have done so much to bring about." A free South Africa should welcome artistic expressions that reveal the complexities and contradictions of South African society, and cultural producers should be encouraged to "express our humanity in all its forms" (Sachs 1991, 188). Njabulo Ndebele (2006, 63) makes a similar call when he urges writers to "free the entire social imagination of the oppressed from laws and perception that have characterised apartheid." According to Ndebele, writers, and other cultural producers, can achieve this by "rediscovering the ordinary," shifting the focus from the grand spectacle of apartheid to the intimacies of the everyday (51). Sachs

and Ndebele are not separating artistic expression from the political but are gesturing toward the limited ways in which humanity is understood and expressed if it is only routed through the antiapartheid struggle.

29. Importantly, both Goniwe (2018) and Khan (2006), in different contexts, have drawn attention to the racialized dynamics of the South African art world after 1994. In *Aluta Continua: Doing It for Daddy,* Khan argues that "a patronizing white mommy has displaced the art world's patriarchal apartheid white daddy." White women have become the new brokers of the art world, and the common justification for the exclusion of black writers, curators, and academics is that there is a lack of qualified black candidates to fulfill these roles. Goniwe published "The Sour Pleasure of the Art Industry" in the *Mail and Guardian* where he critiqued the "cosmetic transformation" of the arts industry and the insidious ways in which black artists, curators, and art academics are constantly under a "white gaze" that works to "police, haunt, and traumatize young and established Black professionals." Furthermore, most, if not all, elite gallery spaces, auction houses, and art brokers are white or white-owned, creating a context where "*white enterprises . . . rent natives for purposes of tokenism and window dressing, legitimacy and political correctness whilst alienating black professionals from the actual means of economic production and creation of wealth*" (Goniwe 2018, my emphasis).

30. In Lowe 2006, the use of the term *intimacy* is twofold. First, it refers to "the world division of labor that emerges in the nineteenth century," which produced overlapping regimes of racialized coercive labor practices (African slavery and Asian indentureship). Lowe's use of the term *intimacy* is twofold ("The Intimacy of Four Continents," 193). Second, intimacy suggests the "volatile contacts of colonized people" (Lowe 2006, 193) produced out of these regimes of racialized labor and "the possibility of cross racial alliance that emerged from this contact" (Gopinath 2010, 166).

31. Passed in June 1946, the act was designed "to curtail Indian property ownership in White areas in Natal" and to "preserve the European orientation of South African society" (Bagwandeen 1984, 63). Although the intention of the act was to curtail the economic success of the trader/merchant class, it was noted by Indian politicians and activists that the act unfairly discriminated against the broader Indian community.

32. From 1860 to 1911, four hundred ships arrived in Natal, each constructing a meticulous register, providing "a detailed account of the individual identities, physical and cultural characteristics" (Breckenridge 2008, 20). Through the indenture number one can trace "information about the person's names, caste or religion; age; physical markings, if any; and places of origin in the form of the village, *thanna* (police circle) and *zilla* (district)" (Bhana 1991, 1–2). According to Breckenridge (20), this registry system intersected with the Natal Immigration Laws, to subtend the colonial state's "draconian pass regime." The law allowed employers of indentured workers "the right 'to apprehend, without warrant, such Coolie immigrant being found a distance of more than two miles from the residence of the person" they were indentured to, "without a written ticket to leave, signed by the master" (quoted in Breckenridge 2008, 20–21).

33. Meer's book, published during the height of political, social, and economic turmoil, is indicative of a broader desire to map out a common humanism as an affront to the state's project of racial segregation. The research and writing of this book would inform her work

with the Institute for Black Research (IBR), established by Meer in the early 1970s. By this stage, the concerns of the Indian working class and poor would be framed through the language of Black Consciousness, indicative of a more capacious understanding of blackness.

34. The longing for belonging, according to Pallavi Rastogi (2008, 1), emerges because of the erasure of Indians from the "apartheid and post-apartheid consciousness." Rastogi coins the phrase *Afrindian identity* to make sense of Indian "desire[s] for South African citizenship . . . a need for national anchorage." Examining the period from the 1970s onward, Rastogi (2008, 3) focuses on the "overtly political nature of South African writing," curating an archive of literary texts that reinscribe the desire for the nation yet to emerge.

35. Some feminist scholars argue that indentured women—often viewed as disrespectful (prostitutes and/or loose women) and dishonorable—were escaping a strict Indian patriarchal society and that indentureship offered (limited) autonomy to escape arranged marriages and the practice of *sati*, for instance.

36. The question of male vulnerability has been recently taken up in US Black masculinity studies. For a recent example, see Bost et al. 2019; see also Ross 2021.

37. Black and queer studies have long engaged with Black and queer temporalities, respectively. For more info, see Freeman 2010; Sharpe 2016; Keeling 2019; Adeyemi 2022; and Fleming, 2022.

38. See studies by scholars like Mphahlele 1962; Nixon 1994; Campbell, 1995; and Chrisman 2005.

1. AFRO-FEMININITIES

1. Even as I recognize my mother's labor in creating the home-space and her influence on my own understanding of beauty and sensuality, I want to also acknowledge that the presence of the black African female domestic worker also informs the textures of the Afro-Indian home-space. The role of the black African domestic worker in the formation of the Afro-Indian home-space and the formation of Afro-Indian femininity remains unexplored at this stage and is an area of research that is much needed in South Africa. Literature and artworks examining the figure of the black African domestic worker are only now beginning to emerge, promising to be a rich site of analysis. See Du Troit 2013 and Jansen 2019. Also see works by artist Mary Sibande.

2. In this project, I play with the African mask. During the rehearsal process, the models were encouraged to develop a familiarity with a mask and to think of it as a prop. In some photos, the mask was used to cover their genitals. In other photos, the mask became an extension of their bodies, a site of sensuality as it was touched and felt. In the twentieth century, the African mask became a global symbol of Africanness and a fetishized object within the global art world. I am interested in how the mask and its use as an art object by the middle class and elite in South Africa and the diaspora have become a way to negotiate a postapartheid African modern. Although I am not aware of any masking traditions within local Indigenous African cultures in South Africa, the African mask becomes a "channel through which all senses of local identity [black, Afro-Indian, African, Colored, white] need to be brokered" (Peterson 2012, 154). By attaching the mask to queer racialized African bodies, I wanted to disrupt the association between the mask and an authentic Africanness (and its association with nativism). Instead, in these assem-

blages, the mask is associated with bodies that are rendered inauthentically African—the Afro-Indian body and the queer black African body. Thus, the mask becomes a catalyst to negotiate regimes of (un)belonging among queer racialized African subjects.

3. For more on surface aesthetics, see Pinney 2003; Stephens 2014; Thompson 2015; and McMillan 2018.

4. In South Africa, the term *brown* in lowercase has been used historically as a colloquial label for coloured people. The Afrikaans term is *bruinmense*, literally translated as brown people. *Bruin*/brown in this context refers to the history of mixing between different groups like European, Malay, Bantu, Khoisan, and Indian.

5. https://www.pressreader.com/south-africa/daily-maverick/20200829/282359747150292.

6. https://www.pressreader.com/south-africa/daily-maverick/20200829/282359747150292.

7. For more on this, see Peffer 2020.

8. https://www.lensculture.com/projects/708951-ke-lefa-laka-heir-story.

2. AFRO-VULNERABILITIES AND THE AESTHETICS OF SLOW DEATH

1. https://www.sahistory.org.za/article/history-slavery-and-early-colonisation-south-africa.

2. Khan indicates that the title *when the moon waxes red* pays homage to Trin T. Minh-ha and her commitment to challenging Western regimes of knowledge production, whereas the lowercase letters commemorate bell hooks.

3. While the *Drowning Durga* series pays homage to women who have turned to suicide to escape gender-based violence, the *After Ana* series remembers Ana Mendieta, the Cuban American artist, who died under suspicious circumstances after a fight with her husband, the artist Carl Andre. The latter series pays homage to the thousands of women who are murdered by the men they love.

4. https://en.wikipedia.org/wiki/Durga_Puja.

5. See Meer 1969 and Desai and Vahed 2010.

6. In 1999, five years after the end of official racial segregation, Meer was once again confronted with the abject lives of the Indian working class and working poor. By this stage, the ANC was losing its "Indian" vote. Sociologist Ashwin Desai writes: "They [the residents of Chatsworth] showed her their dilapidated homes, they showed her their rent slips that contained a baffling myriad of charges, and made their own charge that their lives were steadily getting worse" (Desai 2002, 41). Desai recounts a confrontation between local municipal officers and community members from Chatsworth in 1999, when "one of the designer-bedecked (African) councilors began castigating the crowd" (44) for resisting their attempts at having local community members "sign mortgages and settle all their arrears" related to unpaid rents and fees. Residents were not opposed to signing mortgage papers; they were demanding that houses be upgraded and brought into line with proper living standards. Frustrated by the community's ingratitude, the councilor, described above by Desai, screamed at the crowd, demanding to know why "were Indians resisting evictions and demanding upgrades." According to her, "Indians were just too privileged." Desai recounts a moment that disrupted the racial-identitarian logics and

shifted the politics of community struggle. He recounts an elderly woman, Aunty Girlie, who screamed back at the councilor, "*We are not Indians, we are the poors*." This slogan was adopted by other community members who shouted, "We are not African, we are the poors." Within this context, new politicized identities were being forged around class, which cut across the enduring legacy of colonial-apartheid-era racial categories. Class positionality was being mobilized by residents to disrupt the ways in which Afro-Indians and black Africans occupy the postapartheid national imaginary as oppositional and antagonistic racial categories.

In Chatsworth, Meer would have encountered older folk who remembered the era of mass relocations and displacements from the 1950s, 1960s, and 1970s. Many may have lived in the Tin Towns she studied in the 1960s. Meer encountered the cyclical nature of poverty and trauma, passed down from generation to generation. This cyclical nature rubs against the new nation's narrative of a better life and brings to a halt the linear narrative of progress and development. The "designer-bedecked councilor," a representative of the new black middle class, is unable to see Indian poverty and desperation even when it is all around her. This positionality is an impossibility within the South African imaginary because all Indians have been homogenized into the category of the merchant/trader class. I offer these sociological observations not to flatten out Khan's attention to aesthetics, narrative, performance, and ritual—and not to reduce her aesthetics to a sociological study of the afterlife of indentureship—but because Khan's aesthetic concerns around memory, labor, and trauma grapple with articulating an Afro-Indian positionality in a context where this has been largely rendered impossible. *when the moon waxes red* works with and against this impossibility.

7. In Natal, indentured women were viewed as a cheap and exploitable labor force. According to some colonialists, if women's bodies were harnessed properly, they could be put to work to reproduce the colony's "labor force," emphasizing the biopolitical logics that underpin coercive labor practices (Beall 1990, 58). Indentureship rendered women more vulnerable, disposable, and replaceable than men; see Lal, "Kunti's Cry."

8. The introduction of these feminine artforms into the Indian home-space is directly related to interventions made by colonial missionaries in India. For more information, see Kent 2004.

9. While, in the video, it appears as if the needle punctures the cloth, Khan explains the process as follows: "So only the initial stage of laying down the cordonne (the thicker French cotton outline) works like this, where the cordonne is held down by cheap white cotton thread. The process of needle-lace thereafter does not result in the fabric being pierced—the work is done on the surface and held by the outline (which makes it very difficult to do as the stitches hold on to each other and its relationship to the structure). That means you have to be very careful to ensure that everything holds together. At the end, you then go over with the French cotton over all the outlines to neaten them (but then again also ensuring the whole piece holds together) and you then cut the cheap cotton and the whole piece sits on its own" (email communication with artist, July 5, 2023).

10. See Chen 1992; Lorde 2007b; and Reddy 2016.

11. For more information on the history and politics of Chinese indenture labor and the gold mining industry in South Africa, see Van Onselen 1982; Harris 2004, 2010; and Tu 2008.

12. Robin Cohen (1995, 159) writes: "The intrusions by Arabs in East Africa and Europeans elsewhere on the continent disrupted normal social life of African communities." He continues, "True, there was a long history of violence, kidnapping, enslavement and, in Islamic areas, judicial support for domestic slavery. But the arrival of external social actors solidified the practice of slavery and accelerated the trade into new directions. Many African countries reacted by getting as far away as possible from the slave-traders and in so doing started the melancholy history of 'flight migration' with which the African continent continues to be plagued" (159).

13. According to Cohen (1995, 160), Mozambique turned into a "breeding ground for sleezy labour recruiters." The recruitment depots were run by the Witwatersrand Native Labour Association and the Native Recruiting Corporation. Their sophisticated recruitment strategies included "an elaborate transport structure of ferries, trucks, trains and, latterly, planes to move the migrants south." The depots also controlled the repatriation of money earned by migrant workers on the mines to families in rural areas, designed to discourage the movement of families to urban areas. Migrant laborers from across Southern Africa from different ethnic, linguistic, and regional groups lived with migrant workers recruited from within South Africa, in "regimented, austere, single sex barracks known as compounds or hostels" (Crush 1995, 172). The role of the recruiting agency and the management of the movement and resettlement of African migrant laborers echo the role of the Protector of Indian Immigrants, an office formed in 1872. According to Preben Kaarsholm (2016, 444) "the institution of the Protector of Indian Immigrants . . . guaranteed the clear demarcation between the status of an indentured worker and that of a slave and which therefore provided legitimation of the colonial state's practices of expanding the supply of labor." Kaarsholm (445) writes that "Historical models for the institution of the Protector of Indian Immigrants were the Protector of Slaves, which had been introduced in the Cape in the context of abolition in the later 1820s, and also in British plantation colonies like British Guiana (Demerara), Trinidad, St Lucia and Mauritius." Indian indentureship and African migrant labor are characterized by what Young, drawing on Varma, calls "'unfreedom,' a condition distinct from but related to slavery that is often overlooked or taken as necessary characteristic of colonial capital-labor relations" (Young 2017, 161). In her book, Young writes, "Freedom does not distinguish between slavery and indenture. Instead, discourses of freedom or unfreedom, which are context-specific and adaptive, contributed to the racialized and gendered exploitation of labor. Thus, the notion of freedom worked to the advantage of capitalist and colonialist interests" (161). The practices of recruitment, the management, movement, and settlement of migrant workers, and fetishization of the contract, reveal the ways in which Indian indentured labor and African migrant labor systems imbricate and rub against each other, drawing on the strategies and techniques of control, containment, and criminalization designed in the context of slavery, cutting across the Atlantic and Indian Ocean Worlds.

14. The contradictions between capital and black life were sharply foregrounded in 2012 at Marikana when thirty-four miners were shot dead—most were shot in the back—by police during a strike at the Marikana Platinum Mine. The massacre signaled the suspension of a particular "vision of the after-apartheid" (Nuttall 2019, 44), revealing explicitly the way in which the nation's linear narrative of progress and development

is predicated on the disposability and expendability of black working-class life. The massacre is considered to be "the most lethal use of state violence by South African police against civilians since 1960 [Sharpeville massacre]" (https://www.meer.com/en/29288-summertime).

15. Modisakeng in conversation with Percy Mabandu.

16. https://www.artforum.com/uploads/guide.005/id22404/press_release.pdf.

17. https://tlmagazine.com/moraux-modisakeng-instructions-on-making-sense-of-the-world/.

18. https://tlmagazine.com/moraux-modisakeng-instructions-on-making-sense-of-the-world/.

19. Modisakeng in conversation with Ric Bower, 8.

20. https://www.mohaumodisakengstudio.com/inzilo.

3. AFRO-INTIMACIES

1. https://www.inyourpocket.com/johannesburg/Fordsburg-Delights_73374f.

2. http://archive.stevenson.info/exhibitions/mlangeni/athome_index.html.

3. After 1994, studies on "pensions and remittances," from urban to rural areas, indicate that "the presence of older women in rural households, and absence of older men and husbands, has facilitated the migration of working-age women" (Camlin et al. 2013, 530). The AIDS epidemic also created a context where older African women cared for children dying from AIDS, many of whom returned to the rural areas. Older women also took on the responsibility to care for and raise grandchildren who were orphaned by the epidemic, often in a context with little to no state support. Furthermore, even though colonial-apartheid histories of forced labor practices forced many African men and women to leave the rural areas, African traditional practices around burial necessitate the return to the rural in order that the dead loved one can join the ancestral realm.

4. After 1994, some white communities have employed discourses of vulnerability to position themselves as disenfranchised within the new sociopolitical dispensation. An extreme form of this is visible in Orania, an exclusively white town in the Karoo, a semi-desert area in rural South Africa. Membership in this town is by application and mastery of the Afrikaans language. For studies and further reading on Orania, see Cavanagh 2013 and Majavu 2022.

5. https://www.britannica.com/event/Great-Trek.

6. There is an extensive body of research on the history of same-sex relationships in Africa. See, for instance, Epprecht's book *Hungochani: The History of Dissident Sexuality in Southern Africa* (2013).

7. https://www.tongaat.com/our-business/sugar/.

8. https://www.sahistory.org.za/dated-event/sa-sugar-magnate-sir-hulett-born.

9. The concept of *dostana* has received a lot of attention within South Asian visual cultures, particularly Bollywood. For more information on this, see Gopinath 2000; Jeyathurai 2014; and Dasgupta 2015.

10. For more research on (South) Asian immigration in postapartheid South Africa, see Park and Chen 2009; Munshi 2013; and Pande 2017. To date, much of this emerging research is ethnographic and sociological.

11. For more details on this specific case and a solid analysis of *jahaji bai* (fraternal ship brother) and *jahaji bahin* (ship sisters), see Khan, 2016, 249–80.

12. The 2015 attacks were also exacerbated by King Goodwill Zwelithini, the Zulu monarch, who encouraged a crowd in Pongola to "get our house in order and clean our land of lice." He went on to state that "We need to remove all itching bedbugs and lay them bare in the sun . . . we request that all foreigners should take their baggage and be sent back" (Zwelithini quoted in Landau and Pampalone 2018, 9). His comments in 2015 are linked to his 2012 antigay remarks, where Zwelithini referred to men who engage in same-sex practices as "rotten," eroding the normative African body and politic. In South Africa, the intolerance toward the "foreign-other" is often mapped onto the intolerance toward African same-sex practices, emphasizing the queer limits of Afro-normativity.

13. This is common in South Africa, and the riots that erupted in KZN in 2021, examined in the preface, are a good example of how the political elite mobilize the disenfranchised to do their dirty work. This ensures the fracture between displaced and disadvantaged communities and disallows them from apprehending the intimacies that tie them together across racial-ethnic differences.

4. AFRO-TRANSGRESSIONS

1. "Reshma Chhiba," https://curatingculture.blog/2018/10/25/reshma-chhiba/.
2. See Maditla, "FAKA on Penetrating Art Spaces and Designing a New Sound."
3. For an excellent critique of Gandhi's early politics, see Desai and Vahed 2016.
4. See Davids and Matebeni 2017.

CODA

1. As an academic field, Asian American studies, which includes South Asian American diaspora studies, remains bound within the geopolitics of the United States and is unable to account for the deep and significant differences between the old and the new Indian diasporas. It is important to recognize that South Asian diaspora scholars have not always fitted neatly within Asian American studies. I contend that more comparative studies between Global North and Global South (Indian/South) Asian diasporic formations, from the colonial era to the present, can enrich our analysis of race and racialization, ethnicity, empire, neoliberalism, class, and caste, disrupting how nation and nationalism continue to frame our understanding of diaspora.

References

PRIMARY SOURCES

Achmat, Zackie. 1993. "'Apostles of Civilised Vice': 'Immoral Practices' and 'Unnatural Vice' in South African Prisons and Compounds, 1890–1920." *Social Dynamics* 19 (2): 92–110.

Adeyemi, Kemi. 2022. *Feels Right: Black Queer Women and the Politics of Partying in Chicago*. Durham, NC: Duke University Press.

Adhikari, Mohamed. 2005. *Not White Enough, Not Black Enough: Racial Identity in the South African Coloured Community*. Athens: Ohio University Press.

Adhikari, Mohamed. 2009. *Burdened by Race: Coloured Identities in Southern Africa*. Cape Town: UCT Press.

Ahluwalia, Pal, and Abebe Zegeye. 2003. "Between Black and White: Rethinking Coloured Identity." *African Identities* 1 (2): 253–80.

Ahmed, Sara. 2006. *Queer Phenomenology: Orientations, Objects, Others*. Durham, NC: Duke University Press.

Ahmed, Sara. 2004. *The Cultural Politics of Emotion*. Edinburgh: Edinburgh University Press.

Alexander, M. Jacqui. 2005. *Pedagogies of the Crossing: Meditations on Feminism, Sexual Politics, Memory, and the Sacred*. Durham, NC: Duke University Press.

Alexander, M. Jacqui, and Chandra Talpade Mohanty. 1997. "Introduction: Genealogies, Legacies, Movements." In *Feminist Genealogies, Colonial Legacies, Democratic Futures*, edited by M. Jacqui Alexander and Chandra Talpade Mohanty, xiii–xlii. New York: Routledge.

Amin, Kadji, Amber J. Musser, and Roy Pérez. 2017. "Queer Form: Aesthetics, Race, and the Violences of the Social." *ASAP/Journal* 2 (2): 227–39.

Anderson, Claire. 2009. "Convicts and Coolies: Rethinking Indentured Labour in the Nineteenth Century." *Slavery and Abolition* 30 (1): 93–109.

Angelucci, Federica. 2009. "Sabelo Mlangeni: Men Only." Exhibition Catalogue. Michael Stevenson Gallery.

Arnfred, Signe. 2004. "Re-Thinking Sexualities in Africa: Introduction." In *Re-Thinking Sexualities in Africa*, edited by Signe Arnfred, 7–34. Uppsala, Sweden: Nordic Afrika Institute.

Arondekar, Anjali. 2009. *For the Record: On Sexuality and the Colonial Archive in India*. Durham, NC: Duke University Press.

Baderoon, Gabeba. 2014. *Regarding Muslims: From Slavery to Post-Apartheid*. Johannesburg: Wits University Press.

Bagwandeen, Dowlat. 1984. "Smuts and the 'Ghetto Act' of 1946: The Coup de Grace of Anti-Indian Legislation." *Journal of Natal and Zulu History* 7: 57–73.

Bahadur, Gaiutra. 2014. *Coolie Woman: The Odyssey of Indenture*. Chicago: University of Chicago Press.

Bailey, Marlon. M. 2009. "Performance as Intravention: Ballroom Culture and the Politics of HIV/AIDS in Detroit." *Souls* 11 (3): 253–74.

Beall, Jo. 1990. "Women under Indenture in Colonial Natal 1860–1911." In *South Asians Overseas: Migration and Ethnicity*, edited by Colin Clarke, Ceri Peach, and Steven Vertovec, 57–74. Cambridge: Cambridge University Press.

Belcourt, Billy-Ray. 2017. "Indigenous Studies Besides Itself." *Somatechnics* 7 (2): 182–84.

Berlant, Lauren. 2007. "Slow Death (Sovereignty, Obesity, Lateral Agency)." *Critical Inquiry* 33 (4): 754–80.

Berleant, Arnold. 1964. "The Sensuous and the Sensual in Aesthetics." *Journal of Aesthetics and Art Criticism* 23 (2): 185–92.

Bersani, Leo. "Is the Rectum a Grave?" *October* 43: 197–222.

Bhana, Surendra. 1990. *Essays on Indentured Indians in Natal*. Yorkshire, England: Peepal Tree Press.

Bhana, Surendra. 1991. *Indentured Indian Emigrants to Natal 1860–1902: A Study Based on Ships' Lists*. New Delhi: Promilla.

Bhana, Surendra. 1997. *Gandhi's Legacy: The Natal Indian Congress, 1894–1994*. Pietermaritzburg: University of Natal Press.

Bhana, Surendra, and Joy Brain. 1990. *Settling Down Roots: Indian Migrants in South Africa, 1860–1911*. Johannesburg: Wits University Press.

Bhana, Surendra, and Bridglal Pachal, eds. 1984. *A Documentary History of Indian South Africans*. Cape Town: David Philip.

Bhattacharya, Tithi. 2007. "Tracking the Goddess: Religion, Community, and Identity in the Durga Puja Ceremonies of Nineteenth-Century Calcutta." *Journal of Asian Studies* 66 (4): 919–62.

Biko, Steve. 2017. *I Write What I Like*. 40th Anniversary ed. Johannesburg: Picador Africa.

Bond, Patrick. 2000. *Elite Transition: From Apartheid to Neoliberalism in South Africa*. London: Pluto Press.

Bond, Patrick. 2004. "From Racial to Class Apartheid: South Africa's Frustrating Decade of Freedom." *Monthly Review* 55 (10): 45–59.

Bost, Darius, La Marr Jurelle Bruce, and Brandon J. Manning. 2019. "Introduction: Black Masculinities and the Matter of Vulnerability." *The Black Scholar* 49 (2): 1–10.

Brain, J. B. 1983. *Christian Indians in Natal, 1860–1911: An Historical and Statistical Study*. Oxford: Oxford University Press.

Brand, Dionne. 2001. *A Map to the Door of No Return: Notes to Belonging*. Toronto: Vintage Canada.

Braziel, Jana Evans, and Anita Mannur. 2003. "Nation, Migration, Globalization: Points of Contention in Diaspora Studies." In *Theorizing Diaspora*, edited by Jana Evans Braziel and Anita Mannur, 1–22. Malden, UK: Blackwell Publishing.

Breckenridge, Keith. 2008. "Power without Knowledge: Three Nineteenth Century Colonialisms in South Africa." *Journal of Natal and Zulu History* 2 (1): 3–30.

Breckenridge, Keith. 2014. "The Book of Life: The South African Population Register and the Invention of Racial Descent, 1950–1980." *Kronos: Southern African Histories* 40 (1): 225–40.

Brown, David. 1988. "The Basements of Babylon: Language and Literacy on the South African Gold Mines." *Social Dynamics* 14: 46–56.

Brown, Elspeth H., and Thy Phu. 2014. "Introduction." In *Feeling Photography*, edited by Elspeth H. Brown and Thy Phu, 1–25. Durham, NC: Duke University Press.

Burton, Antoinette. 2016. *Africa in the Indian Imagination: Race and the Politics of Postcolonial Citation*. Durham, NC: Duke University Press.

Butler, Judith. 1994. "Against Proper Objects. Introduction." *differences: A Journal of Feminist Cultural Studies* 6 (2–3): 1–26.

Butler, Judith, Zeynep Gambetti, and Leticia Sabsay. 2016. "Introduction." In *Vulnerability in Resistance*, edited by Judith Butler, Zeynep Gambetti, and Leticia Sabsay, 1–11. Durham, NC: Duke University Press.

Camlin, Carol S., Rachel C. Snow, and Victoria Hosegood. 2014. "Gendered Patterns of Migration in Rural South Africa." *Population, Space and Place* 20 (6): 528–51.

Campbell, James T. 1995. *Songs of Zion: The African Methodist Episcopal Church in the United States and South Africa*. New York: Oxford University Press.

Campt, Tina. 2012. *Image Matters: Archive, Photography, and the African Diaspora in Europe*. Durham, NC: Duke University Press.

Campt, Tina. 2017. *Listening to Images*. Durham, NC: Duke University Press.

Carter, Marina. 1995. *Servants, Sirdars, and Settlers: Indians in Mauritius, 1834–1874*. Oxford: Oxford University Press.

Carter, Marina. 1997. "Indian Indentured Migration and the Forced Labour Debate." *Itinerario* 21 (1): 52–61.

Carter, Marina. 2006. "Slavery and Unfree Labour in the Indian Ocean." *History Compass* 4 (5): 800–813.

Carton, Benedict. 2006. "'We Are Made Quiet by This Annihilation': Historicizing Concepts of Bodily Pollution and Dangerous Sexuality in South Africa." *International Journal of African Historical Studies* 39 (1): 85–106.

Cavanagh, Edward. 2013. "The History of Dispossession at Orania and the Politics of Land Restitution in South Africa." *Journal of Southern African Studies* 39 (2): 391–407.

Chakrabarti, Kunal. 2001. *Religious Process: The Puranas and the Making of a Regional Tradition*. New Delhi: Oxford University Press.

Chatterjee, Partha. 2001. "The Nation in Heterogeneous Time." *Indian Economic and Social History Review* 38: 399–418.

Chen, Nancy N. 1992. "'Speaking Nearby': A Conversation with Trinh T. Minh–ha." *Visual Anthropology Review* 8 (1): 82–91.
Chhiba, Reshma. 2013. "Images of Kali as Reflections of Female Defiance within Selected Examples of Contemporary Asian Arts." MA thesis, University of the Witwatersand.
Chhiba, Reshma. 2017. "The Two Talking Yonis: The Use of Hindu Iconography in Conversations of Race, Politics, and Womanhood within Contemporary South Africa." *Nidan* 2 (2): 44–60.
Chhiba, Reshma, and Nontobeko Ntombela, eds. 2019. *The Yoni Book*. Johannesburg: Self-published.
Chipkin, Ivor. 2002. "The Sublime Object of Blackness." *Cahiers d'Études africaines* 167 (3): 569–84.
Chrisman, Laura. 2005. "Beyond Black Atlantic and Postcolonial Studies: The South African Differences of Sol Plaatje and Peter Abrahams." In *Postcolonial Studies and Beyond*, edited by Ania Loomba, Savir Kaul, Matti Bunzl, Antoinette Burton, and Jed Esty, 252–71. Durham, NC: Duke University Press.
Chuh, Kandice. 2003. *Imagine Otherwise: On Asian Americanist Critique*. Durham, NC: Duke University Press.
Cohen, Cathy J. 2005. "Punks, Bulldaggers, and Welfare Queens: The Radical Potential of Queer Politics." In *Black Queer Studies: A Critical Anthology*, edited by E. Patrick Johnson and Mae G. Henderson, 21–51. Durham, NC: Duke University Press.
Cohen, Cathy J. 2004. "Deviance as Resistance: A New Research Agenda for the Study of Black Politics." *Du Bois Review: Social Science Research on Race* 1 (1): 27–45.
Cohen, Robin, ed. 1995. *The Cambridge Survey of World Migration*. Cambridge: Cambridge University Press.
Cole, D. T. 1953. "Fanakalo and the Bantu Languages in South Africa." *African Studies* 12 (1): 1–14.
Collis-Buthelezi, Victoria, J. 2017. "The Case for Black Studies in South Africa." *The Black Scholar* 47 (2): 7–21.
Coombes, Annie, E. 2011. "Witnessing History/Embodying Testimony: Gender and Memory in Post-Apartheid South Africa." *Journal of the Royal Anthropological Institute*, 17: S92–S112.
Crawley, Ashon. 2016. "Otherwise, Ferguson." *Interfictions Online: A Journal of Interstitial Arts*, 7. http://interfictions.com/otherwise-fergusonashon-crawley/.
Cross, Karen, and Julia Peck. 2010. "Editorial: Special Issue on Photography, Archive and Memory." *photographies* 3 (2): 127–38.
Crush, Jonathan. 1995. "Cheap Gold: Mine Labor in Southern Africa." In *The Cambridge Survey of World Migration*, edited by Robin Cohen, 172–77. Cambridge: Cambridge University Press.
Crush, Jonathan, and Clarence Tshitereke. 2001. "Contesting Migrancy: The Labor Debate in Post-1994 South Africa." *Africa Today* 48 (3): 49–70.
Cunniff Gilson, Erinn. 2016. "Vulnerability and Victimization: Rethinking Key Concepts in Feminist Discourses on Sexual Violence." *Signs: Journal of Women in Culture and Society* 42 (1): 71–98.

Currier, Ashley. 2018. *Politicizing Sex in Contemporary Africa: Homophobia in Malawi*. Cambridge: Cambridge University Press.
Cvetkovich, Ann. 2003. *An Archive of Feeling: Trauma, Sexuality and Lesbian Public Cultures*. Durham, NC: Duke University Press.
Cvetkovich, Ann. 2014. "Photographing Objects as Queer Archival Practices." In *Feeling Photography*, edited by Elspeth H. Brown and Thy Phu, 273–96. Durham, NC: Duke University Press.
Daber, Benedicta N. 2003. "The Gendered Construction of Mourning and Cleansing Rites of Widowhood amongst the Zulu Speaking People of Ndwedwe Community, KwaZulu-Natal." PhD diss., University of KwaZulu-Natal.
Dasgupta, Rohit K. 2015. "The Visual Representation of Queer Bollywood: Mistaken Identities and Misreadings in Dostana." *Journal of Arts Writing by Students* 1 (1): 91–101.
Davids, Nadia, and Zethu Matebeni. 2017. "Queer Politics and Intersectionality in South Africa." *Safundi: Journal of South African and American Studies* 18 (2): 161–67.
Davis, Angela Y. 1998. *Blues Legacy and Black Feminism*. New York: Pantheon Books.
Delius, Peter, Laura Phillips, and Fiona Rankin-Smith, eds. 2014. *A Long Way Home: Migrant Worker Worlds 1800–2014*. Johannesburg: Wits University Press.
Desai, Ashwin. 2002. *We Are the Poors: Community Struggles in Post-Apartheid South Africa*. New York: NYU Press.
Desai, Ashwin. 2015. "Indian South Africans and the Black Consciousness Movement under Apartheid." *Diaspora Studies* 8 (1): 37–50.
Desai, Ashwin, and Goolam Vahed. 2010. *Inside Indian Indenture: A South African Story, 1860–1914*. Cape Town: HSRC Press.
Desai, Ashwin, and Goolam Vahed. 2016. *The South African Gandhi: Stretcher-Bearer of Empire*. New Delhi: Navayana Publishing.
Dlamini, Jacob. 2020. *The Terrorist Album: Apartheid's Insurgents, Collaborators, and the Security Police*. Cambridge, MA: Harvard University Press.
Dhupelia-Mesthrie, Uma. 2000. *From Cane Fields to Freedom: A Chronicle of Indian South African Life*. Cape Town: NB Publishers.
Dhupelia-Mesthrie, Uma. 2009. "The Passenger Indian as Worker: Indian Immigrants in Cape Town in the Early Twentieth Century." *African Studies* 68 (1): 111–34.
Diesel, Alleyn. 1998. "The Empowering Image of the Divine Mother: A South African Hindu Woman Worshipping the Goddess." *Journal of Contemporary Religion* 13 (1): 73–90.
Dooling, Wayne. 2007. *Slavery, Emancipation and Colonial Rule in South Africa*. Athens: Ohio University Press.
Dubow, Saul, and Alan Jeeves, eds. 2005. *South Africa's 1940: Worlds of Possibilities*. Cape Town: Double Storey Books.
Duggan, Lisa. 2002. "The New Homonormativity: The Sexual Politics of Neoliberalism." In *Materializing Democracy: Toward a Revitalized Cultural Politics*, edited by Russ Castronovo and Dana D. Nelson, 175–94. Durham, NC: Duke University Press.
Du Toit, Darcy, ed. 2013. *Exploited, Undervalued—and Essential: Domestic Workers and the Realisation of Their Rights*. Pretoria: PULP.
Ebrahim, Haseenah. 2021. "A Poetics of Sensuality: Xenophobia and Same-Sex Intimacy in *cane/cain*." *Queer Studies in Media and Popular Culture* 6 (2): 141–58.

Ellapen, Jordache A. 2007. "The Cinematic Township: Cinematic Representations of the Township Space and Who Can Claim the Rights to Representation in Post-Apartheid South African Cinema." *Journal of African Cultural Studies* 19 (1): 113–37.
Ellapen, Jordache A. 2017. "*When the moon waxes red*: Afro-Asian Feminist Intimacies and the Aesthetics of Indenture." *Small Axe: A Caribbean Journal of Criticism* 53: 94–111.
Ellapen, Jordache A. 2018. "Queering the Archive: Brown Bodies in Ecstasy: Visual Assemblages and the Pleasure of Transgressive Erotics." *Scholar and Feminist Online* 14 (3): 1–16.
Ellapen, Jordache A. 2020. "The Brown Photo Album: An Archive of Feminist Futurity." *Kronos: Southern African Histories* 42: 1.
Ellapen, Jordache A. 2021a. "*Siyakaka* Feminism: African Anality and the Politics of Deviance in FAKA's Performance Art Praxis." *Feminist Studies* 47 (1): 114–46.
Ellapen, Jordache A. 2021b. "Performing Blackness as Transgressive Erotics: African Futurities and Black Queer Sex in South African Live Art." *Feminist Formations* 33 (2): 52–78.
Ellison, Treva Carrie. 2019. "Black Femme Praxis and the Promise of Black Gender." *Black Scholar: Journal of Black Studies and Research* 49 (1): 6–16.
Enwezor, Okwui. 1996. "A Critical Presence: *Drum* Magazine in Context." In *In/Site: African Photographers, 1940 to the Present*, curated and edited by Clare Bell, Okwui Enwezor, Olu Oguibe, and Octavia Zaya. New York: Guggenheim Museum Publications.
Enwezor, Okwui. 2008. "Archive Fever: Photography between History and Monument." In *Archive Fever: Uses of the Document in Contemporary Art*, edited by Okwui Enwezor, 11–51. New York: International Center of Photography and Steidl Publishers.
Epprecht, Marc. 2013. *Hungochani: The History of a Dissident Sexuality in Southern Africa*. Montreal: McGill-Queen's University Press.
Erasmus, Zimitri. 2000. "Recognition through Pleasure, Recognition through Violence: Gendered Coloured Subjectivities in South Africa." *Current Sociology* 48 (3): 71–85.
Erasmus, Zimitri. 2012. "Apartheid Race Categories: Daring to Question Their Continued Use." *Transformation: Critical Perspectives on Southern Africa* 79: 1–11.
Erasmus, Zimitri. 2017. *Race Otherwise: Forging a New Humanism for South Africa*. Johannesburg: Wits University Press.
Everatt, David. 2009. *The Origins of Non-Racialism: White Opposition to Apartheid in the 1950s*. New York: NYU Press.
Fanon, Frantz. 1986. *Black Skin, White Masks*. London: Pluto Press.
Fanon, Frantz. 2001. *The Wretched of the Earth*. Translated by Constance Farrington. London: Penguin Books.
Ferguson, Roderick. 2004. *Aberrations in Black: Towards a Queer of Color Critique*. Minneapolis: University of Minnesota Press.
Ferguson, Roderick. 2005. "Of Our Normative Strivings: African American Studies and the Histories of Sexuality." *Social Text* 23 (3–4): 85–100.
Fleetwood, Nicole. 2011. *Troubling Vision: Performance, Visuality and Blackness*. Chicago: University of Chicago Press.
Fleetwood, Nicole. 2015. "Posing in Prison: Family Photographs, Emotional Labor, and Carceral Intimacy." *Public Culture* 27 (3): 487–511.

Fleming, Julius B., Jr. 2022. "Anticipating Blackness: Nina Simone, Lorraine Hansberry, and the Time of Black Ontology." *South Atlantic Quarterly* 121 (1): 131–52.
Freeman, Elizabeth. 2010. *Time Binds: Queer Temporalities, Queer Histories*. Durham, NC: Duke University Press.
Freund, Bill. 1995. *Insiders and Outsiders: The Indian Working Class of Durban, 1910–1990*. London: James Currey.
Gillespie, Kelly, and Leigh-Ann Naidoo. 2019. "#MustFall: The South African Student Movement and the Politics of Time." *South Atlantic Quarterly* 118 (1): 190–94.
Gilroy, Paul. 1993. *The Black Atlantic: Modernity and Double Consciousness*. Cambridge, MA: Harvard University Press.
Ginwala, Frene. 1974. "Class Consciousness and Control: Indian South Africans, 1860–1946." PhD diss., Oxford University.
Goffe, Tao Leigh 2019. "Sugarwork: The Gastropoetics of Afro-Asia after the Plantation." *Asian Diasporic Visual Culture and the Americas* 5 (1–2): 31–56.
Goniwe, Thembinkosi. 2017. "Contemporary South African Visual Art and the Postcolonial Imagination, 1992–Present." PhD diss., Cornell University.
Gopinath, Gayatri. 2000. "Queering Bollywood: Alternative Sexualities in Popular Indian Cinema." *Journal of Homosexuality* 39 (3–4): 283–97.
Gopinath, Gayatri. 2005. *Impossible Desires: Queer Diasporas and South Asian Public Cultures*. Durham, NC: Duke University Press.
Gopinath, Gayatri. 2010. "Archive, Affect and the Everyday: Queer Diasporic Re-Vision." In *Political Emotions*, edited by Janet Staiger, Ann Cvetkovich, and Ann Reynolds, 165–92. New York: Routledge.
Gopinath, Gayatri. 2018. *Unruly Visions: The Aesthetic Practices of Queer Diaspora*. Durham, NC: Duke University Press.
Gordon, Avery. 2008. *Ghostly Matters: Haunting and the Sociological Imagination*. Minneapolis: University of Minnesota Press.
Gosine, Andil. 2017. "After Indenture." *Small Axe: A Caribbean Journal of Criticism* 21 (2): 63–67.
Gossett, Reina, Eric A. Stanley, and Johanna Burton. 2017. "Known Unknowns: An Introduction to Trap Door." In *Trap Door: Trans Cultural Production and the Politics of Visibility*, edited by Reina Gossett, Eric A. Stanley, and Johanna Burton, xv–xxvi. Cambridge, MA: MIT Press.
Govinden, Devarakshanam Betty. 2009. "Healing the Wounds of History: South African Indian Writing." *Current Writing* 21 (102): 286–302.
Gqola, Pumla Dineo. 2001. "Contradictory Locations: Blackwomen and the Discourse of the Black Consciousness Movement (BCM) in South Africa." *Meridians: Feminism, Race, Transnationalism* 2 (1): 130–52.
Gqola, Pumla Dineo. 2007. "How the 'Cult of Femininity' and Violent Masculinities Support Endemic Gender-Based Violence in Contemporary South Africa." *African Identities* 5 (1): 111–24.
Gqola, Pumla, Dineo. 2009. "'The Difficult Task of Normalizing Freedom': Spectacular Masculinities, Ndebele's Literary/Cultural Commentary and Post-Apartheid Life." *English in Africa* 36 (1): 61–76.

Gqola, Pumla, Dineo. 2010. *What Is Slavery to Me? Postcolonial/Slave Memory in Post-Apartheid South Africa.* Johannesburg: Wits University Press.

Gqola, Pumla Dineo. 2015. *Rape: A South African Nightmare.* Johannesburg: MF Books.

Gray, Mary L., Colin R. Johnson, and Brian J. Gilley. 2016. "Introduction." In *Queering the Countryside: New Frontiers in Rural Queer Studies*, edited by Mary L. Gray, Colin R. Johnson, and Brian J. Gilley, 1–24. New York: NYU Press.

Halberstam, Jack. 2011. *The Queer Art of Failure.* Durham, NC: Duke University Press.

Halberstam, Jack. 2020. *Wild Things: The Disorder of Desire.* Durham, NC: Duke University Press.

Hall, Stuart. 1993. "What Is This 'Black' in Black Popular Culture?" *Social Text* 20 (1–2): 104–15.

Hall, Stuart. 1996. "New Ethnicities." In *Black British Cultural Studies: A Reader*, edited by Housten A. Baler Jr., Manthia Diawara, and Ruth H. Lindeborg, 163–72. Chicago: University of Chicago Press.

Hall, Stuart. 2003. "Cultural Identity and Diaspora." In *Theorizing Diaspora*, edited by Jana Evans Braziel and Anita Mannur, 233–46. Malden, UK: Blackwell Publishing.

Hall, Stuart. 2017. *Familiar Strangers: A Life between Two Islands.* Durham, NC: Duke University Press.

Hansen, Thomas Blom. 2006. "Sounds of Freedom: Music, Taxis, and Racial Imagination in Urban South Africa." *Public Culture* 18 (1): 185–208.

Hansen, Thomas Blom. 2012. *Melancholia of Freedom: Social Life in an Indian Township in South Africa.* Princeton, NJ: Princeton University Press.

Harris, Karen L. 2004. "Private and Confidential: The Chinese Mine Labourers and 'Unnatural Crime.'" *South African Historical Journal* 50 (1): 115–33.

Harris, Karen L. 2010. "Sugar and Gold: Indentured Indian and Chinese Labour in South Africa." *Journal of Social Sciences* 25 (1–3): 147–58.

Hartman, Saidiya. 2008a. "Venus in Two Acts." *Small Axe: A Caribbean Journal of Criticism* 12 (2): 1–14.

Hartman, Saidiya. 2008b. *Lose Your Mother: A Journey along the Atlantic Slave Trade Route.* New York: Farrar, Straus and Giroux.

Hartman, Saidiya. 2019. *Wayward Lives, Beautiful Experiments: Intimate Histories of Riotous Black Girls, Troublesome Women, and Queer Radicals.* New York: W. W. Norton.

Hartman, Saidiya, and Frank B. Wilderson. 2008. "The Position of the Unthought." *Qui Parle* 12 (2): 183–201.

Hassim, Shireen. 2009. "Democracy's Shadows: Sexual Rights and Gender Politics in the Rape Trial of Jacob Zuma." *African Studies* 68 (1): 57–77.

Hassim, Shireen. 2019. *Fatima Meer: A Free Mind.* Cape Town: HSRC Press.

Hayes, Patricia. 2007. "Power, Secrecy, Proximity: A Short History of South African Photography." *Kronos: Southern African Histories Journal of Cape History* 33: 139–62.

Hernandez, Jillian. 2020. *Aesthetics of Excess: The Art and Politics of Black and Latina Embodiment.* Durham, NC: Duke University Press.

Higginbotham, Evelyn Brooks. 1993. *Righteous Discontent: The Women's Movement in the Black Baptist Church, 1880–1920.* Cambridge, MA: Harvard University Press.

Hill, Robert, A., and Gregory A. Pinto. 1987. "'Africa for the Africans': The Garvey Movement in South Africa, 1920–1940." In *The Politics of Race, Class and Nationalism in Twentieth Century South Africa*, edited by Shula Marks and Stanley Trapido, 209–53. London: Routledge.

Himbara, David. 2007. "The 'Asian Question' in East Africa." *African Studies* 56 (1): 1–18.

Hoad, Neville. 2007. *African Intimacies: Race, Homosexuality, and Globalization*. Minneapolis: University of Minnesota Press.

Hoad, Neville, Karen Martin, and Graeme Reid, eds. 2005. *Sex and Politics in South Africa: The Equality Clause/Gay and Lesbian Movements/the Anti-Apartheid Struggle*. Cape Town: Double Storey Books.

Hofmeyr, Isabel. 2007. "The Black Atlantic Meets the Indian Ocean: Forging New Paradigms of Transnationalism for the Global South—Literary and Cultural Perspectives." *Social Dynamics* 33 (2): 3–32.

Hong, Grace Kyungwon, and Roderick Ferguson. 2011. "Introduction." In *Strange Affinities: The Gender and Sexual Politics of Comparative Racialization*, edited by Grace Kyungwon Hong and Roderick Ferguson, 1–22. Durham, NC: Duke University Press.

Hook, Derek, ed. 2014. *Steve Biko* (Voices of Liberation series). Cape Town: HSRC Press.

Hughes, Heather. 2007. "'The Coolies Will Elbow Us Out of the Country': African Reactions to Indian Immigration in the Colony of Natal, South Africa." *Labour History Review* 72 (2): 155–68.

Islam, Najnin, Kaneesha Persard, and Neelofer Qadir. 2024. "Indenture. Iteration: Race and the Aesthetics of Contract Labor." *Verge: Studies in Global Asias* 10 (1): 1–24.

Jamal, Ashraf. 2016. "Mohau Modisakeng in Conversation with Ashraf Jamal." In *Mohau Modisakeng: Selected Works*, edited by Karin Pernegger, 116–19. Ghent, Belgium: Snoeck Publishers.

Jansen, Ena. 2019. *Like Family: Domestic Workers in South African History and Literature*. Johannesburg: Wits University Press.

Jeyathurai, Dashini. 2014. "Rethinking the Circuits of Male Desires across Multiple Dostanas." In *Masculinity and Its Challenges in India: Essays on Changing Perceptions*, edited by Rohit K. Dasgupta and K. Moti Gokulsing, 227–39. Jefferson, NC: McFarland.

Johnson, E. Patrick. 2001. "'Quare' Studies, or (Almost) Everything I Know about Queer Studies I Learnt from My Grandmother." *Text and Performance Quarterly* 21 (1): 1–25.

Johnson, E. Patrick, and Mae G. Henderson. 2006. *Black Queer Studies: A Critical Anthology*. Durham, NC: Duke University Press.

Jones, Alisha Lola. 2020. *Flaming?: The Peculiar Theopolitics of Fire and Desire in Black Male Gospel Performance*. New York: Oxford University Press.

Josephy, Svea. 2018. "Fractured Compounds: Photographing Post-Apartheid Compounds and Hostels." In *Photography in and out of Africa*, edited by Kylie Thomas and Louise Green, 244–70. New York: Routledge.

Kaarsholm, Preben. 2016. "Indian Ocean Networks and the Transmutations of Servitude: The Protector of Indian Immigrants and the Administration of Freed Slaves and Indentured Labourers in Durban in the 1870s." *Journal of Southern African Studies* 42 (3): 443–61.

Keeling, Kara. 2019. *Queer Times, Black Futures*. New York: NYU Press.
Kelly, Robin D. G. 2003. *Freedom Dreams: The Black Radical Imagination*. Boston: Beacon Press.
Kent, Eliza F. 2004. *Converting Women: Gender and Protestant Christianity in Colonial South India*. New York: Oxford University Press.
Khan, Aliyah. 2016. "Voyages across Indenture: From Ship Sisters to Mannish Women." *GLQ: A Journal of Lesbian and Gay Studies* 22 (2): 249–80.
Khan, Sharlene. 2019a. *when the moon waxes red . . . Negotiating Subjective Terrain as an "Inside-Outsider," an "Outside-Insider."* Johannesburg: Pole Pole Press.
Khan, Sharlene. 2019b. "When Silence Speaks—Gender Performativity in the Visual Art Practice of Reshma Chhiba." In *The Yoni Book*, edited by Reshma Chhiba and Nontobeko Ntombela, 51–71. Johannesburg: Self-published.
Khan, Sharlene. 2006. "Aluta Continua: Doing It for Daddy." *Art South Africa* 4 (3): n.p.
Khan, Sharlene, and Fouad Asfour. 2018. "Whitespeak: How Race Works in South African Art Criticism Texts to Maintain the Arts as the Property of Whiteness." In *The Palgrave Handbook of Race and the Arts in Education*, edited by Amelia M. Kraehe, Rubén Gaztambide-Fernández, and B. Stephen Carpenter II, 187–204. Cham: Palgrave Macmillan.
King, Tiffany L. 2019. *The Black Shoals: Offshore Formations of Black and Native Studies*. Durham, NC: Duke University Press.
Kinsley, David. 1986. *Hindu Goddess: Visions of the Divine Feminine in the Hindu Religious Tradition*. Berkeley: University of California Press.
Kruger, Loren. 2001. "Black Atlantics, White Indians, and Jews: Locations, Locutions, and Syncretic Identities in the Fiction of Achmat Dangor and Others." *South Atlantic Quarterly* 11 (1): 111–43.
Kuhn, Annette. 1995. *Family Secrets: Acts of Memory and Imagination*. New York: Verso.
Kuhn, Jedediah H. 2018. "Indigenous Intimacies: Native Americans and Mexican Americans since 1848." PhD diss., Indiana University.
Lahiri, Madhumita. 2018. "Hearing the Difference: Sexuality, Xenophobia, and South African Melodrama." *Black Camera: An International Film Journal* 9 (12): 295–312.
Lal, Brij V. 1985. "Kunti's Cry: Indentured Women on Fiji Plantations." *The Indian Economic and Social History Review* 22 (1): 55–71.
Landau, Loren B., and Tanya Pampalone. 2018. "Introduction." In *I Want to Go Home Forever: Stories of Becoming and Belonging in South Africa's Great Metropolis*, edited by Loren B. Landau and Tanya Pampalone, 1–18. Johannesburg: Wits University Press.
Legassick, Martin, and Harold Wolpe. 1976. "The Bantustans and Capital Accumulation in South Africa." *Review of African Political Economy* 3 (7): 87–107.
Lehrer, Erica, and Cynthia E. Milton. 2011. *Curating Difficult Knowledge: Violent Pasts in Public Places*. Basingstoke: Palgrave Macmillan.
Lewis, Desiree. 2007. "Feminism and the Radical Imagination." *Agenda: Empowering Women for Gender Equity* 72: 18–31.

Lewis, Desiree, and Gabeba Baderoon. 2021. “Introduction: Being Black and Feminist.” In *Surfacing: On Being Black and Feminist in South Africa*, edited by Desiree Lewis and Gabeba Baderoon, 1–14. Johannesburg: Wits University Press.
Livermon, Xavier. 2012a. “Queer(y)ing Freedom: Black Queer Visibilities in Postapartheid SouthAfrica.” *GLQ: A Journal of Lesbian and Gay Studies* 18 (2–3): 298–323.
Livermon, Xavier. 2012b. “Representations of Sophiatown in Kwaito Music: Mafikizolo and Musical Memory.” In *Music, Performance and African Identities*, edited by Toyin Falola and Tyler Fleming, 169–90. New York: Routledge.
Livermon, Xavier. 2020. *Kwaito Bodies: Remastering Space and Subjectivity in Post-Apartheid South Africa*. Durham, NC: Duke University Press.
Lorde, Audre. 2007a. “The Uses of the Erotic.” In *Sister Outsider: Essays and Speeches by Audre Lorde*, 53–59. Berkeley, CA: Crossing Press.
Lorde, Audre. 2007b. “Age, Race, Class, and Sex: Women Redefining Difference.” In *Sister Outsider: Essays and Speeches by Audre Lorde*, 114–23. Berkeley, CA: Crossing Press.
Lowe, Lisa. 2006. “The Intimacy of Four Continents.” In *Haunted by Empire: Geographies of Intimacy in North American History*, edited by Anne Laura Stoler, 191–212. Durham, NC: Duke University Press.
Lowe, Lisa. 2015. *The Intimacies of Four Continents*. Durham, NC: Duke University Press.
Macharia, Keguro. 2019. *Frottage: Frictions of Intimacy across the Black Diaspora*. New York: NYU Press.
Macharia, Keguro. 2009. “Queering African Studies.” *Criticism* 51 (1): 157–64.
Macharia, Keguro. 2016. “Political Vernaculars: Freedom and Love.” *The New Inquiry*, March 14. https://thenewinquiry.com/political-vernaculars-freedom-and-love/.
Machida, Margo. 2008. *Unsettled Visions: Contemporary Asian American Artists and the Social Imaginary*. Durham, NC: Duke University Press.
Madison, D. Soyini. 2014. “Foreword.” In *Black Performance Theory*, edited by Thomas F. DeFrantz and Anita Gonzalez, vii–ix. Durham, NC: Duke University Press.
Madondo, Bongani. 2017. “Sabelo Mlangeni: Big City.” *Aperture* 227: 54–63.
Magudu, Bulelwa. 2004. “AmaHlubi Women’s Experience and Perceptions of ‘Ukuzila.’” *Agenda* 18 (61): 140–48.
Majavu, Mandisi. 2022. “Orania: A White Homeland in Post-Apartheid South Africa.” *Sociology Compass* 16 (7): e13004.
Makhubu, Nomusa. 2013. “Open Debate: Ephemeral Democracies: Interrogating Commonality in South Africa.” *Third Text* 27 (3): 415–18.
Mamdani, Mahmood. 2020. *Neither Settler nor Native: The Making and Unmaking of Permanent Minorities*. Cambridge, MA: Harvard University Press.
Manalansan, Martin F. 2015. “Queer Worldings: The Messy Art of Being Global in Manila and New York.” *Antipode* 47 (3): 566–79.
Marea, Desire, and Fela Gucci. 2016. “FAKA or Bust.” *Cakeboy* 3 (2016): 10–15.
Masilela, Ntongela. 1996. “The ‘Black Atlantic’ and African Modernity in South Africa.” *Research in African Literatures* 27 (4): 88–96.

Masondo, Ingrid. 2019. "Unstable Forms: Photography, Race, and the Identity Document in South Africa." In *Ambivalent: Photography and Visibility in African History*, edited by Patricia Hayes, 77–104. Athens: Ohio University Press.

Matebeni, Zethu, and Jabu Pereira, eds. 2014. *Reclaiming Afrikan: Queer Perspectives on Sexual and Gender Identities*. Cape Town: Modjaji Books.

McFadden, Patricia. 2003. "Sexual Pleasure as Feminist Choice." *Feminist Africa* 2: 50–60. https://feministafrica.net/wp-content/uploads/2019/10/fa_2_standpoint_1.pdf.

McKittrick, Katherine. 2006. *Demonic Grounds: Black Women and the Cartographies of Struggle*. Minneapolis: University of Minnesota Press.

McMillan, Uri. 2018. "Introduction: Skin, Surface, Sensorium." *Women and Performance: A Journal of Feminist Theory* 28 (1): 1–15.

Meer, Fatima. 1969. *Portrait of Indian South Africans*. Johannesburg: Avon House.

Meer, Y. S., Penny Gains, Shamim Marie, Shereen Motala, Rabia Motala, Zwelakhe O. Msomi, Rehana Padia, Sara Pochee, Farida Pochee, Jane Turner, and Ntombintombi M. Zondi. 1980. *Documents of Indentured Labor: Natal 1851–1917*. Durban: Institute of Black Research.

Mesthrie, Rajend. 1989. "The Origins of Fanagalo." *Journal of Pidgin and Creole Languages* 4(2): 211–40.

Mesthrie, Rajend. 2019. "Fanakalo as a Mining Language in South Africa: A New Overview." *International Journal of the Sociology of Language* 258: 13–33.

Mishra, Vijay. 2005. "The Diasporic Imaginary and the Indian Diaspora." *Asian Studies Institute Occasional Lecture* 2: 1–30. https://ir.wgtn.ac.nz/bitstream/handle/123456789/19272/paper.pdf.

Mishra, Vijay. 2002. *Bollywood Cinema: Temples of Desire*. New York: Routledge.

Mofokeng, Santu. 2013. *The Black Photo Album, Look at Me: 1890–1950*. Göttingen: Steidl.

Mohabir, Nalini. 2010. "Servitude in the Shadow of Slavery? Towards a Relational Account of Indenture." In *Human Bondage in the Cultural Contact Zone*, edited by Raphael Hörmann and Gesa Mackenthun, 227–53. München: Waxmann Verlag GmbH.

Mohabir, Nalini. 2019. "Kala Pani: Aesthetics Deathscapes and the Flow of Water after Indenture." *Asian Diasporic Visual Cultures and the Americas* 5 (3): 293–314.

Mokoena, Hlonipha. 2016. "Isidwaba yini na? What Is That Pleated Leather Skirt?" In *Mohau Modisakeng: Selected Works*, edited by Karen Pernegger, 4–7. Ghent, Belgium: Snoeck Publishers.

Moodie, T. Dunbar. 1988. "Migrancy and Male Sexuality on the South African Gold Mines." *Journal of Southern African Studies* 14 (2): 228–56.

Moore, Madison. 2018. *Fabulous: The Rise of the Beautiful Eccentric*. New Haven, CT: Yale University Press.

Moraga, Cherríe, and Gloria Anzaldúa, eds. 1983. *This Bridge Called My Back: Writings by Radical Women of Color*. New York: Kitchen Table: Women of Color Press.

Moreau, Julie, and T. J. Tallie. 2019. "Queer African Studies and Directions on Methodology." In *Routledge Handbook of Queer African Studies*, edited by S. N. Nyeck, 49–60. New York: Routledge.

Morrell, Robert. 1998. "Of Boys and Men: Masculinity and Gender in Southern African Studies." *Journal of Southern African Studies* 24 (4): 605–30.
Mphahlele, Ezekiel. 1962. *The African Image*. London: Faber and Faber.
Mpumlwana, Malusi, and Thoko Mpumlwana. 2014. "Introduction to Steve Biko's *I Write What I Like*." In *Steve Biko* (Voices of Liberation Series), edited by Derek Hook, 104–116. Cape Town: HSRC Press.
Muñoz, José. 2020. *The Sense of Brown*. Durham, NC: Duke University Press.
Muñoz, José Esteban. 1999. *Disidentifications: Queers of Color and the Performance of Politics*. Vol. 2. Minneapolis: University of Minnesota Press.
Munro, Brenna M. 2012. *South Africa and the Dream of Love to Come: Queer Sexuality and the Struggle for Freedom*. Minneapolis: University of Minnesota Press.
Munshi, Naadria. 2013. "Lived Experiences and Local Spaces: Bangladeshi Migrants in Post-Apartheid South Africa." PhD diss., Northwest University.
Murinik, Tracy. 2019. "The Complex Gendering of 'and': Reshma Chhiba's *The Two Talking Yonis*." In *The Yoni Book*, edited by Reshma Chhiba and Nontobeko Ntombela, 79–90. Johannesburg: Self-published.
Musser, Amber. 2018a. "Race, Affect, and Assemblage: Toward Brown Jouissance." *Social Text* online, October 25. https://socialtextjournal.org/periscope_article/race-affect-and- assemblage-toward-brown-jouissance/.
Musser, Amber. 2018b. *Sensual Excess: Queer Femininity and Brown Jouissance*. New York: NYU Press.
Musser, Amber Jamilla. 2023. "Femininity." *differences* 34 (1): 113–18.
Mzamane, Mbulelo V., Bavusile Maaba, and Nkosinathi Biko. 2014. "The Black Consciousness Movement." In *Steve Biko* (Voices of Liberation Series), edited by Derek Hook, 70–80. Cape Town: HSRC Press.
Naidoo, Riason. 2008. *The Indian in Drum Magazine in the 1950s*. Cape Town: Bell-Roberts Publishing.
Nash, Jennifer C. 2014a. *The Black Body in Ecstasy: Reading Race, Reading Pornography*. Durham, NC: Duke University Press.
Nash, Jennifer. 2014b. "Black Anality." *GLQ: A Journal of Lesbian and Gay Studies* 20 (4): 439–60.
Ndebele, Nhlanhla. 2002. "The African National Congress and the Policy of Non-Racism: A Study of the Membership Issue." *Politikon: South African Journal of Political Studies* 29 (2): 133–46.
Ndebele, Njabulo. 2006. *Rediscovery of the Ordinary: Essays on South African Literature and Culture*. Scottsville: University of KwaZulu-Natal Press.
Newbury, Darren. 2009. *Defiant Images: Photography and Apartheid South Africa*. Pretoria: Unisa Press.
Ngema, Mbongeni. 2002. "Ama-Ndiya." Track 16 on *Jive Madlokovu*. Gallo Record Company, MP3 audio. Apple Music.
Ngoasheng, Asanda. 2021. "Debunking the Apartheid Spatial Grid: Developing a Socially Just Architecture Curriculum at a University of Technology." *Journal of Asian and African Studies* 56 (1): 135–49.
Nguyen, Tan Hoang. 2014. *A View from the Bottom: Asian American Masculinity and Sexual Representation*. Durham, NC: Duke University Press.

Nixon, Rob. 1994. *Homelands, Harlem, and Hollywood: South African Culture and the World Beyond*. London: Routledge.

Ntshangase, Sicelo Ziphozonke. 2018. "The Power of Dreams and Religious Philosophy of the Zulu People as Portrayed in the Novel, *Umshado*." *South African Journal of African Languages* 38 (2): 237–45.

Nuttall, Sarah. 2019. "Upsurge." In *Acts of Transgression: Contemporary Live Art in South Africa*, edited by Jay Pather and Catherine Boulle, 41–59. Johannesburg: Wits University Press.

Nuttall, Sarah, and Carli Coetzee, eds. 1998. *Negotiating the Past: The Making of Memory in South Africa*. Oxford: Oxford University Press.

Oakes, Dougie. 1992. *Illustrated History of South Africa: The Real Story*. Cape Town: Reader's Digest.

Oldfield, Sophie, and Kristian Stokke. 2007. "Political Polemics and Local Practices of Community Organizing and Neoliberal Politics in South Africa." In *Contesting Neoliberalism: Urban Frontiers*, edited by Helga Leitner, Jamie Peck, and Eric Sheppard, 139–56. New York: Guilford.

Oleszkiewicz-Peralba, Malgorzata. 2015. *Fierce Feminine Divinities of Eurasia and Latin America*. New York: Palgrave Macmillan.

Oswin, Natalie. 2007. "Producing Homonormativity in Neoliberal South Africa: Recognition, Redistribution, and the Equality Project." *Signs: Journal of Women in Culture and Society* 32 (3): 649–69.

O'Toole, Sean. 2017. "Sabelo Mlangeni." *Aperture* 229: 118–23.

Outar, Lisa. 2016. "Art, Violence, and Non-Return: An Interview with Guadeloupean Artist Kelly Sinnapah Mary." In *Indo-Caribbean Feminist Thought: Genealogies, Theories, Enactments*, edited by Gabrielle Jamela Hosein and Liza Outar, 193–202. New York: Palgrave Macmillan.

Oyěwùmí, Oyèrónkẹ́. 1997. *The Invention of Women: Making an African Sense of Western Gender Discourses*. Minneapolis: University of Minnesota Press.

Palmer, Fileve Tlaloc. 2015. "Through a Coloured Lens: Post-Apartheid Identity Formation amongst Coloureds in KZN." PhD diss., Indiana University.

Pande, Amrita. 2017. "Mobile Masculinities: Bangladeshi Men in South Africa." *Gender and Society* 31 (3): 383–406.

Park, Yoon Yung, and Ying Chen. 2009. "Recent Chinese Migrants in Small Towns of Post-Apartheid South Africa." *Revue Européenne des Migrations Internationales* 24 (1): 25–44.

Parsard, Kaneesha. 2016. "Cutlass: Objects toward a Theory of Representation." In *Indo-Caribbean Feminist Thought: Genealogies, Theories, Enactments*, edited by Gabrielle Jamela Hosein and Lisa Outar, 241–60. New York: Palgrave Macmillan.

Pather, Jay, and Catherine Boulle. 2019. "Introduction." In *Acts of Transgression: Contemporary Live Art in South Africa*, edited by Jay Pather and Catherine Boulle, 1–16. Johannesburg: Wits University Press.

Peberdy, Sally. 2009. *Selecting Immigrants: National Identity and South Africa's Immigration Policies 1910–2008*. Johannesburg: Wits University Press.

Peffer, John. 2020. "Vernacular Recollections and Popular Photography in South Africa." In *The African Photographic Archive*, 115–33. New York: Routledge.

Peterson, Bheki. 2012. "We Remember Differently and the Intimacies of Our Separateness." In *We Remember Differently: Race, Memory, Imagination*, edited by Jyoti Mistry and Jordache A. Ellapen, 151–60. Pretoria: Unisa Press.

Phillips, Laura, and Deborah James. 2014. "Labour, Lodging and Linkages: Migrant Women's Experiences in South Africa." *African Studies* 73 (3): 410–31.

Pinney, Christopher. 2003. "Notes from the Surface of the Image: Photography, Postcolonialism, and Vernacular Modernism." In *Photography's Other Histories*, edited by Christopher Pinney and Nicolas Peterson, 202–20. Durham, NC: Duke University Press.

Pirbhai, Mariam. 2009. *Mythologies of Migration, Vocabularies of Indenture: Novels of the South Asian Diaspora in Africa, the Caribbean, and Asia-Pacific*. Toronto: University of Toronto Press.

Polak, Henry. 1909. *The Indians of South Africa: Helots within the Empire and How They Are Treated*. Madras: G. A. Natesan and Co.

Posel, Deborah. 2001. "Race as Common Sense: Racial Classification in Twentieth-Century South Africa." *African Studies Review* 4 (2): 87–113.

Posel, Deborah. 2005. "Sex, Death and the Fate of the Nation: Reflections on the Politicization of Sexuality in Post-Apartheid South Africa." *Africa: Journal of the International African Institute* 75 (2): 125–53.

Price, Max. 2015. "Rhodes Must Fall: Max Price's Letter to UCT Alumni," June 19. http://politicsweb.co.za/news-and-analysis/rhodes-must-fall-max-prices-letter-to-uct-alumni.

Puar, Jasbir. 2007. *Terrorist Assemblages: Homonationalism in Queer Times*. Durham, NC: Duke University Press.

Quashie, Kevin. 2021. *Black Aliveness, or A Poetics of Being*. Durham, NC: Duke University Press.

Ramphele, Mamphela. 1991. "The Dynamics of Gender within Black Consciousness Organisations: A Personal View." In *Bounds of Possibility: The Legacy of Steve Biko and Black Consciousness*, edited by N. Barney Pityana, Mamphela Ramphele, Malusi Mpumlwana, and Lindy Wilson, 214–27. Cape Town: David Philip Publishers.

Ramphele, Mamphela. 1996. "Political Widowhood in South Africa: The Embodiment of Ambiguity." *Daedalus* 125 (1): 99–117.

Ramsamy, Edward. 2007. "Between Non-Racialism and Multiculturalism: Indian Identity and Nation Building in South Africa." *Tijdschrift Voor Economische en Sociale Geografie* 98 (4): 468–81.

Rassool, Ciraj. 2019. "The Politics of Nonracialism in South Africa." *Public Culture* 31 (2): 342–71.

Rastogi, Pallavi. 2008. *Afrindian Fictions: Diaspora, Race, and National Desire in South Africa*. Columbus: Ohio University Press.

Ratele, Kopano. 2006. "Ruling Masculinity and Sexuality." *Feminist Africa* 6: 48–64.

Ratele, Kopano. 2016. *Liberating Masculinities*. Cape Town: HSRC Press.

Reddy, Vanita. 2015. "Afro-Asian Intimacies and the Politics and Aesthetics of Cross-Racial Struggle in Mira Nair's *Mississippi Masala*." *Journal of Asian American Studies* 18 (3): 233–63.

Reddy, Vanita. 2016. *Fashioning Diaspora: Beauty, Femininity, and South Asian American Culture*. Philadelphia: Temple University Press.

Reddy, Vanita. 2017. "Affect, Aesthetics, and Afro-Asian Studies." *Journal of Asian American Studies* 20 (2): 290–91.
Reddy, Vanita. 2021. "Beauty, Colorism, and Anti-Colorism in Transnational India." In *The Routledge Companion to Beauty Politics*, edited by Maxine Leeds Craig, 94–102. New York: Routledge.
Reid, Graeme. 2010. "The Canary of the Constitution: Same-Sex Equality in the Public Sphere." *Social Dynamics: A Journal of African Studies* 36 (1): 38–51.
Reid, Graeme. 2013a. "Sabelo Mlangeni: Country Girls." Exhibition catalog. Michael Stevenson Gallery.
Reid, Graeme. 2013b. *How to Be a Real Gay: Gay Identities in Small-Town South Africa*. Scottsville: University of KwaZulu-Natal Press.
Richardson, Matt. 2013. *The Queer Limit of Black Memory: Black Lesbian Literature and Irresolution*. Columbus: Ohio State University Press.
Robertson, Claire C. 1998. "The Feminization of Poverty in Africa: Roots and Branches." *Brown Journal of World Affairs* 5 (2): 195–201.
Ross, Marlon B. 2021. *Sissy Insurgencies: A Racial Anatomy of Unfit Manliness*. Durham, NC: Duke University Press.
Rubin, Gayle. 1993. "Thinking Sex: Notes for a Radical Theory of the Politics of Sexuality." In *The Lesbian and Gay Studies Reader*, edited by Henry Abelove, Michèle Aina Barale, and David M. Halperin, 3–44. New York: Routledge.
Rugunanan, Pragna. 2017. "Migrant Communities, Identities, and Belonging: Exploring the Views of South Asian Migrants in Fordsburg, South Africa." In *Contemporary Issues in the Indian Diaspora of South Africa*, edited by P. Pratap Kumar, 52–84. New Delhi: Serials Publication.
Sachs, Albie. 1991. "Preparing Ourselves for Freedom: Culture and the ANC Constitutional Guidelines." *TDR: The Drama Review* 35 (1): 187–93.
Samuelson, Meg. 2010. "(Un)settled States: Indian Ocean Passages, Performative Belonging and Restless Mobility in Post-Apartheid South African Fiction." *Social Dynamics* 36 (2): 272–87.
Scott, Darieck. 2010. *Extravagant Abjection: Blackness, Power, and Sexuality in the African American Literary Imagination*. New York: NYU Press.
Sharma, Nandita. 2020. *Home Rule: National Sovereignty and the Separation of Natives and Migrants*. Durham, NC: Duke University Press.
Sharpe, Christina. 2009. *Monstrous Intimacies: Making Post-Slavery Subjects*. Durham, NC: Duke University Press.
Sharpe, Christina. 2016. *In the Wake: On Blackness and Being*. Durham, NC: Duke University Press.
Simbao, Ruth. 2016. "Performing Stillness in Order to Move: Mohau Modisakeng's Becoming." In *Mohau Modisakeng: Selected Works*, edited by Karin Pernegger, 68–73. Ghent, Belgium: Snoeck Publishers.
Singh, Julietta. 2018. *Unthinking Mastery: Dehumanism and Decolonial Entanglements*. Durham, NC: Duke University Press.
Singha, Radhika. 2000. "Settle, Mobilize, Verify: Identification Practices in Colonial India." *Studies in History* 16 (2): 151–98.

Skoda, Uwe. 2019. "Worshipping Durga(s) Dasara, Durga Puja and the Dynamics of Goddess Worship in a Former Princely State in Odisha, India." In *Religious Diversity in Asia*, edited by Jørn Borup, Marianne Qvortrup Fibiger, and Lene Kühle, 223–42. Leiden: Brill.

Snorton, C. Riley. 2017. *Black on Both Sides: A Racial History of Trans Identity*. Minneapolis: University of Minnesota Press.

Soske, Jon. 2009. "Wash Me Black Again: African Nationalism, the Indian Diaspora, and Kwa-Zulu Natal, 1944–1960." PhD diss., University of Toronto.

Soske, Jon. 2017. *Internal Frontiers: African Nationalism and the Indian Diaspora in Twentieth-Century South Africa*. Athens: Ohio University Press.

Southall, Roger. 2016. *The New Black Middle Class in South Africa*. Suffolk: James Currey.

Spillers, Hortense. 2003. "Mama's Baby, Papa's Maybe: An American Grammar Book." In *Black, White, and in Color: Essays on American Literature and Culture*, 203–29. Chicago: University of Chicago Press.

Stallings, L. H. 2015. *Funk the Erotic: Transaesthetics and Black Sexual Cultures*. Urbana: University of Illinois Press.

State Information Office. 1949. *Meet the Indian in South Africa: A Pictorial Survey*. Pretoria: Hortors Limited.

Stephens, Michelle Ann. 2014. *Skin Acts: Race, Psychoanalysis, and the Black Male Performer*. Durham, NC: Duke University Press.

Swanson, Maynard W. 1983. "'The Asiatic Menace': Creating Segregation in Durban, 1870–1900." *International Journal of African Historical Studies* 16 (3): 401–21.

Swarr, Amanda Lock, 2009. "'Stabane,' Intersexuality, and Same-Sex Relationships in South Africa." *Feminist Studies* 35 (3): 524–48.

Tallie, T. J. 2019. *Queering Colonial Natal: Indigeneity and the Violence of Belonging in Southern Africa*. Minneapolis: University of Minnesota Press.

Taylor, Diana. 2003. *The Archive and the Repertoire: Performing Cultural Memory in the Americas*. Durham, NC: Duke University Press.

Thompson, Krista A. 2015. *Shine: The Visual Economy of Light in African Diasporic Aesthetic Practice*. Durham, NC: Duke University Press.

Tinker, Hugh. 1974. *A New System of Slavery: The Export of Indian Labour Overseas, 1830–1920*. New York: Oxford University Press.

Tinsley, Omise'eke Natasha. 2008. "Black Atlantic, Queer Atlantic: Queer Imaginings of the Middle Passage." *GLQ: A Journal of Lesbian and Gay Studies* 14 (2–3): 191–215.

Tu, T. Huynh. 2008. "From Demand for Asiatic Labor to Importation of Indentured Chinese Labor: Race Identity in the Recruitment of Unskilled Labor for South Africa's Gold Mining Industry, 1903–1910." *Journal of Chinese Overseas* 4 (1): 51–68.

Twaddle, Michael, ed. 1975. *Expulsion of a Minority: Essays on Ugandan Asians*. London: Athlone Press.

Vahed, Goolam. 2005. "Indentured Masculinity in Colonial Natal, 1860–1910." In *African Masculinities: Men in Africa from the Late Nineteenth Century to the Present*, edited by Lahoucine Ouzgane and Robert Morrell, 239–56. New York: Palgrave Macmillan; Scottsville: University of KwaZulu-Natal Press.

Vahed, Goolam, and Ashwin Desai. 2010a. "Identity and Belonging in Post-Apartheid South Africa: The Case of Indian South Africans." *Journal of Social Sciences* 25 (1–3): 1–12.

Vahed, Goolam, and Ashwin Desai. 2010b. *Inside Indian Indenture: A South African Story, 1860–1914*. Cape Town: HSRC Press.
Van Onselen, Charles. 1982. *Studies in the Social and Economic History of the Witwatersrand, 1886–1914*. Vols. 1 and 2. Johannesburg: Ravan Press.
Van Onselen, Charles. 1985. "Crime and Total Institutions in the Making of Modern South Africa: The Life of 'Nongoloza' Mathebula, 1867–1948." In *History Workshop*, 62–81. Editorial Collective, History Workshop, Ruskin College.
Wahab, Amar. 2018. "Indentureship's Ghostworld: Re-Imagining the Coolie Archive." *Visual Ethnography* 7 (1): 151–69.
Wahab, Amar. 2019. "(Re)tracing Queerness: Archiving Indentureship's 'Coolie Homo/Erotic.'" *Visual Studies* 34 (4): 388–94.
Walcott, Rinaldo. 2009. "Reconstructing Manhood; or, The Drag of Black Masculinity." *Small Axe: A Caribbean Journal of Criticism* 13 (1): 75–89.
Walcott, Rinaldo. 2021. *The Long Emancipation: Moving toward Black Freedom*. Durham, NC: Duke University Press.
Warner, Michael. 1999. *The Trouble with Normal: Sex, Politics, and the Ethics of Queer Life*. Cambridge, MA: Harvard University Press.
Weheliye, Alexander G. 2008. "After Man." *American Literary History* 20 (1–2): 321–36.
Weheliye, Alexander G. 2014. *Habeus Viscus: Racializing Assemblages, Biopolitics, and Black Feminist Theories of the Human*. Durham, NC: Duke University Press.
Weinbaum, Alys Eve, Lynn M. Thomas, Priti Ramamurthy, Uta G. Poiger, Madeleine Yue Dong, and Tani E. Barlow, eds. 2008. *The Modern Girl around the World: Consumption, Modernity, and Globalization*. Durham, NC: Duke University Press.
Wekker, Gloria. 2006. *The Politics of Passion: Women's Sexual Culture in the Afro-Surinamese Diaspora*. New York: Columbia University Press.
Wexler, Laura. 2017. "The State of the Album." *Photography and Culture* 10 (2): 99–103.
White, Melissa Autumn. 2014. "Archives of Intimacy and Trauma: Queer Migration Documents as Technologies of Affect." *Radical History Review* 120: 75–93.
Wright, Michelle M. 2004. *Becoming Black: Creating Identity in the African Diaspora*. Durham, NC: Duke University Press.
Wright, Michelle M. 2015. *The Physics of Blackness: Beyond the Middle Passage Epistemology*. Minneapolis: University of Minnesota Press.
Wynter, Sylvia. 2003. "Unsettling the Coloniality of Being/Power/Truth/Freedom: Towards the Human, after Man, Its Overrepresentation—An Argument." *CR: The New Centennial Review* 3 (3): 257–337.
Young, Hershini Bhana. 2017. *Illegible Will: Coercive Spectacles of Labor in South Africa and the Diaspora*. Durham, NC: Duke University Press.

NEWSPAPERS AND MAGAZINE ARTICLES

Cohen, Jessie. 2016. "Sex Exhibition Is Fair on Representation but Short on Alternative Heterosexual Sex." *Mail and Guardian*, May 26. https://mg.co.za/article/2016-05-26-00-sex-exhibition-is-fair-on-representation-but/.

Ditsie, Bev. 2019. "Love Letter to My Queer Family." *Mail and Guardian*, October 24. https://mg.co.za/article/2019-10-24-00-love-letter-to-my-queer-family/.

Eligon, John. 2020. "A Debate over Identity and Race Asks, Are African-Americans 'Black or 'black'?" *The New York Times*, June 26.

Goniwe, Thembinkosi. 2018. "The Sour Pleasure of the Art Industry." *Mail and Guardian*, September 7. https://mg.co.za/article/2018-09-07-00-the-sour-pleasure-of-the-art-industry/.

Hamblin, Robert, and Ulla Kelly. 2010. "It's Time to Accept Our Diversity." *The Witness*, March 12. https://www.pressreader.com/south-africa/the-witness/20100312/textview.

Hlalethwa, Zaza. 2020. "Wear the Weight of Emotions." *Mail and Guardian*, March 12. https://mg.co.za/article/2020-03-12-wear-the-weight-of-emotions/.

Le Cordeur, Matthew. 2015. "SA's Unemployment Rate Hits 12 Year High." May 26. http://www.fin24.com/Economy/SAs-unemployment-rate-hits-12-year-high-20150526.

Maditla, Neo. 2017. "FAKA on Penetrating Art Spaces and Designing a New Sound." *Design Indaba*, June 30. https://www.designindaba.com/articles/interviews/faka-penetrating-art-spaces-and-designing-new-sound.

Malefane, Moipone. 2009. "ANC Race Row Rages over Cabinet." *The Sunday Times*, August 9.

Mkhwanazi, Katlego. 2016. "Stevenson Curates SEX in the City." *Mail and Guardian*, April 22. https://mg.co.za/article/2016-04-26-stevenson-gallery-curates-sex-in-the-city/.

Modisakeng, Mohau, in conversation with Ric Bower. 2016. "I Can't Help But Make Connections." *CCQ Magazine* 10, August 14, 2–9.

Modisakeng, Mohau, in conversation with Percy Mabandu. 2011. "Chit Chat: Mohau Modisakeng." *City Press*, September 9.

Naidoo, Riason. 2008. "Restoring the Indian Experience." *Mail and Guardian*, September 21. Accessed April 10, 2015. https://mg.co.za/article/2008-09-21-restoring-the-indian-experience/.

Reed, John. 2006. "Zuma Apologises for Comments against Gays." *Financial Times*, September 28. https://www.ft.com/content/fc630030-4e44-11db-bcbc-0000779e2340.

Robins, Steven. 2013. "How Poo Became a Political Issue: Sanitation Is an Old Global Issue." *The Cape Times*, July 2.

Seymour, Tom. 2016. "Mohau Modisakeng: Memories of a Murder." *Financial Times*, September 27. https://www.ft.com/content/2ff46368-4f2e-11e6-8172-e39ecd3b86fc.

Tsapayi, Rory. 2020. "Healing through Family Snapshots–Lebohang Kganye's Ke Lefa Laka: Her Story." *Daily Maverick*, August 29. https://www.pressreader.com/south-africa/daily-maverick/20200829/282359747150292.

WEBSITES

Bakhit, Bakri, 2021. "Lebohang Kganye: The Urgency to Be the Author and Subject." (Interview). October 6, 2021. https://contemporaryand.com/magazines/stories-about-my-granddad/.

Bereng, Lerato. 2016. "Sex." Curatorial Statement published on the Stevenson Gallery website. https://stevenson.info/exhibition/430.
Coopoo, Githan. 2018. "Meet Queer South African Designer Githan Coopoo." Interview with Alok Vaid-Menon. October 9. https://www.papermag.com/githan-coopoo#rebelltitem32.
Corrigall, Mary. 2016. "Sexing Up the Art Scene." *Times Live*, April 26. https://www.timeslive.co.za/news/south-africa/2016-04-26-sexing-up-the-art-scene/.
Davidson, Emma Elizabeth. 2019. "South African Duo FAKA Are Using Music, Art, Photography, and Performance to Amplify the Voices of South Africa's LGBTQ+ Community." Dazed. https://www.dazeddigital.com/projects/article/44183/1/faka-fela-gucci-desire-marea-musician- biography-dazed-100–2019-profile.
FAKA. 2016. Bottom's Revenge . Berlin Biennale. July 20, 2016. http://bb9.berlinbiennale.de/event/bottoms-revenge/.
Khan, Sharlene. 2011. "But What's All Dis Here Talkin' About?" *Artthrob*. http://www.artthrob.co.za/Reviews/But-Whats-All-Dis-Here-Talking-About.aspx.
Khan, Sharlene. 2019. *when the moon waxes red*. Video performance, https://vimeo.com/155281312.
Macharia, Keguro. 2017. "African Pleasure (in 5 Movements)." *Gukira*. https://gukira.wordpress.com/2017/11/07/african-pleasure-in-5-movements/.
Macharia, Keguro. 2013. "Queer Genealogies (Provisional Notes)." January 13. https://bullybloggers.wordpress.com/2013/01/13/queer-genealogies-provisional-notes/.
Macharia, Keguro. 2016. "Political Vernaculars: Freedom and Love." *The New Inquiry*. March 14. https://thenewinquiry.com/political-vernaculars-freedom-and-love/.
Manete, Rofhiwa. 2018. "Umlilo, FAKA, Vusi Makatsi: The Queer South African Artists Breaking Gender Barriers." *True Africa*. February 2. https://trueafrica.co/article/umlilo-faka-vusi-makatsi-queer-south-african-artists-breaking-gender-barriers/.
Marea, Desire. 2016a. "On Visibility and the Illusion of the Safe Space." September 22. https://10and5.com/2016/09/22/on-visibility-and-the-illusion-of-the-safe-space/.
Marea, Desire. 2016b. "SIYAKAKA a Healing Manifesto." Creative Mornings. September 14. https://www.youtube.com/watch?v=kFkgN9PGdMM.
Marea, Desire, and Fela Gucci. 2017. "FAKA." May 14. https://issuu.com/buyani/docs/fakazine_single_pages_17dfde810850e1.
McKenzie, David, Amy Cassidy, and Rob Picheta. 2021. "Former South African President Jacob Zuma sentenced to 15 months in prison for contempt of court." *CNN*. June 29, 2021. https://www.cnn.com/2021/06/29/africa/jacob-zuma-contempt-sentencing-intl/index.html.
McMichael, Christopher. 2016. "FAKA–Speaking with the Gods." *Bubblegumclub*. https://bubblegumclub.co.za/music/faka-speaking-gods/.
Meslani, Zane Leo. n.d. "FAKA in Retrospect." *Faculty Press*. Accessed November 22, 2023. https://www.thebemagugu.com/faculty-press/voice/faka-in-retrospect/.
Mlatsheni, Cecil, and Lauren Graham. 2021. "Young people and women bear the brunt of South Africa's worrying jobless rate." *The Conversation*. September 7, 2021. https://theconversation.com/young-people-and-women-bear-the-brunt-of-south-africas-worrying-jobless-rate-167003.

Modisakeng, Mohau. 2014. "Next Chapter: Mohau Modisakeng Investigating the Impact of Cultural Histories on Contemporary Society." By Houghton Kinsman. September 15. http://www.anotherafrica.net/art-culture/next-chapter-mohau-modisakeng-on-investigating-the- impact-of-cultural-histories-on-contemporary-society.
Monaheng, Tseliso. 2016. "Revolutionary Sex in Johannesburg." *okayafrica* (South African Edition). May 31, 2016. https://www.stevenson.info/sites/default/files/2016_tseliso_monaheng_okayafrica_31_may_2016_.pdf.
Mqombothi, Liduduma'lingani. 2014. "Probing Subliminal Violence." *Africa Is a Country*. June 26. https://africasacountry.com/2014/06/82023.
Saaiq'a. 2020. "Meet the Radical Desi Artists of South Africa's Kutti Collective." November 2. https://www.documentjournal.com/2020/04/meet-the-radical-desi-artists-of-south-africas-kutti-collective/.
Sharpe, Christina. 2019. "Beauty Is a Method." *e-flux Journal* 105, December. https://www.e- flux.com/journal/105/303916/beauty-is-a-method/.
Shezi, Ntombenhle. 2015. "Meet FAKA." September 9. https://web.archive.org/web/20160810022913/.

Index

Bold locators refer to figures